BORDERLINE AMERICANS

BORDERLINE AMERICANS

RACIAL DIVISION AND LABOR WAR IN THE ARIZONA BORDERLANDS

Katherine Benton-Cohen

HARVARD UNIVERSITY PRESS

Cambridge, Massachusetts

London, England

2009

Library of Congress Cataloging-in-Publication Data

Benton-Cohen, Katherine
Borderline Americans : racial division and labor war in the Arizona
borderlands / Katherine Benton-Cohen.
p.   cm.
Includes bibliographical references and index.
ISBN 978-0-674-03277-4 (alk. paper)
1. Working class—Arizona—Cochise County—History.   2. Labor movement—Arizona—
Cochise County—History.   3. Labor disputes—Arizona—Cochise County—History.
4. Social conflict—Arizona—Cochise County—History.   5. Racism—Arizona—Cochise
County—History.   6. Frontier and pioneer life—Arizona—Cochise County.   7. Cochise
County (Ariz.)—Economic conditions.   8. Cochise County (Ariz.)—Race relations.
9. Cochise County (Ariz.)—Social conditions.   10. Mexican-American Border
Region—History.   I. Title.
HD8083.A6B466 2009
305.8009791'53—dc22   2008052251

To the people of Cochise County, Arizona
past, present, and future

Contents

Illustrations

BORDERLINE AMERICANS

Introduction

"Are you an American, or are you not?" This was the question that Harry Wheeler, the sheriff of Cochise County, Arizona, used to determine his targets in one of the most remarkable vigilante actions in U.S. history. It took place in a remote mountain town near the Arizona-Mexico border on July 12, 1917, three months after the United States joined World War I. In the days leading up to the event, Wheeler had appointed more than two thousand temporary deputies, among them miners, foremen, Protestant clergymen, prominent merchants and businessmen, a company doctor, and a Catholic priest. At 4:00 A.M., the deputies—summoned by phone, organized into companies, and identified by white armbands—emerged onto the streets "as if by magic," as the front page of the *New York Times* reported the following day.

The men carried rifles. Some of those firearms were their own, but most, according to reliable sources, came from a company store and from two boxcars of guns and ammunition recently delivered to a mining-company manager. The deputies swarmed through the steep, narrow streets to snatch up fellow residents at home or at work. The targets of the raid were people suspected of participating in or supporting a strike by the Industrial Workers of the World (IWW, or "Wobblies"), a radical union mobilizing against the copper-mining companies of Bisbee, Arizona.[1]

Deputies pounded on doors, rounding up men by threat and by force. They captured not just striking miners, but also restaurant owners, carpen-

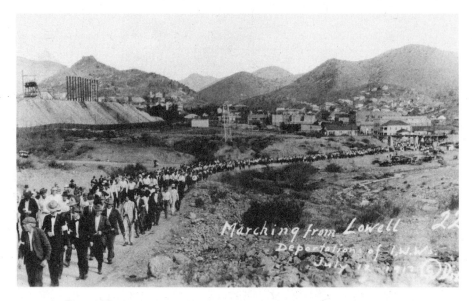

1. Suspected IWW supporters being marched out of Lowell, a suburb of Bisbee, July 12, 1917. Note the deputies' rifles and armbands. Courtesy of the Bisbee Mining and Historical Museum, Bendixen Collection, 75.41.5A.

ters, a lawyer, and a state legislator. Amado Villalovas was buying food for his family when "about ten gunmen all armed came in and told me to get out. I asked them to let me take my groceries home to my family. They dragged me out of the store, hit me and knocked me down." They "pushed me in line and made me go away leaving parcels on the ground."[2] In private homes and boardinghouses, wives and landladies protested and tried to shame the deputies. In the chaos of the roundup, two men—one on each side—were killed. It is astonishing the count was not higher. The *Bisbee Daily Review,* owned by the largest mining company in the area, reported that at 6:30 A.M. "the crash of the musket butts on the pavement stilled the mutterings and murmurs of the trapped 'wobblies' for the rest of the day."[3] In the July sun, a line of nearly two thousand captives snaked along single-file, escorted by armed deputies.

By noon, the men had been marched through town, past the mines, to a suburban baseball field four miles away. Families and neighbors gathered and gaped as deputies weeded through the men and loaded at least 1,186 of them into twenty-three boxcars belonging to the mining-company railroad.

The captives were shipped 180 miles into the New Mexico desert.[4] Some, like Villalovas, had families, but the majority were single and childless. Ninety percent were immigrants. Altogether they included men of thirty-four nationalities, but half came from Mexico or the Slavic regions of eastern Europe.[5] An army camp in nearby Columbus, New Mexico—a border town that had been raided by Mexican revolutionary Pancho Villa a year earlier—rescued the deported men from thirst and starvation. Some stayed there as long as three months. Almost none of them ever returned to Bisbee.

The event became known across the country as the Bisbee Deportation. The term aptly characterized the forcible removal of "undesirables" from a town concerned enough about its racial boundaries to call itself a "white man's camp." Public outcry and national headlines eventually forced President Woodrow Wilson to appoint a mediation commission to investigate labor conflicts across the West, but especially in Arizona's copper camps. It was not an easy decision, because Bisbee's largest mine was owned by the Phelps Dodge Corporation, whose vice president, Cleveland W. Dodge, was Wilson's close friend and former college roommate at Princeton. Wilson named as counsel to the commission a young assistant secretary of labor and Harvard law professor named Felix Frankfurter.

The future Supreme Court justice saw in the strikers' struggles nothing less than a "fight for the status of free manhood" by Mexicans and Slavs who "feel they were not treated as men." After his first glimpse of the Arizona mining camps, Frankfurter wrote to a friend: "As I get deeper and deeper into these marooned outposts of the country, . . . far from the intimacies of my own life, it all seems, it all is, part of the whole. The war, the economic and racial conflicts and cross currents that produced it, the industrial anarchies, our American striving to realize the democratic faith—here."[6] Frankfurter understood that the events unfolding in the Arizona copper camps engaged one of the foundational questions in U.S. history: Who counts as an American?

County sheriff Harry Wheeler might have agreed on the question, but not, perhaps, with Frankfurter's answers. To ask the question Wheeler did—"Are you an American, or are you not?"—was to assume a whole set of answers about who was *not* really an American in his eyes: labor radicals, Mexicans, Slavs, men whom he believed had no roots to family or town. As a patriotic

2. Sheriff Harry Wheeler, ca. 1917. Courtesy of the Bisbee Mining and
Historical Museum, 79.90.3.

citizen and law enforcement officer, Wheeler saw a strike against a vital war
industry as a threat to the nation. He also believed these men threatened the
lives and safety of "American women," as he put it. And so Wheeler joined
causes with mine managers and foremen, appointed his deputies, and began
his roundup.

The story of Cochise County, Arizona, whose citizens elected Harry
Wheeler, is part of a larger national saga of race, belonging, and exclusion. In
the nineteenth century, the abolition of slavery and the passage of the Four-

teenth and the Fifteenth Amendments loosened the racial strictures around U.S. citizenship. But the incorporation of much of northwestern Mexico into the United States after the U.S.-Mexico War in 1848, and, after 1880, the immigration of southern and eastern Europeans, were accompanied by the spread of scientific racism and a fear of radicalism that raised new questions about who qualified as an American. The Bisbee Deportation was one community's answer to those questions, but it was an answer that echoed debates and dilemmas that racked the nation in a time of mass migration, labor struggle, world war, and revolution. As the Deportation lingered in the national spotlight, the men and women of Cochise County found it difficult to avoid the controversy.

County residents had squinted in media glare and succumbed to federal intervention before. Geronimo, the Chiricahua Apache medicine man and resistance leader, ended the nation's Indian Wars when he surrendered at Cochise County's Skeleton Canyon in 1886. Magazines like *Harper's Weekly* kept eastern readers apprised of Geronimo's daring escapes and fascinating encounters with dashing army officers and their Indian scouts. Five years before Geronimo's surrender, the county seat of Tombstone had become infamous, when escalating violence—culminating in the shootout forever associated with the OK Corral—prompted a threat of martial law by President Chester Arthur.

A hundred years later, at the turn of the twenty-first century, the county attracted renewed media attention as the site of the highest number of undocumented migrants apprehended crossing the U.S.-Mexico border. In response, the county became home to several vigilante-type organizations. In 2004, Tombstone gunfight reenactor and newspaper editor Chris Simcox formed the Minutemen Civil Defense Corps, dedicated to monitoring the border and stopping illegal immigration. The group spawned chapters across the nation, and its April 2005 campaign to observe and report undocumented border crossings shot Cochise County bylines across the world, as far away as Great Britain and Australia. Some members believe they are restoring the geographic border between Mexico and the United States—and therefore the strict racial border between Mexican and American—to what it once was. But such a border in fact never existed.

Cochise County changed dramatically between the eras of Wyatt Earp,

Geronimo, and Harry Wheeler on the one hand, and the Minutemen on the other. At its height, military occupation during the Apache Wars involved almost one-fifth of the U.S. Army in chasing Geronimo, and in 1917 a "Citizen's Protective League" maintained checkpoints outside Bisbee to stop deportees from returning. These conditions differ in their particulars from the situation in the twenty-first century: the nearly ubiquitous presence of the Border Patrol and National Guard, joined, in uneasy alliance, by groups like the Minutemen. Still, parallels do exist, and comparisons are worth considering. In both periods, state and private forces policed the boundary between those who belong and those who do not—in terms that often invoked race and nation simultaneously. Anti-Chinese campaigns in Tombstone and Bisbee set a precedent for racial exclusion, and the removal in 1886 of the surrendered Chiricahua Apaches—by boxcar—eerily foreshadowed the Bisbee Deportation three decades later. With the Apaches gone, the racial divisions created and reflected in the labor conflicts of the mines could be embedded in fictions about a natural and bright-line border between "America" and "Mexico."

In the twenty-first century the border can be patrolled as if it were a fixed line (though one easily crossed) between firmly established nation-states, but this is possible only because of a long history in which government officials, corporate interests, and local citizens made that border seem natural by establishing "Mexican" and "white American" as the region's only relevant—and totally separate—racial categories.

This place in the middle of nowhere has been surprisingly central to some of the nation's defining controversies. The story of Cochise County offers a tool for understanding the twinned histories of race and nation in the United States. Although many people continue to think of race in black-white terms, this region of the Southwest contained people from around the globe who were forced to grapple with racial categories and definitions. It's atypical in some ways: not every county in the United States—or the West, for that matter—harbored native resistance like that of the Chiricahua Apaches, a shoot-out like the OK Corral's, or a deportation like Bisbee's. But Cochise County's past offers a window into the ways that race and nation have been linked and unlinked in the nineteenth and twentieth centuries, and how those connections have shaped the lives of everyday people. The personal stories cast in sharp relief the process of race making, which so often seems amorphous and fuzzy.

At the border, "American" was and is simultaneously a local, national, racial, and ideological category. To ask Wheeler's question—"Are you an American, or are you not?"—was scarcely to ponder an abstraction. Not in Apache country, not on an international border, and not, in 1917, during world war abroad *and* the Mexican Revolution just a few miles away. To take the mantle of "American"—or refuse to bestow it on someone else—asserted what you were, but also what you were not.

The men deported from Bisbee on that hot morning were *borderline Americans,* because most were U.S. residents but not citizens (a point carefully considered and recorded in censuses of their camp in New Mexico), but also because, to many local residents, men like the deportees had at best a tenuous claim on whiteness—a concept that even a half-century after the Fourteenth and Fifteenth amendments was still deeply tied to the meaning of U.S. citizenship.

This book, then, is about which borderline Americans became, in the minds of their neighbors and employers, "white Americans," and which ones did not. It is not in the main a book about identity, but rather a book about the evolution of racial categories imposed largely from without, and the power these categories had to shape nearly every aspect of life, from marriage to citizenship to housing to jobs. These categories were never totalizing, of course, but they were powerful.

Treating the whiteness of new European immigrants as inevitable—but not that of Mexicans—erases the complicated racial histories of both groups.[7] The Treaty of Guadalupe Hidalgo of 1848 (which ended the U.S.-Mexico War) and the Gadsden Purchase of 1853 (which included the strip of Mexico that became southern New Mexico and Arizona and that would contain Cochise County) both guaranteed Mexican citizens in those territories the right to U.S. citizenship. Because a 1790 federal law allowed the naturalization only of "white" immigrants, these two treaties thus made Mexicans legally "white."[8] California's and Arizona's first voting laws in the 1850s and 1860s specifically enfranchised "every white male citizen of Mexico" who had "elected to become" a U.S. citizen. It was possible, in other words, to be both white *and* Mexican in the United States.[9]

In the mid-nineteenth century, "Mexican" and "white" were overlapping categories, not opposite poles in a regional racial system. In this world, Apaches were not Americans, but Mexicans might be. These categories were, however, highly contingent on local conditions. During the height of the violence in Tombstone, for instance, many local residents strongly defended Mexicans against American bandits. Building national and racial boundaries required the removal and exclusion of some peoples, and the new inclusion of others. In small irrigated farm and ranch communities, the Apache Wars encouraged close settlement patterns and intermarriage among Mexicans and European Americans. But race relations in places with different economic systems soon became more problematic. Where Mexicans owned ranches and farms, racial categories were blurry and unimportant. But in the industrial copper-mining town of Bisbee, Mexican workers were segregated economically by their lower pay ("Mexican wage") and geographically by new town-planning experiments. To most non-Mexican residents of Bisbee, Mexicans were peon workers or potential public charges, not neighbors or business partners, not co-workers or co-worshipers, and certainly not potential marriage partners.

Eastern and southern Europeans, welcomed as pioneers in the 1880s, had, by the early twentieth century, become objects of suspicion and racially charged commentary. The arrival of growing numbers of new, often unskilled workers from Serbia, Italy, Finland, and elsewhere generated controversy over who qualified as white. Mining officials came to define a white American man as any family breadwinner so long as he was not Mexican. Unmarried European immigrant miners who took wives, bought single-family homes, and raised families found praise as "domestic miners" in the local press, which voiced complaints about single Italian men living in rooming houses "as no white man can." Rural white homesteaders, who had long been hostile to the mining companies, found common ground with mining-town residents in denigrating new immigrants.

Well before the crackdowns on radicals and the restrictions on immigration of the 1920s, public officials and private boosters were using "American" as a quasi-national, quasi-racial category embodied in married, homeowning "white" men. In the 1920s and 1930s, middle-class white women—often the wives or employees of company officials—took on increasingly public roles in social reform and government programs that defined the population by race. Nationally, the immigration restriction laws of the 1920s stopped the flow of southern and eastern Europeans but allowed Mexican immigration to continue. In a place where racial identities were tightly bound up with national ones, "American" increasingly equaled "white," and so "Mexican" came to mean the opposite of both.

Of the West and the Nation

Historians have devoted far less attention to Arizona than to other parts of the Southwest, and the history of the state does not always conform to generalizations about the larger region. Unlike much of the Southwest, southern Arizona had only a very small non-Indian population before U.S. annexation. The Apache Wars, the unforgiving desert climate and terrain, and the region's inaccessibility discouraged permanent settlement in the Spanish, Mexican, and early U.S. periods. Arizona's mining economy attracted a more diverse population than most of the Southwest (with the exception of California Gold Rush country). In Arizona, newcomers of diverse backgrounds brought ideas about race from Mormon colonies in Utah, California mining camps, midwestern farm towns, and the former Confederacy. Industrial mining financed by eastern capital had greater influence in early Arizona than in New Mexico or southern California. Many of Arizona's mining camps boasted international populations that included a sizable Chinese contingent. Cochise County typified these trends.

The county was carved from part of Pima County in 1881 to accommodate the frenzied silver boom at Tombstone. The new county—named for the great leader of the native people who were in the midst of being displaced from this land—occupied an eighty-mile square in the southeastern corner of Arizona, along the borders of New Mexico and Mexico. At more than six thousand square miles, Cochise County is larger than Connecticut and Rhode Island combined. Its environment is one of the most varied in the U.S. Southwest, ranging from desert aridity to riparian habitats along the San Pedro River to the relative lushness of the Chiricahua Mountains, where elevations top nine thousand feet. Bisbee is a mile high, and boasts of having the best year-round weather in Arizona. The climate can be harsh, though. Undocumented migrants attempting to cross the county's long border can—

3. Cochise County, ca. 1881. Map by Philip Schwartzberg.

and do—die of heat stroke in the lowlands and hypothermia in the mountains.

While academic studies of the Southwest often neglect Arizona as a whole, events like the Chiricahua Apache Wars and the shootout at the OK Corral—along with other lesser-known episodes of western lore—have given Cochise County a unique if infamous place in popular western history, and one that stands in for the West in general. Generations of people around the world have watched the shootout reenacted on their movie and television screens. Tombstone, like other parts of the West, was mythologized in real time. Dime novels about Tombstone began circulating as early as 1883, and the first movies about it appeared in the early twentieth century. In 1929, the desiccated town began a survival campaign centered around an annual tourist event called "Helldorado Days," named for a memoir by Earp-era lawman

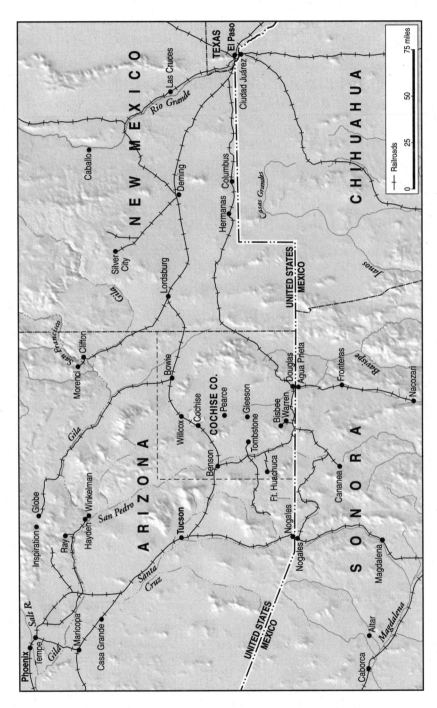

4. The Copper Borderlands, ca. 1917. Map by Philip Schwartzberg.

Billy Breakenridge, that offers fake gunfighting, western fashion shows, and a street carnival.[10]

Cochise County has staged countless gunfights—real and reenacted—but more significantly it has been home to some of the American West's most iconic industries. It contained the important army posts Fort Bowie and Fort Huachuca (home to thousands of African American "Buffalo soldiers"), one of Arizona's most productive cattle ranching regions, irrigated farm communities much like northern New Mexico's, and small family homesteads like those associated with the Great Plains. The Southern Pacific Railroad, completed across the region in 1880, was the first of several railroads to traverse the county, east to smelters and south to mines and workers in Mexico.

But nothing came close to challenging the reign of the copper-mining industry, financed by some of New York's and the Upper Midwest's leading capitalists. Together, the region comprising Arizona, New Mexico, Sonora, and Chihuahua constitutes what geographer D. W. Meinig calls the "Copper Borderlands," a unified economic and geologic region of mineral wealth that is among the richest in the world.[11] For much of the period covered in this book, Cochise County produced more wealth than any other in Arizona, and the overwhelming majority of that wealth came from mining. By the early twentieth century, Bisbee's mines produced almost 40 percent of the state's copper and 12 percent of the nation's.[12] Bisbee was one of the territory's largest cities. By 1910, with Bisbee's help Arizona had surpassed Michigan and Montana in copper production, a status it has never relinquished. Cochise County's mining industry attracted ambitious adventurers from Princeton, Yale, and Amherst as mining engineers and managers, who were catapulted to the halls of Congress, to federal appointments, and to ambassadorships. Even after Phoenix's Maricopa County grew larger than Cochise, the county's mineral wealth and mining magnates guaranteed it lasting political and economic influence.

White women found opportunity and influence, too, in this place dominated by the hypermasculine pursuits of mining and ranching. Despite the West's association with manliness, in fact, most of its political institutions were created in an era of unprecedented political access for some women. Across the West, white women engaged in social reform had a major influence not just on their working-class and nonwhite "charges," but also on state building more generally. Women's prominence is a little-known aspect of Arizona's rather unexpected political past, and of the West's history in general. The term "state building" is quite literal. Ten western territories became states between 1889 and 1912, at the height of the Progressive Era. Several western state constitutions bore the marks of Progressivism, and Arizona—crowned the forty-eighth state in 1912—is among them. By 1912, ten states and territories in the West and Midwest, including Arizona, had approved full woman suffrage. The need to create some kind of social-service net in the West, along with the desire to even out sex ratios in a frontier society, gave white reform women real social power.

This Progressive moment also fostered a political and labor movement intended to protect white miners from new immigrant competition, as well as from mostly absentee corporations. In Arizona the white labor movement controlled territorial and state politics from about 1909 to 1916. This book resurrects the surprising labor-reform chapter in the history of a state associated with Barry Goldwater and John McCain. In doing so, the book probes the racial assumptions of radical thinkers who saw white men and women as the ideal citizens in their hoped-for worker republic.

Race and Relationships

This book relies on the conviction that ideas about race and nation cannot be disentangled from the ways people think about class, gender, and family. This is a claim that many scholars have made, yet it has proven exceedingly difficult to write about these dynamic and often slippery concepts simultaneously. Until recently, the history and study of racial difference in the United States was mapped largely along a black-white axis. Thanks to a generation of scholarship, our racial maps are far more complex. Latino, Asian, Native American, and white experiences with race have become common topics of scholarly investigation. And, as many scholars have shown, the category of "American" is so bound up with whiteness as to be extricable only with great effort and epic social movements, and even then perhaps not completely redeemable from its race-specific roots.[13]

Yet many stories about the links between the history of race and access to citizenship have been told from lofty levels of political rhetoric, or from a legalistic perspective, or from the vantage point of the shop floor or union hall, or simply on the East Coast or in the American South, where racial hierarchies were organized differently. A study rooted on the ground—particularly on diverse and contested ground—offers a way to see how race and nation fit together in lives and communities.

In Cochise County, corporations and governments exerted enormous influence over the creation of racial categories. Ideas about masculinity, femininity, nationhood, and class colored ordinary people's judgments about race in tangible ways (as when Harry Wheeler repeatedly framed his actions in terms of protecting American womanhood). Mexicans could be white, and Italians could fail to be. Rich and poor, immigrant and native, miner and farmer, manager and worker, man and woman: they all fought over how race would be defined and who would benefit from these definitions. The result was the racial conflict that has often been mistaken as natural or inevitable in the borderlands.

In traversing the nineteenth and twentieth centuries, industrial and agricultural landscapes, the histories of people native to the Americas, Africa, Europe, and Asia, and the shifting terrain of the study of gender, this book relies on thousands of historical sources, but it is equally indebted to the insights of other historians. The pioneering Chicano-community studies of the 1970s and 1980s mapped relationships between race, class, and land ownership that make sense of Cochise County's internal variations. Scholarship on the gender and class dynamics of western mining camps links Bisbee to a larger story of the mining frontier. Provocative studies of southern and eastern Europeans, mostly people residing on the East Coast, have cast whiteness as an invented and malleable product of history. A rich literature on women's Progressive reform has informed this book's insistence that white women were as notable for their power as for their lack of it. The work of new borderlands scholars has also shaped this book, even if its focus on U.S. race relations has kept its narrative anchored in the northern side of the border.[14]

Experts in all these subjects may find familiar arguments here, but the particular combination of industries and peoples in Cochise County make new, important insights possible. With only the rarest exceptions, for example, scholars have failed to compare two of the most fascinating and divergent

examples: Mexicans and eastern and southern Europeans.[15] For all the attention historians have given to the creation of the category of "white" (or
"Anglo," as westerners often say), we have still tended to simplify this category—and its putative opposite, "Mexican"—in the American Southwest.
Borderline Americans addresses the question of how southern and eastern
Europeans became white, alongside the uniquely southwestern issue of why
and how the fluid racial system of Mexico shifted and collapsed at the
border.

It should be clear by now that this book proceeds from the premise that
race, in a strictly biological sense, is not "real." Yet, in social practice and
lived experience, race *functions* as something real. The label of "whiteness"
confers powerful privileges—including what W. E. B. Du Bois famously
called the "psychological wage" of being white. It offers advantages and pro-
motes inequalities that are very much material reality. Race is about power
more than biology, privilege more than appearance.[16]

Using race language is tricky. Where possible, I disclose my subjects' class,
citizenship, and nativity, and use the terms "Mexican" and "Mexican American" throughout. Terms like "Spanish American" and "Hispano-American"
appeared inconsistently in Arizona, whereas in New Mexico the term "Hispano" was widely used after 1900 to distinguish native New Mexicans of
purportedly Spanish descent from Mexican immigrants and Indians.[17] In
Arizona, these terms were never clear-cut, but in general the distinctions between "Spanish American" and "Mexican" faded as the racial division between "Mexican" and "American" grew sharper.[18] Meanwhile, I have tried to
use "white" or "American" to describe only those people who, at that particular historical moment, had a firm claim to the label. (Thus, western European mining officials and their wives are white from the outset; Slavs and
Italians not). I sometimes use "Anglo" for the sake of convenience, although
it is a term that appeared in the records only in the 1930s. The term "Anglo"
developed as a synonym for "white" that avoided the problem that Mexicans
were legally white. In the Southwest, Mexicans are never "Anglo"; but people of Jewish, Slavic, and Italian descent can be.[19]

The meaning of the word "race" has changed over time; in 1880 the term
connoted something different from its sense in 1910, something less concrete
and more fluid. Some authors have chosen to use the term "ethnic" or "eth-

noracial" where I have opted for race language.[20] I use phrases like "racial system" to describe social relations in Cochise County, and refer to individuals' racial *status*, not their *race*, as a nod to the concept's artificiality.

The book's first four chapters are snapshots of how four communities in Cochise County organized and divided people by race—or not—in the late nineteenth and early twentieth centuries. Whom one might marry, what one might do for a living, how much one might earn, where one might live, or who one's friends and neighbors might be could vary dramatically over just a few dozen miles. In the agricultural settlement of Tres Alamos, which had roots in the Spanish period, farmers from Mexico, Europe, and the eastern United States lived and worked together, with a camaraderie forged by the demands of the environment and the threat of Apache violence. In 1880s Tombstone, an anti-Chinese campaign, the Apache Wars, and the cattle rustling and murderous raids of white "Cowboys" brought people from Mexico and the United States together in common cause. The rise of industrial copper mining, however, positioned Bisbee to be the most influential community in the county. There mines segregated Mexicans into the worst jobs and paid them less than the "white wage" for the same work, but controversy raged over whether southern and eastern Europeans belonged at all, and in which jobs. In the Bisbee suburb of Warren, designed in 1906 by national planning experts, corporate officials hoped to attract and create the ideal worker, "the robust American with a growing family"—which was a way of referring to white married men without invoking race overtly.

The book's final four chapters tack between town and country up to and after the Bisbee Deportation, to trace the funneling of multiple racial meanings into an increasingly binary world of "Mexican" and "white American." The county's once-distinct communities became more similar. In rural Cochise County, Mexican American landowners persevered, but from 1900 through World War I, thousands of homesteaders from the Midwest and Upper South—15 percent of those who filed homestead claims being women—poured into what had once been open cattle range in the Sulphur Springs Valley. They knew little and cared less about older patterns and cooperation between Mexican and Euro-American pioneers. National and local agricultural promoters tied land ownership to home life, the patriarchal family, and the "Anglo-Saxon race," and encouraged white women to homestead their own claims. The result was deepening racial inequality that matched the divisions starkly evident in the Bisbee Deportation and its terrible aftermath. By the 1930s, schools and New Deal welfare programs were segregated across much of the county. The division between "Mexican" and "white American" seemed complete. Yet, as the conclusion emphasizes, men and women continued to fight—by organizing unions, challenging discriminatory wages, and asserting their rights as U.S. citizens no matter what their national origin or background.

Borderline Americans tells new stories about places both familiar and obscure, and in the process reveals in intimate detail how historical creations such as racial division can come to seem like timeless truths. In Cochise County, the line between "Mexican" and "white American" was at first undefined, then inconsistent. Only by the 1930s was it a bright border—and still, men and women contested it. In this place both unique in its details and typical in its tendencies, race was cast as a governing principle in ways that made racial differences seem natural, when they were in fact the work of men and women, both powerful and ordinary.

1

A Shared World in Tres Alamos

The settlement once known as Tres Alamos does not appear on modern maps or mailing addresses. It has left barely a trace on the landscape. Toll bridge, stagecoach station, general store, old irrigated fields, family home-steads—all gone. People still own ranches in the area, which is reached via a long dirt road, but there is no place called Tres Alamos anymore.

Once, though, here along the San Pedro River, men and women of Mexican, European, and African origin dug irrigation systems, set up businesses, built a school, befriended and married each other, and, inevitably, quarreled with each other, too. Their story is an important place to begin, because it reveals an alternative possibility to the industrialization and division that would soon transform the county, state, and border region. Before Geronimo's surrender in 1886, shared irrigation systems and open-range ranching in the heart of Apache country brought together settlers from many backgrounds.

Community divisions did not cleave to what today might be considered racial (or even ethnic) boundaries, as a dispute between two neighbors in April 1889 illustrates. Maine native Thomas Dunbar operated the town's stagecoach station and owned a ranch whose "beauty and worth, has no superior in Arizona," as one guidebook put it. Antonio Grijalba, scion of an old Tucson family, was also a successful rancher and farmer. Together, the two men had long worked an *acequia,* or irrigation ditch, on the river. But in this particular year, with water so scarce, Grijalba felt that his barley "was in even more danger than [Dunbar's] alfalfa." Grijalba argued he had a right to use the ditch because he had spent six dollars of his own money on it, and had done the digging and the dam building: "I didn't take it from Dunbar, I broke the work [tore out the dam] that I myself done," on a "thing that belonged to me." But Dunbar had a different view: Arizona water rights were granted on a first-come, first-served basis, and he felt his rights had come before Grijalba's. Dunbar also claimed he had spent "in the neighborhood of three thousand dollars" to improve his lands, and that his crops would fail without irrigation.

Grijalba was desperate for water, so he tried to tear down the ditch's temporary dam to irrigate his crops, but Dunbar "didn't want to turn it loose." When Grijalba went to use the water anyway, Dunbar pitched his neighbor straight into the muddy river. Not long afterward, Grijalba took Dunbar to court to demand more of the ditch's water.[1]

In Arizona, water was worth fighting over—but what about race? Tres Alamos had been a part of Mexico well within these men's lifetimes. Grijalba and Dunbar were mad enough to countenance violence and legal action. Yet in more than four hundred pages of court testimony, nary a flicker of antagonism that could be characterized as racial arises between the two. Then again, why should it? In the understandings of the Arizona frontier, the differences in their racial statuses were minimal, and irrelevant. Grijalba's family laid claims to Spanish origin. He was legally white, as Dunbar was. The two men occupied a shared world, and they knew it. A few years earlier, they had served together as witnesses at the wedding of their neighbors and fellow homesteaders John D. Allen and Francesca Díaz.[2] In 1889, Dunbar concurred with Grijalba's attorney that "until this year everything was perfectly friendly" between the two. Dunbar even conceded that Grijalba had "maintained the claim with me and fought other ditches against us" in three other lawsuits.[3] These ditches had varied ownership too. One had been registered and dug by a Mexican American man and his Anglo son-in-law, two other Mexican Americans, an African American, a German immigrant, and an elderly Illinois native who was the wealthiest man in Arizona. A decade later, a Mexican American woman who was the daughter of one owner and the widow of another became a farmer herself and owned water rights alongside all these men.[4]

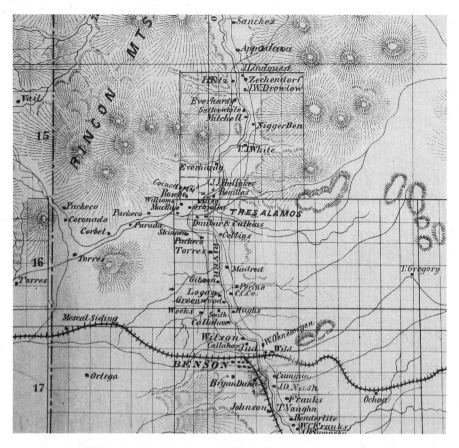

5. Landholdings in the Tres Alamos area, indicated by name of owner, ca. 1881. Braun Research Library, Autry National Center, Map 2047.

The world of Tres Alamos was—to use a word that in today's lexicon is irrevocably tied to race—remarkably "diverse." Yet this hackneyed modern term fails to capture the fluidity of racial status in frontier Arizona, where the perceived racial differences between Mexican pioneers and American newcomers remained sometimes nonexistent and often of little importance. The Treaty of Guadalupe Hidalgo and the Gadsden Treaty theoretically guaranteed that former Mexican citizens could elect to take American citizenship at a time when it was still legal to limit this privilege by race. Land and water rights—not race—were the community's most important status markers, and they were dispersed in complicated webs of connections, including those created by intermarriage. Civil laws that derived from Spain and Mexico allowed married women to own property and maintain economic power in their homes and communities. On the San Pedro River, Mexican Americans were substantial citizens and important economic players, their properties prominently listed on one of Cochise County's earliest official maps.

This place and time, when racial statuses were blurry and some Mexican Americans remained important landholders, complicates an oft-told and seemingly inexorable narrative of Mexican American land loss in the Southwest.[5] The people of Tres Alamos turned United States land law to their advantage by buying public land and proving up homestead claims. Using federal laws to secure land rights, these new citizens assimilated their holdings into the American capitalist economy more easily than could New Mexico's communal land grant holders.[6] In Tres Alamos, Mexican communal canal irrigation combined with American homesteading laws to allow residents to combine the old regime with the new. By joining long tradition with present-day realities, the people of Tres Alamos created an integrated enclave that represented both a bridge to the past and a plausible future for southern Arizona.

Building a Community

Grijalba and Dunbar followed generations of people who had been drawn, over the centuries, to Tres Alamos' lush respite from an arid landscape. The settlement occupied a convenient river-crossing with a year-round water supply on the north-flowing San Pedro. One nineteenth-century settler called it "one of the most beautiful valleys I ever saw," where "the river teemed with fish." It had "wild game in abundance," including beavers and otters.[7] In 1540, several millennia after indigenous peoples first hunted and farmed in the region, Spanish explorer Francisco Vásquez de Coronado passed through. In the 1690s, Jesuit missionary Padre Eusebio F. Kino traveled along the river and found a number of *rancherías* (settlements) on its banks, home to as many as two thousand Pima Indians. Kino named the crossing for the cottonwoods *(alamos)* he found there.[8]

Violence erupted intermittently. After the Spanish military forcibly removed Pima *rancherías* to Tucson and the San Xavier Mission, Western

Apaches filled the vacuum, using the San Pedro Valley as a conduit to Spanish and Indian targets in Arizona. In the 1770s, Tucson presidio commander Juan Bautista de Anza established several forts in the area, including one, Santa Cruz de Terranate, just a few miles north of Tres Alamos.[9] During these years, two officers and more than eighty Spanish soldiers and colonists were killed in Apache raids.[10] By the late eighteenth century, Tucson and the Santa Cruz and San Pedro river valleys were the only Spanish settlements left in Arizona.[11] A rough peace between settlers and Apaches developed during this era of New Spain's Bourbon reforms, marked by increased trade that knit northern hinterlands more tightly into the New World and European economies.[12] But the Pimería Alta ("Land of the Upper Pimas"), which encompassed all of what would become southern Arizona, was the hinterland of the hinterland and was slow to develop, peace or no. After 1810, Mexico's war for independence siphoned funds and soldiers from the frontier, and resistant Apaches soon regained control over most of the region. During one brief détente in the Apache Wars, some *tucsonenses* (Tucsonans) tried to farm at Tres Alamos under armed guard; and on the nearby Babocómari grant, land claimants began running huge herds of cattle. But respite from violence was brief. At its peak in the early 1820s, the Hispanic population of the Pimería Alta was not much more than a thousand. By 1831, Apache violence had thwarted plans for a huge land grant that would have encompassed Tres Alamos.[13]

Mexican officials across northern Mexico countered with deadly intent. In 1837 the Mexican state of Chihuahua offered a bounty on scalps, at first $100 for a man, $50 for a woman, and $25 for a child's; the amounts later doubled. The scalp bounty licensed wholesale slaughter and made the region desperately dangerous. Scalpers cared little whether they were in Sonora (where Tres Alamos was) or Chihuahua, or whether their victim was Mexican, Tohono O'odham, or Apache. Settlers abandoned the San Pedro Valley, and Tucson's population dwindled to just a few hundred inhabitants. In 1842 the Tres Alamos area became a staging and rendezvous point in several skirmishes between Sonorans and Apaches. In 1846, at the beginning of the U.S.-Mexico War, a group of volunteers from Nauvoo, Illinois, known as the Mormon Battalion, passed through on their way to California. On the banks of the San Pedro, the men were attacked by wild cattle abandoned by Mexican ranchers during Apache raids.[14]

In 1848 the Treaty of Guadalupe Hidalgo secured the cession of land from Mexico to the United States that included what would later become central and northern Arizona (it would be part of New Mexico Territory until 1863). Tres Alamos remained in Mexican hands. In 1852, the governor of Sonora made a last attempt to create a large land grant at Tres Alamos and to relocate at least a hundred families there. They never arrived. In 1854, the Gadsden Purchase turned over to the United States the strip of what is today New Mexico and Arizona south of the Gila River, including Tres Alamos and the rest of what would become Cochise County. In Washington, Democrats promoted the Purchase as a route for a southern transcontinental railroad, a sop for southern members of their party and an attempt to mute rising sectional conflicts. On the borderlands, though, the Gadsden Treaty had a more immediate life-and-death impact: it abrogated an article in the Treaty of Guadalupe Hidalgo that had pledged (hollowly) to protect Mexican citizens from Apache attack. U.S. military reports suggested that the small Mexican settlements in the Gadsden Purchase might make effective staging grounds for fighting the Apaches, but the U.S. government now had no responsibility to check raids across the border—and this lack of protection would be a sore point for years to come.[15]

Although southern Arizona was now U.S. land, at Tres Alamos little change occurred until the Civil War. In 1861, army forts were shuttered as troops went east to choose sides and fight in the Civil War. In the early 1860s, the near-murder of Cochise—followed by the murder of his father-in-law, famed Chiricahua Apache leader Mangas Coloradas, by inexperienced army troops—unleashed open warfare in the region, even as Arizona slipped briefly into Confederate control and back out again. The Arizona borderlands—with Tucson and Tubac as lonely outposts—remained almost entirely an Indian enclave until 1865.[16] When American migrants finally joined with native Mexicans at Tucson to create a permanent settlement at Tres Alamos, they were essentially foreigners. In a way, so were the Mexicans, even if their roots there were slightly deeper.

On March 3, 1866, Dolores Heran, Frutozo Castro, John Montgomery, and Hampton Brown (referred to as "Nigger Brown" in early documents) signed a water rights agreement.[17] Their names are less important than the diverse origins they revealed. By the end of the year, fifty-nine people lived in the settlement: thirty-five Hispanics, twenty-one Anglos (both American-

and European-born), and three African Americans. One of them, as Figure 5 shows, appeared as "Nigger Ben" on Cochise County's official map of major landowners.[18]

The settlement had the usual frontier rhythms of sociability. Juan López went hunting with Hampton Brown, "when we didn't have anything else to do." Residents also fished, and found mesquite for firewood. They ran cattle on wild grasses, grew fruits and vegetables, and tried crops as varied as tobacco and sugar cane. In the first year their farms yielded 175 tons of beans, wheat, barley, and corn. Conditions were rough—landowner Jose Valencia lived in a "dugout in the side of a hill"—but this was hardly unusual in new western settlements. The colony steadily grew, and by 1874, Tres Alamos had close to two hundred people, including more than fifty children, mostly on family farms.[19] The following year, Tres Alamos established one of Arizona's first school districts. Its children, school board members (including Grijalba), and teachers were both Mexican and American. One early teacher was the Anglo widow of a prominent Spanish-Mexican freight hauler killed by Indians.[20]

At first, land ownership was informal. Most settlers were technically squatters. "At that time they didn't have any [property] lines," one man recalled. "Everybody would go and take what they could cultivate," usually a "very small piece," ten acres or so. German immigrant William Ohnesorgen called this "the way the Mexicans farm." Land changed hands frequently, and leases were ad hoc. Prominent farmer and territorial legislator John Montgomery purchased a ranch from a man later killed by Apaches, and then leased it to another man in 1872 for "2,000 pounds of good mercheneble corn." Such casual transactions could lead to trouble. Montgomery's tenant pretended to own the land and sold it to a man named Jesús Suáres. Montgomery and Suáres ended up in court.[21]

Loose ownership had its risks, but it also kept land ownership accessible. Mexicans and Anglos alike progressed from laborer to landowner. In the 1870s Severiaño Bonillas was "working wherever I could get anything to do" around Tres Alamos, but eventually bought his own land and married John Montgomery's land-rich widow, María Ruíz. One of her brothers worked for Antonio Grijalba in three-month stretches, while another brother "was working on the river for anybody that would hire him." The Ruíz family held

6. John and María Ruíz de Montgomery, ca. 1870s. Courtesy of the Arizona Historical Society, Tucson, 42040.

several properties, as well as some of the river's oldest water rights. Local transactions of work and farm goods helped everyone to keep their land. Big owners like Grijalba could procure critical labor during harvest and roundup from less prosperous neighbors, who in this way could supplement their own farm income—a pattern with deep Mexican traditions.[22]

As the federal government gradually tightened its control over southern

Arizona, land titles—for public land at least—became more clear-cut. The Pre-Emption Act of 1841 gave squatters "priority" rights to buy outright the land on which they were living. The Homestead Act of 1862 allowed any head of household who was a U.S. citizen (or had signed a declaration of intent to become one) to file a claim for up to 160 acres, known as a quarter-section. Land records suggest many Mexican American landowners preferred direct purchase of public land to the time-consuming homesteading process, which took five years: the homesteader had to develop and "improve" a property by planting crops, digging a well, and building a dwelling. The reward for "proving up," as the process was called, was a land patent, or title, for the property. Although the land was "free," homesteaders paid a total of $18 in federal fees, in addition to the cost of improvements and sometimes private "locator's fees." Locally and nationally, at least half of all homesteaders failed to reach the patent stage, and the odds got worse as the West became more densely settled and good land grew scarce. But the program remained immensely popular.[23]

With the lure of public land, Tres Alamos became one of Arizona's earliest homesteader communities. A few dozen men, including John Montgomery, scoped out land as early as 1866. Antonio Grijalba bought public land in 1872, and later filed homestead claims. A flurry of claims followed, many by Mexican Americans. In the 1870s and 1880s, people with Spanish surnames bought one in four federal land parcels sold in what would become Cochise County. In the 1890s, even after an influx of Anglos to the county, Mexican Americans still accounted for one in seven public land purchases. Spanish-surnamed individuals made up a similar proportion of successful homesteaders, and dozens more Mexican American landholders lived just over the county line. Including those who filed claims but never secured ownership, Mexican Americans likely made up the majority of the population around Tres Alamos.[24]

A few, Grijalba especially, enjoyed considerable success as *rancheros* in the northern Mexican tradition. In 1877 Grijalba was farming forty acres of pre-empted public land on what became known as the Tres Alamos Ranch. In 1886, he patented another quarter-section, where he boarded an immigrant family who worked for him. Grijalba sold his wheat, barley, and beans to neighbors and to Tucson residents, and kept up a good cattle business. By the time of his death in 1906, Grijalba owned houses in Tucson and Tres Alamos, several hundred acres of farm land, water rights, two hundred head of cattle, thirty horses, two mules, stock in a Tucson savings-and-loan, and the rights to two cattle brands. The estate was worth more than $7,000, a sizable sum in the frontier West.[25]

Mestizaje Meets Miscegenation

Grijalba "owned" something else important: access to a Spanish heritage that offered prestige and status defined by both race and class. Travel, filing fees, and land improvements were expensive, and few western homesteaders rose from the poorest, landless classes. Most of Arizona's Mexican American homesteaders belonged to colonial military and commercial elites. Grijalba descended from a family of soldiers, merchants, and politicians of Spanish descent who had lived in southern Arizona since the 1730s. Female homesteader Francisca Comadurán Díaz de Mejía's father was a *criollo* (born in Mexico of Spanish descent) who had been a *comandante* of Tucson during the Mexican era; he was succeeded by his son Joaquín at the time of the Gadsden Purchase. The younger Comadurán's duties included surveying properties and witnessing real estate transactions in Tucson during the transition to American rule—a job that helped friends and kin to navigate new property rights based on English common law rather than Mexican civil codes.[26]

In the 1850s, Comadurán and his compatriots also had to orient the confusing intersection between the slippery racial legacies of colonial Mexico and the more rigid boundaries imposed by the black-white binary in the United States. In the Spanish era, a *casta* system was supposed to measure *limpieza de sangre* ("purity of blood") to create a class hierarchy that used supposed racial differences to make its gradations appear "natural." *Peninsulares* (Spanish-born people of pure Spanish origin) and *criollos*—collectively known as *españoles*—were considered superior to dozens of other categories, most commonly *mestizos* (Indian and Spanish mixture), *mulatos* (part African), and *indios* (a slightly pejorative term for indigenous peoples). These supposedly racial categories were interwoven with a system of *calidad*—roughly, "reputation." *Peninsulares* were supposed to occupy the highest government offices, but *criollos* could hold minor and unfilled positions, especially in remote places like Arizona. Even in the Spanish period, the compilers of Arizona's mission and census records had avoided using racial categories, instead substituting class-based terms like *la gente de razón* ("people of reason"), *vecinos* ("citizens"), and *peónes* ("laborers" or "peasants"). In the eighteenth century, most of Arizona's *gente de razón* were neither *peninsulares* nor *criollos,* but *mestizos* (sometimes called *coyotes* in Arizona).[27] These categories were permeable on the frontier, and by 1812, progeny across the color line (race mixture, or *mestizaje*) had so destabilized racial distinctions that Spain officially eliminated race-based laws and the *casta* system altogether. Less than a decade later, the new government of Mexico decreed that race could no longer be used to determine status. People continued to define themselves and others in terms of race and color, but technically claims of Spanish origins had no legal bearing in the new Mexican state.

Even before the official abandonment of the *casta* system, Spanish American notions of race had been more fluid than those in the United States. There was nothing like the American South's infamous "one-drop rule" (according to which anyone with even a trace of African blood counted as black). In theory, New Spain's elite was Spanish, but in a sparsely settled frontier area, people who were Spanish-speaking, wealthy, or landed qualified as being Spanish, and thus—in the context of American racial codes—white. This was very different from an African American's "passing" as white in the United States, where "changing" one's race meant hiding one's "real" origins, often by separating from one's family. Studies of Los Angeles and Albuquerque have shown that some individuals, tracked under consistent names and addresses, were able to achieve "higher" racial statuses (several beginning as *mulato*) in successive censuses. By 1863, when the Arizona Territory was organized, most children with elite Spanish fathers and *mestizo* mothers had become de facto members of the *español* (Spanish) population. Well into the American period, southern Arizonans distinguished between nomadic Apaches *(indios bárbaros)* and the rest of the population, but many Christianized Indians assimilated into the general *mestizo* population.[28]

It is safe to say that in Tres Alamos the merchant and military classes who made up the first homesteading population were disproportionately "Spanish," but this term obscured as much as it revealed. Homesteading families like the Comaduráns had ancestors of noble stock, marked by the honorifics

"Don" and "Doña" in colonial censuses. On the other hand, one of southern Arizona's most prestigious families, the Pachecos—who would hold more homesteads in Cochise County than any other family of Mexican descent—traced their ancestry to a man listed in an 1801 census as a *coyote (mestizo).*[29]

U.S. social customs and laws made racial categorization more fraught. The Southwest of the mid-nineteenth century was a clash between two different ways of thinking about race, summed up by the different connotations that adhered to the Latin American term *mestizaje* and the North American word "miscegenation."[30] As a practical matter, *mestizaje* destabilized official racial categories. In the twentieth century it would be celebrated by Mexican nationalists as the alchemy by which the Mexican people were created. By contrast, American miscegenation—race mixing—would continue to be proscribed by labyrinthine laws and strong social taboos. American racial systems were rigid by design, and to this day only awkwardly encompass mixed-race identities or categories.[31] In 1863, Democratic politician and travel writer John Ross Browne toured southern Arizona and northern Mexico and concluded, "I think that Sonora can beat the world in the production of villainous races. Miscegenation has prevailed in this country for three centuries. Every generation of that population grows worse; and the Sonorans may now be ranked with their natural comrades—Indians, burros, and coyotes."[32] To many Mexicans, *mestizaje* promoted social mobility and integration; to Americans, it bred degeneracy.

While Mexico's racial categories blurred, those in the United States sharpened and splintered. The ideology of Manifest Destiny that fueled support for the U.S.-Mexico War rested on a notion that not just whites, but Anglo-Saxons in particular, were uniquely suited—indeed destined—to rule over other peoples. At a time of deep dissent over war and expansionism, Anglo-Saxonism could justify the conquest of native peoples, but also of fellow Europeans of Spanish descent. This line of thinking proved powerful, yet Anglo-Saxonism never quite supplanted the view among many Americans that, racially speaking, Spaniards really were not the same as Indians.[33]

Science did little to resolve racial debates. Even as newspaper writers and politicians celebrated Anglo-Saxonism, scientists and philosophers were debating what race really was. Naturalists were hypothesizing about racial difference, while race continued to operate as both a scientific and a cultural idea. As the anthropologist George W. Stocking has argued, the term "race" was more akin to "national character" than to the more concrete and biologically rooted definition it would acquire at scientific racism's zenith in the early twentieth century. Although Charles Darwin avoided the issue of human races, the publication of his book *On the Origin of Species* in 1859 brought into question whether cultural traits could be inherited. The terms "race," "blood," and "nation" were often used interchangeably. In his pioneering study of nativism, John Higham observed that the nineteenth-century "Anglo-Saxon tradition" remained in the realm of philosophy and political theory, not science, because it "lacked a clearly defined physiological basis." Overall, "the leading scientific thinking did not regard race differences as permanent, pure, and unalterable." As a result, in the 1850s and 1860s, "race" meant both more and less than it would by the early twentieth century.[34]

Certainly, the abstract debates agitating Ivy League professors and European scientists never filtered down to the inhabitants of remote Tres Alamos. Yet settlers on the San Pedro did live in a world governed by laws that tried to balance racial "science" and practical diplomacy. Anti-Mexican verbal assaults and occasional violence ensued throughout the Arizona Territory, but by *legal* definition these were not racial conflicts. The Gadsden Treaty and the Treaty of Guadalupe Hidalgo both guaranteed former Mexican citizens in the acquired territories the rights to choose U.S. citizenship and to own property. The treaties were clearly intended to apply to all Mexican citizens, whether Indian, *mestizo,* or Spanish.[35]

So while many—perhaps most—Americans saw Mexicans as nonwhite, the two treaties made these new Americans exceptions to other federal laws that linked race and citizenship. The Naturalization Act of 1790 offered citizenship only to "white" immigrants.[36] The treaties meant that all Mexicans were white, for the purposes of the law, while African Americans, Asian Americans, and American Indians were not. Among these groups, the U.S. Census categorized only Mexicans as white. It was not until the Fourteenth Amendment was ratified in 1868 that immigrants of African descent were afforded the same rights to citizenship. For most Asian immigrants and American Indians, the wait extended well into the twentieth century.

As a result, Mexican-born residents of the Southwest occupied a strange legal position. Voting laws codified the relationship between whiteness and citizenship. In 1863, when Arizona became a territory separate from New Mexico, its new laws made whiteness a voting requirement. Early Arizona offered suffrage to "every white male citizen of the United States, and every white male citizen of Mexico" who had "elected to become" a U.S. citizen by right of the treaties.[37] The meaning of "Mexicanness" varied significantly depending on the context in which it was discussed. Sometimes it was a racial term; other times it was a national term that applied only to one's citizenship or nation of origin.

In any case, citizenship and the right to vote were not coterminous (as woman suffragists were busy reminding fellow Americans). Even after the Fourteenth Amendment made race-based distinctions for native-born citizenship illegal for everyone except American Indians, loopholes restricted the voting rights of nonwhites. An 1868 federal law designed to buttress the amendment denied individual states the right to create their own citizenship requirements. But the law did not apply to American Indians, most of whom remained ineligible for U.S. citizenship until 1924. These restrictions gave wiggle room to western territories and states that wanted to withhold voting rights from Mexicans, most of whom were *mestizo* and thus partly if not wholly Indian. By the twentieth century, Mexican Americans across the West were resorting to the courts to prove their whiteness.[38] If *mestizaje* had created the Mexican people, it had also created the loophole through which they could be denied U.S. citizenship. Since Arizona law forbade Indians from attaining citizenship rights and since the territory's law enfranchised "white" Mexicans, *mestizos* and Mexican Indians were technically ineligible to vote until 1877. Even after that, most Mexican Americans were not registered to vote. In 1884 Cochise County, for example, only 29 out of 2,836 registered voters—just over 1 percent—were Mexican American. Surely some were excluded and others did not want to bother: political citizenship in a U.S. territory conferred few real benefits.[39]

Racial and citizenship status were closely linked, and citizenship was tied to property rights. This was true in both the Mexican and American eras, but in different ways. In colonial New Mexico (then including Arizona), free status, landholding, and Spanish ancestry helped to determine personal and familial honor.[40] In the U.S. period, only those eligible for citizenship could legally homestead—an important way to acquire land. Sometimes neighbors or land-office workers challenged the citizenship status of Mexican American homesteaders who had failed to file the proper documentation because they did not speak English. One might expect them to have become irresistible bait for land sharks.

Yet federal land agents often helped to make things right, even going out of their way to accommodate Spanish-speaking homesteaders.[41] When Tres Alamos resident R. E. Wilson challenged Mrs. Jesús Maldonado de Mejía's right to her land by complaining that, because she was not an American citizen, she was unqualified to homestead claims she had inherited from her late husband, the government gave her sixty days to prove her American citizenship. One agent noted that while she was "ignorant of the English language," she had "faithfully complied with the law in the matter of residence and cultivation" of her claim. Local agents, he advised, should "render her all assistance to enable her to understand" what proof she needed. As it turned out, her husband had filed his declaration of intent to become a citizen, but had died before acquiring citizenship or his land patent. U.S. law granted citizenship to a wife in such a case, and Maldonado kept her land.[42]

Mexican American homesteaders were a self-selected group, comfortable claiming American citizenship, and willing to have it scrutinized. Arizona law, for all its concern over the racial status of Mexicans, failed to define whiteness—which meant that the common assumption of someone's whiteness amounted to their actual possession of it. Legal cases from around the country in the late nineteenth and early twentieth centuries demonstrated this "I know it when I see it" jurisprudence of race.[43] Since many of Arizona's Mexican American homesteaders belonged to families widely considered to be Spanish, perhaps they expected no trouble on this score. Or maybe they thought that homesteading was a way to settle the matter. Homesteading was one of the most popular political movements in American history—and what better way to join the nation? Only voting rivaled the significance of land ownership, and landowners represented the lion's share of Mexican Americans registered to vote.[44]

Mexican American homesteaders seized their American rights, but that did not mean they or Tres Alamos became magically "American" with the signing of the Gadsden Purchase. Southern Arizona in the mid-nineteenth century was like the oval in the center of a Venn diagram, with the United States and Mexico overlapping rather than bordering each other. The few Anglo-Americans were in the minority and essentially foreigners cooperating with a homegrown Mexican elite. Tres Alamos farmers—whether from Mexico or Maine—lived in adobe homes, used Mexican irrigation traditions, grew traditional Mexican crops, ate *frijoles* and *chiles,* and spoke Spanish. Some Mexican Americans, like Antonio Grijalba, were bilingual, and some Anglos spoke Spanish, if only to discuss labor arrangements with employees.[45] Commerce connected a wide web of humanity, even in tiny Tres Alamos. Antonio Grijalba's ledgers and check stubs from the early twentieth century showed accounts with two German immigrants, several German Jews, a Spanish-surnamed lawyer from Bisbee, and a Chinese merchant in Benson.[46]

In its Mexican feel and global connections, Tres Alamos strongly resembled Tucson, whence so many of its settlers had originated. If some writers disparaged Tucson as "un-American" and mired in "the phlegmatic Mexican condition of life," others marveled at a place at once remote yet full of transnational ties. One 1884 guidebook claimed that "a more complete admixture of races and nationalities could not well be gotten together anywhere else—Jews, Swedes, Irish, English, Germans, French, Yankees, Chinese, negroes, Spaniards, Indians, and all conceivable crosses among these"; but, the author noted, "Mexicans largely predominate in numbers." The power of numbers benefited Tucson's majority. By some accounts, "the old pueblo," as Tucson was known, was the most integrated city in the Southwest in the second half of the nineteenth century. Unlike newer American mining settlements like Prescott or Tombstone, where Anglos always dominated, Tucson had substantial Mexican middle and upper classes. They owned important businesses, held elective office, and hosted galas and *bailes* (dances) on Mexican feast days and holidays celebrated by Mexicans and Anglos alike.[47]

This is not to sugarcoat the reality that Anglos were steadily gaining power and influence, if not total control, of the region. As early as 1858, one mining official passing through Tucson found "about forty Americans residing here who monopolize all business and rule the place. The Mexicans fear them," he boasted, "acknowledge them as a superior race, and submit without a murmur."[48] This was an exaggeration, perhaps a wishful one, but for many Mexican families, it is true that prestige had not translated into wealth after the territory passed to American control. As early as 1860, Anglos held 87 percent of the real and personal property in Tucson. Mexican military officials lost their posts after the U.S. takeover, and Mexican-owned freighting firms disintegrated when the Southern Pacific Railroad arrived in 1879–1880.[49]

Farms and ranches carved from the public domain offered a way for Tucson's Mexican elites to diversify imperiled investments. Homestead claims by Mexican Americans along the San Pedro River jumped in 1880, just as the Southern Pacific Railroad was completed—a signal of distress, not prosperity. Antonio Grijalba, a former Tucson merchant, kept his hand in several business ventures, but many Mexican American homesteaders, especially women, were "poor," as Cleófila (or Cleofa) Apodaca described herself in a letter to the U.S. land office in 1892. Desperate for cash during a depression and drought year, she sold some of her homesteaded land back to the government for $640.[50]

In contrast, many Anglos in Tres Alamos were quite wealthy. Mark Aldrich was Arizona Territory's richest man in 1864. Charles Hooker, a storeowner and substantial landowner, was the son of Henry Hooker, the territory's most successful rancher and one of its most powerful men. Though better-off than their Mexican American neighbors, Anglos also branched out to survive in a frontier economy. John Montgomery dabbled in mining and served as postmaster. Thomas Dunbar first ran the stagecoach station, then earned most of his income from farming and stock raising. German immigrant William Ohnesorgen was a rancher, but he also bought Dunbar's station, and built a tollbridge across the river. After silver was discovered at Tombstone, all three men began businesses there.[51]

The successes of these newcomers were all the more reason for Mexican Americans to build a community with them. Many *norteños* (northern Mexicans)—particularly the elites—had more reasons to support American annexation than they did to support the Mexican government. Tucson was a trading center and crossroads for American expansion. Mexican American merchants and businessmen there had cast their lot with the first Americans and Europeans to arrive in the 1850s. Proximity to the United States, economic ties with Anglos, and the desire for rationalized property rights loosened ties to a central Mexican state. *Norteños* could also strengthen their claims to whiteness if they found friends, neighbors, business partners, and even family ties in these newcomers. The alliances of Arizona's Mexican frontier elites with new colonists were part of a larger pattern of similar alliances around the globe. In this way, southern Arizona's links to a world economy were as notable as its seeming isolation.[52]

Water Rights and Women's Rights

Like all communities, Tres Alamos had its own rhythms of cooperation and conflict. Its residents risked droughts, floods, and malaria. The ongoing Apache Wars threatened lives and livelihoods. Tension was inevitable, as Grijalba and Dunbar's dispute demonstrates, but cooperation was also everywhere: in water rights, in marital ties, in civic participation, and in waging war against the Apaches.

In the desert, water is more precious than land. Arizona law was based on the Mexican doctrine of prior appropriation, which says that the first landowner who uses a water source has "first rights." Thus, the law encouraged newly arriving Anglos to partner with Mexicans who had good water rights. Although a water source and the land it irrigated did not need to be contiguous (in this respect, Arizona law differed from English common law), a farmer could not legally sell water rights separate from the land with which they were associated, or use these water rights to irrigate a new land parcel.[53] In practice, however, water rights and land ownership were often uncoupled as they changed hands in a maze of claims and title transfers, which embedded residents in ever more entangled arrangements.

People of varied class, racial, and national backgrounds joined together to dig ditches—and to fight over them. The Ruíz family, John Montgomery, and Antonio Grijalba owned a ditch together, as did the Dunbars and the Madríds. Because law and tradition dictated that water users share proportionately during drought, these agreements often broke down. A descendent of the intermarried Ruíz-Montgomery family explained that "Simón Madríd and Dunbar were our families' mortal enemies." His great-grandmother María Ruíz de Montgomery "threatened Dunbar to have him locked up for stealing her water."[54] The hard work of building ditches—Simón Madríd's mile-long *acequia* took a month of digging by "eight men working with two span of oxen and a good big plow"—could build camaraderie or deepen resentments.[55] A withered crop was infuriating, as Dunbar's dunking of Grijalba so vividly demonstrated. But it was water or the lack of it—not what can only anachronistically be termed "racial tension"—that threw Tres Alamos landowners into fits.

Water agreements became labyrinthine and racial statuses remained supple, in part because so many Tres Alamos residents joined each other's families. Among the original 1865 water users, John Montgomery married María Ruíz, the daughter of his Mexican partner, and water rights transferred freely within the Ruíz-Montgomery family. Teófila León, daughter of a prominent Mexican American politician in Tucson, married Mark Aldrich and inherited her husband's water rights. Other marriages followed similar patterns. From 1872 to 1879, close to one-fourth of all marriages in Pima County (which then included both Tucson and Tres Alamos) were between Anglos and people with Spanish surnames.[56] These were alliances between powerful men and women. Territorial governor A. P. K. Safford married two Mexican women. Half of the Americans who founded the prestigious Arizona Pioneers' Historical Society in 1884 married Mexican women, most from prominent Tucson families like those who had settled on the San Pedro River. Mark Aldrich served as the first Anglo *alcalde* (mayor) of Tucson. He, Allen, Ohnesorgen, and Montgomery—intermarriers all—held elected office at various times.[57]

These marriages at once demonstrated and perpetuated the slippery racial boundaries of southern Arizona. In the United States, marriage law has been one of the most important ways to define and enforce racial difference. The miscegenation laws of the American South, largely concerned with black-white liaisons, are the most famous example. Western U.S. territories and states had complex miscegenation laws; those proscribing marriage with Euro-Americans contained laundry lists of forbidden groups, ranging from American Indians to "Polynesians" to "Mongoloids." Yet unlike almost every other non-European ethnic group in the American West, Mexicans were not barred by law from marrying Anglos.[58] They were legally white; and even if they were sometimes considered to be Indians, only twelve states outlawed Indian-white intermarriage (as did Arizona—and since Mexican Arizonans married Anglos, they were obviously not considered Indian). As for the residents of Tres Alamos, we might guess from their lofty place in the vestigial *casta* system, from their homestead claims, and from their successful voter registration, that they had a status as "white Mexicans" that appealed to the Anglo men who married into these families. The use of racial justifications for strategic marriages seems pernicious today, but it also demonstrates that Anglos in Tres Alamos did not see the category of "Mexican" as racially monolithic.

These were almost always marriages between Anglo men and Mexican women, though there were exceptions. Marriage is rarely a partnership of equals, even among couples with similar economic and cultural backgrounds. Most Anglos were wealthier than even elite Mexicans. Across these kinds of cultural and economic divisions, brides—at least in the eyes of men—have sometimes seemed like mere "collateral" in a loan to Anglo newcomers of colonial prestige and local connections, in return for the bridal family's future financial security and esteem.[59] Intermarriages risked transferring Mexican land or wealth into Anglo hands even as they offered both sides the potential for a good business match. Latin American elites viewed marriages as strategic alliances between families, and a failure to make a "good" match could bring dishonor to a woman and her kin. A wealthy "white" Anglo might prove to be a valuable family asset, but it was a gamble.[60]

Yet surely the content of these couplings varied as much as the individuals they united. Some liaisons were loving unions, some were economic partnerships between fathers and husbands, and others might have been little more than sexual or physical slavery. This latter possibility seems especially likely when men did not bother with marriage. At least one man in Tres Alamos kept a *casa chica,* as Mexican consorts were known. In Tucson, mining official Phocian Way saw the practice as a general rule. "Nearly every man . . . seems to have a lover here—and when the Mail arrives they are always at the station to welcome them. One of our party . . . has a fine looking black eyed girl for his especial favorite."[61]

Stereotypes about "Spanish" and "Mexican" women permeated discussions of sex and marriage across the Southwest. Some men praised "white" Spanish "señoritas" and denigrated darker-skinned women to justify marriage to the former and sexual exploitation of the latter. Many Anglo men assumed that they were inherently more desirable to Mexican women than were Mexican men. Phocian Way reported that some Mexican women "have a great fancy for Americans and a greaser [Mexican man] stands no chance with a white man." Stereotypes about Mexican women's sexuality were common but also contradictory. Phocian Way claimed that "chastity is a virtue unknown" in Tucson—certainly not a compliment in the late nineteenth century. Not everyone agreed, and most Anglo observers found Mexican women attractive, and far more appealing than Mexican men. Charles Poston, one of the first Anglos in Arizona, was typical. "The men of northern Mexico," he announced, "are far inferior to the women in every respect."[62]

Poston claimed that "The Mexican señoritas really had a refining influence on the frontier population. Many of them had been educated at convents, and all of them were good Catholics." Mexican women, according to Poston, were more chaste and ladylike than their Anglo counterparts, and handy to boot. Far from "useless appendages," Mexican women "could keep house, cook some dainty dishes, wash clothes, sew, dance, and sing,—moreover, they were experts at cards, and divested many a miner of his week's wages over a game of monte." Poston was hardly alone in his assessment. Phocian Way described Mexican women as "generally tender hearted and humane—and in sickness they are noted for being good and faithful nurses." Praising Mexican women was often a means of criticizing Mexican men. Mining engineer Raphael Pumpelly called Sonora and southern Arizona a "country where the men are mostly cut-throats and the women angels."[63]

These "angels" hovered in Anglo minds as fleeting symbols of an obsolete, "traditional" world falling away in the face of American modernity. At one of Arizona's new train stations in the early 1880s, travel writer Emma Hildreth Adams encountered "a tall, handsome young woman, dressed in black," with a white head-covering "of gauzy texture, which fell in folds over her shoulders." With the Mexican woman's "eyes fixed upon the engine breathing heavily in front of the train, she remained as still as a statue until the sharp clang of the bell, as we moved off, roused her from her musings. That maiden was the Past of Arizona personified." Only "the shrill bell and piercing shriek of the locomotive" could "break up the chronic reverie of the Territory."[64] Juxtaposing the most blatant symbol of modern, industrial America with the dainty, dreamy Mexican woman was trite prose but telling social commentary—about Anglo assumptions, not Mexican womanhood.

In fact, the Mexican woman at the train station enjoyed economic rights that Emma Adams might have envied. As early as the Spanish period, a few women—including ancestors of Tres Alamos homesteaders—were major landowners in Tucson. Under U.S. control, Arizona's hybrid of Spanish civil law and Anglo-American common law made the territory friendlier to women, and especially widows, than almost anywhere else in the United States. Arizona used the Spanish marriage doctrine of community property, in which a woman owns half of all property acquired by the couple during marriage. Although this property could be controlled by the husband, after 1865 either surviving spouse inherited half of the estate free and clear. In contrast, common law in its strictest form gave widowed women only the use, not ownership, of a mere one-third of their husbands' estates (though this custom had faded). Still, Arizona was generous. By 1887, the widow of a man with other heirs received the one-third portion of her husband's property free and clear, and all of her husband's estate if he had no descendants. Not only that; Arizona's inheritance laws were absolutely gender-neutral: widowed husbands and wives got the same provisions. Widows could even replace a stingy will with the law's more generous provisions.[65]

If Anglo-American commentators saw Mexican women as an empty slate on which to inscribe fantasies of supremacy, the reality was that some Mexican women could exercise real power.[66] So perhaps intermarriage from Mexican women's point of view had some appeal. Some women must have been coerced into these marriages, but others would have been willing partners. Intermarriage might offer a companionable and/or sexual partnership, but also a bond with a wealthy and powerful man. A good match preserved family honor. Women may not always have had a choice in these alliances, but they had incentives to join them. Even in the most traditional marriages, women inherited a fair share of their husbands' estates. Intermarriage might even transfer wealth from Anglos to Mexican Americans, especially because the children of intermarrying families usually became part of the larger Mexican-American community.[67]

One effect of Mexican women's legal rights is evident in Tres Alamos, where women homesteaded and owned land from the start. Most married women were ineligible to homestead, but the practice was open to female heads of households—including single women over twenty-one, widows, and the wives of invalids.[68] Among the twenty-eight Mexican land purchasers and homesteaders in Cochise County before 1900, four were women (14 percent of an admittedly small total number). In the early twentieth century, this proportion increased to about one in three, more than double the county and national averages. Either as sole proprietors or as heirs of their husbands, several women controlled a lot of property. In 1882, Anna Bonillas, a landowning widow and laundress, was one of the first people in Cochise County to buy public land. Mrs. Jesús Maldonado de Mejía, whose inheritance of her husband's homestead had been challenged, was especially tenacious. In addition to proving her right to that claim, in 1888 she patented her own homestead on the San Pedro. At the time of Maldonado's death in 1907 she owned five horses, two hundred head of cattle, and 1,600 acres of land. The estate's appraisers (three male Mexican homesteaders) estimated its total value at a respectable $2,000. María Ruíz de Montgomery took charge of farming barley, wheat, and vegetables on her property, except for two years when she rented her land to Chinese farmers. In 1879, she felt of sufficient standing to threaten to sue her neighbors over water use. Men casually referred to the land she "farmed," and her son noted that she farmed forty acres "for a long time." As a widow, Ruíz de Montgomery hired men to do farm labor, but so did most male landowners, whose status as "farmer" nobody questioned.[69]

Thanks to oral history, we know a little about women's lives on the river. Juana Arcia was born on Antonio Grijalba's Tres Alamos Ranch in 1876, and lived on the river her whole life. Her granddaughter recalled that her *abuela* (grandmother) "knew all about ranching." "She rode a horse; she gathered the cattle and horses and took them to the pastures and brought them back to the corrals. She searched for the cattle on the range when they were lost; she plowed and planted their fields with mule-drawn plows. She took care of the milk cows and fed the chickens and the turkeys they raised." She was, in short, a rancher and a farmer.[70]

Arcia was a ranch hand's daughter, but studies have shown that Mexican American women across the Southwest who owned land had control over their property, even when they did not want it. María Ruíz de Montgomery may have parlayed her land into a marriage proposal from second husband and fellow landholder Severiaño Bonillas. The widowed Teófila León de Aldrich lived in Tucson, first renting out the land and water rights she had inherited, then selling them to Antonio Grijalba.[71]

Women were essential to Tres Alamos, and not just as mothers and house-keepers. Their marriages blurred potential racial boundaries, and their land ownership widened its economic base. In addition to bearing children and managing households, Mexican American women filed homesteads and in-herited them, owned land and fought for water rights, planted crops and rode herd. These facts caused neither consternation nor celebration. Inter-marriage, civil law traditions, and the intricacies of homesteading law all of-fered Mexican women an important role in the settlement and maintenance of Tres Alamos. That they did so without obvious censure or sensationalism rebuts American adventurers' colonial fantasies of pliant Mexican woman-hood and potent American manhood. Frontier or no, Tres Alamos was not just a man's world.

Fighting the Apaches and Getting Along

Bonds of matrimony and kinship linked Mexicans and Anglos in Tres Alamos, but equally important were the bonds of war. Early adventurers from the United States arrived in Arizona confident the Apache "problem" would be easy to solve. They saw Spain and Mexico's failure to conquer the Apaches through the lens of the "Black Legend": the belief, in historian David We-ber's words, that "the Spaniards were unusually cruel, avaricious, treacher-ous, fanatical, superstitious, cowardly, corrupt, decadent, indolent, and au-thoritarian."[72] The Spanish and then the Mexicans had tried to solve the "Indian problem" for more than two hundred years, with limited success. Non-Hispanic Americans argued that Spaniards were simply bad colonial-ists, and that Americans would show them how it was done.

Americans typically made these arguments before actually encountering any Apaches. In 1856 the annual report of the Sonora Exploring and Mining Company, created to search for silver ore in the Gadsden Purchase, assured investors: "No dependence can be placed on the accounts given by the Span-iards, who were cruel colonizers, and have always provoked that barbarity of which they so much complain. I have seen much of Indians, and . . . I have invariably found them kind and harmless, when well treated." The Apaches later attacked and murdered several officers of the company, forcing it to abandon its headquarters in the Spanish colonial village of Tubac in 1861.[73] The Apaches' tactical brilliance and steely defense of their homeland—not

Spanish incompetence—were the real reason that southern Arizona remained sparsely settled.

Some observers disparaged Mexicans by way of expressing grudging praise for the Apaches. One Arizona guidebook claimed, "The Apache Indian, superior in strength to the Mexican, had gradually extirpated every trace of civilization, and roamed, uninterrupted and unmolested, sole possessor of what was once a thriving and popular Spanish province. Thus it remained until its acquisition by the Americans."[74] The part of Mexico that would become Arizona had never been "thriving" or "popular," but this fib conveniently set Europeans—Spanish or Anglo-American—above Mexicans (presumably of mixed race) and Apaches.

Yet if optimistic predictions had once pitted American ingenuity against Spanish and Mexican cruelty, frontier realities promoted cooperation and mutuality. On the ground, adventurers once so sure of American superiority began to rethink their positions. They had fought a war against each other less than two decades earlier, but in the world in which Tres Alamos was founded, Anglos saw Mexicans as comrades, not enemies. Renewed hostilities with the Apaches accelerated an us-versus-them mentality. When federal troops withdrew from nearby forts during the Civil War, settlers were left unprotected. Then, in 1863, inexperienced soldiers tricked and killed Chiricahua leader Mangas Coloradas. In response to the murder, his son-in-law and successor, Cochise, pledged war.[75] Apache raiders used the border to their advantage, slipping back and forth to elude both countries' armies. In the wars against the Apaches, Mexicans and Anglos forged their strongest—and most controversial—bonds.

The people of Tres Alamos had direct experience with the violence of the Apache Wars, as perpetrators and as victims. Francisca Comadurán's brother was killed by the Apaches in 1861. Successful farmer Antonio Campo Soza lost his father and perhaps his first wife to Apache attacks. The most spectacular case was that of Merejildo Grijalba (likely, though not definitely, a relation to Antonio), who was captured by Apaches in 1854 at the age of twelve. He escaped four years later, and went on to serve as a scout and interpreter for the U.S. Army. Kidnappings like these took place on both sides—indeed, they became a bone of contention in Gadsden Treaty negotiations, which forbade the sale of Apache captives. Captivity narratives like Grijalba's took on a mythic quality that reinforced feelings of danger as well as camaraderie among non-Indian residents. Mexican captives of the Apaches, like Grijalba, often assimilated into their captors' worlds, complicating the us-versus-them racial dialogues of Mexicans advocating total war against the Apaches. And Mexicans were not shy about taking Apache captives either, some of whom became household servants as well as valuable sources of privileged information about the enemy.[76]

In the late 1860s and early 1870s Apache attacks intensified in the Tres Alamos area. In a set of petitions sent to the United States Congress in 1871, southern Arizonans detailed various "outrages perpetrated by the Apache Indians" over the previous two years. The report's claims that "nearly all of the early pioneers have already fallen by [Apache] hands" and that "murders and robberies are almost of daily occurrence" are shameless overstatements. Yet the individual affidavits are revealing. One landowner reported that Apaches had taken twenty-five head of cattle worth $2,000 from Tres Alamos in 1869 and 1870. Another San Pedro farmer reported that he abandoned his farm after Apaches murdered two of his neighbors, stole four of his horses, and robbed his home. Mexican American freight haulers and packers described conditions with "no security for life or property on the roads or outside of the towns."[77]

Some people considered Tres Alamos too dangerous to live in. Eugenio Ruíz farmed in Tres Alamos, but left his young family in Tucson for safekeeping. Ruíz survived until old age, but fellow farmer H. C. Long was not so lucky. Long farmed the land of his friend Samuel B. Wise, a Tucson resident who gained title to the ranch in exchange for paying a friend's whiskey tab at a Tucson saloon. Wise never visited the property, but Long set out for "the San Pedro like a gentleman, with a hoe in the wagon," to plant corn. On a visit to Tucson, Long asked Wise why he never visited his own ranch. "I wouldn't go through there for ten thousand dollars," Wise replied, because "the Indians were there." Wise signed the ranch over to Long, who was killed by Apaches shortly after. "In those days," one pioneer recalled, "one could not be a successful Arizona homesteader if he adopted the motto 'safety first.'"[78]

Soon after Long's death, a Tucson posse perpetrated one of the nation's most notorious attacks against Indian peoples. In late April 1871, a group of

43

six prominent Anglos and several dozen Mexican Americans from Tucson (many from families with long histories of Apache fighting in the colonial military) banded together with Tohono O'odham Indians in a brutal attack on a band of Aravaipa Apaches, camped under a white flag outside Camp Grant on the San Pedro River several dozen miles north of Tres Alamos. The Aravaipas had an agreement with the camp commander, who had assured their safety; but according to the best estimate, the posse killed 118 of them, all but eight women and children.[79]

The Camp Grant Massacre, as it came to be known, attracted national outrage, and became a central issue in the debate between advocates of "force policy" and those of "peace policy" in President Ulysses S. Grant's administration. Force policy, represented on the national level by General William Tecumseh Sherman, viewed military conflict between white Americans and native peoples as unavoidable. Proponents of peace policy, mostly missionaries and women reformers, were "endeavoring to conquer by kindness," using the Good Book, not the sword. They took the lead in fashioning Indian policy in Grant's first administration. The 1871 petition to Congress, and to some extent the Camp Grant Massacre itself, were fevered protests to a recent report by General George Stoneman—a "peace" advocate—that the Apache danger was overrated and that the army should withdraw troops and dismantle several forts in Arizona. Influenced by the peace faction, President Grant threatened martial law over southern Arizona if the Camp Grant perpetrators were not arrested.[80]

Insolent locals justified their actions by pointing to incidents like Long's murder at Tres Alamos as justification. The vigilantes believed that the Aravaipa Apaches were using Camp Grant as a home base for raids on nearby communities, including Tres Alamos. Two weeks before the Camp Grant Massacre, John Montgomery reported in the Tucson newspaper that four men were killed along the San Pedro, "and quite surely by Indians fed and protected at Camp Grant."[81] Later, posse leader William Oury recalled running into Montgomery on the streets of Tucson shortly before Oury set out for Fort Grant. According to Oury, Montgomery told him that he "and the few other settlers of the San Pedro, who had escaped the scalping knife of the red-handed Apaches, had determined to abandon their homes and bring their families to safety in Tucson, leaving their crops, the result of their sweat and toil, at the mercy of the pitiless savages." Oury kept mum about his plans, but urged Montgomery to "wait a few days before" leaving Tres Alamos. "Something," he promised, "might . . . obviate the necessity of an absolute abandonment" of their little settlement. That "something" was mass murder, and the Tres Alamos residents stayed.[82]

In response to the president's threats of martial law, Arizona officials agreed to try the participants in the massacre; but the Tucson trial judge instructed the jury to find the men not guilty, which they did, after nineteen minutes of deliberation. The killers remained defiant. In the conflict between the policies of force and peace, many locals, both Mexican and American, placed their faith in force and vigilantism. Throughout the 1870s and 1880s, Tucson's Spanish-language newspapers reiterated the same anti-Apache arguments expressed by their English-language counterparts.[83]

In the years that followed, the men of Tres Alamos continued to form "unofficial militias" to avenge raids and the loss of property and life—Anglo and Mexican American alike.[84] The western tradition of forming posses, a tradition rooted in English common law, dovetailed nicely with Mexican traditions of *compadrazgo* ("godparenthood") and universal male military service to encourage organized retaliation against raiding Apaches. In 1872, John Montgomery reported that Apaches from Fort Grant had escaped and were "prowling around the place, shooting at people; driving the laborers from their fields; lying along the trails; stealing corn, and constantly annoying the people." After "a party of Indians entered the corral of Manuel Caranorno and stole two horses," reported Montgomery, "fourteen men mounted animals" to follow the Apaches' trail. A skirmish followed in which "three horses were killed; also three Indians." Montgomery explained that "the little force of citizens was forced to retire with the loss of one of their companions killed—Ramón Altamirano." When Tres Alamos residents heard about Altamirano's death, a larger group, this time thirty-five men (native Mexicans and American migrants), teamed up and set out. The next year Montgomery reported another raid and horse theft at Tres Alamos. "The people are saddling up to follow them," he wrote, "and will be on their trail in a few minutes." It is safe to say that "the people" were again both Mexican and Anglo.[85]

The Apache wars fostered a sense among landholding Anglos and Mexicans that both groups inhabited and embodied the categories of "white" and "American citizen." The writers of the 1871 petitions to Congress presented themselves as "faithful citizens of the United States, and your own kindred." They emphasized their citizenship, reliability, "hardships," and "fortitude." Mexican Americans, one of them a widowed ranch woman, accounted for thirty-one of the ninety-seven affidavits, and many of the Anglo witnesses had Mexican wives.[86] The very fact that residents would assemble such a group to petition the U.S. Congress reveals the camaraderie created by the Apache Wars. Some petitioners did specify when "Mexicans" were killed by Indians. On the other hand, Antonio Grijalba's brother Francisco described Indians who were "deadly hostile to the whites"—a category in which he surely included himself. Similarly, when an English-language newspaper in Tucson made the dubious claim in 1885 that "the Chiricahua Apaches have killed 1,000 white men, women, and children in the last twelve years," clearly Mexicans counted as whites.[87]

This ecumenical view of whiteness and its membership may not have extended much beyond southern Arizona, however. At least one reader of the 1871 petitions to Congress remained skeptical of dividing lawless Apaches on the one hand from a shared community of law-abiding citizens on the other. To prominent landowner Leopoldo Carrillo's claim that "all of the foregoing depredations were committed by hostile Indians," the cynical reader appended a handwritten "and brother Mexicans" on his private copy.[88] This anonymous comment stands in stark contrast to the way that Tres Alamos residents viewed their own allegiances.

The concept of race existed in Tres Alamos. For both Mexicans and Euro-Americans, the Apaches were a clear racial other. But as a divide between the two settler groups, race was not yet a clearly defined category of social, legal, or class difference—whether in theoretical circles or on the ground. It is not easy to untangle cause and effect in the camaraderie of Tres Alamos' residents. Were the shared *acequias* a motive or a consequence? What about intermarriages and the legal and property rights of Mexican women? Even the contested state of nineteenth-century racial theory and caste systems might have contributed. Yet two factors in particular stand out: a broad base of land ownership and water rights, and the threat of the Apaches. So long as

Mexican Americans represented a sizable proportion of the landowners in an agricultural economy, and so long as Apaches remained a menace to Tres Alamos, the settlement's residents would make common cause.

As the Apache Wars died down and more land-seeking Anglo newcomers poured into the region, Tres Alamos began to change. Prominent black resident Hampton Brown disappeared from the census records by 1880. In 1884, five years before Grijalba and Dunbar's tussle by the river, a promotional guidebook was already claiming that Tres Alamos "contains some 300 souls, principally Mexicans, but at the present writing, is rapidly filling up with Americans. . . . The lowing of herds of the prosperous ranchers and the waving fields of corn and barley, bear silent evidence to the fact that the days of the Apaches are fast fading away, and over the graves of their numerous victims and the ashes of the long-deserted wigwams, are growing and thriving a prosperous community."[89] "Mexican" could still be a national label more than a racial one in the late nineteenth century, and Tres Alamos was proof of that. But this world was vulnerable to the many coming changes in the political and economic climate.

2

Race and Conflict in Tombstone

In early April 1882, Cochise County hosted an illustrious visitor. William Tecumseh Sherman, who had marched across Georgia during the Civil War campaigns and now served as commanding general of the U.S. Army, was touring southeastern Arizona to investigate reports of violent cattle raids and rampant murder by gangs of "Cowboys" (or "Cow-boys," but almost always capitalized). Tombstone residents set off a volley of celebratory gunfire and "Chinese bombs" (firecrackers) to greet the general and his entourage. A parade snaked through the main thoroughfares of Fremont and Allen streets, where revelers swayed to the beat of a brass band. Sherman thanked the "fine looking, intelligent crowd," then retired to wine and dine at the posh Cosmopolitan Hotel, with its Steinway piano, ladies' parlor, and "beautiful veranda in front."[1]

Sherman was "surprised at the appearance of society & order," since he had received credible reports of "lawlessness & disorders" that needed "to be met promptly & efficiently." These reports convinced Sherman to urge the U.S. attorney general to endorse Governor Frederick Tritle's request for $150,000 to raise a posse of deputies "to aid the sheriff & marshals in preventing stage robberies & smuggling, cattle stealing &c." The deputies should be paid professionals, in Sherman's opinion. "It is idle to expect . . . the miners and . . . Ranchmen [to perform] the difficult & dangerous service of posse," he warned the attorney general, especially against "well mounted & well armed" criminals who enjoyed "the sympathy of some of the people."[2]

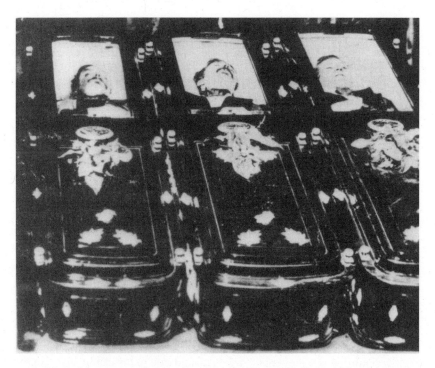

7. Corpses of shootout victims, October 25, 1881: Tom McLaury, Frank McLaury, and Billy Clanton. Photo by C. S. Fly. Arizona State Library, Archives and Public Records, History and Archives Division, Phoenix, 95-2822.

Sherman's visit came six months after a thirty-second gunfight in the streets of Tombstone. On the unseasonably cold afternoon of October 26, 1881, three brothers and their dentist friend had shot and killed three other men 150 feet from the OK Corral. The survivors were Wyatt, Virgil, and Morgan Earp, and John "Doc" Holliday. Their felled opponents were Billy Clanton and Tom and Frank McLaury (or sometimes McLowery), all associated with the Cowboy gang. Over the next six months, the continuing vendetta would leave at least eight more men dead. The shootout near the OK Corral forever changed the way Tombstone's past was remembered—indeed, it is largely *why* Tombstone's past has been remembered—but, as Sherman's visit suggests, it belonged to a larger series of events in a town that was infamous even in its own time.

The shootout was part of a battle over law, order, and border security that threatened a diplomatic emergency with Mexico. In the midst of the Apache

Wars and sporadic local campaigns against Chinese residents, throughout 1881 and 1882 officials in Mexico and the United States struggled over how to govern and police the border. Maintaining a border, then as now, required navigating carefully between local and federal governments and between civil and military authority, and along the fine line between law enforcement and vigilantism. Yet in the 1880s it was violence by American outlaws that prompted these debates, not political battles over Mexican migration. The Apaches and Chinese counted firmly as racial others, but the threat posed by Cowboy violence forced Tombstone's residents to emphasize their common bonds—not their differences—with the neighboring nation and its citizens.[3]

The Mexicans Wore White Hats, the Cowboys Wore Black

In film and popular culture, Tombstone has become a kind of western Anytown, but its real history was firmly rooted to its particular time and place in the Arizona borderlands. In 1877, prospector Ed Schieffelin discovered a rich silver outcropping along the low, conical hills near Goose Flats, east of the San Pedro River. He renamed the site and one of his claims his "Tombstone," a smirking reference to what soldiers at nearby Fort Huachuca told him he would find prospecting in arid Apache country. Four years and thousands of mining claims later, the "embryo city of canvas, frame and adobe, scattered over a slope," was home to almost ten thousand people. In its brief boom from 1879 to 1882, the rough-and-tumble camp generated hundreds of millions of dollars in silver ore.[4]

Like many western mining towns, Tombstone was both cosmopolitan and clannish. Rickety and prone to fire, the town was nonetheless by 1881 a fully realized community with banks and hotels, fine dining and chophouses, physicians and dentists, schools and charities. People of myriad backgrounds jostled for position in the makeshift camp, from the wealthy investor George Randolph Hearst (father of the future newspaper publisher William Randolph Hearst) to anonymous Pennsylvania roustabouts and prospectors from California and Nevada. Episcopal priest Endicott Peabody, future founder of Groton Academy and adviser to Franklin D. Roosevelt, served a six-month ministry in Tombstone, where parishioners found him a "sensible, manly fellow." Church groups, benevolent organizations, volunteer fire companies, ethnic societies like the German Turnverein, the Tombstone Hebrew Association, and the Irish Macabees popped up quickly. So did gambling parlors, opium dens, and at least sixty purveyors of beer and liquor.[5]

Almost half of Tombstone's early residents were born outside the United States. They came from across Europe, as well as from China and Mexico, in a fairly well distributed scattering. Besides the United States, no country, not even Mexico, accounted for more than 10 percent of the town's population.[6] Why so few Mexicans, even so close to the border? The answer lay in the timing of Tombstone's boom, at the tail end of the prospector era and the beginning of the industrial age. The silver camp attracted old-time miners from the California and Nevada gold camps, where they had gained experience not just with pick and shovel, but also with increasingly virulent anti-Mexican and anti-Chinese violence, laws, and union campaigns. These set a precedent for restrictions on civic and economic opportunities. Tombstone also enticed new venture capitalists, who invested in highly industrialized mines that rendered the once-prized skills of Mexican miners obsolete. Some miners across the line in Mexico did benefit from Tombstone's industrialization by guiding ore-laden mules to the town's high-tech smelters and mills for processing. Mexican-American merchant José Castañeda and business partner Joseph Goldwater (Barry's great-uncle) opened shop there briefly. Yet seasoned prospectors' experience excluding Latin American miners from camps, combined with the irrelevance of traditional Spanish-Mexican mining techniques to Tombstone's industrialized mines, added up to the fact that less than 1 percent of the miners listed in Tombstone's 1880 census were Mexican.[7]

Tombstone was also, not surprisingly, a very male place. Women of all backgrounds lived in Tombstone, but they accounted for no more than one in five of the early residents. Thirty women who belonged to what passed for the upper crust founded the Episcopal Ladies' Society, with Reverend Peabody's encouragement. Many women, like Irish boardinghousekeeper Nellie Cashman, and the Earp wives, who took in sewing, earned a respectable living doing domestic labor. Prostitutes of diverse nationalities were also in abundance, paying city license fees to work in the red-light district two blocks from the OK Corral. Rigid class divisions kept a chilly distance between the town's few women. The Earp wives, at least one of whom had once worked as a prostitute, found themselves shunned by "polite society," who attended events like the Valentine's Day "social party" thrown by the Bachelor's Club for the "Spinsters" of Tombstone.[8]

Most people came to Tombstone not to seek valentines, but to make a buck, and not necessarily an honest one. The camp attracted "<u>all men</u> of every shade of character" in a "mad career after money," according to Arizona Territory's acting governor, John Gosper. Some came seeking honest work—long shifts in the mines, or entrepreneurial enterprises such as laundries, grocery stores, and restaurants. But the pursuit of wealth could also mean cutting corners or breaking the law. In 1880, the editor of the new *Tombstone Nugget* promised that he would "fearlessly expose fraud, bogus mining speculations, and all schemes which might result in gain to individuals, but disastrously to the district." He had his work cut out for him. On top of the usual investment scams, rival townsite companies spawned title disputes that robbed innocent people of their property. In early October 1881, the San Francisco *Stock Report* warned entrepreneurs that southeastern Arizona was "honeycombed with corruption."[9]

In addition to Tombstone's boomtown chicanery, the wide-open borderlands supported a band of "desperadoes and outlaws" who were conducting a "reign of terror" on both sides of the border—stealing cattle and horses, holding up stagecoaches, and murdering their mostly Mexican victims. These rustlers were the men known as Cowboys. In West Texas, the term "Cowboy" had retained its familiar meaning of ranch hand and cattle driver. But in Arizona and New Mexico, as the federally appointed U.S. attorney for Arizona explained to the U.S. attorney general, "the name has been corrupted" to include "the lawless element that exists upon the border, who subsist by rapine plunder and highway robbery; and whose amusements are drunken orgies, and murder." Tombstone journalist Clara Spalding Brown declared that "Cowboy" was a "convenient term for villains promiscuously."[10]

The Cowboys were a loose gang of rustlers and hangers-on who numbered anywhere from 30 to 380, depending on who was counting. They used an old mining camp high in the remote Chiricahua Mountains as a hideout, and their origins were shadowy. One source claimed they included "the exiled ranger from Texas, the hunted stage robber from Montana, the murderer from Idaho, the desperate, and criminal of every class, from every place." Gosper thought that many were "fugitives from justice from eastern states," while the *Tombstone Epitaph* reported the Cowboys were "principally from Western Texas & Lincoln Co., New Mexico," another site of recent frontier violence.[11] Whatever their true numbers or origins, the consensus was that the Cowboys came to southeastern Arizona to make money and to escape the law.

Even those who did not actually raid and rustle might benefit from the bloody work, by buying stolen cattle or turning a blind eye to the Cowboys' exploits. The Clanton family, who owned ranches first in the San Pedro Valley then in the Sulphur Springs Valley, belonged squarely in the rustler category, but the McLaurys were likely fences for stolen goods and cattle. Rustlers and ranchers made lucrative contracts with corrupt Indian agents and army procurement officers who did not ask many questions about the origin of beef cattle, even those whose Mexican brands were still visible. These fences and agents were part of the large group who, according to Governor Gosper, were dealing "dishonestly with one hand secretly behind them, handling the stolen property of the 'Cow Boys'" and splitting the proceeds.[12]

This spectrum of criminal behavior complicates the simplest version of the gunfight at the OK Corral—namely, that it was a confrontation between "Cowboys" and "Lawmen." Certainly the latter group preferred to emphasize their law enforcement duties over other, less lofty pursuits. The Earp brothers had come to Tombstone in 1879 and 1880. Virgil, previously Tombstone's acting chief of police, was an assistant U.S. marshal at the time of the shootout. His brother Wyatt was a former deputy sheriff who moonlighted as a guard and detective for the Wells, Fargo stagecoach company. Morgan occasionally pitched in to search for stage robbers and the like. Shortly before the shootout, Virgil swore his brothers in as special deputies, and informally did the same for Doc Holliday. But in addition to their law enforcement duties, the Earp brothers also worked as part-time gamblers, bartenders, and real estate and mining speculators.[13]

A clear division between the "law" and the Cowboys, then, is misleading. Gosper complained that the "civil officers" of Cochise County and Tombstone "sinned to 'wink at crime' . . . for the hope and sake of gain." The Cowboys, he claimed, "have in many cases, no doubt, <u>purchased</u> their liberty, or have paid well to be left unmolested."[14] Gosper was probably referring to county sheriff Johnny Behan, who was closely linked with the Cowboys. But the Earps were no saints, either. Their friend Doc Holliday was wanted for murder, and rumors pinned several recent stagecoach robberies on the Earps.

Personal disputes worsened the situation. Behan and the Earps were bitter rivals. Wyatt Earp had hoped to be appointed sheriff when Cochise County was created in early 1881, but he was passed over in favor of Behan. That summer Wyatt Earp took up with Behan's girlfriend, Josephine Marcus, a German-Jewish dancer and actress from San Francisco. As acting governor, John Gosper visited Tombstone a month before the shootout, and found Behan and the Earps blaming each other for the county's "unsettled state of affairs." Behan accused the Earps of being uncooperative in bringing down the Cowboys, but Wyatt Earp had the "same spirit of complaint against Mr. Behan . . . and his deputies."[15] The Earps and Frank McLaury had argued over some stolen mules. Tubercular, grouchy Doc Holliday clashed with almost everyone but the Earps, who themselves had personal beefs with the Clantons and McLaurys.

Tempers flared the night before the shootout, as bickering at the poker table spilled into the street. Hours before the gunfight, Wyatt Earp reportedly threatened Ike Clanton: "You cattle thieving son of a bitch, and you know that I know you are a cattle thieving son of a bitch. You've threatened my life enough and you've got to fight." (In the end, Ike ran away from the fighting, and left his brothers to fight and die for him.)[16] The "duty of no retreat" demanded that a man respond to such a naked challenge. The Earps, Clantons, and McLaurys knew they were countenancing violence. To back away at this point would mean losing face and losing honor, both unacceptable in a culture that demanded manly bravery.[17]

And it was not just personal pride that was at stake. Regional divisions made preserving honor even more imperative. The shootout, some say, pitted northern Republicans against southern Democrats in a small-scale sequel to the Civil War.[18] The Earps were raised in Iowa and Kansas. Wyatt had hoped to join brothers James and Virgil in the Union Army, but was underage. The family was staunchly Republican. Behan and the Clantons, on the other hand, were Missouri and Tennessee natives who had helped found southern Arizona's Democratic Party in the late 1870s. In some circles, the term "Cowboys" referred not just to the "outlaw element," but to southern Democrats more generally.[19]

"Cowboy" and "Lawman" often translated into "Democrat" and "Republican" in southern Arizona, but not always. The McLaurys were originally from New York and Iowa, not the South. Tom and Frank's brother William, an attorney who came to Tombstone after the shootout to avenge his brothers' death, was considered a Radical Republican back home in Texas.[20] And on the other side, territorial governor John Frémont—the famous retired general known as the "Pathfinder," who had been the Republican Party's first presidential candidate—appointed the Democrat Behan instead of Wyatt Earp as Cochise County's first sheriff. (Frémont, an appointee who feared a backlash from the territory's Democratic majority, split his patronage selections between the two parties.) And Earp's sidekick Doc Holliday was from Georgia. Wyatt Earp could also play both sides of the political game. In 1881, Earp reportedly offered to split the reward for a stagecoach robber with the Clantons and McLaurys, in return for their support for his candidacy in the 1882 elections. The deal went sour. After the shootout, several of the Earps' former allies turned against them and created new, bipartisan alliances in local city elections.[21]

A more precise way to describe Tombstone's factional divide is as a rivalry between the allies of industrial capitalism and strong government, and their opponents. Ultimately, the men linked to Tombstone's mining economy did not want the same things that the Cowboys wanted. Cattle rustlers and their allies did not desire the close scrutiny of efficient law officers, nor did they want a rule-of-law government that could carefully monitor business transactions. They were not eager to welcome every eastern investor with an open checkbook, nor did they care how wild and unsettled the place seemed to outsiders. Cattle rustling relied on a fundamentally local economy and flourished in the absence of outside scrutiny. As Arizona's U.S. attorney put it, "This element in certain isolated sections has long defied the local authorities," and the "element" wanted to keep it that way.[22]

As Tombstone grew, demands for better law enforcement coupled with new competition from outside beef suppliers threatened the Cowboys' livelihood. Mining required the very things the Cowboys resisted: easy access to (and for) outside capital, stable and reliable contracts, and, above all, recourse to rule of law. Mining towns were infamous for spawning more lawyers than miners (or so it sometimes seemed), and Tombstone was no exception. The mining industry and wide-open cattle rustling could not long coexist, and the Tombstone and Cowboy factions knew it. Their differences did not have to end in a gunfight—in fact, they did not end there—but they did require some kind of confrontation. As Gosper predicted three weeks before the shootout, "Something must be done, and that right early."[23]

At first blush, the Tombstone industrial crowd, with its abundant capital and government support, might seem more powerful than a handful of back-country thugs. But the Cowboys enjoyed an important legal advantage. The federal Posse Comitatus Act of 1878 forbade the use of "any part of the army" in the formation of a *posse comitatus,* a common-law term that meant literally the "power of the county," and technically referred to all male residents over the age of fifteen. In practice, a real posse was quite close to the popular image of the armed men on horseback called on by local sheriffs and marshals to exact frontier justice. Prior to the 1878 law, many a *posse comitatus* formed by U.S. marshals included federal troops on active duty, as well as civilians. Although the new law built on the revered American legal tradition of separating military and civil functions, it was a break from common practice and a specific product of post-Reconstruction politics. Southern Democrats in Congress, still angry over the use of military troops as police forces in the South during Reconstruction, had championed the legislation.[24]

The crisis in Cochise County became an important early test of the law, and prompted high-level discussions in Washington about its unintended consequences. Those monitoring the Cowboy Wars had little good to say about the law. The men who ran Arizona wanted to attract capital, and because they were Republican appointees, their loyalties lay with an eastern business class who retained ties to Reconstruction politics and its promotion of federal power. The 1878 federal law meant that local civil law officers and army troops alike were, in Sherman's words, "utterly powerless to prevent marauders from crossing over into Sonora, or to punish them when they return for asylum with stolen booty." Only federal authority, in Sherman's opinion, was "equal to" the task. If troops could only get the power "to do whatever each case demands, the Cowboys will soon cease their forays." But the limitations created by the Posse Comitatus Act were well-known to the Cowboys, who took full advantage of them. "Without the power to pursue, arrest and punish, it is worse than a farce for soldiers to be sent to that border, for the cow-boys are intelligent men and know the law." Sherman denounced the "notorious" law, and demanded either its repeal or a flexible interpretation from the U.S. Department of Justice.[25]

Sherman was not alone. To a man, territorial and federal officials condemned the law. Even Frémont, who treated the governorship as a sinecure and was rarely in Arizona, lobbied Congress for a revision of the act and for federal funds to create a territorial militia modeled after the Texas Rangers. Back in Arizona, Gosper called the law "foolish," and complained that troops were "tied hand and foot" by it. Even "extreme Democrats" would "without any hesitancy vote to repeal" it, Gosper insisted, if they could only understand the "unfortunate situation" in Cochise County. The assassination of President James Garfield forestalled any federal response to the problem. He was shot in July 1881, but did not die until September; the awkward interim paralyzed chains of command, and the new administration yielded several changes in the Cabinet. Two months after the shootout in Tombstone, new president Chester Arthur proposed a law making it a federal crime for outlaws or Indians to cross borders to evade justice. He also recommended a revision to the *comitatus* law. Both ideas went nowhere in Congress.[26]

Military officials in Arizona were desperate enough to propose using Indian scouts to chase down the Cowboys. Across the border, militias of Opata Indians tracked Cowboys for the Mexican government. The U.S. Army used Indian scouts to chase Indians, so why not Cowboys? Army officials and some civilian allies argued that scouts were not technically troops, and thus were not subject to the law's restrictions. Major James Biddle, commander of Camp Grant, and his head of scout operations offered the U.S. marshal's office "two or more parties, each consisting of troops and a company of Indian Scouts; the latter will be found invaluable." The regular troops, he promised, would not lift a finger, much less a rifle, unless civil authorities were directly attacked.[27] The scouts, however, could "make a descent upon . . . any . . . cow-boys ranch where marauders and those thieves are supposed to live."

In so doing, "such ranches can be entirely surrounded and the occupants captured, provided proper secrecy can be maintained." Biddle promised that "the troops or Scouts are [not] to act in anywise as a posse comitatus," and "the subservience of the Military to the Civil Authority will be <u>strictly observed</u>."[28]

J. W. Evans, a deputy U.S. marshal stationed in Tombstone, was interested but skeptical. Like many residents of southern Arizona, he placed little trust in the military, still less in its Indian scouts. He envisioned a citizens' posse of "not . . . less than thirty" men, and ideally a "force of . . . 200 . . . including soldiers Indians and citizens." More civilians would be "advisable if they can be had," because "one good citizen is worth many Indians or soldiers in fighting." "It will be tough on us if we get whipped," he warned, and "this will certainly be the result if we have nothing but Indians & soldiers." His preference for "citizens" over Apache scouts is not surprising, though his desperation is evident in his willingness to consider using the latter at all. His conviction that civilians were preferable to regular troops spoke volumes about the pent-up disgust locals felt for an army (much of it made up of African American "Buffalo soldiers") whose failure to end the Apache wars was enraging. Two months after the offer of troops and Indian scouts, reports of unrest at the huge San Carlos Indian Reservation, involving "even the Apache scouts," scotched any further interest in the plan.[29]

The urgency that fueled plans for Indians to chase Cowboys came from a desperate desire to preserve peaceful relations with Mexico. A war of tit-for-tat between Cowboys and Mexicans had racked up several murders on both sides of the border. In the spring of 1881, a group of Cowboys stealing cattle in Sonora "were attacked by the Mexican citizens," one of whom was killed—in addition to the Cowboys. The incident "caused bad blood" between Cowboys and Sonorans, and conflict escalated. In late July, Cowboys raided a Mexican pack train crossing Skeleton Canyon in far southeastern Cochise County, stole $4,000, and killed four men. Just weeks later, "Old Man" Newman Clanton (Ike and Billy's father) was riding herd, perhaps as camp cook, with six other men through remote Guadalupe Canyon, a hundred miles from Tombstone on a trail that snaked along the U.S. side of the border. During the night, shots rang out; five men, including the Clanton patriarch, were killed by gunfire. The ambush at Guadalupe Canyon was likely committed by Sonoran soldiers retaliating for a recent altercation between the Cowboys and Mexican troops in Sonora.[30]

Even before the incident at Guadalupe Canyon, complaints about attacks on Mexicans were escalating on both sides of the border. In June 1881, Arizona's U.S. attorney C. B. Pomroy warned the federal government that "citizens of the United States . . . are constantly committing depredations of the most barbarous character" in Mexico. "The inhabitants of Northern Sonora and Chihuahua have suffered, and are daily suffering outrages and indignities at the hands of these [American] outlaws." If not stopped, Pomroy warned, their crimes and trespasses "may lead to an open rupture between that country and our own." Officials at every level of government worried that the Cowboy raids would lead to "an international controversy, if not war."[31]

Furious letters passed among officials in Sonora, Arizona, and Washington. The Mexican government was "very much incensed at our seeming neglect," Evans reported from Tombstone, and he could hardly blame them. Sonoran governor Luis Torres implored U.S. officials "to act promptly." "Our border," he observed, is "in continuous alarm," and Mexican citizens "threaten to take matters into their own hands if they are not protected by our government." Torres placed three hundred Mexican troops on his side of the line, and urged American authorities to do their part as well. In Washington, Sherman warned that the failure to use troops to put down the Cowboys might leave the United States "compromised with our neighbor Mexico."[32]

Mexican and American officials alike hoped to maintain burgeoning transnational business ties. After years of warfare and tense relations between the two nations, the ascension of Porfirio Díaz in 1876 brought a regime friendly to U.S. business interests that prized Mexican political stability, even if the price was dictatorship. High-ranking officials on both sides of the border were anxious to protect massive investments by American and British railroad and mining companies, which already controlled the vast majority of assets in Mexico. These men wanted a border permeable to international capital, not to Cowboy raiders. In the early 1870s, Americans had complained about Mexican rebels raiding Arizona; but by the end of the decade, this had reversed, as Mexico began protesting the Cowboys' "acts of lawlessness" in Sonora. If something was not done, Gosper warned the attorney

59

general, "the cow-boy will come to control and 'run' that part of our Territory with terror and destruction and probably cause serious complications with our sister Republic Mexico, with which we are now in fullest peace."[33]

The United States was indebted to Mexico for its restraint, and both locals and officials knew this. Had these crimes "been inflicted upon our people by Mexicans," U.S. attorney Pomroy admitted, they would have "aroused a whirlwind of indignation from the Rio Grande to the Gulf of California, and doubtless long ago led to an invasion of Mexican soil."[34] He seemed genuinely grateful that Mexico did not share his own country's bellicose nature—or capacity.

Cowboy attacks threatened local merchants as well as foreign investment. Arizona's chief U.S. marshal, Crawley Dake, informed the U.S. attorney general that "raiding robbing and murdering on the border . . . is causing great injury to the business interests of our growing territory." In early August 1881, Cowboys attacked a Sonoran supply train returning from a shopping trip in Tombstone. Incidents like this endangered Tombstone commerce, and officials noticed. A report from Mexico's Department of Foreign Relations concluded that the "repression" of the Cowboys would "doubtless have a beneficial influence upon trade between the two Republics," as well as "relations" between the citizens of both nations. Mexican diplomat Manuel de Zamacona forwarded a newspaper editorial to the U.S. secretary of state, James Blaine. Its author warned that while "Sonora is rapidly filling up with Americans," violence threatened to erase the "advantages to be devised from commercial and social intercourse between the two countries." The newspaper was published in Tucson, not Mexico.[35]

Race appeared only fleetingly in discussions about the Cowboys. In hundreds of pages of correspondence between Washington and Arizona, only one exchange directly addressed race. Asked by the U.S. secretary of the interior whether any of the Cowboys were Mexican or Indian, John Gosper noted that a few—not many—belonged to what he called the "Mexican element." (After the shootout, Wyatt Earp shot and killed a man named Florentino Cruz, whom he believed to have been involved in his brother Morgan's murder.) When Gosper insisted that "the Americans, or whites, fully direct and control . . . the American side of the line," he cast "white" and "American" as synonyms. He also noted that "a bitter hatred exists between the 'cowboys' and the Mexican . . . and a spirit of revenge of one race against the other seems to exist." On the Mexican side, this enmity was retaliation for cattle raids and murder. At one point, Gosper grew petulant when he complained that the "Mexicans . . . are equally guilty with Americans in the matter of murder and theft," but went on to catalogue the Cowboys' crimes in lurid detail as he demanded federal aid. When pressed, Gosper had parsed the racial dynamics of the conflict, but it was not his first impulse to do so.[36] "Mexican" was clearly a racial category to Gosper, but this fact did not supersede its use as a more strictly national label. At a time when Americans were eager to appease Mexican authorities, race was not the border's dominant discourse—at least as applied to Sonorans.

More common was genuine sympathy from Anglo-Americans for both Mexican citizens and their government. In February 1881, Tucson's Democratic newspaper implored readers to "let our Mexican neighbors understand that our people are determined to rid them and Arizona of these outlaws and they will be protected in following them across the line into our borders, and treating them in a summary manner."[37] The last comment appeared to endorse Mexican authorities' shooting down Cowboys on U.S. soil. Echoing these sentiments, Tombstone residents defended the Mexican attack on Clanton's party at Guadalupe Canyon. Earp partisan George Parsons wrote in his diary, "This killing business by the Mexicans, in my mind, was perfectly justifiable, as it was in retaliation." Newspaper correspondent Clara Spalding Brown reported that no one was happy about the "great massacre," but "the Mexicans were not the first to inaugurate the present unhappy state of affairs. . . . The Mexicans have lost a great deal of stock, and some of their countrymen have been murdered." Around the same time, Adolfo Dominguez, an assistant to General José Otero, commander of Mexican border troops, visited Tombstone to plead for "united action" in "driv[ing] out these thieves and murderers." Dominguez assured Tombstone residents that Mexicans did not blame all Americans, whose assistance they eagerly sought.[38]

Vigilante justice in the West was often racially motivated and directed, just as it was in the South,[39] and Tombstone had its fair share of racial prejudice. Yet here was a case where calls for vigilantism arose in response to the actions of white Cowboys, whose violence was directed mainly against Mexicans. Frustrated government officials and local citizens resorted to operating outside the law to police the border and to protect Tombstone. Although the Earps always maintained that they constituted a legal posse on the day of the shootout, an extralegal vigilance committee called the "Committee of Safety" was armed and ready to back them up. The vigilantes, many of them leading citizens, stood down when they found the situation under control, but continued to "protect" the Earp faction after the shootout.[40]

The committee's larger goal was to stop the Cowboys altogether. In a report to the U.S. secretary of the interior, the acting governor claimed to have "suggested and encouraged" local citizens to create "this said committee in a secret manner" on his visit to Tombstone a month before the shootout. He urged them to organize "not for the purpose of taking the law into their own hands, but for the purpose of protecting their lives and property from destruction by the murderers, and robbers." Since the committee's creation, he continued, "a number of the worst cowboys have left that vicinity fearing they would be 'lynched,' or stretched up by the neck 'without judge or jury.'" By closing his summary of the committee's work with another plea to repeal the Posse Comitatus Act, Gosper indirectly blamed Congress for Cochise County's resort to vigilante justice.[41]

Neither the shootout nor the vigilantes resolved the problems in Cochise County. If anything, the vendetta set in motion by the gunfight only worsened the situation. In the months that followed, stagecoach robberies escalated, and Virgil and Morgan Earp were both ambushed—Morgan fatally. Wyatt Earp and his posse killed several men in retaliation. Through it all, Congress refused to amend the Posse Comitatus Act or fund a territorial militia. In January 1882, Clara Spalding Brown complained: "An element of lawlessness, an insecurity of life and property, [and] an open disregard of the proper authorities . . . [have] greatly retarded the advancement of the place" and "occasioned much annoyance and loss." "The state of affairs in this camp," she concluded, "is far more unsettled than it was in the early days of the settlement." In March 1882, the *Tombstone Epitaph* was still heartily endorsing vigilantism: "The recent events in Cochise County make it incumbent upon, not only officials, but all good citizens as well, to . . . speedily rid this section of that murderous, thieving element which has made us a reproach before the world, and so seriously retarded the industry and progress of our country."[42]

Officials continued to look for ways they could use federal troops to subdue the Cowboys. U.S. attorney Pomroy suggested that since the territories were under federal control, federal troops could be used to protect them. Three weeks after the shootout, acting U.S. attorney general S. F. Phillips considered characterizing the Cowboys as a "military enterprise" that had "organized with a view to invade the territory of a neighboring people with whom we are at peace." Under such circumstances, "I think the troops may be lawfully employed to prevent them making predatory raids into the territory of Mexico, and in this way to suppress them." It was a legal stretch, and if it did not work, then the president would have to issue an executive order allowing use of the troops, or Congress would have to pass special legislation.[43]

In the end, the president did step in. In a public proclamation on May 4, 1882, Chester Arthur threatened martial law in southeastern Arizona if anyone involved in "obstruction of the laws" failed to "disperse and retire peacefully" by May 15. The president warned "good citizens" of the region to refrain from "aiding, countenancing, [or] abetting" criminal acts. In part, he was responding to pressure from Mexico. Less than a month earlier, Mexican ambassador Matías Romero, who had close ties to New York mining and railroad investors, had lodged an official complaint.[44] In Cochise County, powerful ranchers were closing ranks against the rustlers, and the Cowboys began to scatter.[45] By mid-summer 1882, the Cowboys' power was on the wane, but the Apache Wars ensured that Cochise County remained anything but peaceful.

Apache Wars make Strange Bedfellows

At the height of the Cowboy controversies, the on-again, off-again Apache Wars reignited at a place called Cibecue on the Fort Apache Reservation, more than two hundred miles north of Tombstone. During the summer of 1881, Apache medicine man Noch-ay-del-klinne prophesied the rise of dead chiefs if white interlopers could be expelled from the region. This religious revival, reminiscent of the better-known Ghost Dance Movement among the Sioux a decade later, gained a sizable following of White Mountain and Cibecue Apaches, including several army scouts. On his own, Noch-ay-del-klinne posed little threat to peace on the reservation, but inexperienced civilian and military officers demanded his arrest or death. When soldiers arrested the medicine man in August, several scouts turned against the troops and began shooting. Noch-ay-del-klinne was killed in the confusion. Afterward, many Apaches believed that the attack "was premeditated by the white soldiers" or by corrupt Indian agents, and the head of the army's Department of Arizona, General George Crook, urged caution in retaliating against Indian scouts.[46]

In the aftermath, the Chiricahua Apaches feared renewed attacks against all Apache groups. Chiricahua leaders Naiche (son of Cochise) and Juh (related by marriage to Geronimo) were jittery about army troops massing on the reservations. On September 30, the two men led a group of seventy-four warriors into Mexico's Sierra Madre Mountains, where they joined another band of fugitive Apaches that included Geronimo.[47] Over the next six months, at the height of the Cowboy raids, active warfare between the Apaches and the U.S. Army convulsed the Arizona-Sonora borderlands.

Catching Geronimo and the others demanded following their trail into Mexico, but the Cowboy controversies compromised negotiations for a border-crossing agreement. In December 1881, General Orlando Willcox, who briefly replaced Crook as the commander of the Department of Arizona, wrote to his superiors that Mexican military officials were "shy of making any practical agreement for attacking the renegade Indians. They are very sensitive about our crossing the border, and I think they feel sore because we do nothing to prevent Cow-Boy raids." In the end, Mexico had its own reasons to support an agreement. The Mexican states of Sonora and Chihuahua had lost hundreds of citizens in Apache warfare and wanted to keep the region safe for investment. In July 1882, two months after Chester Arthur's threat of martial law, the United States and Mexico finally hammered out a deal to allow troops from both nations to cross the border in active pursuit of Indian enemies.[48]

As the debate over the border agreement suggested, in some ways the Cowboys and the Apaches presented similar problems in Cochise County. Both defied authorities at every level. Both prompted threats of martial law. Both capitalized on the border's permeability and weak enforcement, and easily retreated to remote hideaways. Both were aided and abetted by arms dealers and fences for stolen goods. In fact, when cooler heads prevailed, many Arizona residents blamed corrupt traders and merchants for stirring up Indian conflict, in order to keep army forts in the area.[49]

Yet the treatment and perception of the two groups had important differences. First and foremost, the Apaches were at war to protect a homeland that had been theirs for hundreds of years before Cowboys or silver miners had appeared; the Cowboys were a criminal operation. But this was not an important distinction to most people at the time, who did not respect Apaches' claims to the land, and saw them as murderers, not warriors. In contrast, recall Acting Attorney General Phillips' suggestion that the Cowboys be considered a "military enterprise."

And then there was race: both Americans and Mexicans viewed the line between themselves and the Apaches as a racial one. In doing so, they took a course common in war by using race to demonize the enemy. But they did not do the same to the Cowboys. In Mexico, the line between Sonora's elite politicos and military leaders and the Cowboys was not a perceived racial line so much as a line between citizen and criminal, between high-class and low-caste. The Sonoran upper crust considered themselves, and were considered, *blanco* (white).[50] In later years, Anglo-Americans would be much less aware of such distinctions, but in the early 1880s, business and political elites on both sides of the border probably understood themselves as sharing the same racial status.

So there was another contrast between the Apaches and the Cowboys: while the Cowboys divided the loyalties of local residents, the Apaches had an amazingly unifying effect. The McLaurys and Earps might shoot each other down in the street, but they shared a hatred—and probably terror—of the Chiricahua Apaches. In early October 1881, reports had circulated that Geronimo and Naiche were near Tombstone. Mayor and newspaper editor John Clum and city marshal Virgil Earp teamed up with their erstwhile rival Sheriff Behan to form an impromptu militia they dubbed the Tombstone Rangers. Accompanying these strange bedfellows were forty other men, among them Wyatt Earp, George Parsons, an African American cook named John Pittman Rankin, and probably Mexican packers. After a day and a half of fruitless searching, sometimes in driving rain, the Rangers rested at the McLaury ranch in the Sulphur Springs Valley. Three weeks before their face-off in Tombstone, the Earps and McLaurys shared a meal, and plotted their pursuit of the Apaches. Later, "things got lively while the whiskey flowed," but no violence among the rivals ensued. Virgil Earp politely greeted the notorious outlaw "Curly Bill" Brocius, who was staying at the ranch, though

Wyatt Earp was reportedly less friendly. Five months later, Wyatt Earp took credit for shooting down Curly Bill in a bloody campaign to avenge his brother Morgan's murder.[51]

After the dinner and camp-out at the McLaury ranch, John Clum caught up with some Apache scouts camping nearby. He knew them from his days at the San Carlos Reservation, where he had served as Indian agent until 1877. The Rangers also visited with "one company or two of Negro or Buffalo soldiers," stationed at nearby Fort Huachuca. George Parsons claimed that the Apaches tended to "deride" the African American troops, but Parsons felt they "fought well enough" in a battle at nearby Dragoon Pass. Nothing could show the dedication to defeating the Apaches more than the enemy-of-my-enemy alliance between Clum and the Earps, Behan and the McLaurys, Apache scouts and Buffalo soldiers. The Cowboys had a reputation for being great Indian fighters, which was why so many people put up with them for as long as they did.[52]

Even for those far removed from the bloody terrain of the Apache Wars, the Chiricahua Apaches were the ultimate racial other—not just as a foe but as an object of scientific study. After the great Chiricahua leader Mangas Coloradas was tricked and murdered by U.S. soldiers under white flag in 1863, his head was removed and boiled for phrenologists to examine. The Apaches found this more barbarous than even what was by all accounts a treacherous murder. As it turned out, the chief's prodigiously large cranium defied "scientific" certainties about brain size and racial hierarchies, and sent phrenologists back to the drawing board.[53]

Back in Arizona and Sonora, for most residents the Chiricahua Apaches represented the outer limits of humanity. Damning the Cowboys by unfavorable comparison to the Apaches justified the conquest of both. In early 1881, one Arizona newspaper complained that the Cowboys "are worse than Apaches and should be treated as such. . . . Wherever found let them be shot down like the Apache." Terrified awe for the Apaches simultaneously elevated them as formidable opponents, then dismissed them as less human than the diverse coalitions assembled to fight them. "Courage they possess to a remarkable degree," one journalist admitted, but "it is the courage of ignorance and of an animal nature." Sonorans called Apaches *broncos* (wild animals) who became *mansos* (domesticated and, by implication, castrated) once they surrendered. Animalistic descriptions were pervasive, and from high authorities. A retired U.S. soldier wrote that "the fiendish cruelties committed by them . . . makes one doubt whether they are human." One military journal reported that Chiricahua Apaches had "all the ferocity of the most savage wild beast . . . rendered more formidable by human cunning." General George Crook, who as the Apaches' greatest foe was also sometimes one of their staunchest defenders, compared them to coyotes and called them "the tiger of the human species." Dehumanizing the Apache served to underscore the common humanity of their opponents.[54]

Yet the Apaches' opponents could also cast them as exemplars of untamed virility at a time when many American men feared the effeteness of modern civilization. General Nelson Miles assigned Leonard Wood, who gained fame as a young army surgeon when he tracked Geronimo into Mexico, to examine the Apaches to see what was hereditary about their "fiber and sinew and nerve power." Wood, who would become a Rough Rider, U.S. Army chief of staff, and candidate for president, called the Chiricahuas a "tough, hardy, well developed race of men." Polarizing images of beastliness and manliness served the same purpose: to justify America's conquest of the Apaches. If the Apaches were the manliest of men, they were a worthy foe. If they were the lowest of men, more brute than animals, then that, too, meant they had to be vanquished.[55]

Gender norms also policed the distinction between "savage" and "civilized." The Chiricahua Apaches included several "women warriors," who fought alongside men. To most Euro-American observers, Chiricahua women were "repulsive, uncouth" members of the "Great Unwashed," as one report put it. Observers disdained Apache divisions of labor. In describing farm techniques at the Fort Apache reservation, General Miles claimed that "the women did nearly all the work, though a few men condescended occasionally to assist." Incidents of wife beating and the punishment of unfaithful women (the tips of their noses were cut off) caused especially deep conflict with reservation officials. Leonard Wood told a story about an American family that had been attacked by Apaches. "The husband was tied up and compelled to witness indescribable tortures inflicted upon his wife until she died. The terrible ordeal rendered him temporarily insane." Apaches could engage in brutal tactics; so could Anglo-Americans, who raped and tortured their own victims. The point is that this sexualized trope of Apache brutality implied, in Wood's telling at least, that it could literally drive a civilized man crazy. Cast against these portrayals of Apaches, the differences between Anglo miners, Mexican ranchers, black Buffalo soldiers, even the Cowboy Clantons and lawmen Earps, could seem insignificant.[56]

In contrast, the Chiricahua Apaches distinguished between their various enemies for diplomatic and practical reasons, but not racial ones. The Apaches viewed the Treaty of Guadalupe Hidalgo and the Gadsden Purchase as agreements between the Mexicans and the Americans that had little bearing on their own territorial boundaries and treaty arrangements: just because the United States had made a deal to take Mexico's land did not mean that it had a deal with the Apaches. In the late 1850s, Chiricahua leader Cochise let American migrants traverse Apache Pass in what would become northeastern Cochise County. But his people continued to attack Mexican wagon trains along the route with no apology. An army officer recalled Cochise saying in 1873, "I made peace with the Americans, but the Mexicans did not come to ask peace from me as the Americans have done." Cochise explained that "young people are liable to go down . . . and do a little damage to the Mexicans" in revenge for the murder of earlier generations. Cochise was referring in part to Geronimo, whose mother, first wife, and three children had been killed by Mexican soldiers in the 1850s. Long before he gained infamy among Americans, Geronimo had reportedly "vowed vengeance" and "ache[d] for revenge" against Mexicans.[57]

Revenge, but not race war. Comparing the racial systems of indigenous peoples and the colonists they encountered is tricky business. But some anthropologists argue convincingly that the Apaches did not have a sense of "race" comparable to that of the Americans and Europeans, whose ideas were influenced by the rationalist science of the Enlightenment. The Apaches did not use a racial concept to divide themselves from whites, or, for that matter, to unite themselves into a cohesive group, which may have explained the willingness of some Apaches to become scouts. The people who became known as the Chiricahuas absorbed other bands as their numbers were depleted by the Apache Wars. Geronimo, for instance, was a Warm Springs (Ojo Caliente) Apache who married into the Chiricahuas. The Chiricahua Apaches, as a collective entity with a distinct name, dated no earlier than the 1540s. For Apache peoples, the issue was one of insider versus outsider rather than one of "racial other." It is reasonable to suggest that the Chirica-hua Apaches acted less out of what today might be called "race pride" than out of a desire to protect their honor, territory, culture, and lives.[58]

As conflict wore on, the army's Apache scouts—always in a tenuous position—became the subject of increasing controversy. Crook relied heavily on Apache scouts, and was always loyal to them, but others were skeptical. Throughout April 1882 Chiricahua leaders Juh and Naiche, en route to Mexico, launched brazen raids across southeastern Arizona. Any remaining benefit of the doubt given to the Apaches evaporated. In early May, the new territorial governor Frederick Tritle suggested that the federal government rethink "the practice of arming and using the Indian as police or scout. You teach him to be a dangerous person." Tritle accused the scouts of amassing government-issue ammunition that later ended up in the hands of Apache warriors.[59]

Over the next three years, Geronimo and his followers moved back and forth between the reservations and their Mexican hideouts, with the army in active pursuit much of the time. Cochise County residents had grown thoroughly tired of the Apache Wars. In May 1885, Geronimo once again fled the San Carlos Reservation. That month, county residents gathered in Tombstone to draft a resolution to the president demanding the defeat and complete removal of the Apache Indians from Arizona. Claiming to reflect "the unanimous sentiment of all the residents of this Territory" (except, the petitioners emphasized, the profiteers who benefited from ongoing hostilities), the resolution pointed to the Chiricahuas' continued raids and evasion of troops, and argued that the San Carlos Reservation had not been able to contain the threat. Comparing the Apaches to the Cowboys, the document noted that "a few years ago we were afflicted with bands of train robbers and outlaws, and every one of them has been either killed whilst resisting arrest or tried and punished by due course of law." Yet Geronimo, "because he is an Indian, seems to possess some potent charm to protect him from punishment." "How much longer are the rules which apply to warfare between civilized nations to be applied to savages who utterly disregard them?" The resolution demanded that all Apaches still at large be captured, and, along with those living peacefully on reservations, be removed from the region altogether—preferably to Indian Territory in Oklahoma.[60]

In the spring of 1886, General Nelson Miles replaced Crook after Geron-

8. Surrender negotiations between General George Crook and Geronimo, Cañon de los Embudos, Sonora, Mexico, March 1886. Geronimo is in bandanna on the left; Crook wears a glove, and is the second from the right. Photograph by C. S. Fly. Arizona State Library, Archives and Public Records, History and Archives Division, Phoenix, 97-2621.

imo and a small band of followers escaped from army supervision in the wake of their reported surrender at Cañon de los Embudos, a few miles south of the border. Crook had regularly assembled scout parties up to four times the size of his regular troops. Miles, in contrast, distrusted Apache scouts, and amassed nearly 5,000 regular troops—almost one-fourth of the nation's standing army—to chase down Geronimo and a few dozen followers. Notwithstanding this show of force, Crook's partisans would later claim that no Chiricahua was ever found by American troops without the use of Apache scouts.[61]

In the end, those who distrusted the loyalties of all Chiricahuas got what they wanted. Five days after Geronimo and his thirty-six followers surrendered to Miles in September 1886, every last Chiricahua Apache that could be found, including the peaceful residents of the overcrowded and desolate San Carlos Reservation, were rounded up, loaded onto trains, and removed to decrepit, dank facilities at Florida's Fort Marion and Fort Pickens. Here was an eerie precedent for the Deportation of 1917. No climate could have proved a crueler contrast to the Chiricahua Mountains in the Arizona high desert. To Crook's horror, even the Apache scouts who had loyally served the U.S. Army were removed. Promises to surrendering fugitives that they would be reunited with their families were denied. When Geronimo heard the news that he and his people would not go to Fort Apache, as he had hoped, he seemed to General Miles "to be wholly unmanned."[62]

Crook and his right-hand man, Lieutenant John Bourke, joined the Indian Rights Association to protest this treachery. Within two years, overcrowding and disease had killed 20 percent of the captives at Fort Marion. In 1894, the remaining survivors were moved again to Fort Sill, Oklahoma. Geronimo died there in 1909. Not until 1913 were the 271 remaining Chiricahuas declared "free," and given the choice of staying in Oklahoma or joining the Mescalero Apache reservation in northwestern New Mexico.[63] Cochise County, named for the great Chiricahua leader, is now one of just two counties in Arizona without any Indian reservations.

The Threat from China

Many Tombstone residents saw a racial threat other than Apaches, and it was not from Mexicans. Instead, many locals feared the Chinese. In 1879 and 1880, an area near the San Pedro River had been temporary home to nearly a thousand Chinese working on the Southern Pacific Railroad, but overall the county's Chinese population was small. At their peak numbers, in mid-1882, Chinese made up only about 4 percent of Tombstone's population, a much lower percentage than in many western mining regions. In Idaho, for instance, Chinese had made up as much as 30 percent of the population in 1870.[64] Small numbers, however, did not stop the Tombstone activists, who, drawing on precedents elsewhere in the West, launched local anti-Chinese campaigns in 1880 and 1886. Both were spasms of political grandstanding that quickly fizzled. Yet they set a chilling example. They demonstrated, like the removal of the Apaches, a persistent commitment to racial exclusion.

Tombstone's Chinese, as in most of the West, were mostly from the area near Canton in the coastal region of Guangdong Province. They fled poverty and hunger, and most had little education, but they also felt the pull of job opportunity and chain migration of family and community members. Before 1882, some Chinese in Tombstone may have come directly from China, with others arriving from California, Nevada, and Tucson. The Chinese Exclusion Act of 1882 barred immigration to the United States for all Chinese except those from a few professional classes. So Tombstone became a popular stop for Chinese who immigrated through Mexico and then crossed the border. This was a legal course until a loophole in the law was closed in 1884, and the practice persisted. All told, the area's permanent Chinese residents never amounted to more than a few hundred, many of whom were small produce growers ("truck" farmers) in the neighboring San Pedro River settlements of Fairbank and Charleston.[65]

Perhaps 10 percent of Tombstone's Chinese were women. Chinese women were associated with unfree labor and the worst kinds of degradation, and many Americans assumed they were all prostitutes. The Page Act of 1875, which was intended to keep Chinese prostitutes out, in effect barred almost all Chinese women from entering the United States. Tombstone's few Chinese women were housewives or worked in family businesses, but a handful regularly appeared in the city's license books as prostitutes. One woman, listed as Ah Sue in city records, plied her trade in a "crib" (a small room) on Allen Street from 1883 until late 1888, long after Tombstone's bust. (During the 1886 recession, prostitutes caught a break when their monthly license fee was reduced from $10 a month to $7.)[66]

Tombstone's Chinese men and women occupied tight quarters in a three-block stretch west of the business district. It was nicknamed "Hoptown," a reference to its opium dens. Typical living quarters were cramped and rudimentary, sometimes a room behind a curtain in the back of a store or restaurant. Most Chinese men belonged to *tongs*, benevolent societies mislabeled by many whites as the "Chinese Masons." Some tongs engaged in violent turf wars, but more often they fostered religious practice, community gatherings, and job networks. While some Chinese did operate opium dens, the majority of Chinese men worked in laundries and restaurants. A woman known as China Mary reportedly dealt in opium and served as a labor agent placing

Chinese domestic servants ("houseboys"), while her husband, Ah Lum, became a well-known restaurateur (and later a suspected human smuggler). Lum was the rare Chinese entrepreneur whose place of business was not in the Chinese district. Sources are alternately prurient or circumspect about Chinese prostitution, but it is possible that China Mary contracted (or forced) workers into the sex trades as well.[67]

Tombstone's first anti-Chinese fever flared in 1880. That year, the census reported just forty-four Chinese residents—about 2 percent of the town's population. Nevertheless, in July, *Tombstone Epitaph* editor and aspiring politician John Clum organized an Anti-Chinese League "to rid the town of evil." Public meetings denounced "the despised Mongolians," but Clum's resolve weakened after the fatal beating of a Chinese restaurant owner. "It may be that 'the Chinese must go,'" Clum wrote, "but that fact will not justify deeds of bloodshed and murder, and good citizens should take a positive stand against such overt acts." Yet Clum's preferred tactic of sending a committee to pressure Chinese residents to pack their bags was plenty menacing. The anti-Chinese meetings themselves, held "in the streets by the light of bonfires," must also have instilled fear. After weeks of Clum's bombast, the anti-Chinese fever died down. Over the next few years, the Chinese "menace" faded into the background as the Cowboys and Apaches took center stage, though racist comments continued to appear in the town's newspapers.[68]

Anti-Chinese campaigns were hardly unique to Tombstone. As demand for railroad labor in the 1850s and 1860s had ushered large numbers of Chinese laborers into the United States, xenophobic campaigns, laws, and vigilante violence mushroomed across the West. As early as 1850, California passed laws taxing foreign owners of mines and laundries, designed to foreclose Chinese and Mexican economic opportunity and eliminate foreign competition. Discriminatory laws and violence escalated, and by the late 1870s an Irish immigrant named Denis Kearney, head of the Workingmen's Party, was whipping up San Francisco crowds with calls to remove the Chinese altogether. Grassroots agitation culminated in the passage of the federal Chinese Exclusion Act of 1882. By barring Chinese immigrants from citizenship and preventing all but the most elite Chinese from entering the United States, it became the first law that defined immigration status by both class and nationality. It helped invent the idea of an "illegal alien" and set a precedent for the immigration exclusion acts of the 1920s.[69]

The Chinese Exclusion Act of 1882 emboldened anti-Chinese activists everywhere, with peak violence in the years that followed.[70] Back in Tombstone, a long, bitter economic decline replaced the brief, spectacular boom. Adding to the woes created by Cowboy and Apache violence, silver prices dropped as new ore discoveries—including Tombstone's—increased supply. In 1884, wage cuts and a strike by Tombstone miners paralyzed the already struggling local economy. By 1885, underground water was flooding the mines, and periodic fires destroyed much of the town and one of its major mine works. In 1886, silver prices had fallen to 63 cents an ounce, about half what they had been in 1881.

In February 1886 local citizens held a public meeting, where they decried a recent "influx of Chinese" and called for a boycott on Chinese businesses. If the "influx" was real, the Chinese Exclusion Act was probably to blame, since it forced Chinese immigrants bound for the United States to enter through Mexico to evade the law. One prominent Chinese merchant reported that some Chinese had felt the boycott's pinch and had left town. Amid the general nastiness, a few people at the meeting emphasized the need for "peaceful measures," and some residents opposed the movement altogether. Local resident George Parsons attended a meeting and scoffed at the whole endeavor. People were making "asses of themselves," Parsons wrote in his diary. "I'm anti-Chinese, but in a practical way. Boycotting doesn't go with me and there is no reason for an anti-Chinese movement here."[71]

There was a reason, though. Politics. Both the 1880 and 1886 campaigns were launched by political aspirants looking for a hot issue. In 1880 John Clum was running successfully for mayor and hoping to sell newspapers. In 1886, a Tombstone "Anti-Chinese Political Party" ran slates of local candidates. Chinese immigrants were an easy target: they could not vote and they employed mostly fellow Chinese. Yet the political successes of the campaigns were limited. The Anti-Chinese League claimed an unlikely eight hundred members, but accomplishments were difficult to quantify. One movement leader, Stanley Bagg, was elected to the city council, where he secured an ordinance to require the health inspection of laundries. Many communities passed such ordinances, which provided a way to harass Chinese businesses

and reflected a fear that the Chinese would spread disease. Bagg's health ordinance lacked an officer to enforce it, however, and people continued to patronize Chinese laundries.[72]

Laundry may seem like a trivial issue, but it became a major flashpoint in
nineteenth-century mining towns for much the same reason it causes friction
in households today: no one wanted to do it. Considered quintessentially
female work, laundry quickly piled up in mining camps filled with single men
who worked in the dirt. Laundry was women's work in China, too, but as
Chinese men were barred from mining and property ownership, they began to fill the demand for laundering services in the American West. The
Epitaph claimed that seven-eighths of Tombstone's Chinese residents were
laundry workers.[73]

Women occupied an ambiguous position in the laundry wars. On the one
hand, anti-Chinese leaders across the West liked to claim that working-class
white women, particularly Irish, needed laundry work to survive.[74] Crusad-
ers harangued middle-class whites, especially women, who hired Chinese
men instead of needy white women. In 1886, one Tombstone speaker urged
residents to pay white women, not Chinese men, to do their washing: "It is
a poor country," he intoned, "where women, willing to work, are driven to
prostitution for a living." By couching Chinese exclusion as a way to protect
women's livelihoods, these campaigns conceded that women's paid labor
was necessary, accepted, even fought over in the young mining communities
of the American West.[75]

Yet in Tombstone, opposition to the 1886 Chinese boycott appeared to
come from women themselves. According to one washing machine advertisement in the *Epitaph,* "The chief argument used by the ladies against the
removal of the Chinamen is the difficulty of getting washing done." In 1886,
an apocryphal account of a meeting of Tombstone's Chinese quoted "Old
Sing Hop" as saying, "You take the average white woman to-day, and she will
not wash under any circumstances, she is too high-toned, and it would hu-
miliate her sense of pride." The reporter almost certainly fabricated the re-
mark, which simultaneously mocked Chinese men and rebuked women who
shirked their domestic responsibilities. One boycott leader urged men to
"find out what women will do washing and give them your work." Still another proposed something much more revolutionary: he urged his listeners

"to wear their shirts, if necessary, for two or three weeks, and, when they be-gan to itch, stick the shirts in the water and wash them themselves." Mrs. Ida Emmerson offered another solution with her new "White Labor Laundry" service, which promised to "do the work as well as Chinamen, and at liberal rates." Yet others observed that Chinese men had "brought the art of wash-ing to a perfection," and white women new to the task simply did not do as good a job.[76]

Here a comparison of Tombstone's Mexican and Chinese populations is instructive. No Mexican members of the Anti-Chinese League in Tombstone were publicly identified, and the town had no roots in the Mexican era. Still, small signs indicated that even Anglo men who were avowed racial exclu-sionists saw Mexicans as vastly preferable to the Chinese. In part, this distinction reflected the hybrid borderlands culture of the 1880s, when Mexican-Anglo intermarriage and business partnerships still flourished, but marriage with Chinese was illegal for both Mexicans and Anglos. Catholics were better than "pagans," to most Protestant minds. In 1886, Tucson busi-nessman L. C. Hughes pledged his city's solidarity with Tombstone's anti-Chinese cause. The Chinese merchants in Tucson, Hughes complained, had "driven out the Mexicans by selling cheap and giving short weight. The stomach of a Chinaman was too small for a white man to compete with."[77] Hughes sided with Mexican merchants—and called them white—by defend-ing Chinese exclusion.

Mexicans often expressed the same objections to the Chinese as other Arizonans did. Tucson's Spanish-language newspaper *El Fronterizo* re-ported on violence between Mexican and Chinese workers. Another Spanish-language paper had warned in 1878 that violence would follow Chinese la-borers recruited to new copper mines in Clifton, Arizona. One article lambasted the state of Sonora for recruiting Chinese and Mormon immi-grants, even as Mexican law made it difficult for Mexican citizens residing in the United States to repatriate. The newspapers also reported opposition to marriage between Mexicans and Chinese. These marriages were illegal, be-cause Mexicans were classified as Caucasian in Arizona's anti-miscegenation laws, but some couples went to New Mexico to tie the knot. In later years, violence and exclusion orders against the Chinese would sweep Sonora.[78]

To be sure, Mexicans in Tombstone were marginalized. Their ranks included merchants and hoteliers, and a few are listed in the voting registers, but they were not listed as participants in any of the anti-Chinese groups or in reports about the 1885 public meeting to write a resolution condemning the Apaches (might they have shied from public gatherings calling for racial exclusion?). The latter document even claimed that "Cochise County is settled principally by Americans."[79] Very few Mexicans found mining jobs in Tombstone. Yet their situation, while less than ideal, was far better than that endured by Chinese targets of removal campaigns. Mexicans, in contrast, were legally white and automatically eligible for U.S. citizenship—at least theoretically. The Chinese did not even have that much; they were legally nonwhite, and ineligible for citizenship.

In the late nineteenth century, Chinese, not Mexicans, were the primary targets of anti-immigrant campaigns in the West. Nobody organized a political party opposed to Mexican immigration, and hardly anybody called for restrictions on Mexican immigration. The Chinese were the nation's first "illegal immigrants," and the first to be refused entry on the basis of nationality alone—which became an easy proxy for race. In the early years of border enforcement, agents were concerned not with excluding Mexicans, but with preventing Chinese from coming in from Mexico. The predecessors of today's Border Patrol were the so-called "Chinese inspectors" first appointed in 1891. Some newspapers in the early twentieth century even referred to "Chinese wetbacks" (though Arizona border crossers trekked on dry land).[80]

Then, as now, the term "wetback" conjured an image of poverty, illegality, and racial otherness. Anti-Chinese activists, especially those who cast themselves as working-class leaders, attacked Chinese as unfair competition because of the lower wages they received. In the 1870s in the copper camp of Clifton, "American" miners earned $70 a month, Mexicans $50, and Chinese $40. In Mexico, some activists claimed that Chinese would accept wages just one-third of what the lowest-paid Mexicans earned.[81]

Critics blamed low wages on the people who earned them, rather than on those who paid them out. The average Chinese man, one California newspaper claimed, was "whipped into servile obedience," and could not "discern that he is a man."[82] In 1882, the *Tombstone Epitaph* took a blame-the-victim approach by claiming: "The people of this country, so largely working people, . . . will not submit to be degraded . . . [by] the coolie, and they will not have their social conditions reduced to the standards of the inhuman beings who cluster in filth [and] who laugh at virtue." Another man stated baldly, "They could live on too little." In 1886, four years after the Chinese Exclusion Act, Arizona's Republican Party platform declared, "The immigration of Coolies to compete with the intelligent white laborers of our land is degrading to their manhood."[83]

Tombstone's Chinese faced boycotts, the threat of violence, and more vicious and dehumanizing stereotypes than it is possible to list. At once feared and ridiculed, those Chinese residents found themselves in an almost impossible position. Their poverty was reviled, and their success resented. Yet they did not disappear. During the 1880 campaign, Clara Spalding Brown observed: "Nearly all the Chinamen have purchased pistols and they seem disposed to defend their rights." Despite anti-Chinese campaigns in 1880 and 1886, Chinese constituted 2 percent of the population in mid-1880, 4 percent in 1882, and 3 percent in 1900.[84] As tourism reinvented Tombstone in the 1920s, Chinese were treated as "local color" and a fascinating curiosity, an ironic postscript to the earlier hostility.

Clear away the smoke from the OK Corral and a different Tombstone comes into view. The Saturday-matinee version has shaped popular understandings of the American West for nearly a hundred years. Yet Tombstone's real history resides firmly in a borderland world far more complex than a simple division between good guys and bad guys—or Mexicans and white Americans. In the minds of many local residents, American criminals, not "illegal" Mexican immigrants, made the border a site of controversy and danger. William Tecumseh Sherman called for greater federal power to patrol the border not because of illegal immigration (an idea that was only just beginning to take shape, and only for the Chinese), but because "the cowboys make use of the boundary line to escape pursuit first on the one side & then on the other."[85] Likewise, Governor Tritle pleaded for a "mounted border patrol" decades before the U.S. Border Patrol was officially established. But he wanted the men to chase American outlaws, not Mexican immigrants.[86] With rare exceptions, Americans sympathized with and saw as their allies those Mexicans caught in the Cowboys' cross-fire. Stopping the Cowboy raids, ending the Apache wars, and containing Chinese immigration all invited greater government power and greater corporate influence in the region.

In the nineteenth century, Mexicans had no need to worry about a dragnet to limit "illegal immigration." Yet Chinese exclusion created a framework for immigration control that would dramatically shape the future of Mexicans and many others. In just the same way, Tombstone would fade from prominence even as its legacy influenced the development of more prosperous communities. In 1881, silver was selling for $1.20 per troy ounce; five years later, the price was 63 cents and still falling. By the early twentieth century, Tombstone was almost a ghost town, saved only by its status as the county seat. Many residents left Arizona altogether, while others dismantled their mining shanties to drag them by wagon to the Bisbee hillsides, where some still stand today. People who moved from Tombstone to the new copper camp brought along their experiences with the Apache Wars, Mexico, and Chinese exclusion. In Bisbee, prospectors and other newcomers would fashion a "white man's camp" designed to avoid Tombstone's troubles.

3

The White Man's Camp in Bisbee

In 1877, the same year Ed Schieffelin found Tombstone's silver, about twenty miles away a "rather slim and raw-boned" civilian army contractor named Jack Dunn noticed the rusty stain of copper while he scouted for Apaches at a mile-high mountain crossing known as Puerta de las Mulas (Mule Pass). He and his scouting companion shared news of their find back at Fort Bowie, where they grubstaked an alcoholic wanderer named George Warren to investigate further. A year later, forty-seven mining claims had been filed at Mule Pass, including one that became the bountiful Copper Queen Mine. Warren died penniless after losing his claims on a bet that he could outrun a horse, but the region became known in his honor as the Warren Mining District. Here "in the heart of a canyon in the last place in the world that one would have imagined a city," Bisbee was born.[1]

Compared to Tombstone, the copper camp was slow to develop. In the 1870s, copper was still used mainly for pots and pans or for alloying with tin to make bronze. Modern uses, such as the manufacture of plumbing pipes and electrical wires, remained rare. Copper mines needed to produce a lot of heavy ore to be worthwhile, and Mule Pass was miles from the railroads that gave access to smelters and markets. In 1880, the census taker who came to the site found just fifteen men: ten Americans, one German, three Mexicans, and an Irishman.[2] By that summer, though, the camp had a post office, some tents and lean-tos, and a handful of real buildings. It also had a permanent name—chosen in honor of San Francisco lawyer DeWitt Bisbee, an early absentee investor in the Copper Queen Mine. The Welsh-born brothers Benjamin and Lewis Williams arrived to run the fledgling mine and built a small smelter that produced seven hundred tons of ore in its first year.

The rudimentary camp relied on the same kind of cosmopolitan cooperation that sustained Tres Alamos. Bisbee's first restaurant was a campfire where the Mexican wife of a Portuguese immigrant served customers under a tree.[3] A Greek fruit stand and a few stores opened, a couple of them owned by women. By the early 1880s, before its founders decamped to Tombstone, the biggest mercantile, or general store, belonged to Joseph Goldwater (great-uncle of the future U.S. senator Barry Goldwater) and his partner from Chihuahua, José Miguel Castañeda. The camp's water was delivered in canvas sacks on burros cajoled up the hillsides by their Mexican tenders. Mexican woodcutters denuded the canyon walls of white oak and juniper to fuel cookstoves and the voracious smelter, whose smoke clogged the canyon. Floods from the violent summer storms known as Arizona monsoons were capable of swallowing every building, wagon, and living creature in their path. Frequent fires would engulf whole blocks. And the Apache threat sent the camp's few schoolchildren running to nearby mine shafts during drills, to prepare for possible Indian raids.

Though Bisbee remained primitive in some ways in the 1880s, it was developing into a small industrial center that relied on wage labor. The question of *whose* wage labor was of growing concern to the area's skilled miners. In 1881, more than half of Bisbee's two hundred residents were foreign born, as in Tombstone. By one account, two-thirds of the copper camp's residents were Mexican, a far higher percentage than in Tombstone.[4] Despite this, Bisbee was gaining a reputation as a "white man's camp," a characterization relying on racial boundaries that changed along with the community's population. The label would retain its power, even as Bisbee outgrew its camp roots and became a modern industrial city. The shifting definitions of the white man's camp reveal how racial categories were changing not just in Cochise County but across the United States in the early twentieth century.

The Rules of the White Man's Camp

On Christmas Eve 1880, prospectors, engineers, saloonkeepers, and merchants huddled in the back of John "Pie" Allen's mercantile to create a district code—essentially a social compact and a set of laws.[5] These codes were the earliest form of government in western mining camps. Similar codes, which were meant to "keep the peace" in such rough-and-tumble settlements, had originated in the lead-mining districts of Cornwall, England, whence many of Bisbee's residents had come—but their technicalities also relied, without acknowledgment, on Spanish and Mexican legal traditions. These quasi-legal district codes spread, in the mid-nineteenth century, to California gold diggings and then across the West. They addressed mine law and sanitation, but could also be used to exclude Chinese and Mexican and South American miners, thus creating what were known as "white man's camps."[6]

These exclusions appeared in Arizona as early as 1863, when miners at the Pioneer Mining District (near today's Prescott) passed a written resolution barring "Asiatics & Sonorians . . . from working this district." Other camps followed suit, usually in areas with no indigenous Mexican landowners or merchants. By the late nineteenth century, Arizona's best-known and largest white man's camps were the copper districts of Jerome, Globe, and Bisbee. Yet where Mexican pioneers did exist, exceptions for individuals could be made. One 1863 code decreed that "no citizens of Mexico shall hold or work claims in this District except the boy Lorenzo Para who is one of the original discoverers." Lines of demarcation were not always clear, however: one group of miners who excluded Mexicans later added an amendment to their code stipulating that a three-man committee "shall decide who are & who are not Mexicans." Occasionally a district code would lay down rules for *inclusion* of a group. One stated that any claims "in the name or names of females in this district, shall be considered legal and valid" and should be "respected in the same manner and form that the laws of this district extend to males."[7]

The Warren District code created at Pie Allen's did not explicitly declare Bisbee to be a white man's camp, at least not in the public record. Yet from Bisbee's earliest years, its reputation as a white man's camp enjoyed, as one local reporter put it, "unanimous unwritten consent." Its first rule forbade any Chinese from living or working in the district. When a Chinese man attempted to open a laundry in Bisbee, local residents burned him in effigy. The man left. Chinese truck farmers along the San Pedro River could sell fruits and vegetables in town, so long as they left by sundown. This rule linked Bisbee with hundreds of other "sundown towns" across the country where racial minorities—usually but not always African Americans—were forbidden to dally after dark, sometimes on pain of death. Bisbee's complete exclusion of Chinese lasted as late as 1920 and probably longer.[8]

This ban was a response to the troubles in Tombstone, which supplied many of Bisbee's early residents. By 1886, a proponent of Tombstone's laundry boycott could point out that "there were no Chinamen in Bisbee, and people seemed to get their washing done there, all right." But some people in Bisbee complied with the "no-Chinese" rule by sending their laundry via stagecoach to Tombstone—hardly a purist's solution.[9]

Women, though scarce in early Bisbee, figured prominently in justifications of the no-Chinese rule. The law, according to one white woman pioneer, was "made for the protection of the widows from foreign countries" who took in laundry to survive. Which countries (England? Mexico?) went unsaid. Yet "naturally the miner's sympathy was for these widows," not for the Chinese.[10] Another story hinted at protecting women from sexual violence. Juanita Tarin remembered some Chinese men being run out of town for doing "what they wanted" with a "white girl, a lady." The "law found out and they were deported from here."[11] The veracity and details of the story (did it happen? was it rape or consensual sex?) are unclear from a remembrance recorded years later. More clear is that focusing on women obscured the fact that the rule protected men by keeping the Chinese out of Bisbee's mines.

The second rule of the white man's camp concerned Mexican workers. Mexican men could live and work in the Warren District—indeed, as the chief road builders and woodcutters, they were essential to its success—but they were barred from working underground, where the best-paid jobs were. Across the Southwest, even highly skilled Mexican men were shunted into positions labeled "helper" or "assistant." "One candid American mechanic" in another mining camp admitted to federal labor investigator Victor Clark in 1908, "They will never pay a Mexican what he's really worth compared with a white man. I know a Mexican that's the best blacksmith I ever knew. . . . But they pay him $1.50 a day as a helper, working under an American blacksmith who gets $7 a day."[12]

Even Mexicans and whites in precisely the same jobs received different

9. Copper Queen Smelter, Bisbee, Arizona, ca. 1902. The smelter was relocated to Douglas in 1903. Courtesy of the Arizona Historical Society, Tucson, 26722.

pay, a practice that was known as the "dual-wage system" and that had existed in the Southwest since at least the 1850s.[13] Early practitioners argued that Mexicans' migratory patterns and lower standard of living justified the lower wages. As early as 1885, the Copper Queen's pay scales had separate columns for "Mexican" and "white" (or "American") wages. Wheeling adobe bricks, for example, earned "whites" at the Copper Queen $2.25 a day, and "Mexicans" $1.50.[14] Mining officials listed these categories in pay scales, and admitted them openly. When asked about the wage scale in 1917, mining engineer J. C. Ryan testified that "it depended on whether they were Mexicans or white men. . . . Mexicans were paid a lower rate."[15]

Reserving the best jobs for white men was common practice across the Southwest, but the rules of the white man's camp made the division formal and explicit. A promotional issue of the *Bisbee Daily Review* published for the St. Louis World's Fair in 1904 explained that Bisbee "is strictly a 'white man's camp.' . . . Mexicans are employed only in the common or rough labor" above ground, and at Mexican wages.[16] The combination of the Southwest's dual-wage system and the job segregation in white man's camps made wage disparities in Bisbee even higher than those in "Mexican camps" like Clifton, Arizona, where Mexicans did work as miners, albeit at lower wages than whites. Overall, Mexicans in Arizona mines earned one-half to two-thirds of the average white wages. But by 1891 Bisbee's average Mexican wage was less than half the average white one.[17]

The year 1891 also marked the tenth anniversary of the presence of Phelps, Dodge & Company (PD) in Bisbee. In 1881, a Canadian metallurgical engineer named Dr. James S. Douglas had urged the venerable New York brass-importing and -trading firm to make its first major mining investment, a claim adjacent to the Copper Queen. In 1884, PD executives negotiated the purchase of the Copper Queen itself, and installed Douglas as mine superintendent and the director of company mining operations. After a tentative beginning, the Copper Queen Mine proved rich in ore, and at just the right time. By the early 1890s, demand for copper started to soar as factories replaced steam power with electricity, and more homes were equipped with indoor plumbing. The Copper Queen Mine itself installed electricity underground in 1887, and the following year PD began building a railroad from Bisbee to a Southern Pacific stop near Tombstone. A rate feud with Southern Pacific at the turn of the century spurred PD to build its own railroad, the El Paso & Southwestern, which eventually spanned the Southwest. In 1899 James Douglas' son Walter took over at the Copper Queen, now the fourth-largest copper mine in the country.[18]

When PD came to Bisbee, the company adopted the rules of the white man's camp that had been established by pioneer prospectors and merchants.[19] By agreeing to exclude Chinese and restrict Mexican work, the Douglases and their foremen were securing the loyalty of their skilled white workers, to forestall union organizing within the company. Mexican wages— but not white wages—actually declined at the Copper Queen after PD took over. By 1904 industry journals could report that "this camp is one of a very few in the West that has never witnessed a strike, or any serious dis-

agreement between the company and the miners—a record equally credit-
able to both parties. . . . It is not unionized and cannot be persuaded into
joining the union." Bisbee, the article claimed, has "acquired that *esprit
de corps* which comes from mutual confidence between employer and employee."[20] That esprit de corps was fostered by white allegiances.

The rules of the white man's camp were designed to protect the white
workers who created them. Chinese were beyond the pale for these men,
who maintained that Mexicans could not perform some jobs as well as whites
could, although Mexicans performed these very same jobs in Mexican camps.
Others argued that it was not skill but work ethic that made Mexicans unfit
for underground work. Federal investigator Victor Clark found that the wages
of white miners in New Mexico and Arizona "are standardized . . . and range
from $3 to $5 a day. Mexicans will accept a rate much lower than this—not
exceeding $2 a day in most places—but they do not do as much work as a
white man."[21] Yet an analysis of Bisbee's wages by the congressional Dillingham Commission—a group that did not shy away from racial and cultural
explanations of wage disparities—concluded that "only racial discrimination
can explain the great differences . . . between the wages of these Mexican surface laborers and those of native-born and north European employees engaged in other kinds of common labor."[22]

The rules of the white man's camp constituted a kind of ideology. They
did much more than create a list of job categories. They also structured local
citizenship, hierarchy, and values, and they did so by projecting a particular
worldview. These rules discriminated, even as they conveyed the notion that
this discrimination was necessary and inevitable. The rules helped some
people and harmed others, yet implied neutrality by invoking explanations
that they reflected the natural order of things. As theorists Trevor Purvis and
Alan Hunt have observed, an ideology "always works to favor some and dis-
advantage others," and makes this disparity seem "natural."[23]

Observers characterized the wealth gap between Americans and Mexicans—indeed the dual-wage system itself—not as an injustice but as the
product of a natural hierarchy. With circular logic, both white workers and
managers used Mexican workers' poverty to contrast them with whites.
Housing was a popular target. Mexican workers did not need much, according to Victor Clark, just "an adobe hut with an earth floor, or even a shelter
of branches against the wind, a few pieces of pottery, a serape or a sheep-

skin to lie on at night." Bisbee's first distinct neighborhood was Chihuahua Town (later Chihuahua Hill), a steep labyrinth of rough shacks and adobes, reachable only by stairs or ladders, above a thoroughfare known as Brewery Gulch. Another Mexican neighborhood on Bisbee's outskirts became known as Tintown, for the scrap metal the residents used to cobble together their homes. Clark concluded that "the wants of the Mexican peon are hardly more complex than those of the Indian from whom he is descended," and therefore low wages did not harm him. The tautological justifications for low Mexican wages—that a lower wage was a function of the lower standard of living, not vice versa—were no less damaging for being sincere. Most Anglos honestly believed that Mexicans did not need a decent wage.[24]

Mexicans felt differently. In 1889, a writer in one of Tucson's Spanish-language newspapers lamented, "It is hard at present to make even enough to live. Work for Mexicans is very scarce and pay is low. Some mining companies only allow Mexicans in the most distressing and low paid jobs, such as woodcutting. . . . What hope do we have living in a country where we are looked at with such prejudice, where justice isn't for us, and where we are treated as the lowest of the human race?"[25]

The term "peon," imported from rural Mexico, emphasized the low place of industrial mine workers who came mostly from the Mexican states of Sonora, Zacatecas, and Chihuahua. Some workers were beholden to forms of debt peonage. But more important, by using the term as a *general* label for Mexican workers, white workers and managers attributed peasant conditions in Mexico to a natural hierarchy of races. One pro-union writer referred to the "peonized Mexican help" and "Mexican slaves" of greedy mining bosses.[26] On the flipside, an American mining-industry journal explained that the "Mexican peon is of a race . . . accustomed for generations to conditions not far removed from actual servitude and who have not yet learned to act on their own initiative."[27] Mexican surface laborers often worked for Mexican *padrones* in contract gangs, rather than for daily wages. Many Mexicans were eager to earn low American wages, which were still high compared to Mexico's, but the contracts made this labor seem less than "free" from the perspective of both employers and white miners. Federal law prohibited contract labor in 1885, but nineteenth-century reformers were more concerned with Chinese workers than Mexicans.[28]

The ideology of the white man's camp assumed that different "races" had naturally different standards of living, and that pitting them against one another would only cause the groups with "higher" standards to decline. Mexicans were particularly suspect, because of the belief that race "mixing" caused degeneracy. Preoccupation with racial standards of living was hardly unique to Bisbee, and it gained force over time. In 1907, John Commons, an eminent labor economist and proponent of immigration restriction, declared, "The competition of races is the competition of standards of living."[29]

As Commons' remarks showed, newly developing scientific racism and the Darwinian sense of "competition" it assumed only bolstered the white-man's-camp ideology in the early twentieth century. If in the 1850s and 1860s ideas about race were still inconsistent and fluid, they had solidified considerably by the late nineteenth century. Racial theorists and politicians increasingly insisted that racial hierarchies were a scientific fact, even as they worried that the white race would "degenerate" without white wages. Twentieth-century race science became focused on differences among Europeans, but this preoccupation only underscored the manifest racial "inferiority" of Mexicans. As concerns about race mixing and decline gathered force, Mexicans—already viewed as a "mongrel" race—did not stand to benefit. Not surprisingly, marriages between Mexicans and Euro-Americans were declining across the Southwest in this period. As race science and industrial capitalism developed, the fellow-feeling between Mexicans and newcomers to the Southwest was disappearing as workers of different nationalities saw themselves in competition, not cooperation.

One common way to illustrate racial hierarchies was to invoke the assumed superiority of men over children and women. In mining camps, white managers and workers, in the words of one historian, "imbued Mexican working class men with less-than-manly qualities," such as docility, laziness, and dependence—this last characteristic considered both womanly and childlike. A 1921 industry journal warned, "The Mexican worker intellectually is a child. He is governed by emotion rather than by reason." So "the Mexican workman will misunderstand an attitude of social equality toward him. . . . He cannot be your equal; he must either be your superior or your inferior." Hierarchies of maturity or masculinity stood for those of class and race, because the supremacy of white over Mexican paralleled the authority of foreman over laborer. An article about the Mexican camp of Clifton in 1904 claimed that workers there needed white bosses they "could look up to," for they "show little initiative and have no sense of responsibility, although they are capable of doing good work under competent direction." (This claim was almost pure fantasy, since Clifton's Mexican workers with supposedly "little initiative," had launched a massive strike the year before.)[30]

In contrast to Clifton's supposedly childlike Mexican followers, Bisbee boasted about its "confident, manly, well-paid men of the mines." The town was famous for its Fourth of July drilling contests, in which burly miners bore holes into a giant granite slab in front of thousands of spectators. In Bisbee, according to a writer in the *Arizona Mining Journal,* one would find "the old-fashioned American miner" who, in contrast to Mexicans, "could do a life-sized, double-fisted, he-man's work with pick or drill or dynamite, who mixed brains with his brawn." Could such a man be managed? Yes, if the right men were in charge. According to a Phelps Dodge company historian, "That independent spirit did not trouble [the] old foreman. Literally a man among men, with strength and courage beyond question, the foreman had elements of the superman. He had often . . . worked his way to authority through the mass of men through sheer persistence. Bone of the miner's bone, flesh of his flesh, the foreman inspired tremendous loyalty among his crews and, as time passed, took on the character of a mythical hero."[31]

In the white man's camp, this mythical hero held the line on Mexican labor to protect the white miners from whose ranks he had risen, and who deserved a "living wage" that could support an "American standard of living." This vague standard, invoked by American labor leaders since the 1830s, referred generally to a man's ability to support a wife and children, and to own his own home ("a comfortable house of at least six rooms," wrote one labor leader in 1898). Labor leaders and reformers presented the American standard of living as a natural fact, rather than a product of gendered assumptions or a burgeoning consumer culture.[32]

The living wage—often called a "family wage," for it assumed that the worker was supporting a family—and the American standard of living were inseparable ideas. They worked in tandem to valorize men's high wages and to denigrate immigrant households, where women so often took in roomers and boarders. Few questioned the assumptions behind the concepts. The idea that a man should earn a wage large enough to support a family was popular with almost everybody: employers believed it reduced turnover, workers used it to demand better wages, and social reformers saw it as a natural ideal. Still, the effects could be pernicious. The family-wage ideal suppressed women's wages by assuming they were just extra pocket change for trifles. Even for men, the family wage was honored more in the breach than in practice. Most men were just a layoff, strike, or injury away from economic peril. Almost all working-class women found ways to supplement their husbands' unsteady incomes, especially in mining camps like Bisbee, where women's laundering, cooking, and housekeeping skills were in high demand.[33]

The "American standard of living" and the "family wage" were as much about race as they were about manhood. The reasoning was reductive: a man should support a family; only a white man earns a family wage; thus, only white men are proper family men. The irony is that "white men" were eligible for family wages even if they were single, but nonwhite "family men" were not. Mexican men at the Copper Queen literally earned *women's* wages—that is, the same pay earned by white women, who began working in its offices at the turn of the century.[34]

In contrast, many of Bisbee's white miners did earn a family wage, largely because managers wanted to attract white married workers with children. As early as 1881, a Copper Queen foreman was recruiting white workers with families.[35] The company paid high wages (that is, white wages) for the industry, offered an eight-hour day by 1903, and, during recessions, laid off single men first. The 1904 World's Fair Edition of the *Bisbee Daily Review* explained, "A man who works in the mine and rests at home with his family is much to be preferred in the community than the one that has no further interests in the community than his individual interest or welfare." This was an ideological belief, but it was also a form of labor control—because of the common though not necessarily accurate assumption that family men would not walk off the job. The family man had become so closely associated with whiteness that the article's description of Bisbee's permanent population flowed directly into the announcement that Bisbee was a white man's camp. Bisbee had "substantiality," according to the article, because "many [men] have been employees of the Copper Queen Mining Company for ten and fifteen years and are known to each other and everybody. This is borne out by the fact that fully two-thirds of the men employed in the mines are married men and that two-thirds of these own their own homes. It is strictly a 'white man's' camp, notwithstanding the contiguity of the city to the International line, and the proximity to cheap labor which could be obtained across that line."[36] The author connected permanence ("substantiality") with marital status and home ownership, then seamlessly praised Bisbee for resisting the lure of "cheap labor" from Mexico.

Yet despite Bisbee's label as a "white man's camp," the town was always Mexican, too. Even surface work in a dual-wage system paid more than jobs in Mexico. Mexican workers came to the Warren District in ever-larger numbers in the twentieth century. In the first decade of the twentieth century, Cochise County's Mexican population quadrupled, from 1,500 to 6,000. And these were census figures, which notoriously undercounted Mexicans. The *Daily Review's* editor estimated that 60,000 to 100,000 Mexicans crossed the border each year. Porfirio Díaz's land policies were displacing hundreds of thousands of peasants from their land, and it was easy for them to get to Arizona. Ángel Baldenegro's parents came to Bisbee "before there was a border," as he put it.[37]

There was still no such thing as a Mexican "illegal immigrant" in any modern sense of the term. The physical border was only occasionally marked, and in some spots its exact location remained in contention. Laws restricting immigration were increasing (crackdowns on paupers, contract laborers, and other "undesirables" proliferated at the turn of the century), but the U.S. government did not require migrants to register at designated border-crossing stations until 1919. Even then, this was a rarely enforced and seldom acknowledged requirement. Families who kept small landholdings in Mexico could send men to earn wages in the United States; the men would return home on holidays and at harvest times. This was one reason employers complained about Mexicans' high turnover. Over time, though, more families began to stay in Bisbee. By the early 1920s, a railroad engineer noted that Mexican workers "will not stay put until they get their families from Mexico."[38]

Families like the Baldenegros maintained ties to their origin communities by living in Chihuahua Hill or Zacatecas Canyon, above Brewery Gulch. Mexican families pieced together work, built homes, grew gardens, and dug wells in their own neighborhoods, attended Sacred Heart Church, and joined *mutualistas* (such as the Alianza Hispano-Americana, founded in Tucson in 1894), to ameliorate their miserable treatment at work. Bisbee native Herlinda Tofoya remembered the "beautiful fiestas" in Tintown's plaza on Mexican Independence Day and on saints' days, especially in honor of the Virgen de Guadalupe. Tofoya grew up in Brewery Gulch, but her father worked with men from Tintown. Otherwise, she claimed, as outsiders, his family "never would have been accepted" at its neighborhood celebrations. Late at night, "someone with enough tequila in them would say, 'What are you doing here?'"[39]

Safely White in the White Man's Camp

The label "white man's camp" obscured not just the reality of a Mexican Bisbee, but also the fact that whiteness itself was hardly obvious. Characterizing Mexicans as passive children and white men as manly leaders helped to fix Mexicanness and whiteness as a simple binary in what was really a more complex world. Ángel Baldenegro described his mother as "Aztec," his father as "Mayo," a Sonoran native group related to the Yaquis. In Bisbee, though, they were just "Mexican," often anonymously ("J. H. Goodman and a Mexican Killed at the Pittsburg & Hecla Mine," ran a typical *Daily Review* headline in 1904).[40] The category "Mexican" lumped together people who had multiple origins and identities, like the Baldenegros, and the label "white" did the same thing to others. In practice, earning white wages meant being white, an accomplishment that was not always self-evident. Many of Bisbee's early skilled miners—the Irish, especially, and to a lesser extent the Cornish—secured their own racial status by defining themselves as whites in the white man's camp.

A large number of Bisbee's early miners were natives of Cornwall, England. From their ranks came several managers and supervisors. By 1910, almost 1,500 English natives and another 500 people with an English parent lived in the county, mostly in Bisbee.[41] Mostly Cornish, and known as "Cousin Jacks," they had a reputation for skill, company loyalty, and hostility to unions (with exceptions, of course). "Racial" characteristics could be invoked to explain mining skill or the lack of it. So instead of crediting Cornwall's centuries-old lead mines with nurturing skills, Bisbee old-timer Joe Chisholm called Cornish men "naturally instinctive miners" who had inherited an "intuitive savvy" about ore from their mining forebears. Chisholm called the Cornish Jack "the world's racial miner." Yet even as he took racial traits to be as self-evident as night and day, Chisholm also revealed how individual actions could deepen and exaggerate "natural" racial advantages. His father had been one of Bisbee's first justices of the peace, and "hardly ever put a white man in jail if he could get his promise to behave."[42]

For Chisholm and others, the Cornish were at once the quintessential whites in the white man's camp, and a "race" unto themselves. Chisholm's usage followed the standard pattern of national experts and pontificators like Theodore Roosevelt, who referred to the "English-speaking race." Bisbee's Cornish certainly saw themselves as a people. One resident recalled that the Cousin Jacks, even those born in the United States, maintained a fierce loyalty to their English "'omeland."[43]

Bisbee's Irish—who were not as numerous as the Cornish—had even more reason to assert their whiteness in the white man's camp. In the mid-nineteenth century, the Irish were pilloried as "niggers turned inside out" who wanted to get "white man's work." The Irish were never truly non-white, but it is clear that the West proved friendlier to the Irish than did the East Coast. Irish immigrants had led the anti-Chinese movement in California in the 1870s, and Bisbee's white man's camp rules were an extension of that sensibility. So was the role of Irish immigrants in the segregation of Bisbee's Catholic church, whose first priest was Irish. Bisbee's first Catholic parish was "built and financed primarily by the Mexican people of Bisbee," but Irish (and Polish) Catholics convinced the priest they needed a separate church, St. Patrick's. Organizations like the Sons of Hibernia, the Lady Macabees, and the Knights of Columbus (who were primarily Irish in Bisbee) became forums to assert Irish identity as well.[44]

Overall, the Irish in Arizona enjoyed a far more privileged racial status than their countrymen farther east. In 1904, when Irish orphans from New York City were sent to Clifton for adoption by Mexican Catholic families, townspeople who identified the foundlings as white whisked the children away and won a custody battle that ended in the U.S. Supreme Court. Marked as Catholic inferiors in New York, the Irish were unequivocally white—and their Catholicism was of little concern—in Clifton and Bisbee. In the very year of the orphan incident, a Bisbee newspaper feature on local churches reported that "many influential and prominent citizens of this city" attended St. Patrick's.[45]

First among them was one of Arizona's most important men, William Brophy, an Irish immigrant. In 1881 he got a job in Bisbee, clerking in a general store owned by one of Bisbee's earliest female entrepreneurs. Phelps Dodge bought her out and named Brophy manager of the renamed Copper Queen Mercantile, PD's first company store. By 1916, the chain of "PD Mercs" run by Brophy employed more than five hundred people, grossed $8.4 million, and boasted hefty profit margins. Brophy became enormously wealthy (among other things, he served as president of the Bank of Bisbee, and then vice president of the Bank of Douglas, the smelter town founded in 1901). He served as patron to Bisbee's Catholic churches, where his wife sponsored Communion classes, and to several Catholic charities. Phoenix's most prestigious parochial school was established by his wife and is named in his honor. Brophy was aware of his role as the token Catholic among PD's staunchly Presbyterian managers, but this reality did not hinder his success or influence.[46] On the contrary, it probably helped "white" Catholics feel more comfortable in Bisbee.

Germans, Scots, and Welsh were likewise safely white. And in the nineteenth century, other groups could also lay claim to white privilege in Bisbee, including the handful of pioneer merchants and saloonkeepers from southern and eastern Europe. Jews settled in Tucson and almost every border town, but few lived in Bisbee, although Sam Levy, who was raised there, claimed he "never knew anti-Semitism as a youngster." Baptiste Caretto, a native of Tuscany who mined in Minnesota and Michigan, came to Bisbee via Tombstone in 1889, and owned a saloon on OK Street at the base of Chihuahua Hill. By 1890 two Serbian immigrants and distant cousins, J. B. Angius and V. G. Medigovich, had passed through several western mining camps before coming to Bisbee. Angius owned a wholesale firm that supplied Medigovich's grocery store, among other ventures. As community builders and financial investors, these few eastern and southern European pioneers—married men with extended families—were white enough for the white man's camp. As their numbers grew in Bisbee and across the nation, however, so did anxiety about their racial status.[47]

Questionably White in the White Man's Camp

In 1899 Midwestern investors formed what became the Calumet & Arizona (C&A) Mining Company, PD's first real competition. C&A's Junction Mine opened in 1903. A third small mine, developed by local entrepreneurs Maurice Denn and Lemuel Shattuck, opened the following year. By then, the Warren District was home to between 10,000 and 15,000 people. In sparsely populated Arizona, this made Bisbee a big city. By 1910, people from more than thirty countries populated Bisbee, and the rate of Mexican immigration was greater than ever.[48]

Bisbee kept its reputation as a white man's camp, but the boundaries of whiteness blurred as more immigrants arrived from southern and eastern Europe to work in the mines. Since racial exclusivity was an established aspect of Bisbee's social compact and economy, one way to object to newcomers was to question their racial status. So in May 1903 the *Bisbee Daily Review* reported, "A question of great moment is agitating the miners—that is, the American miners of Bisbee: viz., the employment of Italian and Slavonic workmen in some of the mines and the readiness with which they are employed by some of the foremen." The article then invoked Bisbee's vaunted reputation: "The American miners contend that Bisbee has always been a 'White Man's Camp,' and much feeling is being manifested by the men who are, as they say, unable to secure employment by the influx of foreign labor."[49] By 1903, the phrase "American miners" implied a three-part hierarchy: "whites" or "Americans" on top, then "foreigners," then Mexicans (on the outside were the Chinese). By 1903, there was little doubt that these were racial, not national, categories—else why would "white" and "foreigner" be juxtaposed? A Cornish miner could be a white "American," while a man born in Arizona could be Mexican. Serbs and Italians? Unclear.

The "American miners" blamed recent conflict on foreign workers (like Mexicans, dubbed "cheap labor" by the *Review*) and on the foremen who employed them, suggesting that both were violating the social compact of the white man's camp. Yet no well-established rules existed about whether Italians or Serbs counted as white or could work underground. Some self-proclaimed white man's camps like Cripple Creek, Colorado, excluded Italians and Slavs.[50] In Bisbee, however, the sons of pioneers Caretto and Medigovich had been working as miners at white men's pay at least as recently as 1898.[51] But what about new immigrants with no claims to the region, to American citizenship, or even to the English language? Were they white? Was the new mining company defying the social compact of Bisbee's pioneers? These questions sparked debate in Bisbee for the next twenty years.

The recruiting and hiring of southern and eastern Europeans signaled a shift in the balance of power, from skilled miners to their corporate managers. C&A recruited hundreds of skilled Cornish miners to Bisbee, where they developed new technology for all three mining companies. But most copper mining was becoming unskilled work. New smelter techniques made low-grade ores profitable, and volume became more important than precision. Production skyrocketed, machines replaced hand drills, and in 1913 Bisbee's manly drilling contest was ended, a victim of obsolescence.[52]

Many Americans understood the tensions between old and new workers in terms that could be called racial—both then and now—but these intersected with distinctions based on national origin, skin color, language, masculinity, and culture. Racial boundaries were porous; they overlapped with other descriptive (and prescriptive) categories. Bisbee was not unique in confronting this dilemma, but the categorizations demanded by the rules of the white man's camp sharpened the debate.

Southern and eastern Europeans began arriving in large numbers in Bisbee at a time when the "high" philosophy of race science and the "low" realm of popular politics and union agitation were employing more elaborate racial definitions. Just a few decades before, Social Darwinists had seen room for optimism: after all, if Anglo-Saxons were the superior race, they had nothing to fear from evolution. But in the 1890s, according to John Higham, racial theorists made a "swing to a defensive outlook." Economic depression in the 1890s coincided with concerns that only the worst specimens of eastern and southern Europe became immigrants. To compete with these supposedly lesser creatures, native-born American citizens were shrinking the size of their families to prevent a decline in their standard of living, which in turn gave immigrants with large families a demographic advantage—leading to fears of "race suicide" among America's best "racial stock." [53] Discussions of standards of living and the plight of the working classes brought inchoate intellectual ideas about race difference to the masses by filtering "scientific" racial concepts through a preoccupation with life's most quotidian and immediate concerns: clothing, housing, family structure, social life, and—not least—wages. Indeed, this last offered the allure of a quantitative measure of racial difference, defined by standards of living.

These discussions began to prompt policy change, with the support of the nation's largest labor unions, the American Federation of Labor (AFL) and the Knights of Labor. In 1898, the Knights' leader, Terence Powderly, was appointed U.S. commissioner-general of immigration. In that capacity, Powderly changed official reporting rules on European immigrants to record "race"—a decision based on his fears about the rising numbers of southern and eastern Europeans. The following year, a young economist at the Massachusetts Institute of Technology named William Z. Ripley released an influential book identifying the three "races" of Europe: Teutonic, Alpine, and Mediterranean, with subcategories splintering from there. By 1900, the new European science of eugenics, or race improvement, was making its way across the Atlantic and influencing American scientists, politicians, and labor leaders. Starting in 1905, articles about "race suicide" (a concern especially of Theodore Roosevelt) increasingly filled the popular press. In 1907, the AFL offered its official endorsement of a bill requiring a literacy test for immigrants, and the U.S. Congress launched the massive investigation of immigration known as the Dillingham Commission, whose findings spurred the restrictions of the 1920s.[54]

Numbers told the story, in the view of immigration's critics. In 1882 the federal government had recorded about 650,000 European immigrants to the United States, only 13 percent of them from southern and eastern Europe. By 1907—the peak year of immigration, prior to the restrictions of the 1920s—the total number of immigrants from Europe had doubled to 1.2 million, in which the proportion of southern and eastern Europeans had ballooned to 81 percent.[55] If these trends continued, the "racial" makeup of the United States—and the very notion of an "American"—would be radically altered.

Bisbee's increases in new immigrants and the racial concerns that accompanied them mirrored the nation's. The Italians are a case in point. In 1882, about fifty Italians lived in Cochise County, mostly in Tombstone. By 1910, about four hundred county residents—now clustered in Bisbee—were either from Italy or had Italian parents. Opera Drive, above Brewery Gulch, became an Italian enclave, and even today the neighborhood is scented by the fennel first planted by its early residents. Many were northern Italians from the Alps region near Torino, not far from Switzerland, which may explain the camp's sizable Swiss population as well. Northern Italians faced far less discrimination in the United States than darker-skinned Sicilians, but, in Bisbee at least, they did not receive a warm welcome.[56]

In the 1903 *Daily Review* story about "foreigners," one man asked, "Why not let well enough alone? This is a peaceful camp, . . . but if Italians are employed it may precipitate trouble." Local mining officials and prominent businessmen also had mixed feelings. C&A general manager John Merrill insisted that "if Italian miners come, I will hire them, as I must have men to work." Merrill was not the type to bow to old traditions created by prospectors ("nothing short of dynamite could ever stop him," one man recalled). For Merrill, mining the ore was the chief goal—not enforcing old rules over who did what work. He laid the blame at the feet of "Americans": "I cannot let this mine be idle for want of men, and if the Americans do not want to work, I must get foreigners." Yet Bisbee's most prominent old-timers disagreed. M. J. Cunningham, a vice president of the Bank of Bisbee who had grown up in Tombstone and who was Brophy's brother-in-law, claimed he was "utterly opposed to the hiring of foreign labor." The article's author concluded that all "the leading business men are in sympathy with the old miners and denounce [foreigners] in strong terms." By interviewing C&A's manager and contrasting his views with PD's local allies, the writer implied that the new company in town was threatening the rules of the white man's camp. The *Daily Review* was owned by Phelps Dodge ("the old reliable family newspaper," it called itself), and although the two mining companies cooperated in setting wages and, later, in responding to strikes, it made sense for PD's newspaper to distance its managers and allies from controversial hiring practices. The situation was resolved temporarily, when a day later mining officials announced that for underground jobs they would employ only men who spoke English. The Cornish could stay, in other words, while Italians and Slavs might have to go.[57]

Still, many Italians remained, and faced discrimination both blatant and subtle, whether they spoke English or not. Both by choice, it would seem, and because of segregation, Italians crossed paths and shared space with Mexicans on lower Chihuahua Hill and Brewery Gulch. They played musical instruments at Mexican celebrations like Cinco de Mayo, and some Italian parents encouraged their children to learn Spanish. A few Italians and Mexicans intermarried. For decades, the Caretto Saloon offered a place where Mexicans, Italians, and African Americans could mingle freely, but it had an unsavory reputation.

Italians differed in some important ways from other European groups. They were, for example, the most likely to return to the home country. Perhaps as many as half went back to Italy, a tendency that characterized Italian migrants across the Americas. This was an undesirable trait in a mining town where turnover among employees was a mark against them and managers wanted a permanent workforce. The lack of Italian organizations in Bisbee was one sign of shallow roots, although in the 1920s Brewery Gulch boasted an Italian-Mexican Club. Italian baker Constantino Aira, who owned the City Bakery, baked *pan de huevo,* a traditional Mexican egg-pastry, and sold it in Tintown, or bartered bread for firewood from Mexican woodcutters. Italians heard epithets like "Dago" on the streets of Bisbee, and rumors of the presence of the Black Hand, an Italian kidnapping syndicate, floated around town. In the 1920s, Ku Klux Klan members planted a burning cross on the Carettos' lawn—a sign that this pioneer family's racial status had declined since the nineteenth century.[58]

Nowhere was the declining status of Italians clearer than in corporate pay scales. When Phelps Dodge took over the Copper Queen Mine in the 1880s, Italians worked at white wages and earned twice what Mexican workers did. By 1898, Italians had slipped down the pay scale. Baptiste Caretto's four sons each earned $3.50 a day working as miners—white men's jobs at white men's pay—while most other Italians worked as "crushers," smashing large chunks of rock into smaller pieces to load onto ore cars. It was a job with low pay but not necessarily "Mexican." By 1911, 85 percent of Italians in Bisbee and Clifton's mines earned less than $3.00 per day (as did 99 percent of

Mexicans) at a time when the lowest underground miner's wage was $4.00. Pay scales in the "Mexican camp" of Clifton had separate categories for Mexicans, Italians/Spaniards, and whites, while Bisbee's divisions were less explicit even as they grew more rigid.[59]

Like Mexicans, Italians supposedly threatened the American standard of living. During the 1903 controversy, one man complained that "the foreign element can live on a mere pittance to what a white man can. . . . All that is necessary [to prove it] is for a man to go up north of the Catholic church and in an oblong building he will find a bunch of Italians living as no white man can." Note the various components of the story—white versus foreign; an "oblong building," not a house; a "bunch of Italians," rather than a family.[60]

In some ways, Italians were "honorary Mexicans." The Dillingham Commission found Italians and Mexicans almost interchangeable in the dual-wage systems of Bisbee and Clifton; both groups were "usually employed at the simplest unskilled labor" and were paid "lower wages than those paid their American and north European competitors." But it was more complicated than that, because Italians were both more white than Mexicans, and nonwhite in a different way. For every bit of common ground shared by Mexicans and Italians, something else set the two groups apart. Italians attended St. Patrick's, the white Catholic church. They went to white schools and worked underground, though not as miners. Unlike African Americans and Asians, Italians, like other Europeans, were legally "white on arrival," as historian Thomas Guglielmo has observed. Even so, in 1898, lawmakers in the racially complex state of Louisiana had seriously contemplated disfranchising Italians along with African Americans. Mexicans, like Italians, were also legally white, but this had little effect by the late nineteenth century. The Italian Carettos' whiteness derived from their status as Bisbee pioneers (it was conferred by a grandfather clause, one might say), while their newer compatriots slipped down the racial hierarchy.[61]

Bisbee's even larger Slavic and Finnish populations also occupied ambiguous racial territories, but they did not share the same affinities with Mexicans that Italians did. Although many border towns had visible Jewish populations, and Bisbee also had Albanians and Greeks, its eastern European population was predominantly Slavic, from Slovenia, Croatia, Montenegro, Bosnia, and especially Serbia. All were part of the Austro-Hungarian Empire, so that many were simply called "Austrians." Kin networks and chain migrations begun by the Medigovich and Angius families drew hundreds of Serbs to Bisbee. By 1910, as many as 1,500 of Bisbee's immigrants and first-generation Americans hailed from Serbia (about the same number as those who came from England). Many settled permanently, in a community anchored by Serbian groceries in Brewery Gulch, where miners cashed their paychecks. The mini-empire established by V. G. Medigovich and J. B. Angius included extensive real estate holdings, mercantiles, a lumber company, and a large commercial building on the Gulch's most prominent corner. The two men helped to form Serbian fraternal lodges in 1903 and 1905. Serbian Orthodox Christmas became a standard part of Bisbee's holiday season as early as 1907, and in later years Serb Hall and a Serbian Orthodox church were built.[62]

A strong ethnic economy and a few pioneer forebears did not save Slavs from discrimination. In 1898, most Slavs in the mines worked in low or middling jobs (for example, as crushers) earning $2.00 a day, when most Mexicans were earning $1.50 and white miners $3.50. Outside the mines, Slavs were treated as exotic primitives. A 1900 news story about a "Slavonian" wedding was peppered with comments about customs "truly . . . peculiar to the race." The guests drank a "strange, weird concoction" (no doubt the plum brandy Slivovitz), and the uncouth party reportedly "showed signs, frequently, of engaging in an all round scrap." The reporter also used his subjects' broken English—like the groom's comment to an interpreter to "shut up, you no good"—to emphasize inferiority and foreignness. When J. B. Angius died four years later, the *Bisbee Daily Review* eulogized him as "one of the pioneer businessmen," but his death came at a time when the growing Serb community badly needed an ally among Bisbee's elites.[63]

Serbs did attend white schools, but that did not mean full inclusion. Children were called "Bohunk" in the street and schoolyard. A child of Serbian immigrants who grew up in Bisbee in the 1910s recalled that "we all felt inferior—kids felt looked down upon." Another woman raised in Bisbee by Serbian-born parents recalled the challenges of her dual identity: "I was like a pendulum—swinging, you see, from this American culture into this Slavic culture and back again, and I had . . . a difficult [time] in really knowing who I was." She married another Serbian American, but her brother used to quip that he and his other siblings had "married white people."[64]

A reputation for radical politics was the biggest mark against Finns, who worked the mines of Minnesota and Wisconsin before moving to Bisbee. Radicalism could create racial ambiguity. In Minnesota, naturalization lawyers tried to deny American citizenship to one radical Finn by arguing he was more "Mongolian" than "Caucasian," but the courts maintained that all European immigrants were legally white.[65] In Cochise County, close to five hundred Finnish-born residents had arrived by 1910, and another three hundred were born in Sweden, many of Finnish descent. Like Slavs and Italians, Finns, when they arrived in Bisbee, often settled in the melting pot of Brewery Gulch, before moving to Bisbee's largest suburb, Lowell, where they built a Finn Hall and lived in rooming houses run by Finnish women. Finns shared a reputation with Italians and Mexicans for being sojourners rather than permanent residents. One man remembered them as a "very secretive group of people" who "didn't mingle with anybody else." Like Slavs, Finns faced a huge language barrier that made "mingling" difficult. Einar Saarela, who grew up in Bisbee, remembered being tremendously bored in school because he did not understand a word.[66]

Whereas a low racial status was the *driver* in the exclusion of Chinese and Mexicans from the white man's camp, for eastern and southern Europeans it was the *result,* as their numbers grew and they presented greater job and wage competition. Old-stock miners saw Italians, Slavs, and Finns as a threat to the gentlemen's agreement that promised miners good wages and "free-labor" arrangements so long as they eschewed unions. Mexican workers' segregation in "top work" kept them from direct competition with "white" workers, but distinctions were less clear with the new "foreigners." Despite laws against contract labor, unscrupulous *padrones* often negotiated with American employers to arrange deals that could border on debt peonage. Einar Saarela's father was a contract miner whose pay varied depending on how much ore he could "blast and deliver out of the mine." Some contract arrangements worked to the advantage of miners, who set their hours and pace. But coerced-labor arrangements made possible by the contract system could challenge the very notion of a free-labor system. White skilled miners who prided themselves on their free agency—being "too independent to be pushed around by boss, foreman, or superintendents, too self-reliant to welcome the activities of labor-union leaders"—did not take this competition lightly.[67]

No mapping of racial boundaries in the white man's camp would be complete without including its small but visible African American population. Blacks were not excluded from Bisbee or any other mining camps in Arizona, or from the white man's camp of Cripple Creek, Colorado.[68] A black miner in Tombstone supposedly once said, "Si White and I were the first white men in Tombstone after [founders] Gird and Schieffelin."[69] It would be a neat truth if, in the white man's camp, blacks were whites, but this was not so. Bisbee's few African Americans—seventy in 1910, compared to 3,473 foreign-born whites—suffered job segmentation somewhat akin to that faced by Mexicans (except they worked in jobs such as porters, barbers, bootblacks, and janitors). They differed, though, in having unthreatening numbers and unquestioned American citizenship.[70] Indeed, citizenship became a bargaining point—and bone of contention—for African Americans. In 1915, Bisbee resident E. G. Hall looked into the possibility of creating a local chapter of the National Association for the Advancement of Colored People (NAACP). "The colored citizens here," he wrote to the national headquarters, "are debarred from all labor except Janitoring. The mining . . . is given to foreigners and there's practically nothing to induce colored people to stay." Noting the availability of jobs for "foreigners" underscored for Hall the injustice of his own situation. Few if any African Americans worked in Bisbee's mines, and it is not clear whether any were deported—or served as deputies—during the Deportation (although Buffalo soldiers at Columbus, New Mexico, guarded the deportee camp there).[71]

Still, segregation was partial at best. In 1910, the legislature passed a Jim Crow law aimed at blacks, and there was talk of placing a "colored school" in an unused corner of the city cemetery, across Brewery Gulch from a black neighborhood at Youngblood Hill; but this proposal seems to have gone nowhere, since the land became a city park a few years later. By the 1920s Bisbee's few black elementary-age pupils—including the children of the vice president of the local NAACP, whose wife was Mexican—went to Franklin School, a school for Mexicans built in 1919. The City of Douglas created a small school for African Americans in a remote location, but local families "banded together" to fight "any attempt . . . to force their children to attend." They would accept the law, but as "property owners and taxpayers," they also demanded "some voice in choosing the site for their school." The outcome in Douglas is unknown, but black teenagers went to Bisbee High (as did a few Mexican Americans). One man recalled that "down in Douglas they wouldn't let niggers go to high school, so they came up and went to Bisbee."[72]

In some ways, African Americans occupied a higher position than Mexicans. During the Mexican Revolution, when African American troops were stationed along the border, being black was better than being Mexican. One Mexican man chased by a racist mob in El Paso yelled, "I'm a nigger! I'm a nigger!" to get them off his trail. An African American woman there noted that when the Klan rose in the 1920s, its members "were after the Mexicans."[73] It is safe to say that in Bisbee, blacks may not have been honorary "whites"—but neither were they the main targets of the white-man's-camp ideology.

From White Man's Camp to Company Town

Nineteenth-century Bisbee had been a one-company town, meaning that Phelps Dodge was the main employer. But it was not a company town in the truest sense—that is, when the company founds the town and owns everything, from the mines to the houses to the grocery store to the land under one's feet. In the twentieth century, PD developed a reputation as a consummate paternalist organization, a "corporation with a full and whole soul for those appearing on the pay roll." The company eventually created schools, playgrounds, a hospital, and other amenities. The Dodge family was a major benefactor of the international movement that created the YMCA and YWCA (Young Men's Christian Association and Young Women's Christian Association), and in Bisbee the Dodges and Douglases, along with the company, funded an impressive "corporate-community" YMCA and a YWCA. Later, the company developed full-scale company towns in Arizona, New Mexico, and Mexico, where PD owned everything, including the kitchen sink. Views of PD's paternalism depended on one's relationship to the white-man's-camp ideology. One Welsh woman, who grew up in the exclusive enclave known as Quality Hill, recalled that "to live in Bisbee was to love our Copper Queen Company, 'the source of every good and perfect gift.'"[74]

But in Bisbee, PD's first mining camp, these gifts were relatively slow in coming. PD's entry into paternalism was reactive and piecemeal—scarcely a full-blown corporate strategy. Even after PD bought the Copper Queen, Bisbee retained an unsavory reputation at odds with the image of a paternalistic company town. In 1883 five people, including a pregnant woman, were murdered during a robbery attempt at Goldwater & Castañeda's mercantile. Vigilantes rounded up and hanged one of the suspects in Tombstone. Later in the decade, some men calling themselves the "45-50 Posse" lynched a Mexican man accused of shooting two men in a bar fight. The posse hanged him from an oak tree on the road into town. One seasoned resident supposedly told an appalled passer-by, "That's nothing; we grow those kind of things on the trees here occasionally." The next morning PD directors arrived from New York, and were shocked to come across the man's lynched body. According to one early resident, the company men had come to Bisbee to announce pay cuts, but "maybe the dangling form of the Mexican and the western way of bringing quick justice made the directors change their minds. They left the camp without cutting wages." PD board members—especially Dr. Douglas—resolved to bring "a more refined and cultured way of life" to Bisbee, starting with a shipment of books to create Bisbee's first library. The collection eventually grew to thousands of volumes, including some in Spanish and newspapers in several languages. The library became the first of many attempts by PD officials to "civilize" Bisbee.[75]

Paternalism was only one way to display corporate benevolence while retaining corporate control. The movement to incorporate the disorganized camp into a chartered city had the same motivations. By the twentieth century, the Warren District had evolved into a sprawling metropolitan area too large and complex to be governed by a simple mining-district code. It faced typical urban problems of overcrowding and public health crises. Kitchen garbage and human waste fouled the makeshift streets, which were "somewhat frightful from a sanitary point of view" and coated with slime that gave off "a nauseating odor." In the town's hillside neighborhoods, the contents of chamber pots were dumped from kitchen windows and landed in neighbors' yards; households still got their water in canvas sacks on mules or from shallow, disease-breeding wells. "Cleanliness is next to Godliness," quipped one local Woman's Club member in 1902, "and some parts of the town seem a long way from Heaven."[76]

10. Postcard image of downtown Bisbee, ca. 1912. Arizona State Library, Archives and Public Records, History and Archives Division, Phoenix, 97-1026.

Bisbee was not a safe place to live. Hard-rock mining was, in fact, the deadliest industry in America, worse even than coal mining. Workers could suffocate, be crushed or impaled, fall to their death in deep mining shafts, drown in floodwaters, succumb to poisonous gas, or be annihilated by dynamite. Lost limbs were common, lung ailments also. Yet in the early years, contagious diseases were even more deadly than mine accidents. Scores of people died in typhoid epidemics from 1888 to 1890, before James Douglas ordered the main well cleaned. The lack of public utilities created a sanitation crisis. Contagious diseases disproportionately affected Mexicans and "foreigners," especially infants who were vulnerable to dysentery. Local boosters dismissed the appalling infant mortality rates as the result of "a foreign population that is ignorant of the care and attention that infants require."[77]

One increasingly popular response to such problems was to incorporate a city. Incorporation gives municipalities the power to levy taxes, issue licenses, pass bonds, appoint public health officers with vaccination and quarantine powers, ban nuisances, contract for public utilities and garbage collection, and regulate food and milk production.[78] The typical company town has no need for incorporation, because the company is the sole landowner. All power resides in the corporate manager's office. But Bisbee was a hybrid version, because its roots as a prospector camp had nurtured an independent merchant class, and because by 1899 it had more than one mining company.

PD officials pursued incorporation in Bisbee (and in Douglas) because creating a city government offered tools to solve problems. City incorporation increased corporate power rather than diminishing it. City contracts for private telephones, ice delivery, and water supply made lucrative personal investments for company officials. When carefully handled, incorporation could also foster alliances with an independent, mostly immigrant bourgeoisie of local merchants and saloon men, who initially opposed incorporation. As many as fifty saloons already paid county licensing fees for liquor, prostitution, and gambling, and their owners did not relish the idea of city taxes too. An anti-incorporation group cropped up in Brewery Gulch, organized by Serb pioneer J. B. Angius, several Scots, a German beer distributor, and a Swiss brewery owner and land speculator.[79]

In response, PD officials offered local businessmen plum appointments and cut them into utility service contracts. In late 1900 a "mass meeting" elected Angius to the committee that recommended the boundaries of the new city, which was officially incorporated on January 9, 1902. Those who were appointed by the county Board of Supervisors to the first City Council (subsequent members were elected) included Angius, mine and saloon owner Lemuel Shattuck, and five other small-time investors and saloon owners—but no PD or C&A officials, since few of them lived full-time in Bisbee. Besides, their absence from the council created a veneer of impartiality. The first mayor, Joseph Muirhead, was a Canadian miner whose wife ran a large roominghouse. Angius and Shattuck also became the only men who were not Copper Queen managers to become shareholders of the newly founded Bisbee Improvement Company, which had a monopoly on gas and telephone service.[80] As one local historian generally sympathetic to PD put it, "The new utility company "was created by the same group of men who owned the mining property, financed the mining industry, built the railroads, published the newspapers, supported the churches, maintained a mercantile business, and operated the banks of the district." Sanitation was eventually improved, after the mining companies—Bisbee's largest taxpayers—gave their seal of approval. The downtown streets were paved, and a water company (run by mining officials) and electricity plant were established. So were a sewer system, a flood control system, and a fire department—though this last only after a huge blaze engulfed three-fourths of the town in 1908.[81]

In a place where racial status determined wages, where the same men set salaries and ran the utilities, and where neighborhoods were clearly segregated, racial differences in public-utility provision followed predictable but also preventable lines. In 1908, sewer lines reached much of Bisbee—but were noticeably absent from Mexican Tintown, Zacatecas Canyon, Chihuahua Hill, and African American Youngblood Hill. Water service, the most important public-health measure, began in late 1902 for eight dollars per month. A flush toilet and a bathtub added a dollar each; so did a supply of water for one horse. At those prices, a water bill was nearly a quarter of the average Mexican salary, and one-sixth of a typical "foreigner" salary. In 1906, the water company had about 1,300 individual users—about a tenth of the total population. Rates fell over time, yet as late as 1914, when the average water bill was just $2.00 per month, at least one in four homes had no running water. It was a recession year, and the combined average utility bills (water, electric, telephone, and gas) added up to about 28 percent of the average Mexican salary and about 21 percent of the average "foreigner" wage. In 1917, the Arizona State Bureau of Mines criticized the "abnormally high rates" of Bisbee utilities and urged the mining companies to address the high cost of living. Since standards of cleanliness are one of the most common measures for expressing racial difference and disdain ("dirty Mexican"), these disparities deepened racial division as much they reflected it.[82]

Municipal power, in theory, could be acquired in open elections by counter-interests such as labor unions, liquor interests, or rival mining companies. Yet that did not happen. Incorporation gave mining officials new tools of social and political control while allowing them to trumpet democratic ideals. The appointment—and co-optation—of the immigrant bourgeoisie to council and utility boards was smart patronage politics, and consolidated the Copper Queen's power. The new city limits carefully skirted PD's mining claims, so that the mines paid no local taxes (though PD did pay taxes on its administrative offices). The city's first business-licensing ordinance also bore the stamp of Walter Douglas' influence. In 1902, Mayor Joseph Muirhead publicly denied the charges, but the city attorney and an alderman both swore he had okayed the bill with Walter Douglas before signing it.[83]

Moving the smelters out of Bisbee's canyons to a new company town, named for Dr. James Douglas by his son Walter, also cemented alliances with local businessmen and consolidated the influence of Phelps Dodge. At the turn of the century, Walter Douglas had secretly located a promising town site in an open valley along the U.S.-Mexico border, twenty-five miles from Bisbee. In 1901, local entrepreneurs led by a Bisbee butcher got wind of the plans, and promptly filed land claims on the proposed site. The original landsite investors, mostly Copper Queen officials, were forced to let the interlopers, among them Lemuel Shattuck and John Slaughter (a powerful rancher and former sheriff) in on the deal. Incorporating the City of Douglas in 1904 became another occasion for dealmaking and for securing loyalty from potential rivals. Years later, Shattuck's daughter characterized the inclusion of the small businessmen as a boon for Douglas, because they "broke the Copper Queen monopoly, and brought into community planning a wealthy and powerful group that rapidly developed Douglas." Yet the deal was no less a boon for PD, because it tied previously independent small businessmen into the corporation's plans.[84]

Moving the smelter to Douglas even bolstered Bisbee's reputation as a white man's camp. C&A and PD completed their smelters in Douglas in 1903 and 1904, during the height of the controversy over Bisbee's foreigners. The move displaced eight hundred jobs, but "no less than three hundred are Mexican laborers," the *Daily Review* reassured its readers. Smelter work became "Mexican work," as surely as mining was "white work." Relocating the new smelters ensured that "Bisbee . . . will become the rival of all the mining camps of The West in more ways than one[:] . . . An American population. Two thousand miners employed. Eight hours work, $3.50 pay. That is the future of Bisbee."[85]

Mapping Race and Place in the White Man's Camp

Moving the smelters cleaned Bisbee's air and siphoned Mexican workers from the white man's camp, but it did not cure all of Bisbee's urban ills. Ten years after incorporation, a tour of Bisbee would have revealed a typical in-

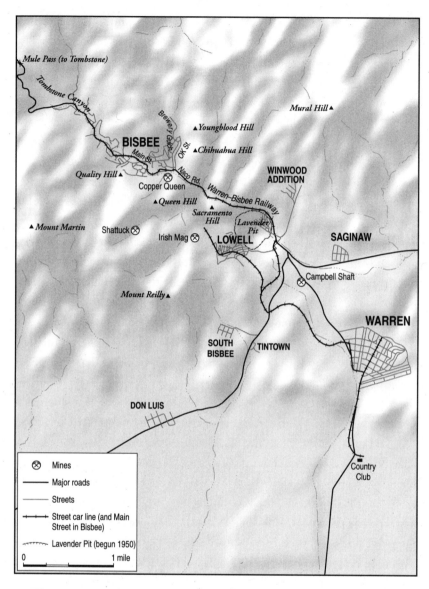

11. The Warren Mining District, ca. 1917. By this time, the City of Bisbee anchored a sprawling metropolitan region. Map by Philip Schwartzberg.

dustrial city in microcosm—think Pittsburgh, only smaller, and in the desert. Urban sprawl is not a new phenomenon, nor is it confined to big cities. From 1910 to 1920, the City of Bisbee grew by fewer than two hundred people (from 9,019 to 9,205), even as the population of the entire metropolitan area peaked during World War I at around 25,000. Many working-class women, disproportionately immigrants, were widowed by mine accidents, or forced to take full economic responsibility after their husbands sustained crippling injuries. The women's roominghouses and hotels adjoined saloons and restaurants, mercantiles and department stores, to fill the narrow canyons. A streetcar now traversed Main Street and Tombstone Canyon. Down Naco Road, the new exurb of Lowell had a population as large as that of the City of Bisbee, and sported several distinct neighborhoods of its own. Across Naco Road from Lowell was Winwood Addition, followed by South Bisbee and Tintown. Further along was Warren, a new suburb being built by corporate newcomer Calumet & Arizona.[86]

Bisbee's residents had once lived wherever they could find a level piece of ground, with little difference in "standard of living." No longer. After Mexican Chihuahua Hill emerged in the late nineteenth century, segregation began in earnest. A report prepared by clergy, PD, and YMCA officials in 1919 listed about twenty distinct neighborhoods in the Warren District, at least half outside the Bisbee city limits. With the exception of Brewery Gulch, the report labeled neighborhoods in Bisbee proper as predominantly "American," "English" (like "Cousin Jack Alley"), and "Welsh." Mexicans and "Americans" were the most segregated groups. Mexicans lived mainly in Tintown and Chihuahua Hill (where they were joined, according to the report's authors, by a "sprinkling" of Slavs). The only places dominated by one group were the "largely American"—and largely elite—neighborhoods of Quality Hill and Warren. Four neighborhoods, all heavily Slavic, had "no Mexicans," according to one report. This social geography nicely matched the racial hierarchy, segregating "Americans" from "Mexicans," with "foreigners" somewhere in the middle. The only exception was Brewery Gulch, whose general area included the predominantly Italian street of Opera Drive, the African American neighborhood of Youngblood Hill, and Chihuahua Hill, which was Mexican, Finnish, and Serbian.[87]

Brewery Gulch was also home to the official red-light district, codified

12. Prostitute walking near "cribs" in upper Brewery Gulch, ca. 1910. Courtesy of the Bisbee Mining and Historical Museum, Kent Collection, 80.115.21.

by City Ordinance No. 1. The city's first ordinance forbade the employment of women in saloons or dance halls, "or in any room or apartment . . . connected therewith." Women were not to "sing, dance, recite, or play on any musical instrument," nor "serve as waitress or bar maid, . . . or take part either as employee or otherwise, in any game of chance or amusement played in any saloon." Yet there was one exception: as part of the ordinance, the city attorney and council members "carefully prepared" a map "showing a line . . . 'across the upper end of Brewery Gulch eight feet south of Clara Allen's place.'" Below this line, women were unwelcome in bars, but above it, they were often the main attraction. The ordinance's purpose was made quite clear by the mention of Allen, a well-known madam and saloon owner who had relocated from Tombstone. Her upscale establishment, with its $100 piano and lavish furnishings, marked the boundary between red light and respectability.[88]

Before city incorporation, Copper Queen officials had monitored prostitution. In 1894, then-constable J. B. Angius arrested the Bisbee sisters Frida and Hilda Miller on a county vice charge. A jury found them not guilty after just twenty minutes of deliberation. The next morning, eight jurors who were employed by the Copper Queen "were informed their services were no longer required." Two days later, the *Tombstone Prospector* reported that "the outcome of the Miller case . . . turned out to be more serious than was anticipated." The Copper Queen management—led by the staunch Presbyterian Scots—had reportedly threatened that "if the women who kept such places did not move" within forty-eight hours, "the mine would be closed for six months." A posse assembled to warn the Millers, Clara Allen, and another local prostitute "that they must move out before tomorrow morning." The latter two had not even been arrested. "Tomorrow Bisbee will contain once more nothing but good and moral citizens," the *Prospector* concluded.[89] Allen's residence in Bisbee eight years later suggests that things did not go quite as the Copper Queen's managers had planned.

PD officials heartily endorsed City Ordinance No. 1. Anti-prostitution campaigns—also known as "social-purity" campaigns—were among the most popular causes of the Progressive Era. Treating prostitution as a civic "disease" defined it as a public-health problem. In Bisbee, William Brophy was "glad to see the stand taken by the council" and called the law "a credit to the city." Yet in 1910, Brewery Gulch was still just "about the busiest place in the camp"—a "blazing myriad of mahogany counters, foaming liquor," and "wild debauch." By then, forty or fifty brothels housed well over a hundred prostitutes.[90]

That the city's vice district was in Bisbee's most diverse neighborhood was no accident. The presence of prostitution there linked Mexicans, eastern and southern Europeans, and the camp's few blacks with degeneracy and immorality, even if the clientele came from all over the city. The newspaper trivialized violence in the tenderloin—like amused reports of prostitutes and their pimps in pitched battles—as colorful spectacle, but concerned citizens did not intend such displays to go any further. In 1905, forty-four men and ten women petitioned the city to crack down on prostitution outside the red-light district. They argued that a bordello would be "perversive [*sic*] of the good morals of the entire community, and a baneful example to the children thereof." There was no mention of the children living in the Gulch, who passed prostitutes and gamblers on their way to school, and earned coins by running errands for them in the neighborhood.[91]

Most proprietors were madams with Anglo names, although there were also Dollie Monbaro and Dolores Díaz, as well as pimps like Jake Kerner and Pete Rossi. Among thirty-seven sex workers identified by the census in 1910 (surely an undercount), fourteen came from the American West or Southwest, fifteen from Texas and the South, one from an unspecified place in the United States; four were French, two were German, and one was English. Crib inhabitant Josephine Cohn, an "Austrian-Yiddish" single woman, occupied a room between a young divorcee from Kentucky and another woman who described herself as a thirty-year-old French divorcee. Bisbee pioneer Joe Chisholm claimed many prostitutes were a "Nordic-Mexican cross," the products of cross-cultural relations that were common in Arizona in the nineteenth century but that by the twentieth century he could exoticize as "some strange barbaric strain."[92]

In practice, city officials had little interest in eradicating prostitution, or the lucrative licensing fees it granted. Many men and women believed prostitution, drinking, and gambling were inevitable in a male-dominated mining town. The city occasionally rounded up prostitutes operating outside the district, but it proved far more zealous about collecting license fees than enforcing the red light's borders. In June 1902 the city charged "bawdy houses" and "houses of ill fame" a quarterly license fee of thirty dollars, and thirty more for a saloon license. A handful of bordellos also owned licensed slot machines. (These were the fees Walter Douglas had reportedly approved.) Later, prostitutes paid a five-dollar monthly head tax. In March 1908, for example, eighty-two women were listed at spots like "Pete's Place," where six women resided, or as "inmates" in an "I.B.H." (individual bawdy house), one of the dreary "cribs" at the shabbier end of the Gulch toward Zacatecas Canyon. No doubt many other sex workers, especially minorities and men, eluded the license collector. Although gambling and alcohol were prohibited in 1907 and 1914, and crackdowns shut most bordellos, prostitution remained in the Gulch publicly until 1917 and surreptitiously afterward. The rusty bed frames and crumbling steps of cribs and bordellos can still be glimpsed amid weeds and rubble.[93]

White Women's Power in the White Man's Camp

At the opposite end of the city's class and racial hierarchies from the red-light district were the white women who became Bisbee's leading philanthropists and social workers. Unlike some mining companies, Phelps Dodge did not have a "sociological department" that employed women for home visits and reform projects. Instead, company officials and civic leaders conducted welfare work via women either married to or funded privately by company officials. These "corporate maternalists" had twin allegiances to typically female social causes and to corporate paternalism. Such women were more than window dressing. Notwithstanding the West's masculine reputation, middle- and upper-class women had significant power in shaping the region's welfare and reform institutions.[94] Bisbee's emphasis on propriety and family life enshrined white women as symbols of respectability and agents of Progressive order. Women's reform worked in tandem with the dual-wage system and white man's camp ideology to sharpen racial difference.

Female benevolent work, like city incorporation, demonstrated the seamless connection between public and private corporate power. The corporate maternalists became centered in three institutions: the Bisbee Woman's Club, the Warren District YWCA, and the Warren District Relief Committee. For members of the Bisbee Woman's Club, founded in 1900, maternalism was married quite literally to paternalism. The Bisbee and Douglas Woman's Clubs were both founded by Helen French, wife of S. W. French, the highest-ranking PD official living full-time in Arizona. Membership was by invitation only, and all but one of the Bisbee club members were married to PD or YMCA officials. Several wives of C&A officials who lived in Michigan were named "honorary members." The club included no Mexican women, and only one woman tied to Bisbee's immigrant bourgeoisie. Danitza Angius, J.B.'s daughter, had joined by 1914. Whether the wives of the immigrant merchant class were deliberately excluded or had no interest in joining (both seem plausible), they clearly traveled in different circles.[95]

Clubwomen slowly moved from socializing to charity work, reform efforts, and lobbying. Their first big fundraising effort was for their own clubhouse on Quality Hill, completed in 1902 with gifts from PD officials, Mrs. Walter Douglas, and Grace Dodge, daughter of PD vice president Cleveland Dodge. The club devoted most of its time to hosting tea parties, discussing literature, and attending genteel lectures. When the clubwomen did turn toward reform, they pursued uncontroversial "civic housekeeping" projects, such as setting up a kindergarten, organizing a manual training program for local schools, installing a water fountain downtown for pedestrians and horses, and, in later years, urging a ban on the "raggery dance" or "one-step" at public dances. By 1908, the club's Civic Committee was working on "the unfavorable sanitary condition" of the city, but records show no evidence of social reform efforts like counseling prostitutes or trying to eradicate the red-light district.[96]

Yet the clubwomen did embrace politics. In 1902, they were invited to guest-edit an issue of the *Bisbee Daily Review* to raise clubhouse funds. The club devoted a full page to its own political endorsements. In a one-party state, where most PD officials were Democrats and where women would not earn full suffrage for another decade, the clubwomen took a decidedly non-partisan approach and endorsed candidates from both parties. Helen French became president of the Arizona Federation of Women's Clubs, from which post she worked as a lobbyist at the legislature and supervised the passage of a bill creating kindergartens across Arizona. In 1907, she enlisted a PD attorney to write her successful bill establishing a territorial juvenile court system.[97]

Bisbee's clubwomen also supported the local YWCA, the nation's first in a mining camp. Founded in 1906, the Bisbee YWCA met in Walter Douglas' former home before receiving its own, impressive building in the heart of downtown Bisbee, overlooking—but light-years away from—the red-light district in Brewery Gulch. The YWCA was funded with $40,000 from Grace Dodge, a major New York philanthropist who served as the first president of the national YWCA board of directors. Bisbee named the building for her when she died before its completion. The women who ran Bisbee's YWCA were professionals hired from outside Bisbee, but the local board of directors consisted largely of mining officials and local clergy loyal to the corporations. YWCA board presidents were always women, several of whom were woman's club officials and/or wives of top PD and C&A officials.[98]

The YWCA deepened racial divisions by providing professional and social opportunities for white women only. Almost without exception, the women who lived in the YWCA's dormitories, ate in its lunchroom, attended its programs, and served on its board were all unequivocally "white." In 1917, at the height of concern over immigrant assimilation, the YWCA did hire a woman (probably Anglo) to "work among the Mexican girls, teaching them home duties, English, etc." But the Protestant roots of the YWCA only buttressed a general tendency to neglect Mexican women. The Dodges were devoted to the YMCA and YWCA in large part because they were devoted Presbyterians. Elsewhere, YWCAs engaged in improving race relations and promoting labor activism, quite unlike the YMCAs. But Bisbee's YWCA, with the Dodge family name emblazoned on the front, did not serve the same purpose.[99]

Bisbee's best-known professional woman, Esther Cummings, also hewed tightly to the racial mores of her corporate benefactors. As secretary of the Bisbee Board of Trade Charity Committee, founded during a recession in 1909, "Miss Cummings," as she was known, did various types of welfare work—though the committee was proud that "not . . . a penny of actual money" was given out. Instead, Cummings distributed clothing and food to widows and families, helped women to secure work, steered the indigent toward medical care, and placed orphans in the California Children's Home. Cummings was a typical maternalist who directed her attention to children and families, and was more than willing to make moral judgments. She blamed juvenile delinquency on "poor and under-nourished families" whose "standard of living is much lower." This is not a huge surprise, but her emphasis on "standard of living" resonated with the racialized arguments about wages and status in Bisbee. By 1914, Cummings' job title was secretary and "investigator," and her job included weeding out the worthy from the unworthy.[100]

Her work was important, because the charity committee served as Bisbee's public-welfare system. By 1916, it had been renamed the Warren District Relief Association, perhaps a way to mask the biases revealed by its previous link to the Board of Trade. Its board of directors, however, remained populated by the city's male and female elite, among them businessmen, the Catholic priest whose benefactor was Brophy, the general manager of C&A, and the secretary of the YWCA. In 1914, woman's club and YWCA officers joined Cummings to lobby for the creation of a state children's home.[101]

Esther Cummings' work increasingly reflected the racialized vision of her benefactors. Her reports from 1910 and 1911 did not mention the race or nationality of any of her cases. By 1915, however, perhaps in response to an influx of refugees from the Mexican Revolution, Cummings had begun reporting her work in racial terms, listing separately the number of Mexican families who received school clothes or Christmas dinners. Besides that, Cummings concluded with what sounded like approval, "The Mexicans have not been a very great expense to this Association during the past year." It was a telling distinction, because in spite of years of debate in the district over the racial status of Serbs and Italians, only Mexicans were a separate category. In a three-page report, Cummings mentioned Mexicans five separate times.[102]

By the twentieth century, the white man's camp was not all-white, all-male, or truly a "camp." Under PD's direction, the little settlement had become an industrialized, class-stratified, and ethnically diverse city. Phelps Dodge itself had become an industry dynamo, and Dr. Douglas and his sons very rich. In 1881, the elder Douglas took a 10 percent interest in the unproven Copper Queen mine as a finder's fee. By 1909, he was president of all of PD (as his son Walter would later be), and was worth as much as $40 million when he died in 1918. Among his many charitable gifts and philanthropies were seed money and radium to establish cancer research at what would become the Memorial Sloan-Kettering Cancer Center in New York. The venerable Dodge family supported their alma mater of Princeton, funded and managed YMCA and YWCA projects around the world, and continued to oversee American University in Beirut, which they had helped to found in 1866 and where several family members served as president. The Copper Queen, in a remote corner of an underpopulated western backwater, funded riches and philanthropies impressive even by the standards of New York's elite.[103]

In comparison, what miners in Bisbee fought over was chump change, but it was all they had. Where white miners had once created the social compact of the white man's camp, mining companies and their allies were now calling the shots. As more Slavs and Italians began to call Bisbee home, the "old miners" of Cornish and Irish stock clung to the label of "white man's camp," even as they debated who belonged in it. The mining companies defended their right to hire "foreigners," even as they created an urban landscape that deepened the perceived racial differences among white, Mexican, and "foreign" workers. The result was a lasting tension over race, and social and geographic inequality that many local residents viewed as racially determined.

In a city where the same men paid wages, funded welfare programs, and operated public utilities, racial inequalities were a by-product of corporate policy. By treating Mexican and "foreign" workers as less than full members of the social compact, the companies created the very conditions that white workers blamed on their new foreign competition. This paradox would have violent manifestations, culminating in the Bisbee Deportation. In the meantime, however, competing mining company C&A pursued more peaceful solutions to Bisbee's problems, as it built a model suburb called Warren to house and create ideal "Americans."

4

"A Better Man for Us" in Warren

While Phelps Dodge and its allies reformed and incorporated, the Calumet & Arizona Company took a different approach. In 1906 C&A's investors created the model suburb of Warren as an alternative to Bisbee, with its overcrowding, poor sanitation, and ethnic tumult. The townsite's designer, Warren Manning (the name was a coincidence; the town was named for pioneering prospector George Warren), was a prominent Massachusetts landscape architect turned urban planner. In early 1906, he came to Bisbee, checked into PD's beautiful new Copper Queen Hotel, and was shocked and fascinated by what he found. "Such a town you . . . never saw in your life," he wrote to his wife. "Its all on edge except where the edges meet at the bottom." On a sheet of hotel stationery, he scribbled a deep *V* to show how "the houses are stuck to the hill sides," and drew haphazard squares along a meandering double squiggle. "Houses are arranged in the streets about like this[,] every possible angle as though they had been tumbled down the hill sides then patched up & made into a house where they happened to land with the streets wiggling thru where it could be squeezed in."[1]

Four miles away, the Warren townsite occupied a triangular valley as gently sloping as Bisbee was craggy and hilly. Three natural arroyos funneled rainwater away to a series of low hills. The development featured widely curving streets in a wheel-and-spoke pattern modeled after Washington, D.C. A park watered by mine runoff and flanked by wide boulevards cut a half-mile swath through town. Water and sewer pipes to every lot, emblems of twentieth-

A Villa of the Better Class.

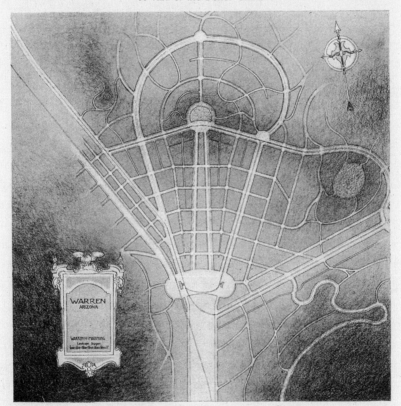

General Plan of the City of Warren, Arizona.

13. The ideal town of Warren, as conceived by Warren Manning and Huger Elliott. From Huger Elliott, "An Ideal City in the West," *Architectural Review,* 15, no. 9 (September 1908): 137–142.

14. A street in the town of Warren, ca. 1918. Courtesy of the Bisbee Mining and Historical Museum, Mihelich Collection, 00.36.1.

century progress, snaked below the streets and parks. A year after the town-site's November 1906 opening, the real estate company's two-story brick office was complete, accompanied by a sprinkling of bungalows and cottages in the townsite's southeast corner.[2]

A decade later, on the eve of the Bisbee Deportation, Warren contained nearly 250 buildings, mostly California-style bungalows and a handful of mining moguls' mansions. The new community of close to a thousand residents boasted a modern streetcar line to downtown Bisbee and the mines, a state-of-the-art baseball stadium, and a new school. Warren was something short of an oasis—one eastern newcomer dismissed it as "a small town surrounded by high hills, all bare and naked"—but its orderliness made quite a contrast with the rest of the district.[3]

Yet, as built, tidy Warren was not what its designers had planned, because C&A modified the town's design for its own purposes. While Manning envisioned a stylized and aesthetically uniform community, with the designer's hand evident throughout, C&A's managers saw Warren as a social laboratory for creating loyal American workers. In their plans and promotions for the town, company officials avoided tangled debates over whiteness by substituting a language of Americanism that was less fraught but just as racialized.

Warren offered a sanitary and orderly alternative to Bisbee's chaotic growth, but in the aftermath of Bisbee's first strike, C&A's efforts would fail to defuse growing racial and class tensions.

Midwestern Roots

The story of Warren's development began far from the Arizona desert, in northern Michigan and Minnesota. Michigan's Upper Peninsula (the U.P.) led the nation in copper production from the 1840s until the turn of the century, when Arizona and Montana took over. From necessity, mining barons of the Great Lakes had built new towns to serve their mines in the northern wilderness. The U.P.'s most extensive housing programs belonged to the enormous Calumet & Hecla Company, founded in 1871 by Alexander Agassiz, the son of famed Harvard naturalist and racial theorist Louis Agassiz. By 1910, Calumet & Hecla was renting out over a thousand company-built houses and was leasing hundreds of home-building sites to miners on company land.[4]

Six of Calumet & Arizona's founding directors came from the copper center of Calumet, Michigan, and two others from the iron-ore-loading depot of Duluth, Minnesota. C&A's most lucrative mining claim, the Irish Mag (named by its first owner for his favorite Brewery Gulch prostitute), developed into one of the most productive copper mines in Arizona history. By 1906, when C&A's plans for Warren solidified, its principals had already developed five other mines in the district, had built a modern smelter in Douglas, and were employing 2,000 people.[5] In 1905, two C&A investors—Thomas H. Cole and H. B. Hoveland—created the Warren Realty & Development Company, and appointed Cole's former personal assistant Lewis W. Powell as its president in early 1906. By the end of that year, C&A took over the real estate venture that would become Warren.[6]

C&A's directors had deep roots with company housing programs. The father of brothers and codirectors James and Thomas Hoatson had been a superintendent for Calumet & Hecla, where he had overseen the company's housing stock as well as its mines. James had also served as a manager at the same company. The Hoatsons' brother-in-law and codirector Thomas Cole had become a rock sorter in the mines at age eight to support his mother, widowed as the result of a mine accident. He worked his way up to book-keeping, before going on to run several mines and a company railroad. Cole moved from Calumet to Duluth to become president of the Oliver Iron Mine Company, a huge subsidiary of Andrew Carnegie's U.S. Steel. Cole created a model community for Oliver in Minnesota. The town, named Coleraine in his honor, was designed by its young mining superintendent, a former Yale baseball star named John Greenway, who moved to Warren in 1910 when Cole hired him to be C&A's new general manager in Bisbee. Greenway would become a prominent leader of the Deportation in 1917.[7]

The men of C&A brought to Bisbee experience with company housing, but also a sincere interest in Progressive reform. Back in Michigan, Calumet & Hecla had sponsored a variety of charity and reform programs. The Midwest's largest cities had pioneered Progressive experiments in civic improvement and sanitary reform. The term "Progressive" is too capacious a term to describe with much precision the philosophy of anyone in the early twentieth century's sweeping "age of reform." The framers of Progressivism painted with broad enough strokes to include sympathizers from the left and the right, men and women, labor unions and corporations, Democrats, Republicans, Socialists, Populists, and other new political parties. C&A officials occupied the conservative end of Progressivism: they advocated social control of underclasses, believed in the primacy of expertise over purely majoritarian rule, and harbored anti-immigrant and anti-labor sentiments in their zeal for Americanism. Their wives were woman's club members who lobbied for maternalist social policies that mirrored paternalist corporate goals. All of these aspects of C&A's Progressivism shaped its officials' plans for Warren.

A company town project could incorporate some—but not all—of Progressives' contradictory impulses. The Progressive tension between efficiency and democracy sometimes pulled reformers in opposing directions.[8] But C&A's choice was easy. Private townsites like Warren could sidestep politics and install experts in all levels of civic management, thus eschewing civic participation but embodying, in the words of one prominent civic reformer, "the best expert service" from engineers, urban planners, scientists, and public health experts.[9]

When C&A chose Cleveland Van Dyke to be manager of the Warren townsite, its decision reflected these goals. Plucked from the Mesabi Iron Range of northern Minnesota, the thirty-one-year-old Minnesotan began work in Warren in February 1906. Van Dyke was a charter member of the National Municipal League, founded in 1894 to campaign for expanded local control over cities ("Home Rule") and for government by experts—both of which were heated issues in Bisbee's own incorporation vote in 1902. A former assistant to a Minnesota governor, Van Dyke also brought political skills that could help C&A carve out influence in a region dominated by Phelps Dodge.[10]

C&A originally envisioned a population of clerks and engineers for Warren. The process of securing housing for middle-class employees followed a typical corporate pattern. As an industry matured and a mining camp became a permanent town, midlevel company employees brought wives and children who needed homes. Lewis Powell wrote to company president Charles Briggs in mid-August 1906 that a few of "our most valuable men are getting married and I have promised them . . . some provision for satisfactory homes." Powell presented home construction as a necessity for retaining this "high class of men," but also noted that C&A could "procure rents which will return us a very good interest." Briggs approved the plan.[11]

But the men of C&A conceived Warren with higher ambitions than merely meeting immediate housing needs. Instead, C&A undertook an ambitious experiment in the new field of urban planning, then evolving from landscape architecture. The fact that C&A retained the up-and-coming Warren Manning to design the site reflected the scale of the company's ambitions. The son of a nurseryman, Manning had trained with Central Park designer Frederick Law Olmsted Sr. at George Vanderbilt's Biltmore Estate and at the 1893 World's Columbian Expo in Chicago, before opening his own firm in 1897. Manning became a charter member and officer in major planning organizations. He did work in large cities like Milwaukee and Minneapolis, but he also brought international design trends to remote places—especially northern Michigan, where over the course of his career he designed more than a hundred projects. After completing his work in Warren, Manning consulted for Calumet & Hecla in Michigan for almost twenty years.[12]

Manning had helped to found the City Beautiful movement. Best-known through Daniel Burnham's Chicago Plan of 1909, the movement combined

Beaux-Arts monumental architecture and urban design with a Progressive emphasis on sanitation, order, efficiency, and expertise. Proponents saw the City Beautiful ideal not just as a beautification scheme, but as a unified philosophy for functional and attractive cities with excellent services, civic participation, and classical beauty—in short, as the "aesthetic expression" of all Progressive urban reform. In 1902, in Harrisburg, Pennsylvania, Manning designed the first city plan to use the term "City Beautiful."[13]

Manning designed Warren as a "western City Beautiful" when both the movement and his place in it were at their zenith. Manning borrowed the "radial plan" of Washington, D.C., in part because it suited Warren's triangular townsite, but he also mimicked the capital's grandiose scale—a key aspect of City Beautiful principles. He planned four phases on the thousand-acre site, to ensure orderly, compact development for up to ten thousand people. In the center of his townsite, three boulevards branched toward the hillsides from the Plaza, a giant hub three hundred feet in diameter. The plan was elegant and compact, but these were not C&A's only considerations.[14]

A Change in Plans

Far from frowning on corporate work, planning pioneers like Manning saw company towns as clean slates upon which to inscribe their aesthetic principles without muddying them in municipal politics and bureaucracy. Yet economic limitations and labor relations issues intruded upon most company town plans. In Warren, the designers and the company quickly parted ways as local labor conditions caused officials to rethink their goals and tinker with Manning's vision.[15]

Warren took shape just as Bisbee miners were organizing their first union, a local branch of the Western Federation of Miners (WFM). Miners from across the West had founded the national union in 1893, in response to deadly retaliation by mine management and law enforcement against strikers in Coeur d'Alene, Idaho, the year before. Led by controversial characters such as William D. ("Wild Bill") Haywood, the WFM engaged in some of the West's most violent and divisive labor conflicts, most notably in Cripple Creek, Colorado, in 1894 and 1903–1904, and again in Idaho from 1899 to 1901. The WFM did not shy away from lawbreaking and sabotage, nor did its opponents, and their disputes have rightly been described as labor wars. While these battles raged, the WFM aggressively expanded, adding a local in Globe, Arizona, in 1896 and an Arizona-wide headquarters in 1903.[16]

In Bisbee, however, the WFM's success was far from assured. Although nearby camps had seen heated labor struggles—Tombstone in 1884 and Clifton in 1903—Bisbee had remained largely free of such conflict. In the year of the Clifton strike, two WFM organizers had come to Bisbee. The first, J. T. Lewis, claimed that PD's opposition had scared off all but twenty-five men from considering WFM membership. The second, Edward Kennedy, reported finding a stable, satisfied, and relatively homogeneous workforce with high wages, an eight-hour day, and little interest in an unproven union. PD's *Bisbee Daily Review* praised Kennedy's "wise conclusion" that he should leave, but the ominous undertones were clear from an industry journal article saying Kennedy "was given to understand in a forceful manner that unionism was not wanted." In public and in private, PD general manager Walter Douglas promised he would shut his mines down rather than accept the WFM. Still, even labor historians agree that workers in the white man's camp were not yet interested in unionization.[17]

Three years later, Bisbee was a town in transition, one deeply divided over both the place of eastern and southern European immigrants in the white man's camp, and what the decline of skilled mining portended for older western European workers. Shared ethnicity bred affinity between old-stock miners and managers who had moved up the ranks, like the Scottish Hoatsons and the Cornish Thomas Cole. But new immigrants, who would form the bulk—though certainly not all—of the WFM's Bisbee membership, were eager to challenge these cross-class alliances.

The WFM had changed during these years, too. In 1905, the WFM joined Socialists and radical AFL members to create the Industrial Workers of the World (IWW, or Wobblies). The IWW touted itself as "One Big Union," open to members of any rank, skill, or—in theory—race. From 1905 until an angry split in 1907, the WFM was formally the mining branch of the Wobblies, making it even more of a nemesis to western mine owners than it already had been. National WFM leaders wanted to organize Europeans, Americans, and Mexicans in the same industrial union, but success depended on the skills of individual organizers and the particularities of local racial systems. In some places, WFM organizers were far more committed to this kind of organizing than in others.[18]

Amid these tense and complicated circumstances, the WFM returned to Bisbee and began recruiting in January 1906. The union question culminated in the first week of March, when two open meetings were held in downtown Bisbee. Thousands of miners and local citizens crowded around to hear speakers from all sides—among them local Socialist restaurateur and organizer Joseph Cannon (later a major national WFM figure), former WFM members from Colorado who opposed organizing Bisbee, and uncompromising company men. Union advocates couched their arguments in the dialectic of labor versus capital; opponents urged peace and pointed out that Bisbee already had higher wages than camps in Michigan, California, and Colorado.[19]

Local businessmen and civic leaders issued thinly veiled threats to would-be union voters. "Let well enough alone," a resolution by the business alliance warned, else its members would "be forced against our will to extend no further credit to our customers." Local Presbyterian minister Harry Shields (a loyal beneficiary of PD largesse) was the first to sign the resolution, which the Merchants' Association sent out to five thousand households—at least one flyer for every four residents. It was well known that the mining companies would sooner close the mines than accept the union (maybe a bluff, but also an appealing move during a recession, and a consistent threat voiced by Phelps Dodge officials, especially Walter Douglas, for more than two decades). One speaker reminded miners that Fort Grant and Fort Huachuca were just a few miles away, and warned, "It isn't any use going up against guns and ammunition and that is what I want to impress on you boys tonight." Sensing intimidation and thus defeat, on the day before a vote on unionization, local organizer John B. Clark publicly withdrew support for the election on the grounds that its impartiality could not be assured, despite the promise of a secret ballot. On March 5, by a margin of more than five to one, local miners defeated a resolution to unionize. The WFM did not recognize the election, nor did it accept defeat, and organizing quietly continued.[20]

The debates in Brewery Gulch were a minor squall in the storm of labor unrest swirling around the mining industry in 1906. The radical implications of the WFM's presence in Bisbee were inescapable. Fifteen hundred miles north, in Boise, Idaho, WFM officials Bill Haywood and Charles Moyer, along with associate George Pettibone, were arrested for conspiracy in the assassination of former Idaho governor Frank Steunenburg. Their defense team, which included the legendary Clarence Darrow, prepared the case as newspapers nationwide reported the sensational story. In Upper Michigan's Keweenaw Peninsula, several years of WFM organizing were followed by two unsuccessful strikes in 1906.[21]

Fifty miles south of Bisbee, another labor conflict erupted that would have a direct impact on C&A's directors. Cananea, in the Mexican state of Sonora, was a copper camp fashioned as an "American town," with a small-town street grid and clapboard cottages, and run by an eccentric Cochise County native named Colonel William C. Greene. Three months after Bisbee's failed strike vote, Cananea's Mexican miners went on strike to protest a dual-wage scale that paid imported Anglo workers twice as much as native-born men. The Partido Liberal Mexicano, a reform group that opposed Porfirio Díaz and was turning toward more radical politics, was also organizing there. Colonel Greene, who had close allies among Bisbee mining officials, reacted to these events by traveling to Bisbee to collect ammunition. Then, at his behest, a cadre of off-duty Arizona Rangers, ranch hands, and Spanish American war veterans crossed the border to become Mexican "volunteers" for Sonora's governor—in actuality, hired guns for Greene. Cananea had already devolved into citywide violence, and by the time it was over, four American officials and at least thirty Mexicans were said to have been killed. Many Mexicans have since come to see Cananea as the opening shot in the Mexican Revolution, which officially began four years later.[22]

C&A officials had a direct financial interest in the Cananea crisis. Thomas Cole cofounded the Cananea Central Copper Company in 1906, with holdings near Greene's. By the end of that year, with Greene's empire in disarray in the strike's aftermath, Cananea Central Copper had swallowed up the colonel's remaining assets. Cole named Greene vice president, but it was a token gesture. By early 1907, Cole was leading a group of investors—several from Duluth—who controlled Cananea.[23]

C&A's officials knew about labor and ethnic conflict, in other words, and they also knew its connections to company housing policies. The Lake

Superior mining districts where C&A's principals had cut their teeth were famously heterogeneous and increasingly prone to labor strife. As early as 1882, *Harper's Weekly* had marveled at Calumet's population of "Swedes, Norwegians, Danes, Finns, Scottish, Cornishmen, Canadians, Bohemians, Spaniards, Italians and Germans." Northern Minnesota's Mesabi Iron Range was no different. At Coleraine, John Greenway—soon to be C&A's general manager—personally rejected the housing applications of most southern and eastern Europeans. In Michigan, Calumet & Hecla parceled out company housing by ethnicity, using it as a carrot for the Cornish, and a stick to push out or punish Finns and Slavs. Mine owners created an international labor force to undermine labor organizing, but they knew they were playing with fire. Mine managers across the Great Lakes region blamed WFM organizing on the Finns, and, later, after a huge strike in 1913–1914, Calumet & Hecla considered eliminating Finns from the district altogether by evicting them from company housing.[24]

Labor dramas and ethnic conflicts from Lake Superior to Sonora galvanized C&A's inchoate plans for Warren, even as the mining companies publicly downplayed any threat from the WFM in Bisbee, where—they claimed—the men "appreciate a good thing when they have it." In August 1906, two months after the Cananea strike, C&A bought up 150 lots in the Warren townsite. The company's goals quickly shifted from reactive to assertive, transforming a middle-class amenity to a labor relations scheme for the rank-and-file. In the same letter that pressed for housing for the "high class" of men, Lewis Powell urged C&A's president to get "as many of our other employees as possible" to buy, not rent, their own homes. "In times of labor trouble," Powell wrote, "the men owning their own homes cause less trouble." He claimed that only one of the men who had voted to join the WFM the year before had been a homeowner. (How this was discovered in an election with supposedly secret ballots went unexplained.) Company director Hubert d'Autremont concurred. "The labor agitator," he proclaimed, "is always the man without a home." When labor disputes inevitably arose, d'Autremont was confident that "employees who have homes of their own . . . will be most likely to stand by us." He concluded, "The more of our men that we can get to buy homes the better for us."[25]

Promoting homeownership for miners was not a lesson C&A's directors had learned in the Great Lakes. Mining companies there leased lots to workers for home building, but homes rented out by the company were the norm. Floor plans carefully delineated class ranking ("Captain's house," "miner's house," etc.), and neighborhoods were segregated by class into monotonous blocks of identical rental units. Company housing was an incentive to work in the mines, as well as a privilege that could be withheld from troublemakers. Managers at Calumet & Hecla complained about the upkeep and paperwork of being landlords, but they did not seriously consider selling these properties to the miners.[26]

Envisioning miners as potential homeowners challenged conventional wisdom about a workforce whose itinerancy the mining companies frequently blamed for labor troubles. Turnover was a common complaint among industrial employers. At least one-third of C&A's workforce was "constantly shifting and changing," according to Warren's manager, Van Dyke. Lack of a stable residence brought a "somewhat undesirable class of citizens to the camp, who had no home, no ambitions and belong to the disturbing elements of labor." Homeownership, like all corporate paternalism, was meant to serve the needs of the company as well as those of the worker. C&A officials wanted to convince employees that home ownership was a better way to display "independence" than voting with one's feet by drifting from job to job.[27]

Yet in designing Warren, C&A's directors also conceded that the mining companies themselves were partly to blame for rampant turnover and dissatisfied workers. Much of Michigan's company housing was grim and decrepit. The living conditions in Bisbee, where there was little company housing, were squalid. Itinerancy was a serious problem. Here was a chicken-egg dilemma, and C&A managers knew it. C&A's directors cared about urban design because they believed that environment was destiny—that a person's living conditions shaped his character and intelligence. This belief, known at the time as "environmentalism," was a backlash against social Darwinism, whose proponents claimed that helping the less fortunate would only undermine the natural order. On a national level, environmentalism influenced important public-health and housing reforms, but it also could justify social-control efforts to monitor people's lives. For corporate officials like

C&A executives, environmentalism and social control went hand-in-hand. Demands by social activists for housing reform and improved sanitation facilities dovetailed with directors' belief that clean living would improve the quality of their workers.[28]

Traditional company towns, meanwhile, were an iffy proposition. The infamous Pullman strike outside Chicago in 1894 had given them a bad reputation. The town of Pullman, built for workers of the well-known railroad car manufacturer, was the classic company settlement, or "proprietary" town, where the company owned everything from the garden to the floorboards. Critics such as social reformer Jane Addams blasted owner George Pullman for an overweening paternalism that sapped worker autonomy and fueled resentment. In the aftermath of the violent Pullman strike, a few corporations laid out basic townsites, but most avoided anything that smacked of social planning.[29]

By the time Warren was planned, the pendulum was already swinging back. In remote mining and lumber camps, companies had no choice but to provide housing. In addition, new ideas about welfare capitalism were developing. Pullman's overt and heavy-handed social control had proven disastrous. Now, instead, most company-town planners genuinely wished to improve workers' living conditions while also reducing turnover. What muckraking journalist Ida Tarbell called the "Golden Rule of Business"— that the interests of the worker and the boss were actually one and the same— became the fundamental tenet of welfare capitalism. Many corporate leaders shared City Beautiful planners' belief in a society defined not by union notions of competing class differences, but by a desire for an "organic totality" and a shared "public good."[30]

Homeownership fit with this new agenda. In 1906 Oliver Iron's parent company, U.S. Steel, created home-buying incentives in Gary, Indiana, where it tried a light touch to avoid the "excess of paternalism" that had put a "blight on Pullman." Surely this influenced Thomas Cole, since C&A hoped "to avoid the mistakes made . . . at Pullman," in the words of Van Dyke, the townsite manager Cole had hired. Deep ore reserves and a strong copper market convinced C&A's leaders that Warren could break the cycle of poor housing, high turnover, labor disputes, and ethnic strife. Homeownership would eliminate transience by keeping workers rooted not only to the civic life of the community but also to their mortgages. Warren's boosters promised that the town "thoroughly extinguished" stereotypes about miners who "would not purchase homes and would not make up a . . . community." Warren was a labor relations plan no less than Pullman was, but it was one couched in the language of independence, not paternalism. As internal correspondence demonstrated, however, this definition of "independence" was particularly well suited to the company's own interests.[31]

Bisbee's First Strike

Just as the plans for Warren were taking shape, a new union called Bisbee's first strike. Bisbee illustrated the very problem C&A's managers had hoped Warren would resolve. After the WFM's failed 1906 election, the union had quietly continued to organize, even as company spotters reported on suspected union members. In February 1907, the WFM opened an office in Brewery Gulch for Local No. 106. Famed orator Mary "Mother" Jones came to sing the praises of unionization. Meanwhile the companies laid off hundreds of workers—what WFM organizer Edward Crough called "indiscriminate firing and black listing." The mines would be shut down, the *Daily Review* warned, before any would accept a closed camp. This was no idle threat. Within a week, mining had ground almost to a halt. In March, the mining companies tried to preempt a strike by announcing a pay raise, claiming to have made the decision "voluntarily and without request or demand" from workers. Miners, carmen, and mule drivers would now make $4.00 a day; shaftsmen, timbermen, pumpmen, and cagers would make $4.50.[32]

The union's chief demand was not higher wages, however. The WFM wanted a union shop and a ban on blacklisting. Local members were also complaining about the use of Mexican labor.[33] Although inconsistent with the union's attempts on the national level to implement cross-ethnic participation, this complaint was indicative of the ways that local activists and concerns could shape WFM organizing plans. In the white man's camp, where class divisions were always already racial divisions, most skilled miners opposed organizing unskilled workers and manual laborers—which meant, most often, Mexicans.[34] In 1907, plans for a strike, fueled by a core of dedicated eastern European miners and radical Anglo-Americans, inched forward. In early April a committee of sixty-seven "mostly Slavonian" WFM miners called on the copper companies for union recognition and an end to blacklisting. They were refused.[35]

The next day, April 10, the WFM announced a strike. "The Struggle Is Now On," read a headline in the *Daily Review*. Mother Jones returned for at least three weeks, shuttling between Bisbee and Douglas to inspire miners and smelter workers. Sources differ on how widespread the walkout was, perhaps because many miners were undecided. WFM organizer Ed Crough claimed 80 percent of the miners joined the strike at the beginning. The *Daily Review* reported that, out of perhaps 3,600 total miners, about three hundred union members went out on strike. As many as nine hundred men left town to avoid choosing between joining the picket line or crossing it. In three days, more than a hundred had quit C&A, besides the hundreds who were fired. William Gohring, a young C&A executive who would later become general manager, wrote to his family that the men "all seemed to be in doubt about what to do and generally waited around to see what was going to happen." The whole town "gathers in little knots and talks things over with union agents." On the first day, C&A was "nearly at a standstill," though with no "sign of violence or even scab talk yet."[36]

The miners faced stiff—and armed—opposition. From the beginning, Crough observed "officers & deputy sheriffs . . . doing their best to start trouble," and over the summer, police rounded up picketers on vagrancy charges. One blow to the strike effort came early, when mining engineers, whose skill won them influence, voted not to join the strike. In July, Copper Queen officials secured an injunction forbidding the use of the U.S. Mail for transmitting any strike information. During the eight-month strike, the copper companies reduced wages and brought in anti-union workers from "Colorado, Joplin & Hannibal [Missouri], and Texas," according to Crough. The strike languished until it was finally called off on Christmas Eve.[37]

Bad timing, rising corporate power, internal union conflicts, and racial divisions among miners had doomed the strike. The Panic of 1907 curtailed copper demand, and in an open camp the mines could hire replacement workers. As WFM organizer Joseph Cannon explained, "They have a closed camp in Bisbee—no one but a scab can work." The WFM's rancorous split from the IWW complicated matters, and left the national union unable to do much, aside from sending cash to aid the strikers over the summer. More important, the WFM failed to convince old-stock "practical miners" to ally with the unskilled and semi-skilled immigrant men who had helped to organize the local. Most newcomers, largely southern Slavs, Finns, and Italians, were not taking the jobs of older, English-speaking miners. But many Irish and Cornish miners were unwilling to join a union in which new immigrants had the potential to outvote them in matters of wage and schedule demands. Even the organizers were ambivalent. On tours through Arizona, Edward Crough wrote in his notebooks that mining camps dominated by Mexican labor were "useless from a Union point of view," even as he hired a Mexican organizer to work in the Douglas smelters.[38]

Most scholars have considered the 1907 strike inconsequential—at most, a symbol of the WFM's bumbling forays into southwestern mining camps, or a mere "rehearsal," in one scholar's words, for the 1917 strike that led to the Deportation. Contemporary organizers knew better. Joseph Cannon told national union leaders, "There is more at stake in that strike . . . than any other strike the Western Federation of Miners ever participated in." Cannon was promoting the strike's national importance, but even clearer were the local implications. The 1907 strike, as historian Philip Mellinger argues, further polarized "American" and "foreigner." Yet there were racial fissures even within the "foreigners": in Bisbee, WFM membership consisted mostly of southern Slavs and Italians (along with a small group of pro-union Irish and Cornish activists), and many local WFM members were at best ambivalent, if not completely hostile, toward Mexican workers. In the 1906 organizing campaign, only underground workers (no Mexicans, in other words) had been allowed to vote on forming a union. The WFM never gained control over the debates about creating a truly multiracial union. In fact, the national WFM buried the Bisbee local's inconvenient anti-Mexicanism. In lengthy discussions of the Bisbee strike at the WFM's national convention, no one mentioned a demand to ban foreign labor. Mother Jones organized Mexican smelter workers even as she was promoting the strike in Bisbee. Her work in Douglas among Mexican workers, and her sympathy for the anarcho-syndicalists of the Partido Liberal Mexicano, were early signs of the division between the WFM and the IWW, the latter of which explicitly welcomed Mexican members.[39]

The bulk of Bisbee's northern European workforce refused to cooperate with a putatively "foreign" WFM, even though both union and nonunion workers opposed Mexican labor in the white man's camp. The strike served as an announcement from Slavs that they, at least, claimed a place in the white man's camp and felt a commitment to determining its future.

Independent Manhood

Calumet & Arizona hoped that Warren would do away with questions about who was "white" in the white man's camp, because it would attract and house "Americans." Or, as it turned out, would *create* them. A lengthy report by Cleveland Van Dyke in December 1907 showed that the strike only strengthened C&A's commitment to Warren's "concrete aims and ambitions." Without directly mentioning the strike, Van Dyke acknowledged that the district was at a turning point. For twenty-five years, it had been free "from strikes[,] . . . labor troubles and agitations." But "now," he concluded, "to bring the miner and mine owner closer together," the company would create "this town plan to build homes for the miners and get them to be permanent residents, thus bringing to the district men of families."[40]

These rank-and-file family men—and the assumptions about wages, race, and gender they embodied—became the heart of C&A's plan. C&A's directors devised the homeownership plan to foster company loyalty, Americanism, family life, and their vision of manly independence. Van Dyke concluded that "the boys who have bought homes in Warren have no radical tendencies and this is not because of a feeling of dependence. There is perhaps no more independent workman in America than those owning homes in Warren." Yet even as Van Dyke praised the independence of C&A's workers, he also called each employee "a unit in the whole mechanism" of the corporation. So at every step that Warren's managers promoted "individualism," they also meant to tighten the hold between worker and company.[41]

The emphasis on independence prompted a new aesthetic for Warren. Manning's street layout remained intact, but C&A officials scrapped an ambitious Mission Revival design—one of the first in the United States—created by Philadelphia architectural consultant Huger Elliott and featured in a lengthy article with full-color renderings in the nation's leading architectural journal. Years before the nation's first comprehensive zoning ordinance (in New York City in 1916), Elliott had proposed a planning commission in Warren to regulate color schemes and architectural design. The urbane Elliott shuddered at tawdry real estate speculation and "patchy street-fronts, like strips torn from bed quilts."[42] Elliott's design was beautiful—the motif was inspired by the early Spanish missions in California—but from C&A's standpoint its emphasis on unity, symmetry, and top-down design smacked of Pullmanesque paternalism. C&A officials wanted control over Warren, but they did not want their puppet strings to show.

Instead, C&A encouraged buyers to choose their own building materials and finishes. The Warren Company built some houses on speculation, but preferred to sell lots or build houses to the buyer's specifications. Elliott sarcastically derided worker control over design as "freedom of the individual," but that was exactly what C&A had in mind, and it reflected a careful management strategy. Van Dyke explained, "The employee goes into the town, looks it over and selects his own home plan." "Permitting the employee" to choose his design was intended to make the homeowner "feel" that his house was "the result of his own ideas" and "more like his own" than one in a row of prefabricated company houses. True to C&A's plans, within a few years of its opening, houses of multiple hues, styles, and construction materials dotted Warren's residential avenues. Some were clapboard, others rusticated cement block.[43]

If exteriors varied, density did not, because almost all of the homes were single-family. There was one set of "flats" on Briggs Avenue, some rooms to let, and a few rental "cottages" (though even these were single-family). The sprawling mansions of mining executives occupied the choicest locations, but California bungalows predominated. In this regard, Warren offered something new. Elsewhere, companies built duplexes and concrete apartment buildings to house their workers. In 1908, two years after Warren opened, a popular exhibit at New York's Museum of Natural History depicted an innovative industrial village of single-family homes as a cutting-edge way to improve the living conditions of the poor. In contrast to Bisbee and Lowell, with their roominghouses and shanties, Warren was promoted for years not just as a City Beautiful but also as a "City of Homes."[44] Today, it represents the largest collection of bungalow architecture in Arizona.

Single-family homes were "American" in a way that the roominghouses of Bisbee and Lowell could never be. Recall the concerns about "Italians living as no white man can" in an "oblong building," not a house. One industry manual on corporate housing noted that "the nativity and racial characteristics of the prospective working force" should "be one of the governing features in selecting the type of house and in districting the site." Implicit in this advice was an admonition against building the wrong kind of housing that would attract the wrong kind of worker. The manual's author also condemned the lodging system, run largely by women, for increasing worker turnover. The association of lodging with immigrants was clear.

C&A officials wanted to promote household economies centered around men's wage earning. Single-family homes were physical embodiments of the family wage and the American standard of living, and thus proof of C&A's superior employment policies. And for the most part, Warren's domestic arrangements did emulate the ideal. In 1910, very few Warren wives appear to have engaged in paid labor, and only eighteen—less than 11 percent—took in lodgers. Out of 193 households, just eight were headed by a woman.[45]

C&A built Warren and paid what it considered family wages not because it abhorred the idea of women's paid labor per se, but because managers believed that good wages and single-family homes would entice family men, whom employers considered to be unlikely strikers. Warren's single-family homes reflected C&A's commitment to family wage ideology. For Cleve Van Dyke, "permanent residents" and "men of families" were indistinguishable—and were ideal citizens. Van Dyke's ideas were not new to the district. In 1904, the *Bisbee Daily Review* had praised "domesticated miners," husbands and fathers who "will become interested in every move that promises to advance the interests of the town."[46]

Workers and managers alike praised homeownership. During the 1906 union debates, two anti-union miners suggested that strikes made homeowning miners vulnerable. By way of opposing the strike, one proclaimed, "Here I have bought a home, and here I want to live." Another counseled, "Men have been able to build homes in Bisbee and save their earnings, and this is the condition we hope to continue." In later years, how-to books on industrial housing offered formulas for creating the ideal "percentage of married to single men carried on the payroll," and the right balance between foreign-born and American workers.[47] The policy of building single-family homes echoed corporate lip service for the American family wage by underscoring the preference for married workers.

The plans for Warren relied on the belief that the home was the basic unit of civil society and the birthplace of citizenship. As one industrial housing reformer put it, "the home is not a mere place of shelter in modern democracy," but a place to develop good citizenship and "strength of character in citizenship." These were characteristics of male heads-of-families in particular, since, as the housing manual explained, "the home connotes the family; and the family and not the individual is the unit of the civil structure."[48] Political theorist Carol Pateman has argued that the first requirement of liberal citizenship is an inherently masculine "independence," defined, in part, by property ownership and by having dependents. These assumptions made an emphasis on home—normally considered feminine—sufficiently masculine for a brawny mining camp, and they became the ideological foundation for building Warren.[49]

Women, while secondary, were still necessary to this vision, in part because they symbolized the "maturing" of a mining camp into a real town, but also because manly independence required a complementary image of womanly dependence. Given the emphasis on housing "choice," promoting single-family home ownership was partly logistical. How could a homeowner express individualism in a shared or rented dwelling? But single-family construction in Warren also promoted a particularly male notion of "independence." By making worker citizenship a goal, and by using single-family housing to promote this ideal, Warren reflected the liberal assumption that modern citizenship rests on male independence in a public-private dichotomy that presupposes women's dependence.[50]

From the viewpoint of corporate officials, home and work fostered a manly independence that the union hall decidedly did not. Collective bargaining was not the "manly way" to deal with a shop grievance, according to the *Bisbee Daily Review*. Better to have a talk with the boss man-to-man. Yet this language cut both ways. Like the family wage, the cult of masculinity attracted labor reformers and managers alike. In the unionization debates in downtown Bisbee in 1906, WFM organizer and Socialist Joseph Cannon proclaimed, "Men, when an insignificant upstart of a jigger boss is your master, and owns you body and soul, it is time something is done to bring back your manhood." During the strike, a union newspaper in Douglas satirized advertisements for replacement workers: "Wanted . . . five hundred SCABS . . . weak minded men, underpaid underfed caricatures of manhood" who "will bow meekly before Her Majesty [the Copper Queen]." The mining companies' ideal worker, according to the editorial, was a "servile hireling" who would "hide his manhood away forever."[51] Mining officials and union leaders shared a language of manliness, even if they differed about to whom it applied.

Paternalism

In spite of all the efforts to promote independence and to avoid Pullman-like dissent, Warren harbored plenty of paternalism. Calumet & Arizona kept a tight grip on its "domesticated miners." A savings-and-loan company that was set up for Warren buyers sold lots at a generously low 6 percent interest, terms "more liberal" than was "customary." But there was a catch. If the homeowner became permanently disabled or moved away, the difference between the payments he had made and the standard rental price was refunded. He walked away without debts, but without assets, too, because he lacked the option to sell the home while it was still mortgaged. This plan helped those who could not make their payments, but it also tied men to their mortgages. Unlike mortgage holders today, Warren's homeowners retained no equity until the loan was completely paid off. If the owner did not complete the payments, the house reverted to the company. Union leaders elsewhere had complained about similar homeowning arrangements, arguing that they tied workers down and made them dependent on employee largesse.[52]

Warren's physical appearance, even stripped of Huger Elliott's Mission Revival motif, also reflected its paternalist intentions. Where other City Beautiful plans made monuments of civic institutions, Warren's plan celebrated corporate hierarchy. Its three major streets were named for C&A principals and for PD general manager Walter Douglas. Two of these streets culminated at the monumental homes of mining managers, while the other led to C&A's Warren mine. Vista Park and the two boulevards that flanked it cut a swath nearly three hundred feet wide through the townsite. At one end—

instead of an "important public building," as Elliott had suggested—the company built the Warren Baseball Field, home of the "City Beautiful" baseball team. (Warren was unincorporated, so a "public building" had no place there.) The other end of the park was anchored by Walter Douglas' forty-room Spanish colonial mansion. The effect was not unlike Washington's Capitol Mall, except that the house of the most powerful man in Bisbee—and arguably in Arizona—was the focal point.[53]

In contrast to downtown Bisbee or nearby Lowell, where grocery stores, saloons, roominghouses, and shanties competed for space and the streets teemed with people, Warren was a private, residential landscape in the modern suburban mold. Public space was carefully monitored. Planners separated residential and commercial areas by reserving Arizona Street, site of the Warren Company office building, for businesses. The company promoted a "good, moral home environment" by donating lots for churches and schools (one later named for C&A manager John Greenway) and by building a playground. Such amenities were promoted heavily in local and mining-industry advertisements.[54]

These were benevolent interventions, but a heavier paternalism could be found in Warren's covenant restrictions. Arizona law had allowed incorporated communities to vote on their own liquor laws since 1901. Warren was unincorporated by design, so C&A unilaterally forbade saloons, gambling dens, and houses of prostitution within its precincts. C&A officials promoted a town with clean water *and* clean living, a temperance ideal they associated with home life. "We had a little difficulty . . . at the start," Van Dyke admitted, but "we have succeeded in convincing people that our ideas on these subjects were absolutely correct." It was not hard to glimpse the iron hand under the velvet glove that gestured with pride at an "absolute temperance town."[55]

As the temperance rule suggested, C&A framed the relationship between masculine independence and citizenship in a way that downplayed direct citizen participation or electoral politics. The company's limited vision of miner citizenship was defined against the political activism of union leaders. During the 1907 strike, the mining corporations founded a company union called the Bisbee Industrial Association, which they dubbed a "patriotic" labor organization.[56] Corporate "patriotism" replaced civic participation, even seemingly benign versions. Civic involvement was central to other City Beautiful plans, including Manning's, but was conspicuously absent from Warren. In the 1910s, Manning created voluntary work weekends, called "Community Days," in Calumet.[57] Warren had no such programs, and decisions about the town's layout, design, and maintenance were decidedly top-down.

This paternalistic approach affected women as well as men. The Warren Company marketed homes to women with descriptions of modern kitchens and careful interior details, but offered little place for women in the governance of the community. Elsewhere, women's clubs played a key role in spurring civic improvement and planning campaigns. The Woman's Club of Harrisburg, Pennsylvania, had led the bond campaign to fund its City Beautiful project. In Calumet, a female landscape architect served as Manning's superintendent. Warren's was a rare City Beautiful plan untouched by women's influence. Although several C&A wives were honorary members of the Bisbee's Woman's Club, it appeared to have no formal involvement in Warren. Neither did a Warren "Ladies' Aid Society" founded in 1910 to support a Sunday school.[58] C&A wanted to foster an "independence" and "individualism" distinct from citizen initiative or public life, or even from white women's rising prominence.

Racial Americanism

Company loyalty, individual "choice," male-headed households, and political passivity came together as part of a deeply racialized vision of Americanism promoted by C&A to replace the foreign allegiances of immigrant workers. Company director Hubert d'Autremont endorsed Warren's home-ownership plans by exclaiming that "a man without a home was almost a man without a country." Cleve Van Dyke summed up the company's true objectives when he noted, "We have learned from experience that the robust American with a growing family is a better man for us than a man without these things." When company men talked about "Americans," they invoked a relationship between employers and employees that contrasted with the one they assumed "foreign agitators" promoted. To mining officials, such men were the quintessential *bad* citizens: vagrant, transient, un-American. During the WFM organizing in 1906, one mining manager laughed at the very idea that a union member could call himself a "free American citizen." He meant not only that union members were not free, but also that they were literally not American. The fact that thousands of union members and "foreigners" in the district owned their own homes was immaterial to C&A officials, either because they were oblivious or because these other homes—like the roominghouses of Brewery Gulch or the shanties of Tintown, mostly owner occupied—were not "American homes."[59]

Still, C&A managers did not see foreignness—at least among Europeans—as a fixed position. Their rhetoric and plans for Warren implied that Americanism was something that could be developed in the right environment. A worker enjoyed independence, in their view, because his employer made an effort to "foster his Americanism" by encouraging homeownership and by providing a proper town layout. They borrowed this idea from Michigan's copper country, where companies, according to a writer for the *Engineering and Mining Journal,* offered "the kind of paternalism that kills unionism and, in one generation, builds out of foreigners, ignorant of Anglo-Saxon institutions, citizens that any community can be proud of."[60] C&A's leaders hewed to the belief—one deeply in their self-interest in a tight labor market, but nevertheless sincere—that "Americans" could be made, not just born.

One family's story suggests the way Warren's Americanization scheme was supposed to work. In the early twentieth century, David Milutinovich lived with his wife, Katie, and their three children in downtown Bisbee. David was one of the "Slavonian" organizers denigrated and then blacklisted by the companies in the 1907 strike. For a while he changed his name and worked in New Mexico. While he was gone, the family's house burned down, so David returned to move his family to South Bisbee, a predominantly Cornish and Serbian suburb. David got a job as a watchman for C&A, while Katie, like many Serbian women, kept chickens and fed six or seven Serbian boarders. When their second house burned, the Milutinoviches moved to Warren. They were the first Serbs there.[61]

The move implied dramatic changes in environment and allegiances. Although the new bungalow was small by today's standards, its two bedrooms, large kitchen, and separate dining room must have seemed palatial. No boarders elbowed for space at the big dining-room table and buffet. In moving to the "city of homes," the family lost the income Katie had brought in by feeding boarders. The Milutinoviches had adopted Warren's ways. In the 1917 strike, David—a former WFM organizer—sided with C&A.[62] The story of the Milutinoviches illustrated C&A's ideal scenario for including in Warren those whose Americanness was suspect.

Mexicans were a different story. Union members and corporate officials alike envisioned fully independent men as white Americans, or perhaps evolved Europeans, but certainly not Mexicans. The catch-22 of the dual-wage system—in which a family wage stood for masculine independence, yet was unavailable to Mexican workers—helped to create the conditions of dependency that C&A and other mining companies blamed on the Mexican workers themselves, and stoked the grievances that led to the 1917 strike.[63]

The dual-wage system made racial covenant restrictions unnecessary in Warren. The few Mexicans in Warren were decidedly special cases. Ignacio Bonillas, whose family briefly lived in Warren, was at the top of the elite: the adopted son of an Anglo territorial governor, a large landowner, an engineering consultant for Colonel Greene in Cananea, and, later, a high-ranking Mexican official and presidential candidate. Another Warren resident, Roberto Redondo, worked for C&A as an assayer, a highly skilled job that entailed examining the mineral content of ore samples. Redondo and his family attended the white Catholic church in Bisbee, though his wife protested about the segregation policy that affected other Mexican Americans. Fewer than five middle-class Mexican families lived in Warren in 1920.[64] The only apparent barrier to Mexicans' living in Warren was financial, but since the mining companies paid Mexicans the low wages that kept them out of Warren, their exclusion can hardly be called an accident.

In all their writings about Americans and Warren, C&A officials never used the term "white man's camp." Instead, they subtly shifted the characterization of ideal workers from "white" men to "American" men. This shift in language reflected an attempt at satisfying the company's competing desires to tap cheap labor and to appease old-time Irish and Cornish miners who wanted Bisbee to stay a white man's camp. A Serbian family in Warren was "American," and thus white, in a way that a single Serb in a downtown roominghouse was not. Warren's planners used a language of Americanism shared by the most skilled miners—the ones who, not coincidentally, were the most likely to move to Warren. Cornish miners' reluctance to join the WFM had reflected their unwillingness to form alliances across perceived racial boundaries. C&A managers, on the other hand, wanted the broadest freedom to hire whichever workers they wanted. C&A officials continued to oppose the old-stock miners' version of racial Americanism, even as they, too, adopted the language of Americanism. Conversely, the flexibility of racial identity for eastern and southern Europeans made the racial category of "Mexican" immutable, and the rigidity of the dual-wage system enforced this division.

Just as the district's racial system was dynamic, so too was Warren. In 1910, 70 percent of Warren homes contained native-born "American" heads-of-household, the largest portion of them from the Great Lakes region. But the World War I boom threatened the sanctity of Warren's vaunted single-family home, as owners subdivided rooms to house the population influx. With these changes, Warren began to reflect the district's larger divisions of nationality and class. In 1910, fifteen households in Warren, or about 9 percent of the total, were headed by Finns or "Swedes" (probably also Finnish). They were clustered in the oldest part of Warren, on Van Dyke Street and Black Knob View, and it is likely they bought homes not from the company but in private resales. In the mid-1910s, a few Serbian families like the Milutinoviches moved into the same area, and their numbers steadily grew. By 1920, the southeast corner of Warren had become something of an ethnic enclave. Townspeople renamed one street "Goat Row" because so many Serbian families there kept goats for milk and cheese.[65]

Yet overall, C&A's attempts to attract working-class buyers to Warren were unsuccessful. Warren had begun as a place for the "better class" of workers, and it remained so. One article claimed that the majority of its homeowners were men who worked underground, but they were largely shift bosses, electricians, timbermen, and foremen. Rank-and-file men, even if they could afford Warren, mostly chose to live elsewhere. In 1908, PD and C&A leaders chose a site near Warren to build a golf course and country club, hardly a fixture of working-class leisure. One miner who worked in the 1910s and 1920s remembered that most of the company officials—"aristocrats," in his words—lived in Warren, while the residents of Bisbee's canyons were "all pretty much working people." If anything, Warren deepened class divides rather than smoothing them, because the new suburb drew middle- and upper-class residents from Bisbee's more economically integrated neighborhoods. As a result, Warren's roots in welfare capitalism for the rank-and-file have been forgotten, hidden away in the private correspondence of C&A officials. Only there did these men write candidly about their attempts to use housing to reinvent their workforce.[66]

Warren's evolution into an elite suburb was not inevitable, and today it is quite diverse. But in its heyday it failed to become a haven for workingmen. This was an outcome of the district's profound divisions and the contradictions in C&A's understanding of them. C&A's management believed that Warren's domestic architecture, rational geography, liberal financing, and moralistic covenant restrictions would create Americans—not in the strict sense of naturalized political citizens, but in the sense of "patriotic" workers defined by their cooperation with management. They hoped Warren would be less a western City Beautiful than a Neighborhood American—a factory for the creation and maintenance of American "citizen-miners."

The idea of the citizen-miner was a hybrid of two seemingly disparate ideals. The citizen was a head-of-household and a homeowner, who would embody traditionally Jeffersonian ideals of a landowning, independent, patriarchal citizenry. The miner would be an able and willing cog in the industrial machine of twentieth-century copper mining. The citizen-miner was inherently male and "American," formed from a deeply imbedded confluence of independence and loyalty. On its face, this idea of Americanism was democratic, but it was also hierarchical. It was a system of duties and obligations to one's family and to one's boss. The head of a patriarchal household would still be a unit in the corporate mechanism. This vision perpetuated and hardened an increasingly rigid division between "American" and "Mexican."

Internal contradictions and compromises doomed C&A's main objective for Warren. In their corporate policies and correspondence, and in the town itself, C&A officials mapped these contradictions onto the "city of homes." The company hired experts, but rejected their advice. It used Warren to showcase welfare capitalism, but denied it had built a "company town." It designed Warren for middle- and upper-level management, but recruited the rank-and-file. Company directors hoped Warren would entice and create the ideal "American" worker in the hopes of promoting industrial peace and company loyalty.

At the same time, a few dozen miles to the northwest, pioneer Mexican landowners in rural Cochise County struggled to adapt an integrated world born in the nineteenth century to changing twentieth-century realities—and they, too, staked claims based on homeownership and Americanism.

5

Mormons and Mexicans
in the San Pedro River Valley

On September 4, 1915, residents of the railroad town of Benson read the following items in the local paper.

The town's "Spanish ladies" were extending a "cordial invitation . . . to all" for an enchilada-and-tamale supper and a concert, to celebrate Mexico's Independence Day (September 16) and to raise money for the Catholic church. Lee Park Lim, a Chinese interpreter from Tucson, was in town "on official business." Local girl "Miss Ernestina Martínez spent the weekend" visiting friends at the San Juan Ranch outside town, while rancher Reyes Mendoza had ridden into Benson for a few days and reported that feed was good on the range. "Miss Rosetta Scott and four children" (note the "Miss" rather than "Mrs.") had just moved from Provo, Utah, to a nearby Mormon settlement, while fellow church member Parley Fenn was planning to move his family to a Mormon agricultural colony in Mexico.[1]

This local news offered a tidy précis of Benson's differences from Bisbee. In northern Cochise County, many Mexican Americans enjoyed pioneer status and a public prominence unimaginable in copper country. They owned large ranches, ran popular businesses, served on civic committees, and were mentioned in local society columns. Chinese settlers lived and worked in Benson and on nearby river farms. So did a sizable Mormon population, which was both part of and separate from the larger Anglo community.

But this world was vulnerable—to economic change, competition for water, and population shifts. Ten miles north of Benson, the old settlement of

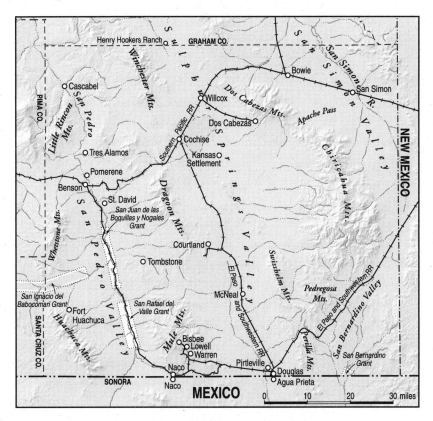

15. Cochise County, ca. 1917. Map by Philip Schwartzberg.

Tres Alamos was slowly dying, while Pomerene, a new Mormon community across the river, thrived. Farther north, in a Mexican American farming and ranching settlement known as Cascabel, integration and intermarriage had once been the rule. Now landowning families joined together to create a mostly Mexican American enclave. The story of four communities—Tres Alamos, Pomerene, Cascabel, and Benson—reveals how race relations continued to differ across the county, but also that no town could remain stable in a twentieth-century world of rapid change.

Mexican Tres Alamos and Mormon Pomerene

Tres Alamos, the county's oldest settlement, was fading away. With the railroad's advent in 1880 and Tombstone's rise and subsequent collapse, the river crossing at Tres Alamos declined in importance. In the 1890s, alternating floods and droughts ruined irrigation canals. Overgrazing and over-hunting devastated the landscape. Disputes over water rights festered, as Benson's growth encroached. The railroad destroyed William Ohnesorgen's stagecoach business and the careers of several Mexican American freight haulers. Yet for those who hung on, the railroad brought work gangs needing food and shelter, and also provided a way to market crops in Tucson, El Paso, Bisbee, and Douglas. A railroad line that ran from Benson to the Sonoran port city of Guaymas was completed in 1882, and nurtured a voluminous international trade.[2]

But farms needed water. As early as 1889, Antonio Grijalba had complained that "from the time the Mormons took the water up the river . . . I haven't had sufficient water to irrigate the ground." Grijalba referred to the residents of St. David, a Mormon farm settlement founded several miles upstream in 1877. Grijalba's son Arturo, also a homesteader and rancher, faced a similar predicament after his father died in 1905. In 1908, Mormons from St. David joined with a local politician to found the Benson Canal Company. Completed in 1912, the Benson Canal was the largest irrigation enterprise yet attempted on the San Pedro. It supplied water to the new Mormon community of Pomerene, across the river from Tres Alamos. While Pomerene blossomed into a village of farmers, the Mexican American landowners downstream found their water supply and population ebbing away.[3]

The Mormons, also known as Latter-Day Saints, represented a sizable percentage of Arizona's early settlers, especially in eastern Arizona and near the Utah border. Mormons and Mexican Americans had much in common— a reliance on kin, close settlement patterns, and experience with irrigation farming. Both faced discrimination and distrust from outsiders, and both simultaneously protected their enclaves and engaged with the larger society. The two groups often lived near each other. In some ways, Mormons functioned as a distinct ethnic group in the American West. They encountered severe prejudice, created close communities, developed distinct patterns of land and water use, and practiced a demanding and sometimes isolating religion.[4]

Yet important differences between Mexicans and Mormons existed. Mormons occupied a unique and anomalous place in western culture and politics as "whites" whose religion—both the practice of it and the opposition to it—set them apart from other people. In Cochise County, one observer found a "lack of cooperation among people in many of the rural communities. In some places this is due in part to the fact that some people are Mormon and others not. Quite generally there seems to be a spirit of jealousy and contention among neighbors." By choice and by necessity, Mormon communities were well known for their insularity. The men belonged to a time-consuming lay priesthood, and the women attended to church benevolent organizations known as Relief Societies, whose meetings they attended, as one Pomerene resident recalled, "no matter how hard life was." In the 1910s, one rural reformer in Cochise County found that it was "impossible to form new organizations" in Mormon communities, because the women were occupied with church work.[5]

Mormons faced bias and persecution, including, in the nineteenth century, laws meant to disfranchise them or alter their marital practices. But they were also unambiguously "white" (not just technically, as was increasingly the case with Mexican Americans). This brought legal and social power that racial minorities lacked. Most Mormons were Democrats and thus allied with Arizona's majority party, in contrast to Mexican Americans, who were mostly Republican (though some Mormon leaders encouraged their followers to register as Republican, so that Mormons would not be seen as a partisan voting bloc).[6]

In spite of suspicion and opposition, Mormons' carefully planned farming communities earned them praise from many people, ranging from famed conservationist John Wesley Powell, in his 1878 *Report on the Lands of the Arid Region,* to "gentiles" (as Mormons called non-Mormons) in neighboring Utah and the Mountain West. Mormon water cooperatives, along with Mexican *acequia* traditions, influenced Arizona water law. Pomerene's Benson Canal was governed by a typical Mormon canal-and-dam association, owned and operated by its members, and funded by assessments in proportion to each owner's share in the company.

Though Mormon irrigation companies served as abstract models for legal codes, in practice they often violated the spirit of complicated water laws. Both Mexican American and Mormon irrigation systems distributed water proportionally and communally, but Mormon cooperatives like the Benson

Canal Company treated water rights as a tradable commodity that shareholders could buy and sell separately from real property. These transactions were
technically illegal, even if government officials tended to look the other way.
When canal shares became valuable and fungible property, this undermined
the communal nature of the enterprise.[7]

So did the scale of the canals, which were much larger than the Mexican *acequias*. The Benson Canal dwarfed the ditches of the nineteenth-
century settlers who technically had "first rights" to the water, and soon siphoned away water that legally belonged to Tres Alamos' residents. A team
of anthropologists concluded that the Canal Company's members appeared
to have given "no thought to how water users downstream" with first rights
would fare or react to the company's diversion of so much water. In his 1889
court case, Antonio Grijalba had demanded enough water to irrigate about
seven acres per day for twelve days, for a total of eighty-four acres, and he
later admitted that he exaggerated how much water he expected to get. The
Benson Canal's original dam was intended to divert almost five times more
than this, enough to cover almost thirty acres per day or as much as six hundred acres in a growing season—in 1890, one-tenth of the irrigated land in
the county. Later estimates rose to more than four thousand acres.[8] Pomerene
could sustain a growing population—but only by draining Tres Alamos' water supply.

After a slow first year, Pomerene's population soon multiplied—along with
its water demands. In early 1912, the Benson Canal's first year, there were
only nine Anglo families in the area, six of them the canal's original investors.
A year later, the town had close to sixty schoolchildren. By 1920, it had fifty-
two households and a population of 257, while Tres Alamos had nearly disappeared.[9]

Many of Pomerene's new residents came from Mormon colonies in Mexico that had been established by American polygamists fleeing federal raids
in the United States in the late nineteenth century. Though the colonies had
little to do with the local Mexican population, Mexican dictator Porfirio Díaz
welcomed the Mormons in order to encourage agricultural development.
Not all Mormons in Mexico were polygamists, but they occupied a world
where plural marriage was neither criminal nor clandestine. A typical case
was that of John Fenn, his wives Lucy and Matilda, and their twenty-one
children. Second wife Lucy spent many of her married years in hiding, "al-

ways under threat and struggle," according to one of Matilda's granddaughters, before they all fled to Mexico. By 1892, the Fenns had settled in Colonia Morelos, Mexico, where John Fenn and his adult sons raised cattle and ran a successful freighting business servicing nearby copper mines. Most members of the Mexico colonies farmed and ranched, including the large family of John Conrad Naegle, a German immigrant and Mormon convert with six wives. For more than two decades, the Mexican colonies offered a safe haven for American polygamists.[10] That changed in 1912, when the Mexican Revolution escalated in Chihuahua and Sonora, and church authorities ordered most colonists to evacuate with just a few hours' notice.

As hundreds of Mormon refugees converged at the border-crossing in Douglas, promoters in St. David convinced some to resettle at Pomerene. John Naegle's now-widowed fifth wife, Pauline, moved there with her children in 1912, as did the Fenns. Relocated families transformed the fledgling settlement into a refugee camp of tents, lean-tos, and rough cabins salvaged from abandoned mining areas. Two years later, at least two-thirds of the families with children in Pomerene were Mormon refugees from Mexico.[11]

Being born in Mexico was very different from being "Mexican," just as being born in the United States did not guarantee that Mexican Americans would be considered "American." Arizona's county school census forms included a column for "Number of white children." The column was followed by a note to "include Mexican children on this list." The U.S. Census had the same rule, though by now it was widely disregarded. In 1880, the federal census taker had marked Mexicans as "W" for "White"; by 1920, Cochise County's local census workers consistently wrote an "M" for "Mexican" in the "Race" column, only to have a supervisor write over it with a "W" for "White."[12]

Mormons fared differently. In 1916, Cochise County's school census taker recorded all of Pomerene's new schoolchildren as "Native born to native parents." This was untrue in most cases, since these were children brought from the Mexico colonies. The federal census taker did mark these children as born in Mexico, but he inserted the notation "American citizen"—also questionable, given their Mexican birth—at the top of the "Nativity" column. The racial status, if not the citizenship, of Mormons from the Mexican colonies was thus made abundantly clear.[13]

The new families settled in quickly. By 1920, the Fenn family spanned five households and included twenty-two people. Lucy Fenn had a homestead, as did her son, Parley. The Naegle family had three homesteads, two belonging to Pauline's sons, the third patented by her.[14] More people in Pomerene bought private land than filed homestead claims, though, perhaps because the refugees lacked U.S. citizenship or were hiding a polygamous past from the federal government. Others planned to return to Mexico. One way or another, by 1920, 85 percent of Pomerene heads-of-household owned their own property.[15]

If the legacy of polygamy deterred some potential homesteaders, it shaped Pomerene in other ways. In 1920, women headed almost one in five of its households (ten out of fifty-two). This was not unique: many Mormon communities "were replete with women living more or less alone," an ironic side effect of polygamy. More wives meant more widows (or abandoned wives), few of whom remarried. In 1920, Pomerene's census listed eight of its ten female heads-of-household as widows. Some, like Pauline Naegle, were the widows of polygamists. A few, like Lucy Fenn, might have been plural wives left to head their own households. Fenn stretched homestead law to fit the realities of polygamy. She lived with her four grown sons, and was listed as married in the census. John Fenn lived in Pomerene, but with his first wife, Matilda. Because Lucy Fenn filed her homestead claim before her husband died, she probably told the Land Office that she was single or widowed. Married women could not homestead, but, after all, her marriage was not legal.[16]

Sixteen percent of Pomerene's homesteaders were women. What this land ownership meant in practice is not clear. Lucy Fenn and Pauline Naegle owned homesteads in their own names, but their sons farmed them. Lucy Fenn's homestead invites several possible interpretations: as a symbol of her independence, as an emblem of John Fenn's abandonment, or simply as a legal fiction to expand the family's landholding. Pauline Naegle's homestead appears to have been a family secret. Her descendents, well versed in family history, knew of the ranch owned by Pauline's son, but learned of *her* homestead only during the research for this book.[17]

Whoever was in charge, Pomerene's homesteads were clearly intended for use as farms, even if their water use imperiled Mexican American agriculture. Fully three-quarters of Pomerene's heads-of-household called themselves farmers in 1920, and they aggressively pursued water supplies. Mormons had peacefully lived in Mexico with the blessing of its president, Porfirio Díaz, and those who had pioneered along the San Pedro River in the 1870s had kind memories of aid from Mexican American neighbors. There is no reason to believe Pomerene's residents set out to displace Mexicans as the county's farmers, or even to take their water. If anything, the opposite—Mexicans opposing Mormons—seems more likely, for elite Mexican Americans had a long history of anti-Mormon attitudes, rooted in Catholic hatred of polygamy and allegiance to the U.S. Republican Party, which was anti-Mormon.[18]

Yet Pomerene's gains were inevitably Tres Alamos's losses, at least where water was concerned. If St. David was draining Antonio Grijalba's water supply in 1889, the situation only worsened after the Benson Canal was built. Because ranching requires far less water than farming, the changing self-identification of Mexican American landowners hints at Pomerene's impact. In the county's first voting rolls, in 1882, thirty-one Mexican Americans called themselves farmers, and only nineteen chose rancher, or *ranchero*. *Ranchero* can mean either "rancher" or "farmer," so if anything, farmers were undercounted. Nearly all of the county's Mexican Americans calling themselves farmers lived on the San Pedro. Doña Jesús Moreno de Soza described her husband, Antonio Soza, who had lived north of Tres Alamos since the 1870s, as a "farmer and rancher," and later recalled that he had "cultivated the land, *as all the neighbors did in those days*."[19]

By 1920, Tres Alamos had essentially ceased to exist, and all but two of the Mexican Americans listed as "farmers" in the remaining Mexican American rural settlement of Cascabel were clearly ranchers. Even these two might have been ranchers as well.[20] In the twentieth century, Antonio Soza's sons and sons-in-law were always identified as ranchers or "cattlemen" in the newspaper. Other Mexican American landholders worked as barbers, general laborers, or railroad employees, which indicated that they were not living off the land. These families raised many crops, but mainly for home use. Their primary occupation was cattle raising. When Doña Moreno de Soza recalled in the 1930s that people along the river farmed "in those days" (the nineteenth and early twentieth centuries), she was alluding to the shift toward ranching.[21]

Ranching meant more cattle, fewer people. In 1894, the Tres Alamos School had served forty-four pupils, making it the fifth-largest district in the county. Seven years later it had half as many students, and, by 1907, just nine. Four years later, the school merged with another predominantly Mexican school, the Apodaca School, while in the same period Pomerene's school enrollment leaped from nineteen to fifty-nine. The Tres Alamos District, with both Mexican American and Anglo pupils, was reestablished in 1916, but its rolls remained dangerously low. In the fall of 1917, one Anglo mother in Tres Alamos felt "so uneasy for fear that our school will lapse. . . . If we lose it will just break our hearts. We would just have to leave here is all." Parents in Tres Alamos fought over whether the district would survive, but increasingly these were disputes among Anglo newcomers, not Mexican American pioneer families. Benson's social pages contained an occasional "local news" section for Tres Alamos—featuring only Anglo names—until early 1920, when reports disappeared once and for all.[22] Today, the site is unoccupied.

Keeping Control in Cascabel

The slow fade of Tres Alamos did not mean the end of Mexican American homesteading. New settlers encroached, but pioneer Mexican Americans continued to farm, ranch, and homestead in isolated spots throughout northern Cochise County. Between 1900 and 1918, people with Spanish surnames made sixty-four successful land claims in the county, almost double the number they had made in the nineteenth century, and this is not counting many other claims clustered just over the Pima County line. New claimants could take advantage of recent legal reforms that offered "dry-farm" plots of 320 acres—double the size of original homesteads—and allowed claimants to live away from their land part-time, which let owners work other jobs or send their children to school in town.[23]

As Tres Alamos declined, Cascabel became the county's largest cluster of Mexican American homesteaders. Tres Alamos lost its post office to Benson in 1880; Cascabel got its first one in 1916.[24] Snug on the Pima County line, Cascabel was more isolated than Tres Alamos, farther from the railroad and from the encroachment of new settlers. Where Mexican landowners in Tres Alamos had once lived with, worked with, and married non-Mexicans almost as a rule, the twentieth-century residents of Cascabel now maintained a decidedly Mexican American enclave.

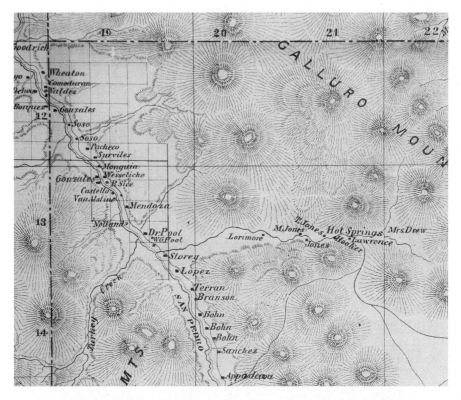

16. Landholdings in the Cascabel area, indicated by name of owner, ca. 1881. Most of the Mexican-American families still remained on their land in the early twentieth century. Braun Research Library, Autry National Center, Map 2047.

Antonio Campo Soza, who had come to the river as a young man in the 1870s, served as Cascabel's patriarch. He married three times and fathered twenty-four children, fifteen of whom made it to adulthood. By the time of his death in 1915, Soza was related by blood or by marriage to more than half of the Mexican American homesteaders on the San Pedro River. Soza belonged to one of Arizona's oldest and most prestigious families, with roots in each of its Spanish colonial outposts. A great-grandfather had been commanding officer of Tucson's Spanish presidio in the 1770s; his grandfather, the administrator of the Tucumcorí Mission; and his father, Tubac's first justice of the peace. Antonio Soza homesteaded in Cascabel in the 1870s alongside his brother, whose land he eventually bought. By 1890, Antonio and third wife, Jesús Moreno de Soza, had extensive land holdings and a tree-shaded, adobe home of 1,400 square feet whose grounds included

17. Antonio Campo Soza and Jesús Moreno Soza, early twentieth century. Courtesy of the Arizona Historical Society, Tucson, 6917.

fenced corrals and a fruit orchard. A farm wagon and a family carriage were likewise signs of prosperity, as well as of mobility.[25]

None of these amenities saved the Soza family from hardship and loss. Antonio lost his first wife and several children to illness, plus several neighbors, and possibly his second wife, to Indian attacks. His third marriage, to Jesús, endured, but they, too, faced challenges. One flood washed out the bridge over the river, and another took their whole house. The ranch's isolation "meant constant fear," as Doña Jesús later recalled, especially from shadowy men who congregated along the river-crossing. She called them "Texans," probably the last strain of Tombstone Cowboys. In 1911, a hired hand robbed and killed their twenty-eight-year-old son, Manuel, whose body would not be found for two months. He left a wife and infant child.[26]

Yet, compared to many homesteaders, Anglos included, the Soza clan led privileged lives. After the flood in 1890, the couple built a sturdy new home. By Jesús' measure, the family harvested "wheat and barley in abundance." They milled their own flour, and kept cattle, dairy cows, and hogs; they produced everything they needed except sugar and salt. Household help—an Apache woman to assist Doña Jesús and hired hands to help Antonio and his sons—lightened their burden, so they had time for leisure at home or in Benson and Tucson, where they attended dances and festivals. The ranch had a cemetery, and a chapel built in 1903. Tucson's bishop blessed it as the Capilla de San Antonio de Padua, where Benson's priest occasionally celebrated Mass, and presided over weddings and funerals.[27]

This world was increasingly insular. Unlike the previous generation, the Mexican American and Anglo landholding families of the twentieth century rarely intermarried. Only one of Antonio Campo Soza's children married an Anglo, and that couple did not live along the San Pedro. Of his other children, at least eight joined neighboring Mexican American families and started their own ranches. Several others married into similar families who ranched outside Tucson. Other landowning families—the Apodacas, the Munguias, the Sánchezes, the Valdezes—also married one another.[28] Nineteenth-century intermarriages had united prestigious Mexican American families with up-and-coming Anglo men; but in the twentieth century, river families began to cross class boundaries to marry fellow Mexican Americans. Antonio Soza's granddaughter married Victor Vásquez, a ranch hand's son ("we were just peons," his niece recalled), who wooed her at a graduation dance at the Soza Ranch's one-room school. The bride's mother, a homesteader named Rosaura Soza Vijil, opposed the marriage, but the couple—who were adults in their twenties—eloped.[29]

Family stories maintain that the bride's father, unlike his wife, supported the marriage, because of his religious ties to the Vásquez family. Rich folk traditions knit together the river's Mexican enclave. In addition to personal saints' days (which were like birthdays) and other festivals, Mexican families on the river "celebrated the Feast of San Isidro, the patron saint of farmers, on the fifteenth of May," one descendant recalled. Her father "had a statue of San Isidro and his oxen," with its own shrine at the Soza ranch. To bless the crops, "the farmers would carry the statue from field to field and ranch to ranch." Mexican women held vigils for the Holy Cross *(la Santa Cruz)* on May 5. They wove elderberry flowers and branches onto a Cross, placed "by the door of the house to bless the house and everyone in it." Families also relied on a local *curandera,* or folk healer, whom they called the "herb lady," and on Laura Gámez, the river's *partera,* or midwife, who belonged to a prominent homesteading family. Mexican families, even those who were less religious, shared a faith and cultural rituals. Anglos established Sunday schools and new Protestant churches in town.[30]

Across the Southwest, marriages between Mexican Americans and Anglos declined as the number of marriageable Anglo women rose. This phenomenon revealed Anglo men's preference for Anglo women, but it also represented a choice on the part of Mexican Americans, who began to see intermarriage as a bad bargain rather than a good deal. The decision of Mexican Americans to marry one another preserved a distinct culture and consolidated land and water rights within the community. Mexican American families had witnessed Anglo land and power grabs, and may have opposed intermarriages to hold on to what they still had.

Some Mexican American ranch families absorbed the children of earlier generations' intermarriages. In the 1890s, for example, the son and daughter of John Montgomery and María Ruíz both married into Mexican homesteading families, as did all of William and María Ohnesorgen's children who stayed in the Benson area. One Ohnesorgen son represented the local Mexican mutual-aid society, the Alianza Hispano-Americano, in the 1930s. Descendents of the intermarried Dunbar family married into the Soto and Vásquez families, and grew up speaking Spanish.[31]

Did these children of intermarriage feel shunned by Anglos? Possibly, in a world of increasing racial division. But Mexican American families also had affirmative reasons to absorb these children of intermarriage. As marriage partners, such offspring posed few cultural challenges to Mexican Americans, because their mothers had spoken Spanish and raised them as Catholics.[32] The majority of people around them had Mexican parents; in the 1870s, Anglo men who had married Mexican women had acculturated to the latter's community, not vice versa. Raised where their Anglo fathers were the newcomers, these children may well have considered themselves more Mexican than Anglo. And for Mexican American families, the advantage of absorbing the children of intermarriage was obvious: it increased the number of landholders, and the amount of land they shared.

Marriage and land consolidation created close kinship ties in Cascabel. In 1910, more than three-fourths of Cascabel's Mexican American households were related to one another in some way. In 1920, this was true of at least two-thirds. In extended families, younger families might live closer to schools, and multiple dwellings on family land made overnight cattle roundups easier. Today, descendants can trace their roots to as many as six river families, entwined in a complex, jungle-like family tree.[33]

Marriages that consolidated land were all the more important because inheritance often dispersed family lands. Arizona's community property laws provided widows with generous inheritance rights. But in the absence of a living spouse, the civil law practice of partible inheritance divided an estate equally among sons and daughters. When single property owners died without wills—as most Mexican Americans did—the state also used the law of partible inheritance.[34] When Rafaela Madrid de Rosas died in Benson in 1904, for instance, the county probate court divided her property between her son and her married daughter. Partible inheritance was far more egalitarian than the English common-law tradition of bequeathing all real property to the eldest son, and nothing to a widow or daughters. But it also split usable plots into ever-smaller parcels that could not support a family. One descendant of the Gámez family attributed the eventual loss of his grandfather's ranch to the decision to divide the land among his several children. With such small plots, descendants worked for wages while they paid taxes on land that could not support them. According to family history, all but one Gámez eventually lost their land in the Great Depression.[35] Some families bucked tradition, bequeathing all the land to one son or daughter.[36] When women inherited land, marrying a neighbor could expand the family acreage.

So could homesteads filed by women themselves. After 1900, women made up about one-third of all Mexican American homesteaders—a percentage about twice as high as that of Anglo women during their peak years of homesteading. Community property and partible inheritance encouraged women's property ownership, as did homesteading's intricacies. Married women could not file new claims, but a single woman could do so before marriage and then keep the land. A widow with inherited land could then homestead and remarry.[37]

The Apodaca family, who had lived along the San Pedro since the 1870s, pursued just such a strategy. Manuel, Ricardo, and the widowed Cleofa (or Cleófila) de Apodaca, along with three other Mexican Americans, patented contiguous claims on the river on the same day in November 1908. Blood or marriage ties connected all six. A few years later, Cleofa married fellow home-steader Jesús María Sánchez. Another female homesteader, Dolores López, also married a Sánchez. Cleofa de Apodaca was the widow from Tres Ala-mos who had sold her homestead back to the government in the 1890s, but she had obviously decided to give homesteading another shot.[38]

Cascabel's patterns of kinship and land ownership in some ways resem-bled those of Mormon Pomerene—except that in Cascabel women's land ownership did not create a single female-headed household in either 1910 or 1920. Some single women left. Some Cascabel widows moved to Benson or Tucson, as Jesús Moreno de Soza did after her husband died in 1915. Several of her children stayed on the river to ranch, but she opened a chain of gro-cery stores and a gas station in Tucson, where she became a successful busi-nesswoman. Other landholding women, like the widow Cleofa de Apodaca, made attractive marriage partners and did not remain single long. Marriage, egalitarian inheritance patterns, and women's homesteading all fostered community cohesion, close-knit families, and economic stability in Casca-bel—at least for the moment.[39]

This world was worth protecting, and Mexican American families did so with tenacity, as a showdown over Cascabel's one-room school illustrates. The San Pedro Valley's three "Mexican schools," as they were known—each a one-room school with its own school district—were the only public institu-tions in the county run entirely by Mexican Americans. They included the old Tres Alamos School and the Soza ranch's school, which was built on family property in 1900 and later moved to the road nearby. The third, Cascabel's Apodaca School, was founded in 1908 (probably coinciding with the Apodaca family's six homestead patents). Cochise County had forty-eight one-room schools by 1920, but only the three "Mexican schools" had Mexican American clerks and trustees. Arturo Grijalba served on the school board of the Tres Alamos School, just as his father Antonio had. At the other two schools, generations of Sozas, Sánchezes, and other families did similar work, sometimes serving alongside Anglos, sometimes not. Pupils were occasionally Anglo, but mostly Mexican American.[40]

The autonomy of the Mexican schools did not go unchallenged. All rural schools were magnets for conflict, because they were often "the only common meeting place and common interest" in small communities, and they became the places where "tensions found an outlet," as county school superintendent Elsie Toles recalled. "The selection of a trustee, the use of a school by different groups, the peculiarities of a teacher—any of these would set off sparks that would explode in community warfare." Disgruntled families could withdraw their children, or petition to dissolve a school district or annex it to another.[41]

By the fall of 1917 the Apodaca School, previously merged with Tres Alamos, was at risk of dissolving. The adobe school's furniture was shabby, and it had just eight books. The school was down to thirteen eligible children (seven fewer than the previous year), with an average daily attendance of only eight—the minimum allowed. A recalcitrant parent, a graduation, or a flu outbreak could shutter the school.[42]

As enrollment fell, an ugly dispute erupted over a controversial teacher named Mrs. Pace. Just before the school year began, twenty local parents petitioned the county superintendent to "get us another teacher" besides Mrs. Pace, because local residents "dont want her" or her husband. Please, they begged, "get us a teacher so that we can keep the children of the district in our home school, instead of their parents sending them else where." The petition was written by district clerk and landowner Jesús Sánchez and signed by ten couples—eight Mexican American, one Anglo, and one intermarried pair. Only two couples in the district failed to sign the petition, one of them Mexican American, the other Anglo. In his accompanying statement, Sánchez dismissed the two couples who supported Mrs. Pace by explaining that they "are not locators here." The term "locator" invoked the technical language of homesteading, as when a potential homesteader "located" a claim. One of the nonsigning men, according to Sánchez, worked "under wages,

18. Apodaca School, ca. 1927. Mrs. Minnie K. Bisby was still teaching.
From Bertha Virmond, "Annual Narrative Report," Cochise County, 1939,
AZ 302, Special Collections, University of Arizona Library.

and no telling how long he will stay"; the other would soon be moving out of
the district. Sánchez used his homestead claim as a moral claim: it meant that
he and his fellow petitioners were virtuous landowners, in contrast to their
rootless adversaries.[43]

The petition worked, at least in the short term, and it was later revealed
that the problem with Mrs. Pace was her hostility to her Mexican American

pupils. That fall, school began with a new teacher, Mrs. Minnie Bisby, who proved to be an excellent fit. (There had not been a Mexican American teacher in the valley since 1902, and there would not be one again until 1919, although Mrs. Pace's predecessor married into a prominent Mexican American family.) Minnie Bisby accused Mrs. Pace of lacking "sympathy" for Mexican students; she herself found "them keen as a rule, ears open for all kinds of facts and stories." In her first two years, the new teacher amassed over a hundred books for the school, and policed attendance carefully to protect the district. Her eloquent letters to the superintendent revealed an extraordinary commitment to her pupils and their families.[44]

Minnie Bisby lived in what she described as a "clean pine shanty" on the Sánchez ranch, facing a stunning rise of sheer red cliffs across the river. It was not the view, however, that drew her there, but the fact that it was on the Sánchez property. As she explained to Superintendent Toles, "I cannot help these people at all by going and living by preference with an ignorant 'Texas' family because they happen to be 'white.'" She wanted to make the Sánchez ranch an "object lesson" in "sanitary and household reforms," with "an extra family room," a bath, "ramadas for shade and summer sleeping," a gasoline-powered washing machine, and concrete floors—all to "eliminate or cover up some of the ancestral germs." By making a model home of the Sánchez ranch, Bisby expected that "a desire for such things soon spreads to other families." She opened the school library to the community, and stocked books about carpentry and concrete, as well as history and patriotism. Her motto was "Progress," which she posted above the schoolhouse door. Bisby brought a sense of superiority to her work, but she also expressed her genuine optimism and devotion to both the parents and children of the district.[45]

The fights over the district were not over, however. In May 1918, the spring of Minnie Bisby's first year, a new petition began circulating. A local Anglo couple, reluctant to accept Mexican American authority over the local school district, wanted to create a new district. But they would not stop there; by drawing pupils from the old school, the petitioners would destroy the Mexican one as well. Bisby defended the families of the Apodaca District with a vehemence that may have surprised even them. "Certain persons," she wrote angrily to the county school superintendent, "would like to throw this district out for personal reasons of gain and retaliation." The new petitioners, Bisby emphasized, shared her predecessor's contempt for her Mexican American employers and pupils. "I have never met Mrs. Pace," Bisby admitted, but "I believe a person who undertakes to teach Mexican children should be in sympathy with them—neither fear or despise them, nor even patronize them." Indeed, she sniffed, "Those whom I have heard speak with the greatest scorn of the Mexicans were persons whose education would not bear inspection and whose breeding was none of the best."[46]

Cascabel's Mexican American families stood firmly together. Casting her lot with the district's oldest residents, Bisby wrote that the trustees "protest strongly against any inroads on the old families. I should, too." "They know of no Mexican patrons who have signed the petition. . . . If any persons attempted then it is not from a desire to be associated with them, as I happen to know, but for a double purpose, to temporarily swell their numbers and to divide and retaliate upon these inoffensive people." Echoing the petition the board had written to oust Mrs. Pace a year earlier, Bisby emphasized Mexican homesteaders' landownership and pioneer status. "The people here own the land along the river," she pointed out, and "I have thought many times that few 'white people' would work so hard to maintain their land and raise their corn, beans, and hay and grain." She was adamant that "these families who have been on this river for two generations . . . are entitled to keep their district intact." "The petitioners," in contrast, were nothing but "a faction of mischief makers."[47] What might her quotation marks around "white people" have meant? Was she challenging the usurpers' entitlement as "whites"? Was she giving a nod to a white identity that her Mexican American school trustees and families might have had? Did she consider them, by virtue of their pioneer status and hard work on the land, "honorary" whites? It is hard to say. But the quotation marks, which she used more than once, surely evoked her own critical stance about the meaning of racial categories in a controversy in which her own allegiances did not follow "racial" lines.[48]

A new petition, written in Bisby's schoolteacher penmanship and signed by the school's trustees, emphasized the families' claims on the land and the rights these should ensure. "We have maintained our homes here for many years. We have given our moral support to the school. The attendance has been maintained, and the school kept alive by our personal efforts. As good citizens, we claim the right of tutelage for our children, and as reasonable persons, [we want to keep our district out of] the hands of mercenary persons, or those careless of our rights." The district's challengers had taken advantage of the busy harvest season and the district's isolation to keep the trustees who were "away on the 'Roundup,' shipping cattle, or otherwise removed" from protesting in person. The trustees could not even hire an attorney to represent them, "because they have no phones to reach him"—a signal of how distant the Apodaca District was both literally and figuratively from the county's seats of power.[49]

Even with no phones or lawyers, the school trustees and Mrs. Bisby saved the school. The designs on the Apodaca District failed. Just as Jesús Sánchez's petition to oust Mrs. Pace had presented landownership as the symbol of true citizenship, Minnie Bisby cast Mexican American homesteaders as the true Americans in the dispute. In a world in which "American" was so frequently contrasted with "Mexican," this was remarkable. Against the backdrop of World War I, Bisby intimated that the German American couple behind the new petition campaign were disloyal, and perhaps alien enemies.[50] In contrast, the Mexican American trustees were landowners and family men, exactly the qualities that defined the ideal citizens in Bisbee's American camp. The families of Cascabel ousted the racist Mrs. Pace after just one year, while Mrs. Bisby stayed for ten years, one of the longest tenures among the county's rural teachers. As late as 1936 Jesús Sánchez served as district clerk and Ricardo Apodaca as school board president. The Apodaca District itself lasted until at least 1950, at times with Anglo and Mexican pupils, as Figure 18 suggests. On the San Pedro, Mexican Americans were holding their tenuous ground.[51]

Integration in Benson

In the years 1880–1910, Benson, the closest real town to Cascabel but still thirty rugged miles away, was the most important railroad hub in Arizona. The Southern Pacific was completed in 1880, and the following year the town became the terminus for a railroad line to the Sonoran port at Guaymas. In 1897, Phelps Dodge's El Paso & Southwestern Railroad opened a route from Benson to Phoenix. Benson's 1880 population of about three hundred had nearly quadrupled by 1910.[52]

In Tucson, the advent of the railroad had destroyed the freighting firms that sustained much of the Mexican American middle class.[53] Yet Benson's growing industrial links did not extinguish the area's unique past, as two of Benson's most important families, headed by José Miguel Castañeda and W. D. Martínez, demonstrated. Castañeda was a *criollo,* a native of Chihuahua with Spanish-born parents, who had begun his merchant career on a trade expedition through Apache country in the 1850s. He then worked for several years in the mercantile business in Los Angeles and along the Colorado River, where he met and married his Sonoran-born wife, Amparo Arvizu. In the early 1880s, Castañeda and Joseph Goldwater moved to Bisbee to open their large store. One Bisbee pioneer revealed the general perception of them when he referred to the pair as a "lean, brown Spaniard" and a "weather-beaten little Jew." After the deadly payroll robbery in 1883, the men moved briefly to Tombstone, where Goldwater married a relative of Amparo, perhaps her sister. By 1890 the two now-related families had relocated to Benson. Goldwater established his own mercantile, and Castañeda opened the Virginia Hotel, which was "first class in every respect" and catered mostly to Anglos. Eventually, Castañeda homesteaded 160 acres, bought Goldwater's store, and turned it over to his son Miguel to manage. Several of José and Amparo's ten sons and daughters attended college in Tucson, and were fixtures of Benson society pages. It is impossible to imagine the same story—the Jewish and thus "white" partner, the swirl of social-page appearances, the proprietorship of the best hotel in town—had the men stayed in the white man's camp of Bisbee.[54]

Like the Castañedas, the Martínez family dominated Benson's society pages. W. D. Martínez served on local holiday and Liberty Loan committees. The family's businesses included Martínez's large grocery store, his brother Nick's billiard hall, a bakery, and extensive mining interests. Kate Martínez worked as the grocery store's bookkeeper, and Laura Martínez was Benson's post office clerk. Mexican Americans in Bisbee and Douglas owned grocery stores and pool halls, but not with Anglo clientele. And Bisbee certainly did not have Mexican American women serving as U.S. postal clerks.[55]

The Castañeda and Martínez families also intermarried with Anglos. Josephine Castañeda married politician and businessman Stephen Roemer in 1919. William Martínez married Sadie Westfield, a schoolteacher in Cascabel. The wedding made front-page news—because of the prominence of the groom's family. The fact that a Mexican American man married an Anglo schoolteacher prompted no commentary. William Martínez was not even the only Mexican American man to marry an Anglo woman in Benson—and this was a very rare practice that showed a high level of Anglo-Mexican integration. Benson resembled northern Mexico, where the merchant classes had long been the most likely to intermarry.[56]

Many of Benson's Mexican American men and women worked in middle-class jobs. Members of almost a dozen Mexican American families in the region held white-collar jobs with the Southern Pacific. A few, like Rudolph Castañeda and Ramón Pacheco, moved to Mexico to take management positions. Other Mexican Americans owned small businesses, such as shoe repairs and garages, that catered to Anglos and Mexicans alike. Young men worked as clerks and salesmen at Jewish mercantiles or the local lumber company, and at least two other Mexican American women followed Laura Martínez at the post office. In a small town with downward fortunes, these were good jobs—the type rarely, if ever, available to Mexicans in Bisbee.[57]

Jobs at the post office, and perhaps indirectly even the railroad, were patronage-related. That Mexican Americans held these jobs was a sign of an active, if circumscribed, role in politics. In 1914, for example, voting rolls included most, if not all, of the middle- and upper-class Mexican Americans in Benson and Cascabel, as well as several more who listed themselves as laborers. That year was the first for full women's suffrage in Arizona. Mexican American women registered as housewives (Guadalupe Sánchez as "ranch-housekeeper"), as well as working in a smattering of paid occupations. Homesteader Cleofa de Apodaca Sánchez was not only registered to vote, but likely served as a Tres Alamos school trustee. Contrary to the stereotype that Mexican American men opposed female suffrage, the Republican Spanish-language newspaper in Tucson had long advocated the right of women to vote, promising that women who vote "will lose none of their dignity or enchantment."[58]

The Bisbee-Douglas area, in contrast, had only a handful of Mexican American voters. In Pirtleville, a suburb for Douglas smelter workers, most residents were Mexican, yet the few Serbs and Italians there outnumbered them in local voting rolls. Although all three groups faced similar citizenship and literacy requirements, Mexicans were much less likely to become U.S. citizens than other immigrants. The few Spanish-surnamed voters tended to have been born in New Mexico or Texas, not Mexico.[59]

By the early twentieth century, Mexican Americans held at best a peripheral place in Arizona politics. Most were Republican, although prominent homesteaders Antonio Soza and Jesús Sánchez were Democrats. A few Mexican American landowners in Cochise County had relatives who had been elected officials in Tucson or Tubac. While *tucsonenses* were never elected in numbers corresponding to their proportion in the population, several Mexican American members of both parties served in elective office in Pima County before 1900. Nabor Pacheco, elected Pima County sheriff in 1894 and chief of the Tucson police in 1910, belonged to an extended family that held a total of eleven homestead claims in Cochise County. But in Cochise County, no one with a Spanish surname was elected to office until the second half of the twentieth century, although Manuel Soza did serve as his precinct's election judge in 1904, and several Mexican Americans served on district court juries in Tombstone.[60]

Barriers to the vote grew during the Progressive Era. In 1900 a poll tax of $2.50 was imposed, followed in 1909 by a literacy requirement. In 1912, Arizona's first state legislature required potential voters to read from the U.S. Constitution in English. This law was explicitly intended to root out the "ignorant Mexican-American vote," but the law was partisan as well as racially motivated, since all but one of the state legislators were Democrats. The 1912 act eliminated so many Mexican Americans from the county rolls that half of its precincts lacked enough voters to hold primary elections that year.[61]

The abundance of Mexican American voters in northern Cochise County and the relative paucity in Bisbee and Douglas reflected the persistence of distinct racial worlds. Landowners and business owners in Benson and along the river were clearly committed to exercising their voting rights, but they also enjoyed advantages most Mexican Americans in Bisbee and Douglas did not. Those who registered in Cascabel and Benson were better educated (often in schools they managed), and much less likely to be immigrants (though there were notable exceptions, like Apodaca School trustee Ángel Arrundeles, who was naturalized in 1903). Most had belonged to Sonora's elite before the U.S. government had taken over Arizona. Yet, citizen or not, literate or not, elite or peon, Mexican American voters could not register without the cooperation of Anglo voting officials. Like Jim Crow voting laws in the South, Arizona's literacy test was not "objective," and registrars had great leeway in administering it.[62] If more Mexican Americans in Benson and Cascabel passed the test, this was largely because Anglo officials chose to pass them. It is hardly surprising that Mexican Americans in Benson wanted to vote. What is noteworthy is the wide acceptance of this right by Anglo officials. It suggests that the Anglos in Benson could countenance Mexican Americans as full citizens in ways that Anglos elsewhere in the county did not.

Equally remarkable was the ease with which Mexican Americans participated in Benson's larger community, even as they maintained ethnic identities and organizations. Three Mexican American mutual-aid societies regularly appeared in the Benson newspaper. From at least 1902 to 1915, Benson contained a local lodge of the Alianza Hispano-Americano, the national mutual-aid society *(mutualista)* founded in Tucson in 1894. The Soza family belonged to it—they received Alianza death benefits for son Manuel in 1911—and as late as 1975, at least half of the remaining nine members in Benson were descendants of ranching families.[63]

Whether Benson's Alianza had working-class members is unknown, but other Mexican American organizations almost certainly did, including a men's group known variously as the Club Mexicano and the Spanish-American Society. La Junta, a "Mexican-American ladies' association," raised funds for Benson's integrated Catholic church. All of the organizations sponsored charity dances *(gran bailes)* with orchestras from Tucson and Cananea. Dances were open to both Anglos and Mexicans, and garnered favorable reviews and newspaper announcements in both Spanish and English. Mexican American organizations marched in Benson's Fourth of July parades, too, at least once "bearing the American and Mexican-American flags" together.[64]

Benson's schools also demonstrated the town's friendly Anglo-Mexican relations. The primary grades had segregated classrooms, but these resembled courses in English as a Second Language rather than "Juan Crow" classrooms, since the children were integrated after the second grade. Mexican American children regularly appeared in grammar school graduations, and when Benson High School opened in 1914, at least four of the school's fifty students were Mexican. This was hardly equality, but in Bisbee, which was ten times as large, the first high-school class and many subsequent ones had no Spanish names at all. At Benson High, Mexican Americans played on the basketball and baseball teams, and graduate Baudelio Martínez became a track star at the University of Arizona. In 1917, two months before the Bisbee Deportation, Francisco Soza was Benson's valedictorian.[65]

Mexican American representation in Benson's newspaper and schools suggested genuine, reflexive inclusion in the town's middle and upper classes. The newspaper occasionally mentioned if someone was "of Mexican-American descent." Some articles elucidated Mexican customs, as when a front-page wedding announcement explained that "a prominent and wealthy Spanish-American family, acted as 'padrinos,' or sponsors for the young couple."[66] Front-page wedding announcements like this were not unusual, and fulsome birth and death announcements of local Mexican Americans regularly appeared. The newspaper reported on local celebrations like San Juan's Day (which celebrates the spring rains and honors St. John the Baptist, patron saint of water), and 16 de Septiembre, Mexican independence day. In 1918, when Mexican American residents chose *not* to celebrate September 16 publicly (no doubt because of World War I), the editor reported on the lack of observance. Similar stories might have appeared in some New Mexico or Texas newspapers, but—outside of Tucson—only rarely in Arizona.[67]

To be sure, few people featured in these articles belonged to Benson's laboring classes, whose lives were quite different from that of Cascabel's ranchers and Benson's merchants. A "Mexican town" of rough barracks emerged on the east side of Benson, even while J. M. Castañeda, W. D. Martínez, and their peers enjoyed prestige downtown. The Southern Pacific controlled Benson's water supply, much of its land, and, to a large extent, the class and racial structure of the community. The same railroad that sustained a small Mexican merchant and farm-ranching class relied on poorly paid Mexican workers. Like the mines, the railroads (one of which was owned by Phelps Dodge) relied on a dual-wage system. Anglo railroad workers excluded Mexicans from union membership and thus from advancement to higher-wage jobs. Together, Southern Pacific managers and white workers created a racial hierarchy nearly identical to that of Bisbee's mines. This exclusion might explain why some of Benson's middle-class Mexican Americans moved to Mexico to take management positions with the Southern Pacific.[68]

Tantalizing but slim evidence exists about class division in Benson's Mexican American organizations. W. D. Martínez headed the "Mexican Citizens" committee for a 1918 Liberty Loan campaign. One might wonder whether railroad laborers and other working-class Mexicans viewed him as an appropriate representative of their interests. Most *baile* organizers had prominent names like Martínez and Ohnesorgen. One 1916 advertisement promised a "refined Spanish and American social dance" at the Benson Auditorium with the "best of band music." "Refined" signaled respectability, as did the emphasis on Spanish *and* American.[69]

Frequent code switching in the Benson paper from "Mexican American" to "Spanish American" (or "Hispano-Americano") mirrored recent developments in northern New Mexico, whose social and racial complexities were similar to those of the San Pedro Valley. In New Mexico, after 1900, people once labeled "Mexican" reemerged in public discourse as "Spanish Americans" or "Hispano-Americans," a language that downplayed Mexican roots in favor of "whiter" Spanish ones. This identity was created both by Hispanos anxious to avoid discrimination, and by Anglos crafting a Spanish "fantasy past" for tourist consumption. As calls for statehood in New Mexico and Arizona grew louder, Spanish Americanism became a counteroffensive against critics who deemed New Mexico racially "unfit" for full inclusion in the United States. Spanish blood was "white" blood, so the language of Spanish Americanism served the interests of Hispano middle and upper classes as well as Anglos.[70]

The same might be said for Benson. New Mexico had what one historian calls an "unusual balance of power" between nearly equal numbers of Anglo-American newcomers and native New Mexicans. A similar situation had prevailed in Tucson and the San Pedro Valley in the late nineteenth century. American migrants had always dominated in Tombstone and Bisbee, but the older mixed communities of northern Cochise County and Tucson invited racial accommodation, even racial blurring. In Benson, the terms "Mexican American," "Spanish American," and "Hispano-Americano" existed simultaneously and were applied to immigrant and native alike. Claims of Spanish origin continued to demarcate racial and class status. José Castañeda's obituaries and biographical sketch emphasized his Spanish descent and Chihuahuan nativity, even though one of Bisbee's "white" pioneers called him "brown." Announcements of whiteness and pioneer status were responses to and reflections of increasing racism in early twentieth-century America. Being *norteño* (hailing from Chihuahua and Sonora) brought with it some claim to whiteness, recognized at least among Mexican American people. (Anglos were becoming much less adept at interpreting the internal differences among Mexicans.) The basis of this claim was the assumption that more *norteños* could trace their ancestry to Spanish roots than those who came from further south, who were more *indio*.[71]

In northern Cochise County, the language of "pioneer" status helped to bind Mexican Americans into a mixed elite. One biography of Castañeda called him a "frontiersman" and a "strong, fearless, and picturesque personality." "Pioneer" status functioned as a class marker by which Anglos differentiated landowning Mexican Americans from working-class or immigrant Mexicans. Ranchers, whether Mexican American or Anglo, would often "share a beef in the summertime when it was hard to keep," or barter labor. Helen Hurtado, who grew up on her family's ranch in Cochise County, eventually realized how unique—and isolated—this shared world was. As a teenager, she went to a movie theater in Phoenix, and remembered being "amazed" when the usher pointed her to worst seats, reserved for Mexicans. Even allowing for the rosy glasses of nostalgia, Hurtado's recollection that in her community "everybody was the same, it seemed like," is revealing.[72]

Hurtado referred to the ranching families she grew up with, who were both Mexican and Anglo. It seems unlikely that most Mexican American elites fully identified with Mexican American laborers, as Rosaura Soza Vijil's opposition to her daughter's marriage revealed. Citizenship often divided landowners and laborers. By emphasizing class divisions, the Mexican American middle class might strengthen its own status, which, in an industrial economy built on the dual-wage system, was increasingly defined by whiteness. Mexican American merchants and wholesalers relied on the railroads just as their Anglo counterparts did, and they favored access to cheap labor. Several of their children worked in railroad management, and

Spanish-language newspapers published and supported by Tucson's Mexican American merchant class sided with the railroads in labor disputes. One article called union members "idle and depraved people."[73]

This is not to say that one had to be considered "white" by Anglos to enjoy some status in Benson. The Chinese, for example, could not claim whiteness, yet their presence in Benson also set it apart from Bisbee. In the 1880s a "Chinese colony" had remained there after railroad work was complete. The Chinese in Benson enjoyed privileges that might seem surprising, given the histories of Tombstone and Bisbee. Prominent Benson merchant Hi Wo, married to a Mexican woman named Emeteria Moreno, appeared regularly in Bisbee's social column and served as the chair of a "Chinese citizens' committee" for the Fourth of July parade and the Liberty Loan campaigns (this would mean local citizenship, since Chinese could not be U.S. citizens). Ong Kee owned a laundry in town that appeared in the newspaper's business—not boycott—news.[74]

More revealing yet is a news story concerning Hi Wo and Emeteria Moreno's daughter in 1918: "The school mates of Victoria Wo . . . , of the eight[h] grade of the grammar school, gave her a very pleasant surprise party at her home Wednesday night. There were refreshments and every one had a good time." The girls' names included Jones, Schwab, Díaz, and Schmidt. The Wo children, half Mexican and half Chinese, occupied an ambiguous place in Benson's social hierarchy. When Hi Wo died in 1931, his widow and children—all with Spanish names—published a bilingual Voto de Gracias / Card of Thanks in the paper. They traveled in both the English-speaking and Spanish-speaking worlds, and downplayed the Chinese component.[75]

Benson's contrasts with Bisbee reveal the extent to which race's meanings could vary over short stretches of time and distance. Benson did not enjoy idyllic race relations, but no one would have called it a white man's camp, either—not when Mexican American merchants were front-page news, or when Mexican American schoolchildren won local prizes, or when the newspaper reported on Mexican *mutualistas* with the same respect and frequency it granted the Methodist Ladies' Aid Society, and certainly not when Anna Schmidt and Hortensea Díaz helped to plan Victoria Wo's birthday party. In northern Cochise County, "Mexican" and "peon" were not interchangeable in the way that they were in Bisbee and Douglas. The copper towns had Mexican American merchants and shopkeepers, but they tended to be invisible to Anglo residents in a way uncharacteristic of Benson. The advent of the railroad in Benson created a hybrid society that combined the internal class hierarchies of places like Tucson and northern New Mexico with the dual-wage system of industrial capitalism.

In the opening years of the twentieth century, Cascabel and Benson remained worlds apart from Bisbee and Douglas, but they could not escape change. Where in the nineteenth century Mexican American and Anglo farmers had settled in close clusters to share water and protect one another from Apaches, now Mexican American families wove a tight web of extended relations as Mormon settlements encroached. Where a few Mexican American women had purchased federal land and filed homesteads in the nineteenth century, now they filed more than one-third of Mexican American claims to expand family holdings. Where Mexican Americans had shared community irrigation systems with Anglos, now they maintained their own religious and fraternal organizations. Where they had created some of the county's first schools, now they worked to keep them.

Linguistic "whitening"—from "Mexican" to "Spanish"—was a defensive maneuver that could not stanch a steady influx of Anglo outsiders who knew little and cared less about such distinctions. No label could disguise the fact that Anglos increasingly controlled the economy. If Mexican American landowners faced difficulty, all the more so for Mexican laborers. When Mexican American homesteaders' settlements could no longer breathe and grow, equality between Mexican Americans and Anglos in the United States grew more difficult to imagine, and believing in a difference based on "race" became easier. Even as Mexican American homesteaders augmented their landholding and preserved cultural autonomy, a veritable land rush in the valleys to their east threatened their enclave settlements and integrated islands.

6

Women and Men in the Sulphur Springs and San Simon Valleys

In 1909, the widowed Mary Cowen, her three daughters, and her father, George Homrighausen, rode the Southern Pacific from Paola, Kansas, to the ranch town of Willcox in northeastern Cochise County. There the family hired two teams of horses, loaded their wagons, and made their way to a spot ten miles south, in the Sulphur Springs Valley. Soon they were filing homesteads, buying land, planting crops, and raising cattle. Over the next year, more plains folks rolled in, several from the same county in Kansas. By 1910, Kansas Settlement boasted eighty-nine people who held Sunday school, ice cream socials, and community dances in the one-room schoolhouse built on the property of Cowen's daughter Nellie. Nellie served as schoolteacher until her marriage six years later.[1]

The Cowens and Homrighausens were among thousands of landseekers converging on rural Cochise County in the early twentieth century. For a brief time, optimistic Anglo homesteaders transformed some of Arizona's most iconic open range into an unlikely patchwork of small family farms whose fences criss-crossed the horizon. From 1900 to World War I, as many as two dozen new rural settlements appeared, along with close to fifty one-room schoolhouses. In 1917, a national travel writer could observe, "Less than a decade ago there were not a hundred families engaged in agriculture in the Sulphur Spring Valley. To-day it is dotted from end to end with prosperous ranch homes, [and] its settlers run into the thousands." Farm acreage multiplied fifteen times over. Within just two decades, drought and crop failure would cut short the farm mania, but at the height of the boom the rural population had grown several times over.[2]

Cochise County's land rush followed a national trend. Although the classic image of the western homesteader resides firmly in the nineteenth century, many more men and women homesteaded in the twentieth, especially before World War I. Most of these claims were in the Northern Plains, but landseekers flocked to the Southwest as well. From 1879 to 1900, only eighty-six successful homesteads were established in Cochise County. Compare that to 2,826 patents (97 percent of all the successful homestead claims ever made there) on claims filed after 1900, the vast majority before World War I. And these figures do not include thousands more landseekers who filed claims but never completed the homesteading process. In some parts of the West, four claims failed for every successful one.[3]

The impact of the homesteaders lasted far longer than their mostly failed farms. Their wells depleted the water supply, while overgrazing and invasive plant species reduced natural forage to nubs.[4] The human impact was also dramatic. New farm communities overwhelmed pioneer Mexican American enclaves, and not just in numbers. Newcomers from the American Midwest and South had no experience with the nuances of shared experience in the county's earliest settlements. On the contrary: the local and national land promoters who drew newcomers westward depicted homesteading as a way to save both rural America and the Anglo-Saxon race. They did so in part by elevating the presence and position of white women in rural America— promoting women's homesteading and celebrating the archetypal American farm wife. Agricultural promoters metaphorically erased Mexican Americans from the land even as their rhetoric about home and independence highlighted white women's place on it. The power of white women was on the rise, while that of Mexican American landowners, male and female alike, was on the decline.

Homes on the Range

Like Mary Cowen and her family, the largest portion of rural newcomers came from the Great Plains, the Midwest, and the Upper South. Almost half of Kansas Settlement's heads-of-households had been born in Kansas, and all but one hailed from the great midsection of the country. In another typical settlement, close to one in four heads-of-households was a Texan.[5] Many resembled the prototypical restless westerners, settling down for a few years before pulling up stakes and moving farther west. Thomas Lewis, who came to Cochise County in 1909, had been born in Indiana, grew up in Iowa, served in the Civil War, married and moved to Kansas, then to Oklahoma, then to New Mexico, and finally to Cochise County, where he died at age eighty-three.[6]

Chain migrations of families and communities preserved older regional identities. J. H. Jaque, an energetic booster from Missouri who owned, edited, and wrote the *Bowie Enterprise* in San Simon Valley, addressed his readers, "Hey Mr. Man in Missouri, Oklahoma, and Arkansaw . . . Come on down and live in the land of sunshine." Place names like Kansas Settlement, Missourizona, the Texas Colony, and Texas Canyon preserved regional ties. The "Arizona-Texas Society" held local reunions and celebrations on San Jacinto Day, commemorating Texas' independence from Mexico.[7]

Why did these people come to Cochise County? The Sulphur Springs and San Simon Valleys were high-desert open range, full of scrub brush but little rain. The valleys were the domain of cattle barons who ran huge herds on a patchwork of private and public land, and were contemptuous of "nesters," as homesteading farmers were known. But times were changing. The end of the Apache Wars in 1886 had made Cochise County safer for settlement. Railroads made getting there easier, and enabled national markets to compete with a local cattle industry reeling from Tombstone's decline, the army's decampment, and, in 1892, a devastating drought that killed one-fourth of the county's livestock. The Panic of 1893, the country's worst depression until the 1930s, finished off most of the remaining big ranches. Their demise cleared the way for new homesteaders, who enjoyed the generous land reforms of the twentieth century that expanded the maximum size of land claims and offered flexibility in the time needed to prove up. The federal government also opened vast stretches of public domain, including parts of the Sulphur Springs Valley, to homesteaders for the first time. Luck played a role, too: in 1905, as the rush was underway, rainfall was double the annual average.[8]

Still, Cochise County was hardly what most people had once considered farm country. Elevations were high, and rainfall was in the range of ten to fifteen inches. The summers were hot enough for corn to have "burned to death," yet killing frosts came as early as Halloween and as late as Easter. In July 1914, homesteader Susie Cundiff Patrick described every day in her diary as "hot" save one—which was "not so hot . . . as it has been." Winter granted little reprieve, and she recorded heavy wind, rain, and snow.[9]

Picking up stakes and starting a farm in such a place required not just a leap of faith, but a new kind of faith altogether—one that prophesied that the desert could bloom. Such confidence was rooted in an almost mystical belief in new theories of irrigation and dry-farming. Progressive optimism—the conviction that, with a scientific system and a little sweat, anything was possible—buoyed homesteaders' faith in agricultural promoters, whose claims relied more on wishful thinking than on hard facts.

In the 1880s, a Nebraskan named Hardy W. Campbell had launched the dry-farming movement by popularizing methods he concocted from ancient practices of crop rotation and deep plowing, so as to create steep furrows meant to preserve moisture in arid soils. Campbell's first attempts at dry-farming came during an unusually rainy cycle in the Great Plains, and, spurred by his successes, he propelled the dry-farming movement farther west. Dry-farming in arid Arizona was mostly hopeless, but the movement's language of "scientific soil culture" made migrants eager and willing to believe. Dry-farm advocates were instrumental in the passage of the Enlarged Homestead Act of 1909, which spurred the surge in homestead claims in Cochise County and elsewhere.[10]

If dry-farmers relied on faith in science, the more successful irrigation movement inspired almost evangelical zeal. Irrigation experts Elwood Smythe and George Maxwell became well-known national figures, and their cause spread far beyond esoteric agricultural journals. The irrigation lobby's crowning achievement was the federal Newlands Reclamation Act of 1902, which was sponsored by a Nevada senator and which used public land sales to finance mammoth dams. One of its earliest projects, the Salt River Project outside Phoenix, offered a shimmering example to Cochise County, but in the end no federal dams were funded there.[11]

The possibility remained alluring, though, and irrigation as redemption permeated local promotional efforts. Another type of irrigation—tapping into water supplies deep underground, via newly discovered artesian wells—also unleashed a frenzy of enthusiasm in the county. The University of Arizona published maps of water supplies for potential farmers, and in 1911 San Simon's school district was named Artesia, its local paper the *Artesian Age*. County irrigation promoters told tales of nine-pound sugar beets and twenty-pound cabbages, and promised nearly sixty marketable crops on what was once grazing land. Local boosters invited prominent national movement leaders to speak, and attended and reported on national agricultural congresses, including one in nearby El Paso. Rural Cochise County also attracted funding from the Southern Pacific Railroad and from Phelps Dodge officials, to build experimental farms advised by national experts like George Maxwell.[12]

At first, national dry-farming and irrigation promoters competed for followers, but the two groups quickly conceded that their movements were more alike than different: both were promoting agriculture where few had once imagined it. In the 1910s, the Dry-Farming Congress and the Irrigation Congress joined forces as the International Farm Congress (also called the Agricultural Congress) and published a popular journal that urged combining seasonal dry-farming with irrigation. In Cochise County, boosters and government scientists always combined dry-farming and irrigation advice.[13]

Swapping science for homier imagery around 1900, national and local promoters began reframing their appeals in rhetoric about "homemaking" designed to appeal to everyday Americans. The journal *National Irrigation* became *The National Homemaker* in 1901, and then, two years later, simply *The Homemaker*. Its counterpart, *Dry-Farming*, became *Scientific Farmer* in 1906, then *Dry Farms and Rural Homes* by 1911.[14]

In Cochise County, special editions of local newspapers offered an "invitation of welcome to every homeseeker," and promised "Free Homes for All in the Sulphur Springs Valley, the Homeseekers' Paradise." Pitches like these refigured the technicalities of plowing, wells, and flowage into the cozy allure of "homes on the land," the official motto of the National Irrigation Congress. Promoters used this "home" motif to fend off accusations that their appeals encouraged speculation, rather than real settlement. In truth, the line between homeseeker and speculator blurred, just as it does today. Many homesteaders were unapologetic "flippers" who hoped to live on a claim, sell it at a profit, and move on.[15]

The "home" rhetoric was meant to disarm critics of speculation, even as it promised financial security and manly independence in an uncertain age. Maxwell, the nation's leading irrigation promoter, promised that the Newlands Reclamation Act of 1902 would create "the man who is free from all the uncertainties of a wage-earner's employment." Back in Cochise County, Bowie newspaper editor J. H. Jaque (who invited Maxwell to speak) advertised his own real estate companies with the headline, "Don't Be a Wage Slave All Your Life. Get on Easy Street. The Road to Independence Leads to a Bowie Valley Farm Tract." Willcox's newspaper editor echoed Jaque when he urged "the throngs in our overcrowded cities to return to the soil, to become producers instead of consumers, and in place of being dependents, and wage earners, to acquire a home, comfort and independence."[16]

When Jaque and his colleague C. O. Anderson advertised "independence," they promised nothing less than real manhood. Reveries about "homemaking" referred to men's work, not women's. The goal was to have dependents, not to be one. Promoters used the image of the family to emphasize productivity, cooperation, kinship, and self-sufficiency. The genius of this vision was that it offered financial independence without social isolation or overly rugged individualism. In a 1911 pamphlet promoting the Sulphur Springs Valley, one relocated Kansan reported:

> We are all heartily satisfied with our new home, so much so that I would advise any person with pluck and a little capital to move in on the government land. I believe that in a very few years the Sulphur Springs Valley will blossom like a rose, and that we will have a big settlement of prosperous and happy farming people. We have fine folks for neighbors, a school house, a church, Sunday school, a literary society, a country store and post office with daily delivery, two railroads not far away, good markets at Douglas and Bisbee, many pianos in our homes and the girls to play them.

Here was the ideal homesteader community, one whose members had character ("pluck"), community institutions (neighbors, school, church), access to outside commerce (a store, a post office, the railroad, local markets), culture and family life ("pianos in our homes and the girls to play them"). "What more," he asked, "could any man settling in a new land want?"[17]

"Desirable White Settlers"

Boosters maintained that homesteading would save not just the man and the family, but also the nation and the white race. Each issue of *The National Homemaker* ran a boilerplate quotation from Theodore Roosevelt: "Throughout our history the success of the homemaker has been but another name for the upbuilding of the nation."[18] "Upbuilding" referred to ideas about racial improvement that on their face had nothing to do with family farms. Homesteading has become so enmeshed in the nostalgic American past that its political nature has been largely forgotten. Yet it always hummed with a political and cultural resonance far greater than mere land ownership. More than just a way to get land, homesteading was also a social movement about race and regionalism. Before the Civil War, its proponents promised a northern vision of independent white farm families populating the American West. The sectional ideal that the Homestead Act represented is one reason it did not become law until 1862, after the South had seceded.

By the twentieth century, homesteading advocates had shifted their rhetoric from a north-south axis to an urban-rural, east-west one. The 1909 founding of the "Country Life" movement, endorsed by Theodore Roosevelt, reflected this new perspective. Promoters translated the abstractions of "science" into emotional appeals to the hopes and fears of the Progressive Era— hopes of efficiency and independence, fears of wage dependence and "race suicide," because white Anglo-Saxon women were not having enough children to keep pace with the influx of new immigrants. The bitter depression of the 1890s, ugly class division, and untrammeled urban growth and immigration prompted fears among policymakers and everyday citizens alike that a land of agricultural plenty would become one of teeming urban want.[19]

In 1907, prominent irrigation lobbyist Dr. Samuel Fortier announced at the National Irrigation Congress that "the greatest need in arid America is desirable white settlers." That same year, Roosevelt echoed him: "It would be a calamity to have our farms occupied by a lower type of people than the

... manly and womanly men and women who have hitherto constituted the most typically American, and on the whole the most valuable, element in our entire nation. Ambitious native-born young men and women who now tend away from the farm must be brought back to it." In 1912, an assistant secretary of agriculture instructed the Women's Congress of a dry-farming convention that "if our best blood will here [in rural America] multiply more rapidly on the average; and if the worst blood will remain in the city and will multiply less rapidly," farms could supply the cities with a better "race," as well as better crops. Dry-farming's "science," he hoped, could work in tandem with eugenic race improvement.[20]

In an era of great controversy over the meanings of race and whiteness, agricultural promoters who used racial arguments had to tread lightly. "It is true the West needs settlers," the agriculture secretary told his audience, for it is a "white man's country. . . . But its needs are not so great that it can afford to adopt everyone who crosses either the Pacific or the Missouri." No, he went on,

> It wants the sons and daughters of the pioneers of the Mississippi Valley who have grown tired of raising corn to try the more interesting and more profitable irrigated agriculture. It stands ready to hand over its dairies to the Norsemen, its sugar beets to the Germans and its vineyards to the Italians. With one hand toward New England and the other toward the South it extends an invitation to the children of both Puritan and Cavalier to settle in the West and blend forever into the highest type of civilization what is best in both races.[21]

This blending suggested his confidence in national unity (Puritan and Cavalier referred to Northerner and Southerner) and racial improvement, even as it set Italy as the outer limit of whiteness. His vision for the rural West was remarkably similar to that of the architects of Bisbee's transformation from a white man's camp to an "American" camp. He excluded the Chinese and Japanese, and left the precise place of Mexicans obscure.

Mexican Americans rarely appeared in agricultural promotions, and then in only two forms: as cheap wage-labor competition, or as quaint vestiges of old-world primitivism that "American" homesteading would render obsolete. A 1906 *Scientific Farmer* article warned potential migrants to Las Vegas, New Mexico, "There are too many dollar-a-day Mexicans . . . to make it profitable for the American . . . wage worker." Mexican landowners, the author allowed, were "thorough businessmen," but also "slouchy, unkempt," wearing "shoes . . . full of holes." These sloppy, poorly shod farmers did not stand a chance against (in his words) the wave of "progress" that "American" farmers would bring. "The future of the town is in its American immigration," the article concluded. "The Mexican population is slow, unprogressive and asleep in the sun." Even the article's title, "New Mexico: To-day and To-Morrow," cast "Mexicans" as the past and "Americans" as the future. Mexican American farmers became like the vanishing Indian, a group whose exclusion could be justified by the inevitability of Anglo-American "progress."[22]

A few commentators noted a basic irony: that native peoples and Mexicans had pioneered the desert farming practices that would now eliminate them. John Wesley Powell praised the cooperative customs of water use in New Mexico's *acequias*. Thirty years earlier, Antonio Grijalba had experimented with deep furrows around his crops in Tres Alamos. Yet Apache fighter and retired general Nelson Miles included in his memoirs a chapter describing irrigation as the final frontier in conquering the West. Aridity was "the only bar to the complete victory of that vanguard which the soldiers led. It must be conquered now by science." He conceded that irrigation was "a system of farming new to the . . . Saxon mind, though it is one of the oldest arts of civilization." Yet, Miles promised, "with this man, to whom it is new, it is more successful . . . than it is in any other hands." Arizona's state agronomist saw the "Anglo-Saxon, with his capacity for invention in government," as the savior of the "semi-arid regions" of Australia, Africa, and the United States.[23]

Back in Cochise County, Willcox newsman C. O. Anderson was promoting well-water irrigation by denigrating older, communal traditions. In 1909, as if speaking directly about the conflict between Antonio Grijalba and Thomas Dunbar in Tres Alamos twenty years earlier, he promised that with your own well "you have no troublesome neighbors to cut off your water, no dispute with the canal company over shortage of water, no prorating of water during a dry season, no breakage of canals. . . . You are your own master."[24]

Those who relied on communal irrigation methods, he seemed to suggest, were foolishly dependent on others.

Ultimately, agricultural promotion was for whites only. *Scientific Farmer*'s 1906 foray into the Arizona and New Mexico statehood debates, which on their face had little to do with dry-farming, made this clear. A 1905 proposal by Congress to combine the Arizona and New Mexico territories into one state unleashed a spate of racist rhetoric from lawmakers in Arizona and their Democratic allies, especially in the South. Republicans in Congress favored joint statehood because New Mexico's predominantly Republican Hispanic population vastly outnumbered Arizona's mostly Democratic Anglos. Anglos in Arizona were incensed at the prospect of relinquishing political control to Hispanic New Mexicans. A *Scientific Farmer* editorial, probably written by Hardy Webster Campbell, bluntly summarized the racial dichotomies of the debate. "Arizona is American. New Mexico is Mexican, to the extent of 60 per cent of its population. Even the legislature of the latter territory is controlled by the Spanish-American element, while in the Arizona body there is but one member of the Latin race." Anglo Arizona would wait for statehood, even if it meant less political representation: "Arizona doesn't want senators; she wants home rule, and by all the right of American citizenship she ought to have what she wants." For Campbell and many others, "home rule" meant white rule. "American citizenship" was more about white supremacy than political representation, since he was arguing that Arizonans preferred living in a territory—where they had few electoral privileges—to living in a state with a Mexican American majority.[25]

White Women Ascendant

In the new agricultural utopia, Mexican Americans were marginalized, but white women were central. Agricultural promoters embraced women's rights as part of the agenda to save the white rural family. Calls for more women on the land—as wives, mothers, daughters, and homesteaders in their own right—came at a moment when white women were uniquely situated to benefit from racial appeals. Southern politicians routinely justified lynchings of African Americans in protection of white women's virtue, while leaders of the campaign for national woman suffrage argued that white women were superior to nonwhite and immigrant men. Rural women, though less visible than their urban counterparts, benefited from white women's increasing public presence in the Progressive Era. When a 1913 *Collier's Magazine* article praised single white women such as the "girl from Omaha" who homesteaded on former Sioux reservation land in South Dakota, it happily included these women in the white triumph over the West.[26] Many Americans believed that only white women could truly civilize an unruly, multiracial West. For eugenics enthusiasts like Theodore Roosevelt, the mere presence of white women in the West promised a better "race" of rural Americans.

Within the dry-farming and irrigation movements, paeans to white womanhood created a platform—one might even say a pedestal—from which women activists could make demands. Some turned "homemaking" rhetoric to their own purposes. "The principles of home-making should be taught to men as well as women," proclaimed one woman at a 1918 agricultural convention. Men, she insisted, must "be trained to turn their thoughts back towards the home, the wife and the family." Other women decried the way western farmers exalted independence even as their wives sounded "a gospel of despair" stemming from overwork and loneliness. These critics attacked the male biases of "scientific" farming, such as buying fancy farm equipment or lighting the barn before installing indoor plumbing. Female farm reformers maintained that farmwomen needed "labor-saving devices for the home" as much as men needed new plows and water systems for their barns. Farm women themselves—not just spokeswomen—often complained of the same.[27]

Farm life, female boosters insisted, should foster independence for women as well as for men. A Texan named Mrs. Warner recommended that "every mother and every boy and girl on the farm have a pocketbook and a bank account of their own." Only then, she believed, could "the farm home . . . become a happy, domestic democracy, instead of a one-man monarchy."[28] Warner's "domestic democracy" differed sharply from the vision of men like the one in Cochise County who pictured a republic of independent men in rural households stocked with pianos and girls to play them.

If men could be homemakers and homeseekers, and if women deserved their own pocketbooks and bank accounts, why couldn't women be homesteaders in their own right? Before 1900, women accounted for fewer than 10 percent of American homesteaders; but by the early twentieth century, 10 to

18 percent was more common, and in some places up to one-third of claimants were female. The Enlarged Homestead Act of 1909 opened more land to homesteading at a time when Anglo women enjoyed increasing freedoms, especially in the West. The 1912 and 1914 homesteading laws easing residency requirements and allowing men and women to keep their claims after marriage also helped women. Not coincidentally, these were the peak years of publicity about single woman homesteaders. In Cochise County, even in the nineteenth century, women had made up a relatively high proportion (13 percent) of successful Anglo homesteaders. In the period 1900–1918, the boom years of Cochise County's land rush, 14 to 21 percent of the county's homesteaders were women.[29]

Homesteading women contended with the same steep odds and daunting hard work that their male counterparts faced, but they also rode a wave of public support for a new kind of womanhood—one that was always assumed to be white. The iconic single woman homesteader became both a rural version of the emergent New Woman and a female counterpart to the masculine frontier image trumpeted by Roosevelt and others. Women homesteaders appeared in dozens of newspaper and magazine articles in the early twentieth century. Their most famous imagemaker was a Wyoming homesteader named Elinore Pruitt Stewart, who published romanticized testimonials in the *Atlantic Monthly* and later issued them as a popular book in 1914. Echoing calls to men, the former laundress urged "troops of tired, worried women, . . . scared to death of losing their places at work," to leave the cities and take up their own homestead claims. Stewart's work served as entertainment and ideological fodder for eastern New Women, and her literary self became the model for the idealized woman homesteader. Although such images did not reflect the far more complex reality, they were meant to inspire women seeking personal and financial independence.[30]

Cochise County's women homesteaders had their own promoter in Lortah Stanbery, a former writer for the New York *World* and *Sun* who filed a claim in the San Simon Valley. In a 1914 article in the local *Artesian Belt: Homeseekers' Edition,* Stanbery argued that men's and women's goals were fundamentally similar—to acquire a home, self-sufficiency, and an independent life through land ownership. To Stanbery, the major difference between the sexes was their *access* to these goals. Men were choosy about what land they might own, but women saw land ownership in itself as precious. "After years of living in other people's houses . . . the prospect of sitting down and getting up, sleeping and waking, working or idling on MY land was a new and seriously absorbing sensation. Men who come to the valley homeseeking go about in critical attitude, disdaining this, discarding that, objecting to something else, but not I. I took the first claim I found, and sat down on it at once." Women wanted a place of their own, in Stanbery's view, and they should seize the opportunity to have it. In contrast to the vision laid out for male homeseekers, the one promoted by Stanbery—a teacher and principal—focused on a distinctly female independence attained through property ownership, rather than self-employment per se. Back-to-the-land promoters urged city dwellers to "build up a home and an independent fortune,"[31] but Stanbery emphasized the home, not the fortune.

Stanbery had plenty of male allies. Beneath the bombast of most pitchmen was a casual but genuine acceptance of women homesteaders and women's work. Willcox land promoter W. B. Dickey detailed women's homesteading rights in his pamphlet "Free Homes for All in the Sulphur Springs Valley." A 1912 article in *Arizona: The New State Magazine* celebrated single woman homesteaders as "energetic bachelor maids" whose work as "waitresses, nurses, stenographers, [and] teachers" was "contributing . . . to the common good." Small-town gossip columns reported on women's work just as they did on men's. Mrs. Alice Armstrong, for instance, was busy "proving up on her desert claim," and Mrs. Mary J. Contraman had "advanced ideas" about running a "well conducted hog and poultry ranch." Everybody knew Arizona needed women workers, and homesteading was a good way to get them.[32]

The need to attract women is the most common explanation for the fact that the West pioneered woman suffrage. Most western states allowed women to vote long before the Nineteenth Amendment was ratified in 1920. Arizona women had voted in school board elections since 1883, and the state's first legislature approved woman suffrage in 1912 (even as it enacted poll taxes and literacy tests that disfranchised Mexican voters). Rural newspaper editors Jaque and Anderson wholeheartedly supported woman suffrage, and promoted female political candidates. Cochise County voters elected a female county superintendent of schools in 1914, the first year women were allowed to vote and to run in regular elections.[33]

Two years later, twenty-four-year-old Republican Elsie Toles beat two

other women candidates for the post. Toles impressed rural voters by becoming the first candidate to visit all eighty-nine of the county's school districts, a daunting journey by Model T that she made an annual event. As
the only Republican in county office, she benefited from the fact that women
harbored an "indifference to party lines" that was "infuriating to their men
folks." In 1920, Toles was elected state superintendent of public instruction.
She was the first woman to hold statewide office in Arizona, but she lost in a
Democratic landslide two years later.[34]

Toles's assistant superintendent, Helen Benedict, a homesteader and
teacher, became one of her best political assets. Benedict proudly publicized
her landownership on the campaign trail. After losing an egg race at a community picnic, she quipped "that the proper race for her" was "a plowing
contest, as she felt positive that she could plow more acres of a dry farm in
one hour than any other female homesteader in the valley." In the best tradition of stump politics, she tooted her own horn even as she emphasized her
shared experience with an important constituency.[35]

Toles and Benedict did not have husbands (indeed, their shared residence
and social calendar suggest that they were life partners as well as business
partners), but political power was not reserved only for the unmarried. Lortah Stanbery, herself a widow or divorcee, claimed that married women had
just as much gumption as their single counterparts, and that one could not
understand rural society without them.

> What community has its story written without a record of its women?
> And San Simon has a type of woman not to be overlooked or even
> noted indifferently. To hear a woman speak of her political activities,
> voting for one official while her husband favored the opposing candi-
> date, gives an impression of moral courage quite as distinctive in its way
> as that of another woman killing a rattler and tossing [it] . . . to one side
> with small concern.

Stanbery was single, but she readily conceded that rural wives and daughters
could display genuine independence, too. Rural families and single woman
homesteaders both complicated promoters' smooth promises of manly independence.[36]

Women were integral to the farm economy, and not just in the household or kitchen garden. "The women work so hard in the fields," wrote one observer, "that they have neither energy or inclination to do more than is necessary in the house." The terse diary of homesteader Susie Cundiff Patrick chronicled endless work: sewing, washing, ironing, and baking; but also plowing, post-hole digging, and making "doba" (adobe) bricks. Her entry for November 1, 1916 ("Washed today. Shot at a coyote.") speaks volumes about homestead life. In rural Cochise County, women's work, broadly defined, was a simple indispensable fact. It included unpaid labor on women's own property and on that of their husbands or fathers, as well as work for wages. Susie Patrick plowed and sewed at home, but also did domestic wage labor on far-flung farms, where she boarded days and weeks at a time, at least sometimes doing "work I don't like."[37]

Across the West, most women who homesteaded were not single women making a new start, as folks like Elinore Pruitt Stewart would have it; rather, they were consolidating family landholdings. In North Dakota, where many women filed for public land, only 7 percent matched the stereotype of the "lone homesteader." The vast majority came with siblings, parents, other kin, or acquaintances. The same was true in Cochise County, where sometimes five or more members of a family filed individual claims, or several family members were listed on the same claim. Diarist Susie Patrick came from Missouri with her father, mother, and several of her eight siblings. Reforms in 1912 and 1914 allowed homesteaders to live away from their property five months of the year. This change helped all homesteaders, but especially women, who worked as schoolteachers (the way Stanbery did) or lived with their families for part of the year.[38]

Young couples learned to work the system. One change, instituted in 1914, allowed homesteading men and women to keep their own claims after marriage, provided the claims had been filed at least a year earlier. Some young, single women filed homesteads with the intent of bringing their property to a marriage. Others, like Susie Patrick, wanted title to that land before they tied the knot. Diary entries from October 1916 make this clear:

> [October] 26. Went to Courtland today to prove up on my homestead.

27. Made my wedding dress.

28. Pat and I were married today. Warm and sunny.[39]

The vagaries of homesteading law—residence requirements, rules about wives' separate homestead entries—altered family dynamics. No doubt many engaged couples who lived on their own claims for a year before marrying established more egalitarian decision making than did couples where the husband bought and controlled the family's property. Susie Patrick's homestead claim was near that of her parents, but she had her own 10-by-16-foot plank house to fulfill the law's residency requirements. After her marriage, she moved to her husband's homestead near the San Pedro River, but her parents kept her land. Homesteading daughters could also find new opportunities and even new identities. The father of assistant county school superintendent Helen Benedict was a well-known minister and rancher, but her claim was miles from her parents' land. She proudly identified herself as a woman homesteader while she supported herself as a teacher and administrator. Women like Benedict lived on their land and made the day-to-day decisions, even if the claim was one of many family holdings.[40]

A good example is Mary Cowen's youngest daughter, Katie, who came to Kansas Settlement with her family at age seventeen, and fashioned a life deeply tied to family but full of independent choices. Katie married another homesteader in late 1911, had a child, and divorced a few years later. Then she opened a boarding house with her mother at the nearby Dos Cabezas mining camp. In 1919 Katie patented her own desert claim, near but not contiguous with other family land. Two years later she remarried, and eventually bore three more children. Katie's new husband Louis Flick, like most men in the area, picked up mine and carpentry work to make ends meet. The family moved several times before returning to Dos Cabezas in 1931. All the while, according to her descendants, Katie continued to make the primary decisions about ranching and farming her land. It would be wrong to assume that homesteading women made all their own decisions about the land in their name, but it would be equally silly to suppose they made none. It is clear that many, if not most, women had a fair amount of control over their own property.[41]

The realities of women's homesteading demand a recasting of the manly "independence" formula. Most women came with families, but then so did

19. Wedding portrait of Susie Cundiff and Frank Emmitt ("Pat")
Patrick, 1916. Cundiff patented her homestead claim two days
before the wedding. Courtesy of Rebecca Orozco.

most men. Consider the Cowen family story from a different perspective.
At least seven family members, including George Homrighausen's brother,
daughter, son-in-law, and two of his granddaughters, bought or homesteaded
public land. Most of the family claims were contiguous, together comprising a 640-acre section, or one square mile. After a couple of years in Arizona,

George's brother deeded his land, a parcel worth $1,000, to his niece Mary Cowen. Family labor was indispensable. One granddaughter drove her wagon alongside Homrighausen's as they ferried lumber from Willcox for their first home, while another taught the school that enticed more migrants. George Homrighausen was just as dependent on his "dependents" as they were on him. He died just two years after he arrived. His daughter and granddaughters stayed.[42]

Depictions of women homesteaders tend to occupy the two ends of a spectrum. One version is a casual dismissal of women's homesteads as mere "dummy claims," legal fictions to allow male ranchers and large cattle companies to acquire more land. The other version is a hagiography that portrays single woman homesteaders alone against the world. The latter image was sometimes perpetuated by women homesteaders themselves, especially Elinore Pruitt Stewart. The popular author presented herself as the iconic single woman homesteader. In reality she married her employer, with whom she lodged, less than a month after filing a claim—which she eventually relinquished and failed to patent. Stewart recognized that a romanticized image of the single woman homesteader was more appealing to her eastern New Woman readers, and more redolent of western tropes of independence. The reality was more complicated for men and women alike, but women—white ones, at least—found surprising possibilities in the West in those years.[43]

This was far less true for Mexican Americans. In many ways, Mary Cowen's Kansas Settlement in 1909 and 1910 was little different from María Ruíz de Montgomery's Tres Alamos of the 1870s. Both were settled by family groups. Both used men's and women's homesteads to build the family economy. Both found men and women making strategic marriages to help themselves and their families, and both required hard work of their residents. Yet the stark distinctions between "Americans" and "Mexicans" made by promoters implied that these experiences were worlds apart. Rural promoters marginalized or ignored Mexican American farmers. They treated whiteness as something separate from Mexicanness, and celebrated a racialized vision of rural life as the protector of a eugenic American greatness.

Words were one thing, but the crushing force of numbers was another. The newcomers constituted a large bloc of American-born, rural citizens who did not share a past with their Mexican peers. A few numbers tell a stark story. Before 1900, people with Spanish surnames represented slightly fewer than one in seven successful homesteaders. After 1900, the actual *number* of homestead patents held by Mexican Americans rose by 75 percent, even as their *proportion* of the county's total number of successful homesteaders plummeted to just over one in fifty. The decline in the percentage of public land sales by Mexican Americans was even more dramatic—from one in four before 1890 to fewer than one in a hundred after 1900. In short, while the number of Mexican Americans acquiring federal land rose, their share of the total homesteading population became minuscule.[44] The combination of these phenomena—a large, relatively homogeneous bloc of newcomers to the region and the exclusionary promotional rhetoric that lured them there—boded ill for Mexican American homesteaders.

Even at the height of the homesteading rush, rural Cochise County and copper country were hardly sealed off from each other, or even totally distinct: ranchers and homesteaders worked in the mines from time to time, and rural pockets of the county continued to attract mining development. Yet there were genuine political and cultural divides. While most voters in the county—and Arizona—were Democrats (all but one in the state's first legislature), this label disguised a broad range of political beliefs. Homesteaders were largely of the conservative "Texas" or "Missouri" Democrat variety (and advertised as such in campaigns), with interests distinct from that of mining-town electorates. Voters in the San Simon and Sulphur Springs Valley, desperate for better transportation, opposed by large margins the road bills that favored Bisbee and Douglas. Ranchers and farmers also railed against mine assessments as low as 2 percent of actual values, which left agricultural lands taxed disproportionately. These tax disputes caused rural voters to resent "absentee capitalists," a cause and rallying cry they shared with unionizing miners. In 1916, for example, Bowie's J. H. Jaque applauded labor Democrat George W. P. Hunt for a recent victory, which he achieved despite "a corrupt fund of nearly $400,000 . . . spent by the Copper Barons" to defeat him. Boosters like Jaque favored splitting the county north-south to escape copper-country dominance. Farmers sued the copper companies because of crop damage resulting from smelter smoke. Amid these resentments, Phelps Dodge and its allies tried fence mending, such as the following advertisement in the county farm bureau report. "Bisbee Welcomes the Farmer!" the Chamber of Commerce promised. "You've got what we want, and we've got what you want. Let's get together." Bisbee was "just a hospitable western mining camp that welcomes all strangers and tries to make them feel at home."[45] Yet the conservative homesteading families who organized the Sulphur Springs Sunday School Association probably did not agree that Brewery Gulch was homelike, friendly territory. In 1914, Arizona voters approved a long-shot Prohibition initiative. The triumph of teetotalers in "what romantic Western literature regards as the 'wettest' state in the Union," as a *New Republic* writer put it, shocked the nation. Mormons, new rural voters, and woman suffrage combined to put Prohibition over the top. The success of Prohibition, despite a well-funded opposition campaign by saloon owners in Bisbee and other mining camps, was the high mark of rural political power, and an early sign of women's ascendance.[46]

Yet beneath the real differences between rural values and mining-town mores were some developments that would have a deep impact on the Bisbee Deportation and how it would play out: a rising number of white voters, the symbolic and actual importance of middle-class white women, and—above all—the 1911 election of future Deportation leader Harry Wheeler as county sheriff. From 1903 to 1909, as an officer and then captain of the Arizona Rangers, Wheeler had been stationed all over Cochise County, where his pursuit of cattle rustlers endeared him to rural residents. So did his strong support of Prohibition and his opposition to gambling. Without the endorsement of Phelps Dodge (in 1908, Wheeler confided to a friend that "the Copper Queen does not want me and that settles it in this County"), Wheeler rode to his first victory on rural support. In 1916, the year of his third victory, Wheeler won forty-two out of fifty-two precincts.[47]

Despite the different economic positions of Cochise County's homesteaders and the men who would become Wheeler's deputies in 1917, the white homesteading rhetoric of loyalty, patriotism, and nationalism strongly resembled the assumptions of mining officials and their allies. Both defined "American" by invoking an optimistic eugenic scheme of European amalgamation, and both used Mexicans as the foil against which the American "race" could be defined. Both exalted the role of white women in achieving this racial success, and both accepted—even embraced—increasing opportunities for white women as a desirable side effect of casting them as a symbol of progress. Together, the growing if unacknowledged convergence of rural and urban racial ideas, along with the rising public stature of white women, would help to explain the explosive events that unfolded in Bisbee in the summer of 1917.

7

The Bisbee Deportation

While midwestern newcomers quietly transformed rural Cochise County, the entire world seemed to be exploding—across the border in Mexico, then in Europe, and closer to home in Arizona's mining camps and the new state capital of Phoenix. In 1910, Arizona was finally shaking off its frontier reputation to gain statehood, while just next door the Yaqui Wars and the Mexican Revolution were erupting from the long-smoldering resentment against Porfirio Díaz's repressive regime. In Cochise County, the revolution was no distant abstraction. First in 1911, then in 1914 and 1915, major battles ensued just over the Mexican border, in Naco and in Douglas' sister city of Agua Prieta. In 1914, World War I erupted in Europe. By the time the United States entered the war in April 1917, the demand for munitions metals was fueling the biggest surge the copper industry had ever seen.

Statehood, revolution, world war: together, these events energized radicals on union lines and in electoral politics, and left corporations scrambling to protect investments, capitalize on rising copper prices, and search for reliable workers. Simultaneously, while the old Western Federation of Miners foundered, the colorful and infamous Wobblies (International Workers of the World) launched strikes across the American West. Their success in a series of free-speech battles in Seattle and elsewhere renewed the organizing energy and publicity of the nation's most controversial union, even as their anti-war rhetoric infuriated most Americans.

Bisbee's IWW strike and the Deportation were consequences of all these national and global upheavals, but they were also the unique product of local events: the rise of union radicalism among both native-born and immigrant workers in Arizona, the intensity of the forces aligned to oppose it, and the ways that both miners and managers were rethinking the racial politics of the mining industry. Though much had changed, old divisions of race and old assumptions about the rights and responsibilities of white manhood still shaped how Bisbee residents understood the events that occurred in the summer of 1917.

Arizona Transformed

Although the WFM's 1907 strike in Bisbee had failed, union membership continued to grow across Arizona. At the long-awaited state constitutional convention in 1910, a savvy alliance between labor-friendly Democrats and members of an incipient Labor Party—many of them WFM veterans from Cochise County—managed to seize control of the proceedings and write one of the nation's most Progressive state constitutions. The final version included provisions for an eight-hour workday, child labor and employer liability laws, workmen's compensation, a state mine inspector, a corporation commission to regulate business, and the direct-democracy measures of voter initiative, referendum, and recall. One radical delegate from Douglas proclaimed the new constitution the "greatest and grandest document since the Declaration of Independence," while the appointed governor, Richard E. Sloan, called it the "worst affair ever turned out, and objectionable to all classes." Apparently it wasn't, since Arizona voters approved the new constitution in large numbers—by a margin of three to one in Cochise County. The constitution's most controversial provision, which allowed voters to recall judges, was excised when President W. H. Taft threatened to veto it, but was promptly added back in after statehood became official on Valentine's Day, 1912.[1]

The political ascendancy of union activists was steep and heady. By 1912, the most powerful politician in Arizona was Progressive Democrat George W. Hunt, who had brokered the alliance between leftists and centrists as president of the statehood convention. A colorful former miner, mayor of Globe, and territorial legislator, Hunt privately referred to the mining companies as the "Beast."[2] In 1912, he won the state's first governorship in a landslide victory for Democrats. That same year, insurgents from the Western Federation of Miners founded the Arizona State Federation of Labor, whose first convention was devoted to developing ballot initiatives for the 1914 election. Together the legislature and voters—who now included women—passed a raft of reforms, including prohibition of alcohol, anti-blacklist and anti-injunction laws to protect labor picketers, one of the nation's earliest pension laws for mothers (an early form of welfare), and a bill that barred state officials from amending or vetoing laws passed by popular vote. One historian has called the set of laws passed in 1914 the most complete labor agenda ever enacted.[3]

By that time Arizona's WFM, based in the copper community of Globe-Miami, was arguably the strongest in the nation. At the national level, the union was foundering under the weak leadership of its president, Charles Moyer, who in 1916 changed its name to the International Union of Mine, Mill, and Smelter Workers (IUMMSW, or Mine-Mill) hoping to reshape its faltering identity. In Arizona, though, the union remained on the rise. When Calumet & Arizona superintendent William Gohring complained to federal investigators in 1917 that "the companies here in Bisbee have less influence on recent laws—on Arizona laws, than any other element in the state," he made a good point. The copper companies continued to control the Arizona economy, many local governments, several newspapers, and a few members of the legislature, but they faced unprecedented opposition and a robust state government where weak federal appointees had once given them a free pass.[4]

Although white labor emerged triumphant in the statehood battles, Mexican Americans did not. The 1910 statehood convention led by labor champion Hunt brought to a head decades of racial tension over the battle to give Arizona and New Mexico separate statehood. Arizona's desire for separate statehood, as one South Carolina senator put it, was the "cry of a pure blooded white community against the domination of a mixed breed" New Mexico. Organized labor in Arizona had opposed joint statehood in 1906, when a referendum vote overwhelmingly rejected it. In 1910, New Mexico's statehood convention had several members of Mexican descent. Arizona's had none.[5]

Arizona's lily-white delegation quickly made its mark. One measure known as the Alien Labor Act—or, more popularly, the Eighty Percent Law—required that four out of every five employees in any workplace be native-born Americans or "qualified electors" (that is, naturalized citizens). Another proposal, by a Bisbee delegate, would have required 80 percent of workers "in underground or other hazardous occupations" to be English-speaking. Cochise County labor delegates argued that it was a safety measure, but the bill amounted to creating a statewide white man's camp. English and Irish immigrants—safely white—could speak English; most Mexicans and Slavs could not. Both proposals were defeated at the 1910 convention, but labor leaders got the first one (based on citizenship, not language) onto the statewide ballot in 1914. In Bisbee, Phelps Dodge ran ads warning that the law would mean "changing out" immigrant miners "for negroes from the Southern States." Another ad emphasized that the men likely to lose their jobs were "men with families, good neighbors, [who] own, or are paying for their own homes.... You know them, they are your personal friends." Here were all the qualities of the ideal "American" worker—traits that had motivated the construction of Warren—applied to immigrant workers. The arguments rang hollow to voters. The initiative received 64 percent of the statewide vote, and four out of five votes in Cochise County.[6]

Opposition to the law was immediate. The Italian ambassador and Great Britain's vice consul (whose citizens were not the main target but were technically subject to the law) both lodged official protests. Governor Hunt was unmoved. In Bisbee, Phelps Dodge funded a test case filed by an Austrian waiter at the English Kitchen restaurant against his bosses, William Truax Sr. and Jr., who had close ties to PD (one deportee argued that the company actually operated the English Kitchen). The suit alleged that the Truaxes, and by extension the state, had denied him equal protection by firing him to comply with the new law. The law clearly violated the Fourteenth Amendment, and was overturned by the Federal District Court in San Francisco. The U.S. Supreme Court affirmed the decision in early 1915.[7]

A year later, the English Kitchen inspired another landmark case when the Bisbee Waiters' Union went on strike against the restaurant. The Truaxes and their supporters challenged one of the nation's strongest anti-injunction laws, designed to protect union pickets from cease-and-desist orders. The case, *Truax v. Corrigan,* produced a key piece of the Deportation's organizational infrastructure. The Citizens' Protective League, whose leaders would organize and participate in the Deportation, was founded to fight the anti-injunction law. Members contributed to the Truax legal fund with checks "made as donations to the Citizens' Protective League," which assessed mining companies and supportive local merchants "proportionately to the amount of property they own." During the IWW strike in 1917, the Citizens' Protective League paid for "agents"—spies—in the unions, and both Truaxes participated in the Deportation.[8]

The Truax cases demonstrated the animus between white unionists and company leaders, but also the close connection between anti-foreigner and "pro-union" laws. The fact that both cases made it to the U.S. Supreme Court reflected the degree to which Arizona's labor laws were radical and untested. The court challenges mounted by Phelps Dodge revealed a deep commitment to nullifying the new laws, while the funding mechanism established by the Citizens' Protective League formalized the growing alliances between the copper companies and small-business owners. But different kinds of alliances were also in the works—namely, those between Mexican and Slavic workers and Anglo Wobbly organizers.

The Alien Labor Act was the brainchild of white unionists and a scourge to Phelps Dodge. But allegiances were changing. Many white unionists had finally decided that Mexicans were not the enemy. Bisbee lawyer William Cleary showed how an individual could veer from one side to the other. In a 1909 court trial, he served as defense attorney for the Flores Magón brothers of the Partido Liberal Mexicano—an early sign of his radical allegiances. In 1910, he sought election to the statehood convention, but was considered too radical. Yet in 1915, he joined the state's legal team to defend the Eighty Percent Law. Then, just two years later, he would be one of the Bisbee strike leaders—rounded up and deported alongside his immigrant comrades. Hunt and the white leadership of the Western Federation of Miners were changing, too, cheering on the struggle of Mexican and Mexican American miners who held strikes in the town of Ray and in Clifton-Morenci. By the time of the Deportation, it was the companies and their allies—not white unionists—who had become the most ardent defenders of the American camp ideology.[9]

The people responsible for this change in perspective were Mexican workers themselves. As infighting weakened the mostly Anglo WFM, Mexican
workers challenged the dual-wage system and everything it stood for. Strikes
in the Mexican camp of Clifton-Morenci in 1903 and 1907, and the Cananea
strike of 1906, had warned mine managers of the sleeping giant in their midst.
The Mexican workers they once dismissed as docile and passive had organized—despite indifference and opposition from white unions—to demand
higher wages.[10]

The Mexican Revolution sharpened conflict between Mexican workers
and American managers. Under Porfirio Díaz's regime, foreign investors had
acquired close to 75 percent of Mexican capital, while workers' wages stag-
nated and fell. In the northern border states of Chihuahua and Sonora, foreign mining and railroad companies fueled revolutionary fury. In "Mexican
camps" like Clifton north of the border, malingering, brief sit-downs, and
other minor work stoppages became so common that a new Spanglish term
arose to describe them: *strikitos*. But the sustained, organized campaigns
were even more impressive. Major strikes in the years 1913–1915 erupted at
the ASARCO smelter owned by New York's Guggenheim family in nearby
El Paso, Texas, then in the Arizona mining towns of Ray, Clifton, and Ajo.
All were organized and carried out by largely Mexican workforces. Although
the 1913 strike in El Paso failed, it was, according to one scholar, the first time
the WFM and the IWW fought "for the allegiance of Mexican and other Hispanic workers." Though few would have realized it, this was a harbinger of
the Wobblies' rise in Bisbee.[11]

The 1914 strike at the Guggenheim mine in Ray was a turning point in the
effort to enlist white union support for Mexican workers in Arizona. Workers
from Mexico and Spain, independent of any *mutualistas* or Anglo organizers, had founded their own organization, the Comité por Trabajadores en
General (General Workers' Committee), which later affiliated with the Western Federation of Miners. The Ray strikers demanded what was known as
the Miami scale (named for a camp near Globe), a sliding pay rate based on
white men's wages. Although the strikers in Ray did not secure Miami wages,
they declared victory and were "highly jubilant" after negotiating a sizable
pay hike of 60 cents per day.[12]

The Mexican revolution colored how both sides viewed the Ray strike.

Mine owners asked white men to cross the picket line by appealing to their "American 'patriotism' to 'defend'" Arizona against "Mexican revolutionarists," as the *Arizona Labor Journal* put it. But white workers refused to break ranks with the strikers. Although only about ten strikers were Anglo, the *Arizona Labor Journal* reported no "imminent danger of racial trouble." Strike leader Jose Miranda convinced the journal's editor that the mining companies were stirring up what he dubbed "racial patriotism," in order to spur Americans to become "strikebreakers or . . . to wield clubs and guns."[13]

Shortly after the strike in Ray, organizers there moved to Clifton-Morenci, which was dominated by Phelps Dodge. New York reporter Robert Bruère called this "the most important strike of 1915," because it "resulted in a measurable increase in wages and the embryonic beginnings of democratic control" for Mexican workers. Their grievances about dangerous conditions and unequal pay scales were little different from those made in earlier, failed strikes in 1903 and 1907, but the Mexican Revolution imbued the 1915 strike with rich symbolic importance. In 1917, the President's Mediation Commission, appointed by Woodrow Wilson, found that Mexicans in Clifton had gone on strike because of "their political beliefs and the ideas of what they term their conception of the social struggle." No doubt many workers there *were* influenced by revolution; but corporate officials, for their part, also played the revolution card in order to discount locally specific grievances. One PD official in Clifton complained that his Mexican employees had "assumed an attitude of independence amounting to arrogance which has made it exceedingly trying and exasperating to those in authority." He expressed frustrations typical of a manager during times of labor trouble, but his remarks are also inseparable from the racial hierarchy in which they were made: he saw (white) mining managers' "authority" over (Mexican) workers as natural. White managers claimed to foster white workers' "independence," but the same quality in Mexican workers was unwelcome, even offensive.[14]

Yet what infuriated mine managers impressed white unionists, who supported both the Ray and Clifton strikes. In August 1914, Governor Hunt, erstwhile champion of the Eighty Percent Law, visited Ray and called conditions there "feudalism." The next year, he gave a rousing speech to the Mexican strikers at Clifton, prompting Phelps Dodge to launch an unsuccessful recall bid. The AFL-affiliated *Arizona Labor Journal* supported the Mexican workers' strikes, which it characterized as living-wage campaigns. White unionists were finally blaming employers—not Mexican labor—for the low wages of the dual-wage system. The *Labor Journal* also began a regular Spanish-language feature, edited and translated by Clifton organizer Canuto Vargas. By 1917 Clifton mine managers were protesting Hunt's appointment as federal labor mediator not because of his support for the Eighty Percent Law, but because of his aid to "Mexicans and other foreigners in the labor troubles in this district in 1915."[15]

On the eve of the Bisbee strike, then, the relationship between white unionists and Mexican and other foreign miners was complicated. Hunt and Cleary were fighting for the Eighty Percent Law one moment, praising Mexican strikers in public speeches the next. At the heart of this apparent contradiction was the fight for an "American standard of living," laden with ideas about manliness and race. In 1915, Cleary gave a Fourth of July speech on the front steps of Bisbee's PD Mercantile, in which he claimed that the only way to Americanize immigrants was "to Americanize the industries." But he did not mean a racial purging. The way to make the United States a nation of "contented homes and patriotic citizens is to raise the wage from the boarding house standard of single men to the home standard of family men. Can a man support a family on $1.60 a day[?]"[16] Cleary grasped how wages, manliness, and racial difference intertwined.

In 1917, Arizona miners were at a crossroads. White unionists were lobbying for laws that would turn the entire state into a white man's camp, even as the national Mine-Mill was falling apart; and labor activism in Arizona was increasingly that of Mexican strikers, for whom white unionists were developing a grudging respect. Whether they all would join in common cause—and why—remained to be seen.

The Strikers

In Bisbee, too, these were years of excitement and uncertainty. The war in Europe turned the camp into a bona fide boomtown. Newcomers flooded in. Others left: long before the United States entered World War I, Bisbee was hosting parades to see off its Serbian citizens drafted to fight in the Balkan Wars. A recession hung over Bisbee in 1914 and early 1915, but every rifle cartridge sent to the European warfront used a half-ounce of copper, and prices soon rebounded. Copper leaped from 26.5 cents a pound in the summer of 1916 to 37 cents by March of the following year. The Bisbee area's population peaked at around 25,000, with the mines running twenty-four hours a day. Landlords subdivided Warren's bungalows, and in Lowell and Bisbee roominghouses were renting beds in shifts.[17]

Meanwhile, anti-union Bisbee was becoming a labor powerhouse. In 1906, the WFM had organized the camp in secret only to call an ineffective strike. Yet by 1914, the city boasted not just the miners' WFM Local 106, but also unions for bakers, bartenders, butchers, cooks and waiters, teamsters, paperhangers, carpenters, and general trades.[18]

Before becoming part of the IWW in 1917, the Bisbee Miners Union— whose leaders included some of the most radical alumni of the Arizona Labor Party—had severed financial ties with the national Mine-Mill headquarters and joined up with the insurgents in the Globe-Miami organization. But even these upstarts were unnerved by Bisbee's radicalism. Bisbee contained one of Arizona's few remaining Socialist Party locals, whose members had helped to elect Labor Democrat Rosa McKay to the state legislature in 1916. The Miami union men did not want to charter Bisbee's local, so IWW organizers seized the opportunity. By early February 1917, Grover H. Perry, the lead IWW organizer in Arizona, could report to national leader Bill Haywood that the president of the Arizona State Federation of Labor "wanted to know what so many Wobblies were doing in Arizona." In March, the Wobblies took over the Bisbee Miners Union, now part of Arizona's IWW Metal Mine Workers Union No. 800. By April, the IWW had more than six thousand members in Arizona, thanks especially to Bisbee.[19]

On June 26, 1917, six months after the Wobblies began organizing, the Bisbee Miners Union called a general strike against the copper mines. The Wobblies capitalized on miners' anger over blacklisting practices and skyrocketing inflation. Miners resented what they saw as Phelps Dodge's dictatorial manner, and the "ground rentals, water charges, power and light charges, insurance charges, Y.M.C.A. charges, library charges and dozens of other false infamous charges"—in addition to "war charges" (probably pressure to buy Liberty Bonds)—deducted from their paychecks. Wages were on a sliding scale, but lagged behind wartime inflation and soaring profits, even as PD Mercantile raised prices, "starving the men out who have families."[20]

The Wobblies talked revolution, but bread-and-butter issues brought in the rank-and-file. Three weeks before the strike, one IWW organizer reported that "we sure are a power" in Bisbee. Organizer A. S. Embree called a meeting the day before the strike "a success beyond our best expectations," with the crowd "pretty solid with us." Evidence suggests as much as 90 percent of the mining labor force went out on strike. Many participants declined to join the IWW, but supported its demands for pay increases, improved safety practices, and an end to the blacklisting of union members. The AFL's *Arizona Labor Journal* considered the Wobblies deplorable, but labor conditions in Bisbee even worse. According to state legislator Rosa McKay, Bisbee's strikers joined up "not because they were in sympathy with the I.W.W.'s," but because "the I.W.W.'s happened to present the demands . . . that the men were deserving of." Critics of the IWW (and unions in general) accused organizers of manipulating local workers; but by using the Wobblies' strike to address their own concerns, the miners were, in turn, using the IWW.[21]

Changes in Bisbee's workforce also helped the Wobblies. Unskilled laborers were rapidly replacing experienced miners. By 1917, Bisbee had unprecedented numbers of Slavic, Finnish, and Mexican workers—the groups most likely to support unions and strikes. In the 1907 strike, Slavs had brought the demands to the mining companies and had represented the bulk of the WFM membership. In 1917 eastern Europeans represented one in four (207) of the men recorded in the deportee camp. Finns—more than 100 of them were deported—also played an outsized role. Finn Hall became an unofficial IWW headquarters, where the union held public meetings. The Wobblies welcomed people of all skills, races, and sexes, and their wide-ranging political and social critiques—as well as their concrete demands—appealed to more than just the miners themselves. "Some of the women were as bad or worse than the men," one deputy sheriff complained. During the strike, "the Finnish women openly assaulted men in Lowell on their way to work, while their men cheered them on."[22]

Other women also joined the picket lines alongside the men. Striker Robert Noble mentioned to his wife that some women were picketing, so she "went with him, and . . . stood there with the boys." Finding women on picket lines irked Sheriff Harry Wheeler, but it was a logical outcome of the disparity between the companies' pro-family rhetoric and the less rosy reality.

Women imbibed the same talk of family wages and the American standard of living that the men did. If a miner's wage was meant to support a family, the family had a right to fight for better wages.[23]

If women picketers shocked some people, even more unsettling was the massive turnout of Mexican militants in the white man's camp. By the summer of 1917, Mexicans made up a significant portion of Bisbee's population and workforce. The Copper Queen Mine had about three hundred Mexican workers, second in number only to "Americans," and hundreds of Mexican immigrants had recently come to town looking for work, though how many were on payrolls is unclear.[24] Several witnesses claimed that at least half of the men on strike were Mexican.[25] Mexicans constituted about 13 percent of Bisbee's mining labor force but more than a quarter of the deportees—and probably more.[26] Partly, as we shall see, this was because Mexicans were targeted in the roundup. Still, one mining manager echoed a common sentiment when he said that Mexicans, alone among the workingmen, quit "practically in a body at the first announcement of the strike." At one mine, 300 out of 350 Mexican workers appeared on the picket line the first day of the strike.[27] In 1919, Sheriff Wheeler recalled seeing Mexican strikers fill two lines stretching "probably four or five hundred yards in length . . . marching up to I.W.W. headquarters" each day. By that time, Wheeler had reason to exaggerate the extent of Mexican participation, but strike statistics suggest his comment had some basis in reality.[28]

Mexican strikers were rejecting the unequal social compact of the white man's camp by demanding a family wage and an American standard of living. One strike demand proposed to more than double the wages of *all* surface laborers, regardless of race, from $2.50 to $5.50 per day, while raising the wages of underground (white) miners from $5.75 to $6.00—an increase of less than 5 percent. Had both these demands been met, the wages of surface laborers would have been within fifty cents of what underground white workers earned. If surface workers earned $5.50 per day and underground workers earned $6.00, the dual-wage labor system would effectively have ceased to exist.[29]

This was the strike's most radical demand, because it threatened to topple Bisbee's racial hierarchy. Miles Merrill, a miner who led the Workman's Loyalty League, protested "the inconsistency of that wage scale. . . . Miners would much prefer to work on top for five and a half than underground for six [dollars]. I would prefer to."[30] The "inconsistency" was that Mexican and American jobs would pay nearly the same. Merrill had a point. Underground jobs were more dangerous, and, until recently, more skilled. But with that danger came prestige and manly credentials. Raising the wages of surface workers to near those of underground miners might entice men other than Mexicans to these jobs. It might, then, destroy racially defined job categories, along with the discriminatory wage scales: a two-pronged attack on the dual-wage system. If whites worked surface jobs that paid almost as much as underground work, there would be no reason to keep Mexicans from working underground. Although underground work was not an explicit demand of Mexican workers in 1917, proposing such high wages for surface work hinted at a wholesale reordering of mining's race-based labor system.

Anglo IWW leaders from headquarters concocted this extraordinary wage demand to entice Mexican workers to their cause, not because they felt a genuine commitment to it. Organizer A. S. Embree saw Mexican workers as "a sure bet, as we are demanding a minimum of $5.50 for all topmen." But this demand was never a main priority. Anglo strike leaders intended the Bisbee strike to show support for other strikes by the Wobblies, especially in the copper mines of Butte, Montana. One IWW spokesperson wrote privately, "This is a solidarity strike and we must concentrate on that phase of it. The demands made are wholly secondary." Anglo leaders had a national political agenda, while Mexican miners and their organizers pursued locally specific demands with broad consequences. The spiraling demands of strike leaders made their cause look less and less reasonable. Organizer Grover Perry's call for a six-hour day during the wartime boom was, from the standpoint of almost everyone except professed labor radicals, absurd.[31]

Despite differences with Anglo leaders, Mexican workers had good reason to join the Wobblies. The IWW was the first American union to take a genuine interest in Bisbee's Mexican workers, and it hired Bisbee's first Mexican organizers, Benito García and Joseph Robles. Rosendo F. Doramé—a cofounder of the Phoenix IWW—also organized in town. Sheriff Wheeler liked to believe that Mexicans joined the Wobblies because the union handed out daily rations, but this was about more than a breadline. While some strikers—Mexican, Slavic, or Anglo—were surely ignorant of the finer points of the Wobblies' doctrine, many knew about the connections between the IWW and the Partido Liberal Mexicano, the once-liberal but now anarcho-syndicalist organization headed by the Flores Magón brothers. One of the Partido Liberal's largest cells, with three hundred members, was in Douglas. In 1907, its leader was arrested by the Arizona Rangers for planning an attack on Cananea. Many Bisbee miners had come from Cananea, where the Partido Liberal had supported the 1906 strike, and where, more recently, Pancho Villa's followers had ousted American citizens. The Partido Liberal had played an important role in Clifton-Morenci's recent strikes. In Bisbee, the Sheriff's Department used the terms "Magonistas" and "Mexican IWW" synonymously, and the leader of this "Mexican IWW" was also a representative for the Partido Liberal's newspaper. In other words, Bisbee's Mexican workers, far from being the Wobblies' dupes, knew exactly what they were doing. "We ran you out of Cananea and we will run you out of here," one deputy claimed a Wobbly told him.[32]

By going on strike, Mexican workers took the mantle of manhood—and with it the respect—long denied to them in Bisbee. Federal and state investigators ignored Mexican workers when they collected testimony in Bisbee. The result is a dearth of sources from the Mexican point of view in Bisbee, a reflection of the power of the white-man's-camp ideology to render part of its population invisible. But the views of Mexican workers are apparent in statements gleaned from Clifton (where Mexican workers represented such an overwhelming majority that investigators could not disregard them). When reporter Robert Bruère asked Mexican miners in Clifton why they were on strike, "they said it was for an American standard of living" and for more of a say in improving working conditions. Mediation Commission member Felix Frankfurter described the strikes as "a fight for the status of free manhood" by Mexicans and Slavs who "feel they were not treated as men." One Mexican striker in Clifton characterized their effort as a freedom struggle and solidarity campaign. Critics "were sure that the Mexican element and the Spaniards and Italians would not hold together. [But] the times in which the master class were imposing on us are past and gone. . . . The times of slavery are gone forever."[33]

As this Clifton striker recognized, perhaps the most revolutionary aspect of the Bisbee strike was its ability to subvert established "racial" truths. One white union carpenter observed that "the much vaunted superiority of the so-called Anglo-Saxon fades into a myth" in the face of the dedicated resolve of Mexican strikers, who "lived on less than half of what the average [white] striker would consent to remain loyal on."[34] Surviving on a "Mexican standard of living" had been outstanding training for a war between capital and labor. Now, by claiming their manhood and demanding the American standard of living, Mexican strikers were gutting the most basic ideological principles of the white man's camp. Outsiders like Bruère and Frankfurter recognized this, but most local Anglos could not. For white workers and managers to admit the equal manhood of Mexican workers would be to topple the teetering racial hierarchy of the white man's camp.

And So It Began

Mexicans were bad enough; Wobblies, even worse. During the summer of 1917, the IWW and its opponents clashed in a series of encounters across the American West and Great Plains. They were not alone on the nation's picket lines: that year saw more than 4,500 work stoppages in the United States, at least twenty in Arizona, including another IWW strike in Globe. But in the patriotic fervor of World War I, the Wobblies in particular infuriated many Americans. The union's constitution began, "The working class and the employing class have nothing in common," and the Wobblies were among the nation's most vocal anti-war activists. The federal Espionage Act, which made most anti-war activities illegal, was passed into law just days before the Bisbee strike began. The law aimed squarely at the IWW. By September 1917, hundreds of Wobblies, including Bill Haywood, would be arrested. Some towns tarred and feathered suspected Wobblies. In Jerome, Arizona, where Walter Douglas' brother James owned a mine, vigilantes deported a few dozen striking workers just two days before the Bisbee purge. Two weeks afterward, IWW organizer Frank Little, who had been in Globe during the Arizona strikes, was lynched in Butte, Montana.[35]

Nowhere, however, did anti-IWW responses reach the precision and scale of those in Bisbee. In the hours leading up to July 12, county sheriff Harry Wheeler began appointing his 2,200 temporary deputies in Bisbee and Douglas. Why? The strike, claimed the *New Republic,* had ignited "a flame

20. Loading the deportees, July 12, 1917. Note the little girl in the foreground, standing behind a gunman. Arizona State Library, Archives and Public Records, History and Archives Division, Phoenix, 97–0629.

of terror . . . from Bisbee throughout the West."[36] But had it? Just days before the roundup, strike leader A. S. Embree reported "no disorder and no boot leg booze" among his men. He was sure the companies "can find no excuse to use violence." A more credible observer, a deputy U.S. marshal, called it "the most peaceful, orderly strike I ever saw." The President's Mediation Commission concluded that strike "conditions in Bisbee were, in fact, peaceful and free from . . . disorder or violence."[37]

Even so, on the morning of July 12, mining officials silenced all outgoing phone calls and telegrams, shut down the train station, and set up a command station at the YMCA. At dawn, Sheriff Wheeler climbed into an open-top Ford which he'd borrowed from St. Patrick's Father Mandin and which had been mounted with a machine gun. Deputies, guns in hand, began their sweep of the district. From upper Tombstone Canyon to Lowell and Tintown, deputies broke down doors and forced men from their homes and rooming houses, their bedrooms and their workplaces. Men were collected under armed guard in front of the downtown post office, then marched through town at gunpoint, past the mines to the Warren baseball field, where neighbors and kin gathered and gawked.[38]

Among those who watched—and protested—were hundreds of women. When the roundup began, women reacted quickly. The wealthier got phone calls from friends, but in poor neighborhoods, especially Mexican ones, women banged on doors or shouted warnings to neighbors. Mrs. Richard Denning "ran and got my husband's six-shooter and put it in a sack and dressed the baby," then sprinted down the hill to her friend Mrs. Campbell, who taunted an armed deputy, "You are not man enough to take my husband." A few women managed to stop the gunmen. Bridget Gerity used her homeownership as her trump card. "I own my house," she explained, "and I ordered them [the deputies] . . . away from my house; I made them get away. They didn't get him [her husband]." When three gunmen came to get Evaristo Martínez, his daughter Gloria remembers that her mother "put her hand against the screen door and said, 'You cannot come in.' The men left."[39]

Sheriff Wheeler's front-page announcement in the *Bisbee Daily Review* telling women and children to stay off the streets went unheeded. When the gunmen told Mrs. Myrtle Reep, "No women allowed down town today," she announced, "I am going anyway." Susie Rice, an unmarried clerk at a downtown department store, hissed at a deputy who took her arm, "Kindly keep your dirty hand off me." When she ran into her armbanded boss, she quit on the spot: "I refused to work for a gunman." At the ballfield, one of the deputies announced, "You ladies keep still or we will have to arrest you," and Rice replied, "Yes, you try it. . . . The Constitution allows free speech and I intend to say what I want to."[40]

And then there is Anna Payne, a sixty-year-old Colorado native with an amputated leg, whose two sons were initially rounded up. Hobbling down to the ballfield, she "walked straight to the fence" and asked for her sons. When an officer grabbed her arm, she warned him, "Be careful there, I got to have this hand to carry the crutch with." She told the deputy that his mother should be ashamed of him, but he shoved her into the pen with the men.

Anna Payne nearly got deported. "I stirred up quite a time," she recalled.

21. Anna Payne, July 12, 1917. She and her sons were nearly deported. Courtesy of the Bisbee Mining and Historical Museum, Brophy Collection, 74.115.89A.

"I got on the platform and made them a speech." When she spied an arm-banded Dr. Nelson Bledsoe, a C&A company doctor known for using physical exams to exclude union members, she "told him off." Then she warned Sheriff Wheeler, "I think you have fired your last shot. . . . You are a dirty coward." The sheriff made no reply. When she went to her boys, a deputy tried to stop her. "I pulled back my fist and says, 'Let me by or I will just smack you in the jaw, I don't care how big you are.'" At that, they let her sons go, and the Payne family went home. Some reports initially claimed that three

Francisco.M.Barba
worked for the Copper Queen
15 years in whose service
he lost his arm.

Deported Jul
12.1917

22. Francisco Barba, deportee, Columbus, New Mexico, August 1917. Hunt Collection, Arizona State Library, Archives and Public Records, History and Archives Division, Phoenix, 01 3099.

women were deported. In reality, when the boxcars came, Sheriff Wheeler released the women. No doubt he realized what a political debacle it would have been to deport women.[41]

The union membership in Bisbee included a few women, mostly telephone operators and theater workers. There is no evidence that women formed an auxiliary to the miners' union in Bisbee, as their peers did in Globe and Miami, but their support was clear. One group of women shouted to the Wobblies, "Hurrah for you fellows!" Anna Payne, a lifelong union supporter, told the deputy guarding her sons, "We belong to the working class"—a sentiment echoed by several other women.[42]

Anna Payne and her sons were lucky to get out. The others were piled onto twenty-three boxcars owned by PD's El Paso & Southwestern Railroad and shipped into open desert 180 miles across state lines to Hermanas, New Mexico. Reports differed on the adequacy of food and water for the ride, but there is no question that conditions were unpleasant and dangerous in those freightcars packed with men at the height of summer. When they got to New Mexico, the men were relocated to the border town of Columbus, where the U.S. Army set them up in a "bull pen" last used by Mormon refugees, and by Chinese camp staff during General John J. Pershing's futile Punitive Expedition in search of Pancho Villa after Villa's raid on the town a year earlier. Some deportees, guarded by the African American members of the 24th Infantry, stayed in New Mexico for three months.[43]

The Sheriff and His Deputies

Even by the standards of World War I, a time of grave assaults on civil liberties, the Bisbee Deportation stands out. How could one-fifth of a small city's adult males essentially kidnap a similar number of their neighbors and run them out of town? To understand why the Deportation happened the way it did requires an understanding of how its participants and organizers—especially Harry Wheeler—thought about it and justified it. As soon as the trains pulled away from Warren, participants and observers began offering explanations: they have blamed nativism, class conflict, the tension between wartime vigilance and vigilantism, race war, even a violent attempt to preserve domestic tranquillity (in both senses of "domestic": national and familial). All of these interpretations have abundant evidence to support them; they are all, in important ways, true.[44] But no one reason can explain an event that involved thousands of people and their individual perspectives. On the border—and everywhere—ideas about nationality, race, class conflict, family life, sexual difference, even where and how people live, were deeply intertwined. Men and women on both sides of the fight invoked all of these factors as justifications. But as they groped for rationales, they referred especially to manliness and proper womanhood, because these concepts were a convenient and deeply personal way to talk about a muddy amalgam of other ideas. Invoking manhood or womanhood allowed people to understand their complex motives as something reflexive and natural.[45]

Paternalism, privilege, and self-interest shaped the manly ideals of mining men like John Greenway and Walter Douglas. C&A general manager John ("Jack") Greenway—known as Captain Greenway—was a former Yale baseball star who served as a Rough Rider in Cuba, where he became assistant and protégé to Theodore Roosevelt (who staunchly supported the Deportation). Like his mentor, Greenway sculpted his romantic past into a larger-than-life reputation as a "big fine man of the highest ideals and impulses," who was "part and parcel of the West." As reporter Robert Bruère put it, "The mine managers of to-day, though many of them were born in the East and bred at Columbia and Harvard and Yale, claim direct spiritual descent from the early prospectors to whom the treachery of the Apaches and the hellbent luck of Roaring Camp and Brewery Gulch gave zest to the hunt for treasure." Greenway was a Southerner, born in Alabama, whose charisma combined southern gentility, eastern elitism, and western bonhomie. He took his gambling risks at both the stock exchange and the faro table; he could sip champagne or down a tumbler of whiskey. In 1911, he had rescued "American ladies" and children from Cananea, where managers feared they were threatened by Mexican insurrectionaries.[46]

The motives of Bisbee's managers are the easiest to understand. Greenway defended the Deportation as an action against "alien enemies" engaged in a nationwide conspiracy. Phelps Dodge managers maintained that the IWW could not represent "loyal American citizens," and Lemuel Shattuck—considered the mine manager who was most sympathetic to labor—called the strikers "the floating population of the district." But all of these men had a financial interest in ending the strike, viewed Bisbee as their private fiefdom, and had made it clear they were willing to eliminate Wobblies and "alien enemies" at almost any cost. Walter Douglas (who now ran the Phelps Dodge Corporation and arrived by private train car in Bisbee on the eve of the Deportation) was elected president of the American Mining Congress in 1916 as a staunch anti-unionist who was especially opposed to the IWW. He had famously said about unions, "We will not compromise with rattle-snakes."[47] Felix Frankfurter, the lawyer for the President's Mediation Commission, was unimpressed: "These old bags, who have fought labor, and unions as poison for decades, now wrap themselves in the flag and are confirmed in their biases. . . . Gee, but it's awful." These men "control a quarry and forget it's also a community." Yet Frankfurter sensed moral complexity in the managers, too, who were "otherwise perfectly nice, decent people." Greenway was "doubtless a good man in all relations of life in which passion didn't supplant his fairness and reason." This frightening dichotomy, Frankfurter reflected years later, "left a deep impression on me."[48]

The motif of good men doing bad things reached its fullest expression in the story of Sheriff Harry Wheeler, whose motivations on July 12 are more obscure than that of the mining magnates, and thus more interesting. "Perhaps the best known man in Cochise County," Wheeler cultivated the persona of the homespun, straight-shooting country lawman, and with it a reputation for fairness. Though shorter than five-foot-seven (some said five-foot-four) and slightly built, Wheeler had authentic western manly credentials. The son of a West Point graduate, Wheeler was born in Florida but raised at western army forts. After serving in the U.S. Cavalry in the Spanish American War years (though not, as some people claimed, in Cuba), Wheeler moved to Willcox and then to Tombstone, before joining the Arizona Rangers in 1903. He served as their captain from 1907 until they disbanded, in 1909. In 1917, at age forty-one, married (though divorced shortly after the Deportation) and still mourning the death of his only son two years earlier, Wheeler was an upright military man—stern, teetotaling, moralistic. A memo he wrote to his men while captain of the Rangers summed up his personal philosophy: "Obedience constitutes discipline; without discipline, we would lack system, without system we would have chaos." He did not mean military decorum, imposed from without, but was referring to "a higher discipline; that which a man's honor enforces upon himself. 'To obey is honorable. To disobey, dishonorable, in this Organization.'" A previous sheriff called him "a man of splended judgement, cool—skillful, daring, and the right man in the right place at all times."[49]

Critics and defenders alike described the sheriff as moral, honest, and empathetic. He knew men were made, not born. He once admitted that he "fought down some personal habits, but it took me a long time . . . before I gained the mastery over myself." Some Rangers found their captain inflexible and condescending (twenty-six resigned during his tenure), but he could also be forgiving. He "grieved" after dismissing an officer whom he had found drunk. Praising the fallen man's "exceedingly good character and most lovable traits," he decided to reinstate him.[50]

Living in Phelps Dodge's citadel had not cowed Wheeler. One member of the Medigovich family recalled that Wheeler was known around the county as "a man of character *but highly independent.*" The Rangers' hands-off approach to the 1907 Bisbee strike had earned Wheeler a reputation not as a tool of the mining companies, but as a fair-minded arbiter who insisted that "all parties should receive justice and protection while within their rights." No less than Mother Jones had attested to Wheeler's good character, calling him "a pretty fine fellow" after she met him in 1907. Thanks to his reputation for fairness, Wheeler was not beloved by the mining establishment. When Democrats and Republicans from across the county first asked him to run for sheriff, "the Copper outfit shut their foot down on the proposition," and his supporters turned "still as mice."[51] Nevertheless, Wheeler's support from farmers, ranchers, and the rank-and-file of Bisbee won him several county elections and immense popularity.

It is fair to say, then, that the nature of Wheeler's participation on July 12 was not a foregone conclusion. Before the roundup, a planning meeting of "business and professional men" (perhaps the Citizens' Protective League) discussed "the importance of Wheeler's decision [to participate], a decision definitely in the balance," according to George Medigovich. "I was sure Harry would make it on his own," and with "aloofness from persuasion." Medigovich was "rather surprised" when he saw Wheeler sitting next to a mounted machine gun in an open car on the morning of the Deportation. Perhaps Walter Douglas was surprised, too. Just two weeks before the Deportation, he announced that "the sheriff has completely lost his nerve." Clearly, something had changed.[52]

One biographer claims that Wheeler had an unexplained twelve thousand dollars in a New York bank account, a lot of money—even a suspicious amount—for a rural sheriff. Yet everything about Wheeler argues against its being a bribe. After meeting with Wheeler for hours, the members of the Mediation Commission dismissed veiled allegations by other witnesses that Wheeler had been paid off by the mining companies. They condemned the sheriff's actions, even as they marveled at his decision to stick by his guns in the face of intense criticism and potential indictments. One commissioner, an AFL leader from Illinois, echoed the sentiments of several others when he admitted, "I don't like to disagree with a man that I believe is absolutely honest and clean and courageous." U.S. secretary of labor William Wilson called Wheeler immune "to any corrupt influence of any kind of character whatever."[53]

Wheeler was not a company man, nor did he appear to be crooked. So why cooperate with the mining officials? William Beeman, an organizer with the Workingmen's Loyalty League, maintained that it had taken powerful inducement. When the strike broke out, mining-company managers allegedly asked Wheeler if they could deputize men to protect company property from trespass. He refused. Beeman claimed that John Greenway and C&A head watchman George Willcox, another former Rough Rider, pulled Wheeler aside and somehow convinced him (by what means, we'll never know) that the Germans were financing the strike, and that the union's only goal was to tie up the copper industry, not to improve workers' conditions. According to Beeman, Wheeler told him less than two hours later that "had they not convinced him that there was German influence behind the strike he would have died rather than deputize men to take sides against labor."[54]

Wheeler may have worked on the mining companies' behalf, but he fully believed that he did so for his own reasons and on his own terms, and so did the Mediation Commission. The sheriff believed that maintaining wartime industrial production was a patriotic responsibility, and he stuck to this theme in grueling investigative interviews and hearings. In the weeks leading up to the Deportation, he published newspaper announcements around the county calling for "every able-bodied loyal American in Cochise County to assist me." In Wheeler's mind, he was protecting national interests, not material ones. He claimed to have no knowledge that some deputies had asked potential deportees whether they were "at work or not" as the litmus test for being deported. A week after the Deportation, the sheriff invited anyone "caught up in the roundup by mistake to return. . . . We will welcome those who have homes and families here and are not agitators but we will not let the agitators and 'wobblies' come back. . . . We intend to make this an American camp where American working men may enjoy life, liberty and the pursuit of happiness unmolested by any alien enemies of whatever breed."[55]

Sheriff Wheeler even insisted, "This is no labor disturbance. We are sure of that." That he could make the extraordinary statement that a strike was not about labor indicated how thoroughly the class system was also about race and nation. Wheeler believed that anyone striking against a war industry was potentially treasonous. He defined his Americanism against the actions of "foreigners," because "appeals of patriotism do not move them, nor do appeals to reason."[56]

The Mexican Revolution weighed on Wheeler even more than the war in Europe. In 1914, the sheriff interrupted his own re-election campaign to patrol the U.S. side of Naco during battles that sent stray gunfire across the line, and he threatened to create an international incident by bringing five hundred men across the U.S.-Mexico line to halt the fighting. In 1916, tensions in Douglas' Sonoran twin city of Agua Prieta prompted Wheeler to ask the U.S. government to impose martial law along the border, but the request was denied. When Wheeler defended his role in the Deportation, he repeatedly referenced "border troubles" in general and the Battle of Naco, Sonora, in particular as precipitants. The sheriff was furious at Woodrow Wilson's failure to protect the border. By the time of the Deportation, Wheeler felt he was on his own.[57]

To Wheeler and many others, the Bisbee strike was the work of pro-German provocateurs who had allied with the Mexicans in the aftermath of the Zimmermann telegram. In the intercepted missive, the Germans had promised to return Arizona, New Mexico, and Texas to Mexico, if Mexico would attack the United States. The telegram, sent just five months before the Bisbee strike, confirmed Harry Wheeler's worst suspicions. Wheeler believed German agents had convinced Pancho Villa's followers to attack U.S. copper mines. After the Deportation, he told members of the President's Mediation Commission that they would have done what he did, had any of them "been a sheriff on this border for six or seven years, and a captain of the Rangers years before it[,] and had seen the things which occurred on the border as I have seen them." Living on the border, he explained, "put a new complexion on" the strike. His choice of the term "complexion" unconsciously captured the racial subtext of the labor dispute.[58]

And what of his "deputies," the men sworn in by Sheriff Wheeler in the days leading up to July 12? Participants understood their own motives—a blend of racial fear, job protection, and patriotism—as part of the manly protection of white women and children. The main organizations that provided deputies, the Citizens' Protective League and the Workingmen's Loyalty League, linked anti-labor and anti-immigration concerns. The Protective League had been created to combat the anti-injunction law in 1915, but appears not to have gone public until 1916, when the *Tombstone Prospector* reported that it was created to protect against "agitators of the type" involved in the recent strikes in Clifton-Morenci.[59] Its membership, according to the Warren District Trades Assembly, was "composed largely of men desirous of company favor, receiving their goods over the company railroad, and tied to the company banks." Here was the local bourgeoisie who had allied with mining managers during the debates over the city's incorporation fifteen years earlier. The Workingmen's Loyalty League, meanwhile, was a group of "loyal workers," in the words of John Greenway, whose numbers grew from eight hundred to two thousand in the days leading up to the Deportation. Its founder was mine foreman Miles Merrill, who used it to launch a nationwide Loyalty League movement.[60]

But the league was not created from scratch. According to Wheeler, it was "the remnants of an old organization that I helped to organize here long ago. . . . We formed a military organization here and in Douglas, and in all the little towns in this County for the purpose of resisting an invasion from Mexico, which was threatening." Membership had changed over time, but "the captains were practically the same captains . . . [and] I had organized them in a semi-military manner."[61] By 1917, though, the Loyalty League represented "the voice of the mining companies," according to the Warren District Trades Assembly Committee. At least one man claimed that the mining companies themselves had set up the Loyalty League. But Merrill backed up Wheeler's statement, saying that the league dated to early 1915. "At the time of the border trouble . . . a good many men had sent out for Krug-Jorgensen rifles, and we got them cheap, and we got some ammunition." The "talk" was that Mexicans might raid Bisbee, and "that the people should go to their respective places and guard the women and children or the residence, and when this affair came up we done about the same thing." He told the President's Mediation Commission, "You eastern people haven't had much experience with Mexicans, but I know for a good while after the Mexican trouble we figured they might do anything, and we took some precautionary measures against the Villa men, as we provided for anything that might happen."[62] The Loyalty League was a vigilante answer to the demise of Wheeler's old organization, the Arizona Rangers, which had been disbanded in 1909 by pro-labor legislators who saw it as a tool of the mining companies.

Evidence contradicted Merrill and Wheeler's belief that Mexican revolutionary activity was imminent. Deputy Sheriff Bert Watkins told the federal mediators that Bisbee had suffered no "tensions" during the "Mexican troubles" two years previous. A year before the Deportation, Sheriff Wheeler's own informant in Tintown had reported, "There does not seem to be any plotting and organizing going on among" Mexicans in Bisbee. If anything, "they are somewhat timid for fear that they might be molested by the Americans, [they] say that they could not make a living or stay in Mexico and that all they want is to be protected with their families here." The informant found perhaps twenty men at a meeting of Magonistas—the "Mexican IWW"—but found no "plots" against the government being organized. "In general," he concluded, "things seem to be very satisfactory among the Mexicans in the District just at this time." These reports went straight to Sheriff Wheeler. Yet by the summer of 1917, Harry Wheeler was claiming that "all Mexicans hate Americans," and his every action flowed from this premise.[63]

For Wheeler, border violence counteracted any reassurances his informant's reports from Tintown might have offered. The Naco violence alone had injured or killed more than forty American spectators and peacekeeping soldiers from Fort Huachuca. In 1916, Pancho Villa's attack on Columbus, New Mexico, must have rightfully alarmed all border sheriffs. Wheeler heard rumors that Mexicans in Tintown had hidden weapons in Bisbee and the Ajo Mountains, and he had been in the Arizona Rangers when they helped to arrest Magonistas in Douglas several years earlier. In June 1917, C&A director Chester Congdon wrote to Jack Greenway, "There is no telling what sort of a rumpus the Mexicans may kick up in case this war should last any length of time, and it will take somebody along the border with lots of ability in organization who has the confidence of the people of the state to take the lead in any measures which may be necessary."[64] Wheeler was the man.

To men like Wheeler and Congdon, Mexicans were now dangerous revolutionaries, not childlike innocents. Neither stereotype, however, resembled the ideal resident of the white man's camp—the independent, loyal, manly, family-supporting American worker. In Sheriff Wheeler's view, Mexicans remained docile; they had simply switched their allegiance from "American" foremen to foreign provocateurs. Mexican strikers were dangerous because now they had fallen under the sway of "Prussians." Even sympathizers reified this passive stereotype of Mexicans. Mining officials warned Robert Bruère that Clifton and Morenci were "unsafe" because of the "terrible Mexicans." On the contrary, the muckraking journalist reported, with apparent disappointment, that he found them to be "the most docile people imaginable."[65]

Wheeler saw it differently, of course, and his sense of manly duty was inseparable from his decision to take a leadership role in the event. "I don't shirk anything," he told investigators. "If I have done wrong, I am willing to suffer for it. I am not the kind of man who will whimper, and I am not running away from it." He wanted to protect Bisbee's most precious social boundaries—those that separated working-class Mexican men from "white women." He worried for weeks, he said, about "foreigners" bothering "women."[66]

When Mexican strikers approached a group of white female laundry workers to join the union, this was the last straw. The IWW was famous for organizing women, but in Wheeler's words, the women at the laundry "were so terrorized by visitations of a committee of Mexicans . . . that the women one day left in a body in abject terror. Think of white women in an American town so terrorized by foreigners that they were compelled to quit work in terror of their lives."[67] Bisbee, the white man's camp, was also supposed to be an "American town," and that meant racialized patriotism, brave manliness, and white women's protection—from threats real or imagined.

Although the incident at the laundry was fairly minor, it came up again and again when vigilantes defended their actions. To their mind, the situation was bad enough when Mexican workers demanded nearly the same wages as Anglo men in Anglo jobs. But when Mexican strikers approached white women to join their union, to make common cause with them, the strikers were also challenging relations between men and women that built on racial fears. In a world where class differences were built on race, and where racial boundaries were built on rules about manliness and proper femininity, to have single white women joining a mixed-race miners' union was literally unthinkable. Sheriff Wheeler could not conceive of it as anything except a potentially violent threat to white womanhood, indeed to "pure Americanism itself."[68]

Americanism was about race, of course, perhaps just as much as it was about nationality. On July 12, 1917, almost all of the identifiable deputies were Anglo-American, British, or Canadian. Two members of the Medigovich clan also wore guns that day. There is even evidence that three people of Mexican descent served as deputies. But many Bisbee residents, Wheeler included, saw the conflict in racial terms and considered all Mexicans "the enemy." Wheeler and the deputies targeted Mexicans as a group, regardless of whether they were on strike. "It is hard for an American to tell the faces among the Mexicans," one deputy explained. As a result, according to one source, "innocent suffered alike with guilty." Witnesses reported that Mexican men were singled out for rough treatment. When U.S. secretary of labor William Wilson asked Wheeler how he had ascertained which residents of Mexican descent were revolutionaries, or at least "alien," Wheeler responded, "They were practically all aliens, Mr. Wilson." The secretary pressed on, "What steps were taken to take charge of those Mexicans" who were Villistas? Wheeler's response was, "How could you separate one Mexican from another?" When Secretary Wilson continued to needle him, he added, "I would repeat the operation any time I find my own people endangered by a mob composed of eighty per cent aliens and enemies of my Government."[69]

Aftermath

Wheeler's numbers were close to the mark. About 90 percent of the deportees were born outside the United States. They claimed thirty-four nationalities, but fully half of those deported were either Mexican or eastern European, the men who had always been at the margins of the white man's camp. Only a quarter of those whose citizenship can be identified were American citizens. By removing radical activists, most of them immigrants, "white" Bisbee decisively declared who enjoyed real citizenship in the white man's camp, and who did not.[70]

Bisbee's female citizens played prominent roles in the events of July 12, and in the aftermath as well. The Deportation's champions relied on a vision of patriotic white women as passive beneficiaries of men's protection and decisions. In October, Felix Frankfurter asked mining engineer J. C. Ryan whether women had attended a recent mass meeting. Ryan replied, "No, the women . . . would [not] be at a meeting held by men." But "women vote in Arizona," Frankfurter protested. "They don't vote on questions of this kind," Ryan retorted. "They have sense."[71]

Sense, yes, but not necessarily the kind he meant. White women in Bisbee were frankly more notable for their power than for their deference. A week before the Deportation, some women had met at the YWCA to create a Women's Loyalty League. After the Deportation, Thomas Campbell, a Republican temporarily in the governor's seat while George Hunt challenged election results (successfully, as it would turn out), came to Bisbee, where he was met at the Copper Queen Hotel by a crush of four hundred women on both sides of the issue. In early August, state attorney general Wiley Jones interviewed dozens of local women about the Deportation. All but one denounced the roundup.[72]

The presences and absences of women in the records of that summer reflected Bisbee's shifting racial gradations. Attorney General Jones did not interview a single Mexican woman—one reason that Mexican voices are sadly lacking in the historical evidence about the Deportation. In contrast, he took statements from more than a dozen Slavic women, most of them wives or widows, whose mere presence discredited the stereotype of eastern European men as single drifters. Maybe the Mexican women were afraid to talk; more probably, they were never asked. For officials who saw the Deportation as a class conflict, Mexican women complicated the story by adding an indisputably racial element. For advocates of the Deportation as a manly defense, the heartrending stories of Mexican families were an unwelcome intrusion. A rare glimpse hinted at the roundup's personal toll. An Anglo woman "saw one little Mexican woman come up and bid her husband good bye, and she fainted down at the [box]car, just at the car her husband was in and he jumped out and picked her up." A deputy told him, "Get back in that car, that is your place." The husband replied, "My God, man, this is my wife." The response was, "We don't give a damn, get in the car." The story is all the more chilling alongside reliable evidence that at least 174 Mexican families were separated by the Deportation.[73]

Brutality gripped Bisbee long after July 12. Two weeks after the Deportation, a deported AFL member told George Hunt, "People only discuss the events of that day in whispers. In short they are still terrorized." In November, state legislator Rosa McKay, a miner's wife and former boardinghouse-keeper, told investigators, "I went through four strikes. I seen the [WFM's] Cripple Creek strike in Colorado; I seen that was awful, like war, but it never put the horror in me that this one did. . . . The condition is worse in this place than any place. . . . You have no idea of the things that have been done here."[74]

There were other ways to rid the town of "undesirables." Before Harry Wheeler joined the Army Reserve Corps in 1918, he headed the county draft board. When the draft numbers of strike sympathizers came up, Wheeler waived their medical exams so that they would be inducted immediately. The irony was profound: the same men who had failed Dr. Bledsoe's company physicals because of their suspected union sympathies were exempted from medical exams before leaving for war. Now the men deported at gunpoint would carry guns overseas.[75]

Bisbee was a police state. Deportations continued, in the guise of vagrancy arrests—"sandbagging with velvet gloves," in the words of a police court judge. In order for deportees to get back into town, a kangaroo court (a sham tribunal common on the nineteenth-century frontier) run by the Loyalty League—renamed the Vigilance Committee—forced them to submit letters of recommendation and sign loyalty oaths to the country and the company.[76]

Word got out. News coverage in every Arizona newspaper, on the front page of the *New York Times,* and in national magazines such as the *Nation* and the *New Republic* bombarded state and federal officials. George Hunt, while awaiting the results of his election challenge, in the meantime was appointed a federal mediator and traveled to the deportees' camp in New Mexico in late August. That month, Woodrow Wilson finally agreed to appoint the Presidential Mediation Commission, headed by U.S. secretary of labor William B. Wilson, to investigate several labor conflicts across the West.[77]

When commission members interviewed Bisbee witnesses at the end of

October, they noticed their cowed expression and behavior (McKay cried through most of her testimony). Felix Frankfurter's assistant Max Lowenthal nearly had a nervous breakdown after listening to testimony there—even after a month in other Arizona mining camps. It was a "just response," his boss felt, "to the cruelty, ruthlessness and callousness that were involved in what was done in Bisbee." As late as January 1919, when industrial health reformer Dr. Alice Hamilton investigated the miners' working conditions, "the shadow of the Deportation still lay heavy on the copper country. There was a state of armed truce in the camps, everyone lined up on one side of the other, eyeing his adversaries with suspicion and hatred, peaceful for the moment, but ready to fight again at the drop of a hat." Hamilton found "no neutrals anywhere"—not among miners, nor clergymen, doctors or lawyers, all labeled by locals as either "labor" or "copper." In Ajo, a C&A company town in southwestern Arizona designed by John Greenway, one mining official defended the Bisbee deputies as decent men "who couldn't act any way but white and square."[78]

U.S. Army troops remained stationed in Bisbee's suburb of Lowell until 1920, ostensibly to handle border problems, but their presence in a working-class Slavic and Finnish stronghold was probably not an accident. For decades, people rarely talked about those days, but not because they forgot. As retired miner Fred Watson told his wife, "I'll forget it when I die."[79]

The erasure of the deportees from Bisbee was nearly total. A news article in September said that only thirty-four of them had returned, each searched by the sheriff, and that twenty of those were immediately sent packing. At the end of 1917, only 6 percent of identifiable deportees—61 out of 1,003 men—appeared in the city directory. By 1920, the census showed that somewhere between thirty-four and forty-five of those original 1,003 were still living in the Bisbee area.[80] Some men probably stayed in town and changed their names to avoid the blacklists, but hardly enough to make a meaningful difference. One deportee spoke for many when he predicted, "Life would be made, in one way or another, unendurable for them in Bisbee, and it is altogether likely that even those with established homes would soon move away, rather than endure the persecution." The Deportation "disrupted everything," another Bisbee resident explained. Churches and fraternal organizations "lost a whole lot" of members. Two miners concluded that "thousands of good miners . . . are today scattered all over the map." Production was down, because manpower remained short.[81]

Bisbee's immigrant communities were devastated. Census reporting methods make it difficult to track Mexicans, but anecdotal evidence clearly shows that they were purged. Deputies "cleaned out" Finn Hall, the site of several IWW meetings. Cochise County's almost 500 Finns in 1910 dwindled to 135 in 1920, many of them living in towns other than Bisbee. The Slavic population shrank by perhaps half (aided by the Balkan Wars, into which some were drafted), Italians by about 20 percent.[82]

Deputies fared better. In late 1917, more than two-thirds of the deputies—321 out of 503 identifiable men—appeared in the city directory. A severe recession in the years 1918–1920 reduced the county's population by several thousand. Yet in 1920, almost two hundred deputies still lived in and around Bisbee.[83] Anecdotal evidence shows that many moved up the corporate ranks even during a recession. Henry Hillman went from carpenter to foreman; the miner Frank Salmon became a chief watchman. Sidney Harris, a watchman in 1917, became an employment agent for the mines—both jobs were meant to forestall labor trouble. Deputy Allie Howe, meanwhile, was living proof of the *Bisbee Daily Review's* allegiances. He went from newspaper reporter in 1917 to mine detective—company spy, that is—in 1920.[84]

In 1917, Phelps Dodge bought the Warren Realty Company from Calumet & Arizona and began a new homeownership campaign. Dozens of employees signed up for the new mortgage plans, perhaps eager to demonstrate their loyalty to the company and their desire to be permanent residents. Mexicans were not the target market. Walter Douglas argued that Mexicans were not interested in buying homes, and that rental "tenements"—separated from the "American" neighborhoods in Warren—could be made available to them instead. In contrast, Serbs began to move into Warren, although no homes in Warren belonged to single foreign men.[85]

The politics of nativism were reversed. After fighting the Eighty Percent Law, Phelps Dodge and C&A publicly committed to maintaining an American camp. By the fall of 1917, C&A's underground workforce was more than 70 percent "American," compared to just under 50 percent a year earlier. The proportion made up of "Austrians" (who were, as part of the Austro-Hungarian empire, mostly Slavs) fell from 15 percent to 4 percent. The city directory published in December 1917 by a former deputy even claimed, "No foreign labor is employed in the mines, thus making Bisbee stand out as the leading American industrial center of the Southwest." During the postwar downturn, the companies preserved jobs—mostly underground and for married men—that strongly favored American-born men over immigrants, especially Mexicans. "The [single] fellas moved out," one man recalled, "and it became more of a family town after that"—so much so, that "around 1919 they built one, two, three, four new schools. Families kept moving in. After that, it was never the same town."[86]

Defenders proudly credited the Deportation for these changes. In 1918, Fred Sutter, a Bisbee attorney turned state senator, addressed the Arizona Senate with an update on Bisbee.

> And what are the results in Bisbee since the Deportation? They are . . . a practically one hundred per cent American Camp. A foreigner to get a job there today has to give a pretty good account of himself; an increase of thirty-three percent in the number of children attending school; the erection of three new school buildings and the completion of over three hundred new dwelling houses. More miners own their homes in the Warren District than in any other mining camp in the United States. The mines are today producing more copper than ever before and we are a quiet, peaceful, law-abiding community.[87]

The commitment to an American camp persisted. In 1920, G. H. Dowell, new manager of the Copper Queen Mine, promised that "the reputation of Bisbee as an American camp will be maintained." Dowell boasted that 80 percent of the men underground were American citizens, exactly the figure white unionists had pursued in the Alien Labor Act. In 1922, 82 percent of all Copper Queen employees were American citizens. Underground the figure was much higher, because the overall percentage included "the large number of Mexicans employed in the surface labor division." More than three-fourths of the workers were married, and "a large percentage of these men are home owners . . . whose hopes and plans are co-ordinated with other permanent residents in an endeavor to build a bigger and better Bisbee district." The company's own numbers showed that, in comparison to the

"Americans," a greater portion of Mexican workers were married—though this fact went unmentioned. As late as 1929 promotional articles in the *Arizona Labor Journal* boasted that Bisbee "has rightfully earned the reputation of being the 'last stand of the white miner,' because more than ninety per cent of them are American citizens."[88]

Mexican workers found themselves excluded in ways both blatant and subtle. For the duration of the war, Walter Douglas ordered the mines to concentrate on high-grade ore, which relied on skilled (white) labor. When Bisbee's first open-pit mining was halted after the war, top men lost their jobs. In an eerie replay of the Deportation, some Mexican families were "offered" transportation to cotton fields to work as pickers. If they refused, they were cut off from local relief. Besides this, according to Charles Willis, "director of community welfare" at Phelps Dodge, "nothing of a distinct nature" had been aimed at the Mexican population. On the contrary: PD's new insurance plan and "Employees' Representation Plan"—a company union—excluded only the Mexican workers. While other mining camps complained about "Mexicanization," Bisbee remained the exception. As one mining-industry author noted, "In some camps they are using Mexicans for open work and other miners for underground. At Bisbee a definite policy to this effect has been adopted on the theory that the two classes will not mix."[89]

Those Mexicans who did live in Bisbee found it increasingly segregated. Mexican residents helped to pay for and build the beautiful new St. Patrick's Catholic Church, completed two months after the Deportation. Yet Bisbee's parish priest, Constant Mandin (who had allegedly served as a deputy and lent Harry Wheeler his car), barred Mexicans from attending. Instead, the old St. Patrick's was renamed Sagrado Corazón (Sacred Heart) and "given" to the town's Mexican population. When Mandin told the congregation about his desire "to exclude Mexicans from the new church," Louisa Redondo, the wife of an assayer for C&A, and one of the most elite Mexicans in Bisbee, was "very indignant," even though her family was allowed to attend St. Patrick's.[90] In October 1920, Bisbee opened the Franklin School, which was intended specifically for Mexican children and which concentrated them in vocational programs. In a weird reprise of the Deportation, the four hundred Mexican schoolchildren were paraded through town from the old school to the new one.[91]

Bisbee's most prominent white women brushed Mexicans aside. This was true even of the prolabor Rosa McKay. On the one hand, she defended the strikers, even driving to the Columbus camp to deliver food and supplies. On the day of the Deportation, she tried to send telegrams to President Wilson demanding that "we women of the Warren District . . . be protected, for we fear harm at the hands of the gunmen." (She failed; the mining companies shut down the telegraph lines.)[92] On the other hand, she always skimmed over the fact that most of the deportees were immigrants. Unlike Sheriff Wheeler, McKay insisted that "this strike . . . is not treason," but rather "a fight between capital and labor," plain and simple. [93] Maybe, but she was refusing to address the very factors others used to defend the Deportation. Her most notable legislative achievement, a minimum-wage law for women passed in 1916, excluded domestic workers—who were almost all Mexican women. [94] In Arizona, work was defined by race, and labor politics often sank to the racial antagonisms used by men like Sheriff Wheeler. So McKay's decision to ignore race altogether was only avoiding the issue.

In contrast, social worker Esther Cummings focused on both class and race and benefited handsomely. As the secretary of the Warren District Relief Committee since 1909, Cummings had been parceling out charity in racially specific terms for years. She did the same after the Deportation, to finish what the Deportation had started—a purging of undesirables. Wives of strikers received groceries (since company officials feared newspaper headlines about starving families) but no rental assistance. At least sixty-four women received one-way tickets out of town as their "relief." Flora Davis, the pregnant wife of a deportee, went into labor on the day of the Deportation. Two weeks later, Cummings and the president of the Bisbee Woman's Club, Harriet Bledsoe (whose husband was Dr. Bledsoe), "gave her a ticket and $1.75, marked 'charity'" to visit her aunt in Los Angeles. Flora Davis' sister-in-law called this "charity" what it was—a Deportation for women. Ironically, Miss Cummings was creating the itinerant miners that company homeowning programs were supposed to eliminate.[95]

Unlike McKay, Cummings acknowledged that the Deportation involved divisions beyond those of class. In Columbus, women complained to their husbands that the strike leaders' wives were well-fed, "but the Mexican families and Slavonian and those they consider of no importance are neglected."[96]

A telegram sent to attorney general Wiley Jones warned, "Prominent families [are] furnished all relief. . . . Mexican and others neglected. . . . Transportation forced on many families to other points." These were decisions and handouts meted out by Cummings. She had some decision-making power, but not ultimate authority. Cummings had to clear her questionable cases with the same kangaroo court in charge of keeping the deportees out of town.[97]

McKay was elected, and Cummings was appointed by Bisbee's most powerful men. Cummings did their bidding, while McKay—an elected official—fled to Globe not long after being shot at by vigilantes outside Bisbee. Depicting the strike as a fight between a union and a corporation was not acceptable in a town now controlled by pro-company gunmen. McKay was elected to the legislature in Globe, but by then organized labor had lost most of its power. Her minimum-wage law was nullified, along with those of many other states, by a U.S. Supreme Court ruling in 1925. She died in early 1934.[98]

McKay interpreted what happened in Bisbee as a struggle over class, not race, and she paid dearly. Cummings fared better. Within three months of the Deportation, she was promoted to the county's child welfare board, and several prestigious social service positions followed. By the time of the New Deal, Cummings was chair of Bisbee's civilian relief for the American Red Cross, which helped to administer public relief programs. Her power was acceptable so long as she wielded it in ways that ameliorated, but did not upend, the social relations of the white man's camp.[99]

The racial politics of the Deportation—and the shift to an "American camp" rather than a "white man's camp"—seem initially to have benefited black men, too. In a fascinating episode, in November 1917 Sheriff Harry Wheeler and Loyalty League leader Miles Merrill urged the state government to heed the "protest of colored citizens everywhere" and ban circulation of the D. W. Griffith film *Birth of a Nation* (1915), which celebrated the Ku Klux Klan. This "consideration of colored men's feelings" was fair reward, they argued, for such "loyal response and service" as wartime volunteers and draftees. Bisbee's mayor concurred, and the town "turned down" the film.[100]

Yet African Americans soon discovered that race left them vulnerable to charges of disloyalty, too. In 1919, the federal government's Bureau of Investigation (forerunner of the FBI) looked into charges that German agents were contacting black soldiers stationed on the U.S.-Mexico border and recruiting them to their cause. That July, the federal government also investigated rumors of a "race riot" in Bisbee between Negro soldiers and local civilians. The talk was that some Wobblies (how many could possibly have been left in Bisbee?) had provoked the conflict, presumably to turn black troops against the local population. Two months later, Bisbee residents established an NAACP local with fifty-five charter members. Its vice president, a porter at City Hall who came from Alabama and whose name was James Nash, was married to a Mexican American woman named Josefina (who also joined the organization). Perhaps Nash's mixed-race family felt especially threatened by the rumors of disloyalty, though they did stay in Bisbee. By the mid-1920s, however, the NAACP branch was too small to keep its charter, despite attracting two-thirds of Bisbee's black population.[101]

No Redress

While African Americans received glancing blows in the post-Deportation battles, the main protagonists of 1917 were never punished—not Harry Wheeler, or a single mining manager, or any rank-and-file deputies. Federal and state attempts to prosecute Sheriff Wheeler, mining officials, and the deputies all failed, despite the conclusion of the Mediation Commission that the Deportation was "wholly illegal," carried out by a "vigilance committee, having no authority whatever in law."[102] On May 15, 1918, federal attorneys secured the arrest of twenty-one mining officials, businessmen, and other deputies on charges of conspiracy and kidnapping. But a federal judge in San Francisco ruled that no federal laws had been broken, and dismissed the case. Two years later, the U.S. Supreme Court upheld his decision. That was the end of federal attempts at legal redress.

Attempts in state court were unsuccessful as well. In 1919, five hundred deportees filed a civil suit against Phelps Dodge and the El Paso & Southwestern Railroad for damages totaling $61.5 million. PD initially offered to fund out-of-court settlements of $1,250 for married men with children, $1,000 for childless married men, and $500 for single men (family men were literally worth more). Only a handful of the plaintiffs were Mexican. Most must have been long gone—back to Mexico or to new jobs. Those who remained may well have been too cynical about U.S. justice to seek any. Even if they had wanted to fight, most were not U.S. citizens and would have lacked the money and support for an extended legal battle.

In early 1920, before the civil suit was settled, a criminal case charging 210 Bisbee citizens with kidnapping opened in state court in Tombstone. Phelps Dodge officials sensed that a not-guilty verdict would let them get away with paying nothing in the civil case. State senator Fred Sutter was part of a defense team that used a novel argument invoking the "law of necessity," essentially self-defense akin to justified homicide. The trial lasted three months, and the men were acquitted on the jury's first ballot. Phelps Dodge revoked its civil settlement offer, and the attempts at legal redress for the Deportation were officially over.[103]

Outside Bisbee, even longtime critics of the mining companies defended the Deportation, or remained oddly neutral. Harry Wheeler's popularity in cattle country helped to cement rural support. Bowie's loquacious newspaper editor J. H. Jaque, who had once railed against the mining companies, also supported the Eighty Percent Law and condemned the trend of "Mexican miners . . . taking the jobs of Americans." But he hated the Wobblies, and published anti-IWW reports for several months. The Farmers and Merchants Club of Bowie, with Jacque as secretary, sent a resolution to the county attorney asking him to end criminal investigations into the incident. The father of Loyalty League leader Miles Merrill was a prominent Mormon bishop from one of the San Pedro Valley's oldest families. The jury included two Mormons, and Merrill's father—who looked like a patriarch out of the Bible—appeared conspicuously at the long kidnapping trial. The *Courtland Arizonan,* a small rural weekly, reprinted a Bisbee newspaper article telling readers that if any of the deportees tried to return, "summon all your manhood and put in a positive 'NO.' The rubbish is gone. Keep it GONE." Wartime patriotism made it easy for rural newspapermen and politicians to see the IWW as a far more threatening menace than the copper industry. This meant the death knell of effective political opposition to the mining companies, both in the county and the state, for a very long time.[104]

Many county residents had grown weary of the whole saga and the spiraling court costs, as the case generated hundreds of subpoenas and requests for witnesses' travel expenses. To rural observers, the Deportation just meant that Bisbee would attract more attention while places like Bowie struggled to survive. Jaque praised the not-guilty ruling in the criminal case as the "consensus of opinion of the 'all American citizenship' of Cochise County." Those who called for a new trial were "mostly composed of the floater or non-taxpayer class, or those who pay very little taxes." Benson's newspaper editor was more circumspect, but warned that the trials "should not be made a political game at the expense of the innocent taxpayer."[105]

Labor unions effectively ceased to exist in Bisbee and Cochise County. After the IWW was crushed, AFL and Mine-Mill organizers found Bisbee to be hostile territory. In 1919, a state labor leader scheduled to speak in Bisbee on the Fourth of July could not secure a "speaking place in the stronghold of the copper barons of deporting fame, and the general committee who have charge of the 4th of July program were of the opinion that 'this is not the time to hold labor meetings.'" At first, only the miners' union disappeared, replaced by a company union in which "the management has the power of vetoing any of its recommendations." Union membership continued to dwindle, and by 1925, Cochise County could not muster a single delegate to the annual convention of the Arizona State Federation of Labor. Effective labor organizing would not resume until the passage of the National Industrial Recovery Act in 1933.[106]

Across Arizona, organized labor collapsed or acquiesced to corporate power. As early as November 1918, a future editor of the *Arizona Labor Journal* announced that "Big Business" was trying to take over the journal. The journal's Spanish-language column disappeared in 1919. The labor paper became a mouthpiece for conservative Phoenix unions, and coverage of mining communities waned. Editorial stances grew more and more conservative, and in 1925 the *Labor Journal* published articles written by Calumet & Arizona superintendent William Gohring and Phelps Dodge spokesperson Charles Willis. In the 1926 congressional race, the journal endorsed Lewis W. Douglas, nephew of Walter Douglas and owner of the United Verde Copper Company in Jerome. Douglas won, and remained in office until President Franklin D. Roosevelt named him federal budget director in 1933. The *Arizona Labor Journal,* which despite its opposition to the IWW had warmly denounced the Deportation through 1919, never mentioned the incident in the 1920s. The mining companies may not have won all of Arizona's hearts and minds, but they had scared the others into silence.[107]

By combining modern corporate discipline with Wild West brio, the Deportation's leaders finished off any effective competition the mining corporations might have faced in Arizona's politics and economy, and this situation lasted until the 1930s. The Deportation foreclosed the possibility of peaceful conciliation among those who saw a place for unions in Bisbee and those who did not. And it deepened racial divides even as it cast in stark relief the constituent parts from which these divides were created: unfair pay scales, cultural stereotypes, and visceral defense of white women in the name of pure "American" manliness. In the aftermath of the Deportation, the racial category of "foreigner" faded with a renewed commitment to an "American camp," the latest guise of the white man's camp. Phelps Dodge's American camp strongly resembled the racially exclusionary workforce that skilled white miners had long been demanding. By creating a white man's camp by force, the company had beaten white miners at their own game. Purging "foreigners" increased the distance between "Mexican" and "American," and being European increasingly meant being "white."

The Deportation was an extreme version of the World War I demand for 100 percent Americanism. But for Mexicans it was impossible to be 100 percent American. Not in a community so close to the border, and not in a wage system predicated on their inferiority. In the end, the Deportation reinforced the dual-wage system's division between white "Americans" and "Mexicans," because ultimately the loudest voices defending the deportees were not challenging the *terms* of the "white man's camp" ideology. Instead they complained about its incomplete implementation, because of the mine owners' lack of commitment to its tenets. Newspaper editor John O. Dunbar assailed the hypocrisy of the mining companies by pointing out that the Copper Queen, "after twenty-five years of effort in preventing American miners from finding employment in its various mines, now comes forth with loud sounding trumpets and tell[s] the people of Arizona that 'none' but Americans will be 'employed' in their mines."[108]

Mexican men challenged the dual-wage system by demanding a huge raise for surface workers, but their message was lost—at least for the moment.

Defenders of the deportees argued that no Mexicans or "foreigners" would have needed to be removed in the first place if the companies had simply agreed to treat white workers as the independent republican citizens, masters of their own households, that the "white man's camp" ideal seemed to promise. In Dunbar's words, reasonable unions "come like white men to talk" with managers about grievances; foreigners join the Wobblies and strike.[109] When Clifton's Mexican miners told reporter Robert Bruère that they were fighting for "the American standard of living," they knew that this meant much more than simply white wages. So did Bruère and Felix Frankfurter, who both saw the strikes of Arizona copper miners as a fight for democracy. But the Deportation foreclosed these possibilities for Mexican workers—and, indeed, for anyone who challenged the terms of the agreement—until new federal remedies were implemented in the 1930s.

8

One County, Two Races

World War I turned out to be the high point of Cochise County's prosperity and political influence. Drought and glutted agricultural markets halted the homesteading movement and devastated the ranching economy. Mining fared no better. From 1918 to 1921, copper prices fell by almost two-thirds, production by three-quarters. In 1921, every mine in Arizona but one closed. Bisbee mines retained a few hundred underground men, many part-time. Work halted at open-pit operations. The Phelps Dodge smelter in Douglas kept only a skeleton crew. Conditions throughout the 1920s remained unsteady, and during the Depression, mine and smelter employment rolls shrank by the thousands. From 1917 to 1940, the county's population fell by 30 percent. Bisbee lost a third of its population, and several rural settlements completely disappeared.[1]

All the while, Phelps Dodge tightened its grip on the copper industry, Cochise County, and Arizona. As the economy weakened, the company swallowed up its struggling competitors to become the dominant force in the Arizona economy. By the late 1930s, the company employed more than half of the workers in the state's most important industry.

Racial divisions deepened. New federal policies restricted European immigration, tightened the border, and cast Mexicans as "aliens." In Cochise County, PD's cadre of white women reformers—now involved in federal programs like the Agricultural Extension Service and the New Deal—brought the racial mores of copper country to places where more fluid ideas had once reigned. Aided by these women and their male patrons and allies, Arizona's New Deal was created in the mining industry's image, and brought the stark racial division of the mining economy into the public sector. By the 1930s, "Mexican" and "white American" had become mutually exclusive racial categories that divided nearly the entire population—not just in Bisbee and Douglas, but across the county and the state.

Women's Networks and Racial Division

By making anti-unionism a patriotic cause, the Bisbee Deportation silenced much of the rural dissent against Phelps Dodge. But the recession and drought that followed World War I played a role, too, as farmers relinquished their homestead claims or sold off their property and moved away. A series of misfortunes—the 1918 flu pandemic (which killed tens of millions of people worldwide), a national downturn in agriculture, and a severe drought beginning in 1919—spelled disaster for many homesteader communities. "Nearly all of the homesteaders lived in the most depressing poverty," county school superintendent Elsie Toles recalled, "often in houses built of railroad ties, roofed and floored with dirt." They had no wells, "too little to eat, too little to wear, and practically no recreation." As late as 1929, one study found only 12 percent of Anglo farm families in the county had running water. Dry-farming had not saved the Anglo-Saxon family; instead it had brought failure, "hardship, and privation," according to a sympathetic Toles.[2]

The land homesteaders had once coveted now lay worthless and unwanted. Between 1900 and 1918, Cochise County residents had filed about 2,600 successful homestead claims. For the rest of the century, they filed only 179 more. "The day of the homesteader has come and gone," one land promoter admitted. "Present land values are low and can do nothing but increase." Some homesteaders hung on by finding part-time wage work on big ranches or in the mines, but many, Toles observed, "sold out to the cattlemen, and the land reverted to the only thing it was good for—grazing." Courtland had nearly a thousand people in 1910, barely a hundred by 1930. The homesteading settlement of Light went from 441 people to 69 in the same period. Both are gone now.[3]

While the fortunes of rural families declined, those of professional women remained on the rise. No one made this clearer than Elsie Toles, whose family epitomized the changes Bisbee and the county had seen. Her prospector father, George Toles, had allegedly participated in the 1880s lynching of a Mexican man—a crime that had shocked Phelps Dodge managers into their first paternalist measures. Later the elder Toles ran the Red Light Saloon in Brewery Gulch. Yet his daughter, born in 1892, was eminently respectable. She belonged to Bisbee High School's first graduating class—four students, all women—and attended a teachers' college and the University of Michigan. She had come a long way from her father's rough roots, but she still benefited from them: she considered her status as a "pioneer daughter" an important factor in her political victories.[4]

Elsie Toles became a polished Progressive with unbridled faith in expertise and efficiency. As county school superintendent, she sympathized with rural families even as she promoted centralized power at the expense of democratic and local control. She had exacting standards, in everything from chalkboard height to school map orders. But she also treated her mostly female teachers as professionals and advocated for them assiduously. Her first report as state superintendent included detailed graphs to expose the gross underpayment of rural teachers and women, compared to city teachers and men.[5]

Toles championed professional teachers, but she wanted to abolish local trustees, whom she felt too often selected a teacher because of "her good looks, her bad looks," nepotism, or financial need, "but rarely because she is efficient." Autonomous school districts might have been a necessity in a "pioneer period," Toles believed, but they were an "anachronism in this day of modern development." She also believed that county and state superintendents should be appointed, not elected, to ensure they were efficient professionals. Although she failed to do away with district trustees or to replace elections with appointments, her efforts to centralize rural-school administration were successful enough for one observer to declare that Cochise's schools were "welded together" as "no other county in the state have been." "Miss Toles has been allowed to proceed, not in disregard of the law, but as if there were no code at all." Most striking about this description of Toles's sweeping, self-defined power was that it was not a critique but an endorsement.[6]

Her views of "efficient" public administration were at odds with local autonomy. Minnie Bisby, the Cascabel teacher who helped Mexican American families to save their school, was a fan of Toles, but she opposed her boss's proposals to appoint county superintendents and centralize rural-school administration. Bisby knew how important local control was for districts run by families with little political capital. Toles's measures, she warned, "would concentrate too much authority to be practical at present."[7]

Like many other "nonpartisan" reforms, Toles's ideas had more political and racial implications than she let on. Bisbee's school system was her model for a powerful administration that would "increase efficiency and the standard of teachers, eliminate waste and take the schools out of politics." Centralized power was certainly "efficient," but it did not make schools any less political. In Bisbee, Phelps Dodge controlled the schools financially, through corporate taxes and donations, and culturally, through its maternalist wing, the Bisbee Woman's Club, which oversaw kindergarten and industrial-training programs. Bisbee's school superintendent, C. F. Philbrook, was a close ally of Phelps Dodge (one observer noted, "to hear him talk you would conclude he has been a mining capitalist all his life"). He oversaw the segregation of Bisbee's schools and curriculum.[8] Using Bisbee as a model for rural schools had implications far beyond "efficiency."

But it was Toles's relationship with assistant county superintendent and woman homesteader Helen Benedict that created the most interesting ties between mining-town and rural culture. After they had spent some time living and working together in Tombstone, Toles was elected state superintendent in 1920. She then hired Benedict as her assistant in Phoenix. Months earlier, the women had jointly purchased a summer ranch and fruit orchard on Cave Creek, in the Chiricahua Mountains. Toles and Benedict were mentioned often in the society pages. One article announced that the "2 women politicians" were "in the market for a good name" for their ranch. Suggestions included "Amazonia's Domain," the "Kitchen Cabinet" (referring to their political careers), the "Hen House," and even the "Manless Eden." Toles and Benedict rejected one of the most obvious, the "Old Maid's Retreat," as "certainly" unacceptable, since, in Toles's words, "an old maid never retreats." Publicly, Elsie addressed her personal life with self-effacement and rumor deflection, by joking about her independence and attesting to her heterosexual desirability. The women's partnership never seemed to be a political liability. On the contrary, theirs was a smart alliance that cemented ties between a mining-town stalwart and a bona fide woman homesteader from an influential rural family.[9]

Benedict's father, Reverend Arthur J. Benedict, had close ties to a Bisbee minister named Reverend A. D. Raley, a YMCA leader and staunch critic of the Democratic-Socialist state legislator Rosa McKay. In August 1917, Raley had published an editorial in the *Arizona Mining Journal* entitled "Deportations Justified," in which he called Bisbee residents "cultured" and "law abiding," and quoted people who declared the Deportation "a great day." While a teacher in Bisbee, Toles had taught Raley's children. When she ran for state office, he launched an anti-Mormon smear campaign against her opponent. Allies like Raley prompted one critic to claim that Toles was "running on the Copper Queen ticket and is dependent on the mining bosses to put her over."[10]

As county superintendent, Elsie Toles created a nascent network of maternalist social reformers who linked Bisbee with its struggling rural hinterland. One positive example created in Bisbee was a school health program promoted by Phelps Dodge. With it as a model, Toles hired Arizona's first rural school nurse, Ruth Fuess. Fuess lived at the Bisbee YWCA, and traveled by horseback and Model T to almost fifty rural schools. Her commute from the citadel of corporate maternalism to the county's most remote outposts traced the deepening connections between Bisbee and rural Cochise County.[11]

New federal programs extended the reach of this network. The Home Extension Service, created by Congress in 1914, was designed to improve the lives of farm families through education by experts. Male agricultural agents offered farming advice; female agents (known first as home demonstration agents and later as homemakers' extension agents) conducted home visits and group demonstrations of housewifery skills such as canning and home decoration. The Extension Service reflected the same assumptions about rural virtue that motivated dry-farming and irrigation promoters. It was quintessentially "Progressive," with all of the possibilities and shortcomings that this amorphous label implied. It offered professional careers to college-educated women, while reaffirming the traditional role of housewives. It offered federal dollars for intensely local activities, creating webs of connection between home demonstration agents and volunteers and officials on the local, county, state, and federal levels. And like other Progressive reformers, Home Extension agents encountered educational, racial, and economic gaps between their clients and themselves, as well as between their own lofty goals and resource-poor reality.

Although New Mexico had Hispano agents and the South had a segregated program with black agents, Cochise County's agents were always white.[12] Their shifting priorities were a barometer of the county's changing racial alignments. The county's first full-time agent, Louise Sporleder, who was hired in 1918, genuinely tried to transcend racial and class boundaries. She focused on some of the county's poorest residents—the Mexican families who lived outside Douglas and Bisbee. Louise Sporleder's background may explain this choice: her previous job had been teaching home economics at Benson High School, in the heart of Cochise County's integrated enclave.[13]

In Pirtleville, a Mexican smelter-worker settlement outside Douglas, Sporleder joined a female reform network at the local school, which had been organized "along the lines of social settlement work"—a reference to the urban reform centers made famous by Jane Addams' Hull House in Chicago and run largely by women.[14] In January 1919 Louise Sporleder started the Pirtleville Home Bureau, a "homemakers' club" of eighteen Mexican women to whom she offered lessons in sewing, cooking (no doubt American, not Mexican, food), child care (which were unpopular), and home canning. But the Home Bureau's most important project was a hot-lunch program run by Pirtleville women for local children, mostly their own. The clubwomen elected as their leader a Mrs. Lambert, a Mexican woman married to an Anglo man. Lambert accompanied Sporleder on countless personal calls to club members. Her language skills and background made her an indispensable intermediary between the agent and the Pirtleville women, whose cultural distance Sporleder marked by observing that many wore "shawls on their heads."[15]

Louise Sporleder's ill-defined mission—to create "community spirit" among the Mexican mothers—reflected Anglo attitudes, rather than the actual state of affairs in Pirtleville. One Anglo volunteer told the women "how much good this club was doing for them," something they no doubt could have determined for themselves. Sporleder reported to her superiors, "The

23. Women of the Pirtleville Home Bureau, 1919. From Louise Sporleder, "Annual Narrative Report," Cochise County, 1919, AZ 302, Special Collections, University of Arizona Library.

women of Pirtleville seem to have a very much happier expression than they did a year ago. They are developing more of a community spirit which absolutely was not there before." She did not acknowledge that Pirtleville had its own community life and indigenous social welfare organizations: neighborhood networks, an altar society, a Society of St. Vincent de Paul for helping the poor and homeless.[16] Yet Sporleder had gained the people's trust and offered real assistance—no small gesture two years after the Deportation.

Sporleder devoted more energy to helping Mexican women and children than any other Home Extension agent before World War II. In addition to creating the Pirtleville Home Bureau, she organized sewing groups for Mexican girls and women in Pirtleville and Tintown, something no subsequent agent did, and even "obtained work for three Mexican women," a service that went above and beyond her duties. This kind of work represented one of the best hopes for bridging Cochise County's ever-deepening racial divides.[17]

Yet, even as Sporleder persisted, cross-cultural extension work was on the wane. In the 1920s, the "social settlement" experiment at Pirtleville inspired the Douglas schools to institute special programs for Mexican girls— but these were segregated classes to train the girls to be "efficient domestic help" in "American homes." This hardly counted as transcending racial inequality—was more like affirming it.[18]

Postwar federal budget cuts shrank extension programs, while women in Cochise County needed more help than ever. Sporleder's last year in Cochise County was 1920, and subsequent agents covered more than one county. "Many people of this county need greater prosperity," observed Home Extension agent Laura Mae Seward in 1926. "Any farmer who could come into this county and show people how to make money would be the most popular person here. We need it."[19] In the face of these challenges, Home Extension agents had ceased to organize Mexican women and began to focus on rural Anglos. In 1921, an agent named Grace Ryan resumed Home Extension work in Cochise County after a year-long hiatus. The county's size, farm women's isolation, and poor transportation led her to work "through already established organizations," like "the Women's Club, a Civic Club, a Community Club or a Church Club"—groups that tended to be homogeneous and relatively well-off (although she did list Pirtleville's Altar Society). Relying on existing local women's groups allowed agents to avoid differences of class, religion, or simply of personality.[20]

Home Extension agents in the 1920s found it difficult to bridge class, cultural, and religious divisions among rural Anglo women, much less with Mexican women. Ryan's attitude of superiority had elicited "antagonism to the work," according to her successor, Laura Mae Seward, and in several places "women . . . frankly talked against" any similar programs. But most difficulties stemmed from lack of time and money. "Many of the farm women seem to be working harder than ever to make a living here," Seward noted.

"It is hard work to be interested in advancement perhaps when one is tired out and rather discouraged."[21]

Throughout the 1920s, programming for Mexican women was haphazard, nonexistent, or incidental. And for all the desperate need, agents during those years tended to aid the women who needed it the least. Grace Ryan fawned over a woman who belonged to "rather a high type of the pioneer group," and raised 250 turkeys for sale with Ryan's assistance. Yet few homesteading families could have afforded such a scheme: one woman spent nearly $1,000 on her poultry before she made a profit of $850.[22]

The only extension efforts that included Mexican women in these years were large food-conservation or sewing demonstrations, one-time events for large crowds that did not require community organizing. But Slavic and Italian women—like one housewife who did a ravioli-making demonstration for her club—were part of white groups.[23] Children's programs, which became what are now known as 4-H clubs, were also run by Home Extension agents. These were integrated by default at one-room schools, but were segregated elsewhere. In 1934, Home Extension agent Bertha Virmond observed that she was now "contacting the same centers that [Sporleder] used in her pioneer work *with the exception of Pirtleville.*" Virmond noticed that "the 1918, 1919, and 1920 reports show much work with the Mexican girls and mothers in Douglas and Bisbee," but that this trend had not continued. The agents who had followed Sporleder took the path of least resistance—latching onto preexisting groups and calling this a federal program. In doing so, they gave government sanction to deepening class, race, and religious divisions among women.[24]

These divisions increased during a watershed era in federal immigration policy and the history of the U.S.-Mexico border. In 1921, when the government set new immigration quotas for southern and eastern Europeans, Mexicans were exempted from numerical limits thanks to lobbying by southwestern employers. But by the end of the decade, in the face of growing anti-Mexican sentiment, Mexican migration garnered unprecedented scrutiny. The Border Patrol was created in 1924. Although the number of agents was minuscule compared to the size of the border, the symbolism of having federal agents police migrants' movement and treat them as criminals hardened the border as never before. Several early border patrol agents belonged to the Ku Klux Klan, which surged in popularity in the 1920s. In 1928 and 1929, the federal government began imposing stricter interpretations on existing laws (such as an old law barring entry to any immigrants "likely to become a public charge"), in order to prevent some Mexicans from crossing the border. Requirements for head taxes, literacy tests, and visas were increasingly—if intermittently—enforced. At border stations, degrading physical examinations and bathing requirements reinforced the notion of Mexicans as unwelcome and "alien" (a term dating to this era). Closer scrutiny at the border meant that more migrants stayed in the United States and sought citizenship, even as the stricter policies and souring public sentiment made the terms "Mexican" and "illegal alien" increasingly synonymous.[25]

Depression and Division

In the midst of these changes, the Great Depression hit the copper industry with the force and devastation of a cave-in. Few industries are as recession-prone as mineral extraction, the first link in the chain of industrial manufacturing. When the stock market crashed, so did copper prices: from 18 cents per pound in 1929 to just 5.6 cents three years later. In 1933, copper production was the lowest it had been since 1897. With huge inventory surpluses, companies cut their workforces to skeleton crews. In 1929, Arizona's twelve largest copper companies had employed 12,043 men. Four years later, only 2,226 still had jobs. Bisbee, where one in four copper workers remained on the payroll, was actually better-off than many mining towns, though most of the jobs were part-time. From 1920 to 1940, the total number of adult men in Bisbee fell by more than 40 percent, and the number of schoolchildren fell by a third. The loss would have been greater, but many people were reluctant to leave because they owned their homes—precisely the situation that Phelps Dodge and Calumet & Arizona had encouraged.[26]

Statistics do not begin to capture the suffering and sadness caused by copper's collapse. A state report observed, "Mines closing down left thousands of people homeless and starving. . . . There was nothing the miner could do for himself and his family." Florence Warner, a Chicago social worker hired as an administrator for the Arizona Board of Public Welfare, arrived in Arizona in early 1933. She reported to Roosevelt's relief director,

Harry Hopkins, "I did not realize how difficult is the situation of the unemployed in the mining towns of this state until I visited one or two of them . . . [where] there is no other industry in town." Another report two months later warned that "the situation is indeed desperate" and that, especially, "conditions are very uncertain with Phelps-Dodge." One federal official in Arizona concluded, "Some of our problems here defy solution, had one the wisdom of Solomon."[27]

Outside Bisbee and Douglas, things were only slightly better. In Tombstone, the situation was dire; the town hovered at the brink of extinction when Bisbee took over as the county seat in 1929. The Apache Powder Company, a dynamite factory owned by Phelps Dodge, opened outside Benson in the late 1920s and kept a full workforce throughout the 1930s. It offered welcome (if dangerous) jobs, even as it expanded PD's influence in northern Cochise County. But the Southern Pacific Railroad, northern Cochise County's major employer, reeled from the loss of mining business. In early 1931, Benson's banks failed, and Pomerene's Benson Canal Company went bankrupt after its dam collapsed.[28]

Only the luckiest farmers and ranchers scraped by. In 1933 and 1934, prices for alfalfa hay and beef cattle were less than half of what they had been a decade before. Worse, the early 1930s brought a new period of drought, which was nearly as devastating in Arizona as it was in the region farther east that became known as the Dust Bowl. Overgrazing was severe, and many cattle were diseased and near starvation. This was the end for many farm and ranch families, some of whom had been on the land for sixty years. The Gámez family, to name just one example, lost almost all of the San Pedro Valley land they had owned since the nineteenth century.[29]

Everywhere, people struggled to survive. They grew their own food, or butchered cattle when there was no forage. Some ranchers banded together to open a soup kitchen. In Bisbee, families like the Ruízes of Dubaker Canyon cobbled together a living. Mauricio Ruíz worked intermittently for Phelps Dodge, and on off-days cut mesquite wood to trade for things the family needed. The Ruízes shared a garden plot with ten other families, and wife Sofía kept chickens. When Bisbee's PD Mercantile burned down in 1939, Sofía Ruíz sewed smoky, salvaged fabric into clothes that she sold to neighbors. She also cleaned, took in washing, and made tortillas for money.

Mauricio and Sofía Ruíz shielded their family from the worst of the Depression's effects, but others were not so lucky.[30]

Governments long reluctant to fund large welfare programs felt compelled to respond. Yet far from diluting the power of Phelps Dodge, relief programs strengthened it.[31] In 1931, Esther Cummings' former employer, the Warren District Relief Committee, was reinvented as the Warren District Unemployment Committee to hand out clothing, food, medicine, and small work assignments. Subcommittee chairs included the former state senator and Deportation defender Fred Sutter, a Woman's Club president whose husband was a PD official, and mine owner Lemuel Shattuck. Following a tradition dating to at least 1909, the committee granted Mexicans separate and unequal cash relief. It also provided "transportation back to Mexico or [to] . . . work in cotton fields." Mexican Americans (U.S. citizens) were offered local work assignments, but with only half the hours offered to some whites, an amount that the committee "found sufficient to care for their situations." Naturalized citizens from Europe got "white" hours and assignments.[32]

As the largest taxpayer in the county and state, Phelps Dodge indirectly funded the bulk of government relief. The need was staggering. By January 1932, the relief rolls in the Bisbee area alone included 3,281 people, and 900 more had been bumped off because of insufficient funds. Property tax revenues declined calamitously. PD officials claimed that because of low copper prices, the company's property assessments were too high. In 1933 the company stopped paying property taxes altogether. Phelps Dodge and the state wrangled in court for more than three years, while the company racked up $5,196,074 in back taxes. Much of this was owed to Cochise County, which in the meantime had to turn away hundreds of needy families for lack of funds. Among thousands of tax delinquents across the state, Phelps Dodge was "the most severe offender," according to one historian. The state increased sales taxes to make up the lost revenue, but with little success.[33]

Yet Phelps Dodge wielded more political and economic influence than ever. The Depression destroyed smaller mining companies, and their loss was PD's gain. A "hard-working and hard-riding" new company president, Louis Cates, who took over when Walter Douglas retired in 1930, began buying competitors, including Calumet & Arizona. Shattuck-Denn folded, too, and for the first time in the twentieth century, Bisbee and Douglas were one-company towns. PD officials no longer needed to consult other corporate managers about wages, benefits, and labor management. In 1938, a local historian wrote that "every educational, civic, and industrial undertaking, while not instituted directly by the Phelps Dodge Corporation, is done with its approval." By 1942, Phelps Dodge was responsible for 17 percent of the state's annual revenue. The *Los Angeles Times* called the company "the biggest single creature in the state of Arizona, next to Harold Ickes and the Interior Department."[34]

The comparison to Ickes was apt, because industry leaders now wielded their power from public posts, including those in Washington. Lewis Douglas, who had inherited control of the United Verde Extension Mining Company in Jerome (where in 1917 mining officials had deported sixty-seven workers two days before the Bisbee Deportation) was Walter Douglas' nephew. His uncle and grandfather were PD managers who had wielded public influence from behind the scenes, but Lewis did so in the open, as Arizona's sole member of Congress from 1927 until 1932, when President Roosevelt named him his first federal budget director. Douglas was a Democrat, but hardly a New Dealer. A staunch fiscal conservative, he was aghast at New Deal spending. He resigned in less than a year to give speeches and publish a book skewering Roosevelt's excesses, and later served as U.S. ambassador to Great Britain. During his short tenure in Washington, Douglas spent much of his time arguing that states—not the federal government— should provide Depression relief, a policy that would have guaranteed the Douglas family business even more control than it already had.[35]

His successor in Congress, Arizona's first female representative and one of only eight in the House in 1933, was Isabella Greenway, widow of the former C&A general manager and Deportation leader John Greenway. In 1939, the congresswoman married businessman Harry O. King, who created the National Recovery Administration's Copper Code (the labor component of which union miners in Bisbee called "a betrayal of the Copper miners of the nation") and later became the copper division chief of the War Production Board. In spite of a lifelong friendship with Eleanor Roosevelt (for whom she served as bridesmaid), Isabella Greenway also turned against the New Deal. One sympathetic critic in Arizona felt that Representative Greenway's "heart is really for those in distress," but "she is repressed by being of the corporation caste."[36]

Though they opposed the New Deal, Douglas and Greenway had connections to the Roosevelt administration that guaranteed attention to Arizona's copper industry. After a dismal report to Harry Hopkins on the Arizona mines, one relief administrator added, in parentheses, "If any confirmation of this is desired, consult budget director Lewis W. Douglas." In Arizona, local administration of New Deal programs tightened the corporate grip on government spending. The largest New Deal relief programs, like the Federal Emergency Relief Administration (FERA) and the Works Progress Administration (WPA), relied on local administration. As abundant research has shown, in southern and southwestern states this policy preserved racial segregation and excluded outsiders.[37]

State officials consolidated private and public relief, which only exacerbated these tendencies. In 1933 Arizona created state and county Boards of Public Welfare to oversee county, state, federal, and private programs. Cochise County's board relied on private donations and cooperated with the Red Cross, where Bisbee's Esther Cummings had become an officer. "The County Welfare Boards thus became a directing unit and clearing house for private agencies as well as public," one WPA report explained; the result was an "almost absolute lack of duplication" in the administration of relief. But there was, as well, almost absolute centralization of power.[38]

Much of this power belonged to mining officials. Labor champion George W. P. Hunt was reelected to the governorship in 1929 after a term as U.S. ambassador to Siam, but since the Progressive era he had softened his views of the corporations. In mid-1932, before the New Deal went into effect, Hunt appointed as the state's emergency director of Unemployment Relief a corporate manager on loan from Lewis Douglas' United Verde Copper Company. By the time the federal WPA was implemented in 1935, Arizona's New Deal administration had become a kind of jobs program for former mining officials. Both the chief officer and the personnel director of the state WPA were veterans of United Verde, and two of the five appointed members of the Arizona State Board of Public Welfare were mining executives. One of these was Hubert d'Autremont, the Calumet & Arizona director who in 1906 had urged the company to build Warren because "a man without a home was almost a man without a country." The board chairman was T. H. O'Brien, who owned the Inspiration Mining Company in Miami, a citadel of the dual-wage system. In a nod to the nickname of Louisiana's powerful governor

Huey Long, the *Arizona Labor Journal* denounced O'Brien as a "'kingfish' in the mismanaged Arizona relief set-up." In addition to filling appointed and professional New Deal positions, company allies often served as advisors or sponsors of local programs.[39]

Connecting the dots between the mining industry and the New Deal is not the same thing as tracing a conspiracy. Most members of the New Deal coalition took their work seriously and probably saw themselves as objective. When a small Mine-Mill affiliate called a strike in Bisbee in 1935, state officials conferred with Washington about whether strikers were eligible for relief. They were, and they received it. Here was an example of mining-related officials who were "bend[ing] over backwards in trying to be square," in the words of state board secretary Florence Warner. Warner made this observation after one Washington official appeared "distressed" about copper men's prominence on the board. Not to worry, she assured the national headquarters, the state board was a "grand group of people." But this was beside the point. Phelps Dodge left its mark on almost every aspect of the New Deal's implementation in Arizona—how wages were set, how relief was distributed by region and race, and who administered programs. The company, as one Bisbee man explained in a letter to President Roosevelt, was "the dominating power in the community and in many instances state affairs."[40]

In Cochise County, Phelps Dodge controlled how relief wages were determined and distributed. In March 1934, the state welfare board decided to reclassify relief wages based on local prevailing rates, which in Cochise County were of course those of the mines. The mechanics of wage selection worked in the mining industry's favor. Each county was supposed to create a wage classification committee and a grievance committee, in addition to a board of welfare. But the state board allowed county welfare boards to serve in all three capacities—that is, it permitted a single committee to set policy, determine wages, distribute relief, and handle complaints. In Cochise County, Phelps Dodge partisans, including the superintendent of the PD smelter and a Bisbee YMCA leader, dominated the board.[41]

Phelps Dodge's control of public works projects did not escape notice. Local residents protested to the federal government about corporate influence over public relief. These complaints often came in the form of letters reeling off the litany of mining executives in important appointed positions.

In the summer of 1933, one Douglas resident sent U.S. secretary of labor Frances Perkins a history lesson and a plea. A year and a half before, "the local Phelps-Dodge Corporation . . . commenced to get control of local government relief, and to stack the whole thing with . . . their own henchmen. It is the same corporation that pulled off the Bisbee deportation in 1917. . . . We plead with you, for the love of Christ, to do something about this situation— and that right promptly." In May 1935, new guidelines allowed middle-class professionals who were not on relief rolls to work in supervisory jobs in Civil Works Administration programs. A veterans' group in Lowell protested the rule, claiming that it "tends to promote domination . . . of relief money" by "certain politically controlled individuals and groups." A similar resolution declared that Douglas residents "resent and are opposed to the dictatorial attitude . . . of the local Relief Board." Though neither letter named Phelps Dodge, the target of their complaints was obvious.[42]

One group willing to name names was a nascent AFL local. The group began organizing after the passage in 1933 of the National Industrial Recovery Act, whose section 7(a) guaranteed the right of collective bargaining. In 1935, the union sent a letter of protest to President Roosevelt about the local Civil Works Administration's oversight committee. The union claimed that all thirty members, who had been appointed by the chair of the Cochise County relief board, were either "executives of the Phelps Dodge Mining Corp." or "inclined to be influenced in favor of" the company. The superintendent of construction for the Civil Works Administration was a PD "carpenter construction boss," while the assistant superintendent was a former PD motorman. Phelps Dodge, the union's letter continued with considerable understatement, "is apposed [*sic*] to organized labor and has fired men who have become union members," and it hardly seemed fair that the company should supply all the supervisory positions. A federal labor relations adviser was unmoved by the union complaints, stressing the need for "trained administrative personnel," regardless of financial need or labor policies.[43]

Phelps Dodge's influence combined with New Deal regulations meant that Bisbee and Douglas got the lion's share of the county's funding allocations. Early FERA rules provided wage work (as opposed to direct cash relief) only to towns of five thousand or more—which meant that in Cochise County only Bisbee and Douglas qualified. By April 1934, there were twenty-eight FERA projects in the county. Eight projects in northern Cochise County cost just over $10,000; nine projects in the Bisbee area totaled $176,148. Funds evened out slightly over time, but Bisbee and Douglas continued to monopolize federal work funds. One WPA administrator made a telling mistake when she mistakenly mentioned "Bisbee County" in official correspondence.[44]

Bisbee and Douglas had the greatest number of unemployed citizens, which partly explains the *amount* of work there; but the *type* of work benefited those who least needed it. In 1934, Warren—by far the county's wealthiest community—was awarded four FERA projects. Two of these were the county's largest that year. In addition to $60,000 in street improvements (in the one part of the county with professional urban planning), workers built a new fence around the entire Warren townsite to protect its lawns and foliage from cattle who "molest . . . the inhabitants." Upon completion of the fence, Phelps Dodge and the Southern Pacific Railroad donated trees to shade the suburb, where, as one author in the WPA Writers Program put it, "many of Bisbee's mine officials and business men have expensive homes with landscaped grounds." FERA also allocated extravagant sums for golf courses near Bisbee and Douglas, equivalent to more than half the total spent on northern Cochise County. The Bisbee course was at the Warren Country Club, site of the annual meeting of Phelps Dodge's foremen, and, after the Deportation, of a congratulatory banquet for Harry Wheeler. The funds were granted even after Governor B. B. Moeur complained specifically about using federal money for golf courses.[45]

Building golf courses was annoying, but even more insidious was the way federal relief aped the dual-wage system of the mining industry. Although FERA guidelines forbade discrimination based on "religion, race, color, non-citizenship, political affiliations, et cetera,"[46] in practice, local administration accommodated local inequalities. Like the mines, public relief programs granted Mexicans lower salaries (these were, of course, the "prevailing wages" of the dual-wage system) and lower levels of aid. In 1932, W. Val de Camp, the former United Verde employee who had become head of the State's Emergency Relief Fund, conserved funds by allotting only $3.66 per month to Hispanic and Indian families of four, while white families received $6.69. Direct food handouts also varied by race. All families were allotted flour, milk, sugar, fresh vegetables, rice, and beans, but only white families received potatoes, lard, baking powder, and cereal.[47]

Federal programs run by the state and county operated similarly. Cochise County's administrators made no apologies for their dual-relief system. In 1935, Douglas resident A. C. García wrote to labor secretary Frances Perkins to protest "gross irregularity in the distribution of relief work in this district." "Spanish-American citizens are being discriminated against, whether native born or naturalized," he explained. "This fact is shown on the posted lists and freely admitted by our relief boards." He informed the labor secretary that "we deeply resent" this inequality, and "we as Americans desire and demand this injustice be abolished." Upon receiving a copy of García's letter, the executive secretary of the Cochise County board explained flatly, "The budget for Spanish-American people for man and wife is $12.00 per month," leaving unmentioned the higher amount paid to white Americans. A regional social worker promptly explained to Washington, "a difference is made between budgets for Spanish-Americans and others on relief rolls." No one forced a change. A group led by Willcox resident Pete Gonzales made a similar protest, and in July 1934 a Latin-American Club of Cochise County complained to the state Board of Public Welfare about the "amount of relief given to Mexicans as compared to other families." The board replied that "relief was given on the basis of need only." This was a sly answer that did not deny the club's allegation—because state administrators widely agreed that Mexicans had less "need" than did whites. The careful new terminology of "Spanish American" and "Latin American," which was meant to downplay racial difference, had done not a whit of good.[48]

The few aid programs that did not discriminate annoyed white recipients and administrators, both of whom took the dual-wage economy's racial assumptions for granted. White county residents complained that funds distributed on the basis of family size actually *favored* Mexican Americans, who tended to have larger families. In 1934, state administrator Florence Warner urged FERA's national director to increase the number of professional projects in Arizona. "It has been bitter for the educated people," she argued, "to have to see the peon type of Mexican receiving the same relief as they." Thousands of Mexican workers, she explained, have a "standard of living [that] is very low but if they are citizens we are obliged to give them the same amount

24. Bisbee's *Arizona Miner*. The public-works project was dedicated in 1935 to "those virile men the copper miners" by Representative Isabella Greenway. Photo by Russell Lee, 1940. Library of Congress, Prints and Photographs Division, FSA-OWI Collection, LC-DIG-fsa-8a28440 DLC.

of relief as the people who have a high standard of living. Consequently, many American-Mexicans are living fatter than they have for a good many years.... On the other hand we have a group of people whose morale is almost at the breaking point." She saw equal wages and relief not as simple justice, but as a humiliation of whites.[49]

Here was a morale boost, though. In 1935, public money funded a monument to white men—literally. Bisbee had finally managed to seize the county seat from Tombstone in 1929, and in front of the gorgeous new courthouse, a sculptor on public relief fashioned a giant statue called *The Arizona Miner.* Sheathed in copper, smooth and sensual in the fascist style, the figure towers atop a granite slab once used in Bisbee's manly drilling contests.[50] The plaque affixed to its base reads: "Dedicated to Those Virile Men the Copper Miners Whose Contribution to the Development of the Wealth and Lore of the State of Arizona Has Been Magnificent." The statue remains one of Bisbee's most noted landmarks.

Relief administrators and Anglo residents treated whiteness and American citizenship as inextricable, a long-standing assumption of mining-town housing and salary policies. One report by the Civil Works Administration included in its "alien class" category not just natives of Mexico (there was no mention of their current citizenship), but also "American born men and women of Mexican descent, and Negroes who have been attracted from the southern states by the cotton growing." These were explicitly contrasted with the (implicitly white) "settlers and pioneers who have slowly made their way westward from the midwestern and southern states." By this reasoning, the twentieth-century settlers of Kansas Settlement were pioneers, but Mexican Americans who had settled in the San Pedro Valley in the nineteenth century were not. Calling African Americans an "alien class" only underscored racial assumptions about who "belonged" in Arizona—and perhaps the United States. Federal rules forbade the use of FERA funds in small communities, which prompted the State Board of Public Welfare to complain to Washington, "Some urban communities have a large foreign born population whose citizenship is of a few years duration and these will be qualified for employment while many communities have a population made up of citizens native born who will be deprived of any chance of employment." This letter was referring to Mexican, not European, immigrants, since the work-force in most Arizona mining towns other than Bisbee was largely Mexican by 1930. These were American citizens by the board's own admission, yet decidedly second-class ones.[51]

Aid for citizens of Mexico living in the county was even more politically fraught, especially in an era of tightened immigration laws. "Cochise County has always refused to allow the aliens to work," the state board explained to Washington in early February 1935. Unlike most other counties, Cochise obeyed an obscure Progressive-era state law that barred noncitizens from public works projects. The attorney general ruled that working for food rations would not violate the law, so the two FERA projects Cochise County created for resident aliens—cleaning out cemeteries—did not pay cash wages. Still, some white residents resented providing anything to Mexican citizens, and blamed Phelps Dodge for the policy. A Douglas man complained that the company "dumped tons of flour into the Mexican Consul's office here [in Douglas] to feed alien Mexicans, imported to [be] peon American labor, while between twelve and thirteen hundred American citizens were working four and five days a month and getting orders on company stores—while the corporation got the government money. Now they are still feeding the aliens, while twelve or thirteen hundred Americans, with families, have been cut off." Here were the old antagonisms between white miners and mine managers about race and labor (and about how Phelps Dodge profited by funneling government vouchers to company stores).[52]

Even as Mexicans were marked in new ways, local parables of assimilation praised eastern and southern Europeans for becoming "Americans." By the end of the New Deal, the middle category of "foreigner" for eastern and southern Europeans had ceased to exist, while the dual-wage system of the mining industry became public policy. Mexicans remained in a separate category (indeed, since citizenship was required for almost all relief programs, the category "Mexican" really meant "Mexican American"). Complementing the rising notion of Mexican as "alien," in 1930 the federal census, which had previously categorized Mexicans as white (even if many Arizona enumerators insisted on putting an *M* instead of a *W* in the race column), added a new racial category, "Mexicans." So Mexicans became officially nonwhite, while eastern and southern European immigrants became "Americans." In

Cochise County, first the Deportation of 1917 and then federal immigration restrictions reduced the number of European-born residents, while complaints about Mexican immigrants continued to grow.[53]

Another stark difference between Mexican and European immigrants in Cochise County was that the former faced the threat of deportation, while the latter did not. Repatriation (deportation) of Mexican workers occurred mostly in agricultural areas, but Bisbee created a small-scale deportation, modeled after Los Angeles. Many more were forced out of Phelps Dodge's "Mexican camp" of Clifton-Morenci. In Cochise County, the company merged its Douglas smelter with Calumet & Arizona's in 1931, which cut over a thousand jobs. Phelps Dodge kept the "American" workers and paid many of Mexican origin to leave. Douglas Chamber of Commerce officials discussed a larger-scale deportation with the U.S. State Department, but nearby truck farmers and ranchers who wanted cheap labor talked them out of its plans. Contemporary expert Paul S. Taylor estimated that 18,520 Mexicans, or 16 percent of Arizona's Mexican population, were repatriated in the years 1930–1932. Cochise County had an active Ku Klux Klan in the 1920s that targeted Catholics like the Carettos. But no one seriously suggested sending the Milutinoviches or Medigoviches to Serbia or the Carettos to Italy.[54]

So Slavs became "Americans" in the American camp, but Mexicans did not. A manuscript created by the WPA Writer's Project in about 1940 characterized Slavs as the successful culmination of all of the Americanization rhetoric that had saturated Bisbee for forty years. No longer were Slavs a "foreign" race bent on destroying American jobs. On the contrary, according to the author, they had become the finest miners of all: "The Balkan Kingdoms, now united in the post–World War nation of Jugoslavia . . . carved from sections of the old Austrian empire, have provided the mining industry with the most dependable underground labor men" (note they were "underground"—the bastion of white men). This was a far cry from the situation in 1903, when there were complaints that "foreign labor" was threatening the white man's camp; in 1907, when the strike was blamed on Slavs; and in 1917, when Slavs were targeted in the Deportation. The author then offered a triumphalist history of the Americanization of Slavs, a "hard-working, industrious, home-building and assimilable contingent of aliens who have rapidly acquired American citizenship." Nine out of ten were naturalized, according to the report, and these immigrants have kept "little to remind one of the alien either in manner or garb. . . . Their American-born children are an integral part of young America." Another WPA writer claimed that second-generation Serbian Americans were "becoming a part of the great American melting pot," intermarrying with "other nationalities." Slavs had been run out of town in 1907 and 1917, but the ones that remained were now thoroughly American in the American camp.[55]

The switch to labeling Bisbee an "American camp" instead of a "white man's camp" cleverly avoided racial categorization. One WPA manuscript that discussed the Slavs' magical Americanization was titled "Racial Groups in Arizona," but it did not confront "racial" questions directly. One version of it called "Serb" a "national group classification." Indeed, this document contrasted Slavs with Mexican immigrants, whom the WPA author called "as yet unassimilated aliens." The final draft concluded, "The present day Mexican in Arizona maintains his group identity; there is little intermarriage except when there is mixed blood. They are in a measure segregated." While Slavs had become white Americans, the federal census and local sentiment concurred that Mexicans had not.[56]

The New Deal also brought segregation of "Mexicans" and "Americans" to places where the division had once not been important or clear-cut. On the one hand, contrasts in racial patterns in Bisbee and Benson persisted. In 1934, the few Mexican students at Bisbee High School appeared alongside two lonely African American girls on a page by themselves, separate from "white" students (many of them Serbs), in the school yearbook. At the same time, Benson High elected William Molina to two different student council offices. Benson included Mexican Americans in its Depression planning, while Bisbee did not. Benson's local advisory committee of the National Recovery Administration included Paul Blanco, a Southern Pacific employee with deep family roots in both Arizona and Mexico, and Ed Ohnesorgen, the grandson of German and Mexican pioneers from Tres Alamos. Blanco represented the Mexican Woodmen's Lodge, and Ed Ohnesorgen represented Benson's still-thriving branch of the *mutualista* La Alianza, indicating how intermixed the early population of Benson had been.[57]

Yet when the New Deal offered relief, it forced formal racial divisions on

Benson as well as Bisbee. In 1934, FERA sponsored summer camps in the Chiricahua Mountains for children on relief rolls. Forty "American" children from Benson, St. David, and Pomerene attended one week, and forty "Spanish" children attended separately. Which camp would the children of Paul Blanco and Ed Ohnesorgen have attended? Would William Molina have gone to camp separately from the rest of the student council?[58]

In Tombstone, too, WPA policy sometimes clashed with local culture. Juanita Parra, the American-born daughter of Mexican immigrants, described Tombstone as the sort of place where "There was no, 'You go there, because you are an American.' or 'You go there, because you are a Mexican.' No difference. That's what I liked about it." Parra saw race segregation and class difference as closely associated, and she believed that Tombstone was integrated because everyone—whether Mexican or Anglo—was poor. When the Depression hit, Parra's father got a job installing outdoor toilets for the WPA, but "they stopped him because he was not an American citizen," she recalled. So Juanita Parra "came in and said, 'Well, I am an American citizen, and I'm going to help my dad, . . . and I'll do it.'" Installing toilets was a job for men, but "we needed the money *so* bad, because we didn't have anything to eat." She did the job.[59]

Women of the New Deal

Most women, whatever their racial or ethnic classification, did not build public toilets. Instead they worked on women's projects designed and run by female administrators. Women occupied important paid and unpaid positions in New Deal programs for men and women alike. With only a shoestring budget, Governor Hunt's first statewide response to the Depression, the Emergency Relief Fund, relied heavily on women volunteers—among them Woman's Club members and other philanthropists. Professional women headed several important relief agencies. Florence Warner was the state's chief professional welfare administrator. Jane Rider served as the head of women's programs for first the Civil Works Administration, and then the WPA; after 1939, she was one of only seven women in the nation to serve as a state director for the coed National Youth Administration. The head of the state's WPA Professional and Service Projects was a woman, as was the state supervisor of Americanization—a former Bisbee High School teacher. The Cochise County Board of Public Welfare employed fourteen social workers, likely all women.[60]

Gender-specific women's work was an important part of New Deal relief everywhere. Sewing rooms became some of the county's largest works projects, with sites in Bisbee, Douglas, Benson, Tombstone, and Willcox. Other programs included a nursery school for the children of relief workers and the creation of a children's library in Bisbee. One women's WPA project preserved more than two thousand legal documents left in the Tombstone courthouse after the county seat moved to Bisbee.[61]

Local administration of federal programs ensured that corporate maternalists would keep control over women's programs in Cochise County, because the deep pockets of Phelps Dodge gave it the power to determine which nominally federal programs would run and which would not. The National Youth Administration, for instance, relied on the county board of public welfare to determine eligibility. In practice, this meant mining-company allies determined its employment rules. Many programs relied on local philanthropic institutions like the YWCA and women's clubs for supplementary funding, administrative support, and volunteers. The sponsor of Bisbee's first sewing room was Nellie B. Hoy, a Bisbee Woman's Club member, former newspaper publisher, and county probation officer, who also served as the secretary of the Cochise County Child Welfare Board. The Lowell Woman's Club sponsored a WPA day nursery, while the Douglas and Bisbee YWCAs housed several New Deal recreation projects. An advisory panel of Bisbee women, inspired by a "shortage of domestic help," oversaw a domestic training course for teenage girls, as did Hubert d'Autremont's wife in Tucson. Here was a program designed to benefit the well-off as much as, if not more than, the program's participants—much like the programs for Mexican girls in the Douglas schools. Like the women on relief in Tucson who complained that the YWCA there was "snooty," participants might have correctly sensed that class privilege motivated some programs.[62]

Reliance on Woman's Club members and YWCA staff was not mandatory. In fact, it exasperated Chicago native Florence Warner. When she arrived in Arizona in mid-1933, the secretary of the state welfare board confronted a distressing "lack of any trained personnel." She complained that the "Boards and Powers That Be" refused to "import" trained social workers, even though there were "no such animals in the state of Arizona." The situation, she admitted, "distresses me greatly."[63]

Local control ensured that there would be segregation in the Cochise County programs run by the National Youth Administration and the Works Progress Administration. Sometimes participants were divided three ways, into white, Mexican, and African American groups, because federal law required access if not integration for minorities. Yet segregation contrasted sharply with the views of Aubrey Williams, federal director of the National Youth Administration, who pushed for racial equality and integration. In Cochise County, programs went beyond mere physical segregation, and signified very different ideas about Mexican and white women. In the sewing rooms, all women did the same work, but in separate locations. Other programming was race specific—for instance, housekeepers' aide programs were set up for Mexican and African American women, but not for white women. The most egregious case was a WPA professional program that hired white women to organize naturalization records at Cochise County's border station in Naco, in order to weed out Mexican nationals from the ranks of relief workers. This program achieved two primary objectives of Arizona's New Deal programs: employing middle-class white women and excluding aliens from the relief rolls. State director Jane Rider lavished praise on the program, grateful because "in that county we have never been able to provide sufficient white collar projects to give a proper sort of employment to that class of relief clients." It was a small program, but it spoke volumes about the ways that Arizona's racial hierarchies benefited white women at others' expense.[64]

Rural Home Extension programs, flush with increased funding, also absorbed the New Deal's mining-town racial politics. In 1932, in a highly symbolic move, Home Extension agent Bertha Virmond relocated her offices from northern Cochise County's ranch center Willcox to the new county seat in Bisbee, so that Home Extension could collaborate with other county and federal social programs. The number of communities she organized doubled, and work specifically intended for Mexican women and children appeared for the first time since the Progressive Era. 4-H clubs were established in majority-Mexican communities. These programs contained a few

Anglo children, just as children's programs in a few places in the northern part of the county continued to be integrated.[65]

At the same time, though, segregation was developing where it had not existed before. In the ranch town of Willcox, for example, children's programs had been integrated in the 1920s, but now there was a Willcox Mexican First-Year Garment-Making Club for girls. In McNeal, a very active 4-H area, both children's and adult groups were segregated. Finns who lived in McNeal belonged to the white groups. The entrenchment of a racial binary peeked through Virmond's proud report in 1932, which noted, "Every girl, Mexican and white[,] within a radius of ten miles of McNeal has been enrolled in some 4-H Club Project this year." Her report reflected the expansion of 4-H programming for Mexican children, but also evinced strong assumptions about how the population was divided.[66]

In a way, it was ironic that Lewis Douglas and Isabella Greenway both opposed the New Deal, since the mining industry that produced and supported them controlled federal programs in much of Arizona. As a result, New Deal work programs—really, local fiefdoms made possible by federal funding—replicated the race relations of Bisbee and Douglas in government programs across the county. We might wonder whether a purely local relief effort in Benson would have segregated its children, or whether one in Tombstone would have prevented Juanita Parra's father from working. In Cochise County, local control meant that Phelps Dodge called the shots, that Bisbee and Douglas received the lion's share of funds, and that public welfare and work programs incorporated the racial inequalities of the dual-wage system. All the same arguments about race, citizenship, gender, standards of living, and wages that for decades had buttressed the dual-wage system now appeared in New Deal work and direct relief efforts, administered by mining officials and their corporate maternalist allies. Just as city incorporation had increased rather than diminished the power of Phelps Dodge thirty years before, the New Deal did the same.

Where once diverse ideas about race had competed or coexisted, by the 1930s the line between Mexican and white was well entrenched. New border policies were crucial. But this deep racial divide was also enacted in 1917 by Esther Cummings' division of whites and Mexicans in Deportation relief;

in the 1920s by Home Extension agents, who abandoned the challenge of cross-racial work for a comfortable reliance on white women's organizations; and in the 1930s by New Deal administrators whose programs reinforced the racial hierarchies of mine work. At each new stage, white women reformers had new opportunities, even as they helped to stamp the divisions between "Mexican" and "white" ever deeper into the social landscape of Cochise County. These women's successes—however much they were deserved, however much they reflected good intentions—came at a steep price: the maintenance of racial inequalities that were neither natural nor inevitable.

Conclusion

By the 1930s, the line between "Mexican" and "white" was well entrenched, but it was never completely stable. The New Deal and World War II gave workers new tools to dig away at its foundation, the dual-wage system. The New Deal had two faces: one that offered local elites greater power, and another that granted union rights where none had existed before. Thanks to the right to collective bargaining, granted in the National Industrial Recovery Act and the Wagner Act, a new era of unionizing began in Cochise County. A small Mine-Mill local organized in 1933 went on strike at the Copper Queen Mine in 1935. One supervisor told a striker, "in 300 years we will not give you fellows a job again." Another striker was told, "If you want a job you will have to go to a union camp to get it."[1] The men challenged their firing and blacklisting by filing a complaint with the National Labor Relations Board. The case ended up in the U.S. Supreme Court, which in 1941 ruled in favor of the strikers. The ruling stated that the company could not blacklist the workers and that it owed them back pay. *Phelps Dodge v. National Labor Relations Board* became a major legal precedent in protecting union workers from blacklists. The Supreme Court's decision was written by a justice who knew a great deal about Bisbee labor practices: Felix Frankfurter.[2]

The men who launched the strike had names like Kalastro, Caretto, Curtis, Vaclav, Bateman, Mortenson, and Erkkila. They represented the new, broader definition of "whiteness," and they were not newcomers to Bisbee. One man had first worked for the mine in 1908. Another, Verne Curtis, signed on as an organizer with Mine-Mill, which left the American Federation of Labor for the Congress of Industrial Organizations in 1937, and began aggressively organizing Mexican workers. Curtis went on to help organize Mexican American workers at the Empire Zinc Mine near Silver City, New Mexico. Empire became the site of a 1950 strike made famous by the 1953 film *Salt of the Earth,* which focused on the decision of Mexican American miners' wives to take over the picket line after a court injunction.[3] Although the 1935 Bisbee strike did not address the disparate pay scales of Mexican and "white American" workers, it was one of a series of worker actions against the Arizona copper industry that eventually led to the dismantling of the dual-wage system.

Like the more famous Silver City strike—and the 1917 strike that had led to the Deportation—the 1935 strike at Bisbee involved more than just miners. Brothers Anson, Grover, and William Windsor, for example, walked out together, along "with all the rest of the family." Clyde and William Bigelow, also brothers, were joined by their wives *and* their mother.[4] Meanwhile, women in Bisbee, Douglas, and Globe organized union auxiliaries and label leagues that encouraged the buying of union goods. In the WPA sewing rooms, women on relief protested working conditions and hours, and threatened to go on strike.[5] Men and women correctly saw the local relief programs and mining-company policy as two sides of the same copper coin. Mine-Mill's national president no doubt spoke for many residents when he wrote to a federal official, "The mining companies have dominated every phase of the . . . life of the workers and it is time that something is done to allow these people the opportunity to exercise their constitutional rights."[6]

Unionizing was legal now, but ending the dual-wage system was not an issue that all union members embraced. In the 1930s, the American Federation of Labor and the Congress of Industrial Organizations competed for copper workers, with the former often holding the line against Mexican wage parity. After the federal government ordered Phelps Dodge to dismantle its company union, PD simply reorganized the union as a sympathetic AFL local. As one federal official noted with considerable understatement, "The employment practices of the industries of the Southwest have become so traditional and the Companies . . . have for so long dominated the political as well as the economic life of their communities, that it will be difficult to get them to change their ways."[7]

Mexican Americans fought the dual-wage system by emphasizing that they, too, were Americans. They emphatically denied that "American" and "Mexican" were opposites, or that "American" had to equal "white." White bosses often disagreed. One day in 1936, the Copper Queen smelter in Douglas was short-handed. Carlos Rivera briefly took over as a puncher, traditionally a "whiteman's job." Soon after, Rivera got "bumped off" by a new white worker. When Rivera complained, the foreman said, "I am putting an American in the American job." Rivera replied, "I was born and raised here in the United States of America and . . . [I am] an American." The foreman replied: "I don't care if you were born in China you are still a Mexican and I am putting a whiteman on the job."[8]

Jose Estrada, another experienced smelter worker in Douglas, complained that he was forced to work with the "Mexican gang" doing menial work, even though he had "broken in fifty or sixty Anglos" since he started at the smelter. "I taught them their jobs, but I got the Mexican scale while I was teaching them their work and they got the so-called white scale. The Anglos got approximately $1.52 per day more while I was breaking them in." Estrada emphasized that "I feel I am subjected to discrimination because of my race."[9] Co-worker Bob Hart asked the boss why Estrada was not promoted to a recent opening, and the boss replied, "Bob, you know how it is. We have to save all of the best jobs for the Americans because they pay more money and that's the rule of the company." Hart clarified for federal investigators that "I understood the term American, as he used it, to mean Anglo-American."[10]

Language was changing. Smelter workers like Jose Chavez used the terms "Latin American" and "of Spanish extraction" to describe themselves, while relating that what they earned was "the so-called Mexican rate."[11] The terms downplayed race, as political leaders did in New Mexico and Texas, where organizations like the League of United Latin American Citizens were arguing that Mexicans were white Caucasians and thus should not be segregated. Burgeoning civil rights efforts in Arizona were doing the same. These terms were also a way for American citizens of Mexican descent to assert their rights in contradistinction to immigrants with Mexican citizenship. Whether claiming whiteness or not, Mexican American workers and their defenders were insisting that people of Mexican descent could be Americans—and skilled workers, for that matter.[12]

Managers continued to blame tradition and the opposition of white workers for the endurance of the dual-wage system, but Phelps Dodge had its own reasons for keeping things the way they were. One manager "frankly admitted" that the company did not want to stir up labor troubles by promoting Mexican miners against white workers' objections. More important, though, the status quo was profitable. In the early 1940s, two federal investigators calculated how much money the company earned by preserving the system. If five thousand miners in Arizona worked for $1.52 less than Anglos in the same jobs (the differential Estrada had used), the dual-wage system saved Arizona copper companies $2,371,200 in wages per year.[13]

New federal tools combined with the activism of ordinary men and women to challenge the dual-wage system as never before. With the aid first of Mine-Mill and, by the middle of World War II, of some AFL locals, Mexican American workers attacked the dual-wage system and their exclusion from high-paying jobs. Their plight was detailed in hundreds of affidavits collected by the Fair Employment Practices Commission (FEPC). In response to black union activist A. Philip Randolph's threat to launch a massive march on Washington in 1941, President Roosevelt created the FEPC to investigate complaints of racial discrimination in the nation's war industries. Although FEPC representatives interviewed copper workers like Carlos Rivera and Jose Estrada across the Southwest who experienced discrimination, pressure to keep good relations with Mexico and foot-dragging by corporate attorneys meant that the FEPC failed to hold a proposed public hearing in El Paso on their findings. The FEPC's concrete accomplishments proved limited, and its institutional dedication to ending discrimination against Mexicans was lukewarm. Individual investigators, however, were devoted to the cause.[14]

The FEPC fell short of its mission, but its extensive investigations in the Southwest cast light on a shadowy industry and a region of the country where racially discriminatory labor practices had been an unchallenged norm since 1917. Even though the FEPC had failed to hold hearings, in 1942 the mostly Mexican American workers of Douglas' Copper Queen smelter secured an early contract in what would become a whole series of agreements across the copper industry, guaranteeing substantial pay hikes, union rights, grievance procedures, and paid vacation time.[15]

In 1917, the patriotic xenophobia of World War I had blunted the attack against the dual-wage system. But in World War II, racially inclusive rhetoric and manpower shortages combined to open up new opportunities for equal wages and job advancement. In 1942, an Anglo officer in a Bisbee union wrote to an FEPC official, "We know that racial discrimination is greater in the Southwestern part of the country than else where. We feel that racial discrimination is one of the major factors contributing to the man power crisis and must be tackled quickly. Discrimination against minority groups is obviously working on Hitler's side and not ours."[16] In Bisbee, a handful of Mexican workers began working underground, and across the industry Mine-Mill continued to fight the dead-end job classification schemes that had replaced explicit racial job categories as a means of keeping Mexican workers in menial positions. A report on New Year's Day, 1944, warned that it would take "drastic measures . . . to obtain the copper necessary to successfully fight the war." The "drastic measure" was finally to dismantle the racial hierarchy of mine work. The War Production Board and the Nonferrous Metals Commission supported efforts to end racial discrimination in the copper industry. The "Victory Campaigns" conducted that year by union leaders got more AFL locals to cooperate with the Congress of Industrial Organizations, in its efforts to push for an end to racially discriminatory wage scales.[17]

In the years that followed, Mexican Americans made significant advances in the copper industry, tearing down more job barriers and wage differentials, and building powerful unions. They fought even as Mine-Mill, which had Communist allies and members, became a target of continual attack at the height of the Red Scare. By the late 1960s, the United Steelworkers had destroyed Mine-Mill's dominance among southwestern mine workers. A legacy of union organizing centered on racial equality continued, though. The United Steelworkers launched an industry-wide strike in 1967, and intermittent ones regularly followed. By the late 1960s, Mexican American union activism cast increased attention to electoral politics. The union experiences of their parents influenced many young men and women of the "Chicano generation," who came of age in the 1960s and began to launch social movements in college and to run for public office. One of these was Representative Ed Pastor, who replaced Morris Udall, descended from Mormon pioneers, to become Arizona's first Mexican American member of Congress in 1991.[18] In an industry slump in the 1980s, an industry-wide strike led to massive defeat for the unions, however, and more than thirty union locals lost their right to collective bargaining in Phelps Dodge mining towns across the Southwest.[19]

Since that time, copper prices have rebounded and fallen again, but union membership has not increased. In 2006, Phelps Dodge was sold to Freeport McMoran, a gold-mining corporation that was based in New Orleans until Hurricane Katrina and is now the world's biggest copper producer. Yet, with the huge growth of service industries and high-tech firms in the Phoenix and Tucson metropolitan areas, copper has nowhere near the same power over Arizona it once had. In late 2008, Freeport announced hundreds of layoffs in Arizona.

Long before that sale, Cochise County had already entered a new phase—one as unique and typical of the American Southwest as ever. Following a shift from underground to open-pit mining during the 1950s, Bisbee's mines closed in 1975. The Douglas smelter closed in 1987. The county relies mostly on military spending related to Fort Huachuca and on tourist dollars, spent during the 1940s and 1950s at dude ranches, and more recently in Tombstone and in Bisbee, which has become a little Santa Fe resettled by hippies and retirees in the late 1970s. Mexican Americans live in Bisbee, as always, but I have also heard it called the "whitest border town."

RV parks have replaced ranches in Benson, and tract homes surround Sierra Vista, the military town that has sprung up around Fort Huachuca. Most—but not all—of the remaining family ranchers and farmers in the rural parts of the county have been forced to sell out or subdivide, as drought devastates the landscape and their livelihoods. Open range has been carved into ranchettes in some parts of the county, yet some local ranch owners are working with the Bureau of Land Management and environmental organizations to protect open space and endangered species.[20] There is still no Apache reservation in the county, although the place where Cochise is buried is a state park, and the Chiricahua Mountains are a National Monument.

Cascabel, the tiny Mexican American enclave in the northwestern corner of the county, remains accessible only by a fifty-mile dirt road and had no phone service until 1993. Most pioneering Mexican families sold or lost their land, but a few descendants are buying some of it back and are returning to the area. There they find a unique community—resettled in part by social activists (many of them Quakers) involved in Tucson's Sanctuary Movement, which offers protection and support for undocumented immigrants.

Others in the county take a less welcoming view of border-crossers. The biggest story in Cochise County remains the border, which is still—even with an unprecedented amount of enforcement—more permeable than it is concrete. Since 1994, Border Patrol policies have funneled illegal immigration away from cities like San Diego and Nogales, where it is easy to hide among the crowds, and toward the open desert of southern Arizona. By 2000, the number of migrants detained in Arizona was double that of the entire rest of the border *combined*. In 2004, the Border Patrol made 235,648 apprehensions of undocumented immigrants in Cochise County, about double the county's entire permanent population. Numbers were down considerably in subsequent years, but the county remains an epicenter of migration. From Fall 2007 to September 2008, at least 167 people died while traversing the southern Arizona deserts.

The vast majority of border crossers do so with no other intent than to find work or reunite with family. In 2006, the county sheriff estimated that immigrants accounted for only 3 to 4 percent of the county's criminal violations (not counting trespassing and littering). But the scale of the migration and its furtive nature have done serious damage to residents' property and sense of security. Ranchers' fences have been cut; their lands have been covered with trash and clothing abandoned by migrants. Thefts and break-ins are a real fear.[21]

The Border Patrol has become ubiquitous. In October 2001, 699 agents were stationed in Cochise County, and by 2005 there were 909 (to put this into context, note that Bisbee's current population is about six thousand). At one ranch outside Bisbee with more than seven miles of land along the border, fifteen to twenty Border Patrol agents have worked at a time, because dozens of immigrants cross the property almost daily. Border Patrol agents set up checkpoints outside Tombstone and on rural roads across the county. In 2007 three thousand National Guardsmen also served at the Arizona border. Some residents oppose what amounts to a military buildup along the border, while others lament that it is not nearly enough. Some, like the men who created the Minutemen Project, have launched private organizations that monitor the border, build fences, or apprehend migrants. Other groups, alarmed at the number of migrant deaths, have provided water stations and maps for migrants. Bisbee, in a turn from its past as an exclusionary white man's camp, has become a regional haven for pro-immigrant activists. Both sides in the debate over the county's undocumented immigrants see the situation as a crisis.[22]

As the shootout at the OK Corral celebrated its 125th anniversary, then, Cochise County had come full circle from Tombstone's Cowboy era. The Tombstone marshal's office has a federal grant to increase its ability to apprehend lawbreaking immigrants. Nowadays, the National Guard is called out to protect the border from immigrants and drug traffickers, not from white American bandits. The governor who made this decision, Janet Napolitano, is expected to be President Obama's secretary of the Department of Homeland Security, in large part because of her border-enforcement experience. Most residents of the border region would be surprised to hear that the Border Patrol's roots lie in the late nineteenth century, in attempts to find Chinese immigrants. And in the early twenty-first century, the Department of Homeland Security has emphasized the national-security threat posed by people from many nations crossing illegally at the Mexico border. But more than 96 percent of those who cross the southern border illegally are of Mexican descent—everyone else detained there by the Border Patrol is referred to as "OTM" (other than Mexican). This nomenclature reinforces the fiction that the border line is a natural divide between Mexicans and Americans.[23]

What the future holds at the county's and nation's border is hard to say. But in Cochise County, as in the rest of the United States, race and nation have proved difficult to extricate from each other. Over time, the division between "Mexican" and "white" sharpened, but it was a binary distilled from myriad other possible outcomes. Along the way, ideas about race became wrapped up in assumptions about manliness, womanhood, nation, family, work, and class. The collusion of private and public power on the local and state levels bolstered the power of corporate leaders and their allies in defining racial difference, even as individual citizens fought back and formulated their own ideas—for both good and ill. Intellectual discussions of the social origins of race can seem rarefied and theoretical, divorced from lived experience. Cochise County's history demonstrates that the lived experience of race—on the border and elsewhere—has daunting and even tragic power. Yet this history also testifies that realities can change, and this gives us cause for hope.

ABBREVIATIONS

NOTES

ACKNOWLEDGMENTS

INDEX

Abbreviations

AHF	Arizona Historical Foundation, Arizona State University, Tempe, Arizona
AHS	Arizona Historical Society, Tucson, Arizona.
ALJ	*Arizona Labor Journal*
ANC	Autry National Center, Los Angeles, California
ASLAPR	Arizona State Library, Archives and Public Records, Phoenix, Arizona
BDR	*Bisbee Daily Review*
BMHM	Bisbee Mining and Historical Museum, Bisbee, Arizona
Byrkit, *Forging*	James W. Byrkit, *Forging the Copper Collar: Arizona's Labor-Management War of 1901–21* (Tucson, 1982).
CCHS	Cochise County Historical Society, Douglas, Arizona
EMJ	*Engineering and Mining Journal*
Manuscript Census, 1880	Bureau of the U.S. Census, *Tenth Census of the United States,* 1880, Arizona, Pima County, federal microfilm T9A, roll 36, National Archives Record Group 29, Records of the Bureau of the Census
Manuscript Census, 1910	Bureau of the U.S. Census, *Thirteenth Census of the United States,* 1910, Census Schedules, Arizona, Cochise County, federal microfilm T624, roll 38, National Archives Record Group 29, Records of the Bureau of the Census
Manuscript Census, 1920	Bureau of the U.S. Census, *Fourteenth Census of the United States,* 1920, Census Schedules, Arizona, Cochise County, federal

	microfilm T625, rolls 46–47, National Archives Record Group 29, Records of the Bureau of the Census
MC 2028	Claire Prechtel-Kluskens and Sherman Landau, comps., microcopy 2028, *Records Relating to U.S. Marshal Crawley P. Duke, the Earp Brothers, and Lawlessness and 'Cowboy Depredations' in Arizona, Territory, 1881–1885,* National Archives and Records Administration (Washington, D.C., 1996)
MC 429	*Interior Department Territorial Papers Arizona 1868–1913,* microcopy 429, roll 3, "Letters Received Relating to Disturbances along Mexican Border, December 13, 1878–January 25, 1884 and Miscellaneous Subjects February 14, 1868–January 24, 1888," National Archives and Record Administration (Washington, D.C., 1963), originally contained in Record Group 48, Records of the Office of the Secretary of the Interior
MTUCCC	Michigan Technological University Copper Country Collection, Houghton, Michigan
NACP	National Archives at College Park, College Park, Maryland
PMC hearings	E. W. Powers, ed., "President's Mediation Commission Hearings at Bisbee, Arizona, November 5–11, 1917," U.S. Department of Labor, in *Papers of the President's Mediation Commission, 1917–1919,* ed. Melvyn Dubofsky, rev. ed., microfilm (Frederick, Md., 1986)
SPVAHM	San Pedro Valley Arts and Historical Museum, Benson, Arizona
UACES	University of Arizona, Cooperative Extension Service
UASC	University of Arizona Special Collections, Tucson, Arizona
WHQ	*Western Historical Quarterly*

Notes

I have corrected minor errors of punctuation and obvious typographical errors in primary sources. Otherwise, I have left grammar and spelling in their original form. Since early primary sources created or transcribed by English speakers rarely used accent marks, I have added accent marks to Spanish names where appropriate.

Unless otherwise noted, I generated all Cochise County homestead and public land data from a database of the county's public land patents created by analyst Rick Selbach at the Phoenix office of the Bureau of Land Management (cited throughout as "BLM database"). Further information on homestead claims (whether patented or not) is derived from genealogist Edward Soza's research (see parentseyes.arizona.edu). Individual land patents (but not claims that failed to go to patent) can also be found in an online federal database at www.glorecords.blm.gov.

Introduction

1. Harry Wheeler testimony, PMC hearings, 154; "Sheriff Wheeler's Statement on Strike," *Courtland Arizonan,* 21 July 1917, 2; "Arizona Sheriff Ships 1,100 IWW's Out in Cattle Cars," *New York Times,* 13 July 1917, 1. Rifle information in Byrkit, *Forging,* 192, 369 n. 23.

2. Amado Villalovas testimony, cited in reports to Governor George W. P. Hunt, July 1917, probably from sworn statements to Arizona's attorney general, Wiley Jones, or taken by Ben Dorcy. See reports in Record Group 1, Governor's Office, George W. P. Hunt Papers, Box 8, ASLAPR.

3. *BDR,* 15 July 1917, 7, quoted in Byrkit, *Forging,* 193.

4. This number (1,186) was the official count at the deportee camp in New Mexico; some of the deportees escaped or were released before the count was made. See Ben

Dorcy, census conducted at Columbus camp, in Hunt Papers, ASLAPR (also in PMC hearings).

5. These figures are based on a database of more than 1,500 deputies and deportees, which was compiled by the author and is detailed in the notes to Chapter 7.

6. Felix Frankfurter, quoted in Michael E. Parrish, *Felix Frankfurter and His Times: The Reform Years* (New York, 1982), 95, 87–88.

7. I am not suggesting here that new European immigrants were categorically non-white, as some critics of whiteness studies have accused its practitioners of doing. What I *am* saying is that their relationship to whiteness was not always clear, and meant more in some arenas—the law, voting, housing, job status—than in others.

8. On the naturalization law's requirements of whiteness, see Matthew Frye Jacobson, *Whiteness of a Different Color: European Immigrants and the Alchemy of Race* (Cambridge, Mass., 1998), 7. On the legal relationship between whiteness and Mexicanness, see Ian F. Haney-López, *White by Law: The Legal Construction of Race* (New York, 1996); Neil Foley, "Becoming Hispanic: Mexican Americans and the Faustian Pact with Whiteness," in Foley, ed., *Reflexiones 1997: New Directions in Mexican American Studies* (Austin, 1998), 53–70; idem, "Partly Colored or Other White: Mexican Americans and Their Problem with the Color Line," in Stephanie Cole and Alison M. Parker, eds., *Beyond Black and White: Race, Ethnicity, and Gender in the U.S. South and Southwest* (College Station, Tex., 2004), 123–144; Dara Orenstein, "Void for Vagueness: Mexicans and the Collapse of Miscegenation Law in California," *Pacific Historical Review,* 74 (August 2005): 367–407; and the special issue of *Law and History Review,* 21, no. 1 (Spring 2003): passim. But see Carlos K. Blanton, "George I. Sánchez, Ideology, and Whiteness in the Making of the Mexican American Civil Rights Movement, 1930–1960," *Journal of Southern History,* 72, no. 3 (2006): 569–604.

9. Richard Griswold del Castillo, *The Treaty of Guadalupe Hidalgo: A Legacy of Conflict* (Norman, Okla., 1990), 66–72; Coles Bashford, comp., *The Compiled Laws of the Territory of Arizona from 1864 to 1871, Inclusive* (Albany, N.Y., 1871), 231.

10. Joseph E. Badger, *The Old Boy of Tombstone; or, Wagering a Life on a Card* (New York, 1883); William M. Breakenridge, *Helldorado: Bringing Law to the Mesquite* (New York, 1928); see also Walter Noble Burns, *Tombstone: An Iliad of the Old West* (New York, 1927). The first Wyatt Earp film came out in 1932, according to Allen Barra, *Inventing Wyatt Earp: His Life and Many Legends,* 2nd ed. (New York, 2005), photo insert preceding page 90.

11. D. W. Meinig, *The Shaping of America: A Geographical Perspective on Five Hundred Years of History,* vol. 3, *Transcontinental America, 1850–1915* (New Haven, 1998), 152–157; and see Samuel Truett, *Fugitive Landscapes: The Forgotten History of the U.S.-Mexico Borderlands* (New Haven, 2006), 6, 8.

12. Warren District Commercial Club, "Arizona's Treasure House: Bisbee and the Warren Mining District" (Bisbee, 1913), 11; see also "Cochise Empire in Self," *BDR,* 1915 Mining Edition.

13. On race and Americanism I have been influenced by Gary Gerstle, *American Crucible: Race and Nation in the Twentieth Century* (Princeton, 2001). Major studies of whiteness include Alexander Saxton, *The Rise and Fall of the White Republic: Class Politics and Mass Culture in Nineteenth-Century America,* 2nd ed. (London, 2003); David R. Roediger, *The Wages of Whiteness: Race and the Making of the American Working Class,* rev. ed. (New York, 1999); idem, *Towards the Abolition of Whiteness: Essays on Race, Politics, and Working Class History* (New York, 1994); Jacobson, *Whiteness of a Different Color;* and George Lipsitz, *The Possessive Investment in Whiteness: How White People Profit from Identity Politics* (Philadelphia, 1998). On the South, see esp. Grace Elizabeth Hale, *Making Whiteness: The Culture of Segregation in the South, 1890–1940* (New York, 1999). Critiques of whiteness studies include Peter Kolchin, "Whiteness Studies: The New History of Race in America," *Journal of American History,* 89 (June 2002): 154–173; Eric Arnesen, "Whiteness and the Historians' Imagination," *International Labor and Working-Class History,* 60 (Fall 2001): 3–32; Barbara J. Fields, "Whiteness, Racism, and Identity," *International Labor and Working-Class History,* 60 (Fall 2001): 48–56; Daniel Wickberg, "Heterosexual White Male; Some Recent Inversions in American Cultural History," *Journal of American History,* 92 (June 2005): 136–157; and Hasia Diner, "The World of Whiteness," *Historically Speaking* (September–October 2007): 20–22.

14. These debts, too vast to summarize here, are acknowledged in notes throughout the book.

15. Among the few books that consider the racial status of both Mexicans and eastern Europeans are Gunther Peck, *Reinventing Free Labor: Padrones and Immigrant Workers in the North American West, 1880–1930* (New York, 2000); Nancy Foner, *In a New Land: A Comparative View of Immigration* (New York, 2005); and Linda Gordon, *The Great Arizona Orphan Abduction* (Cambridge, Mass., 1999). On Arizona, also see Eric Meeks, *Border Citizens: The Making of Indians, Mexicans, and Anglos in Arizona* (Austin, 2007). The body of work that comes closest is on California. See, e.g., Natalia Molina, *Fit To Be Citizens? Public Health and Race in Los Angeles, 1879–1939* (Berkeley, 2006); Kevin Leonard, *The Battle for Los Angeles: Racial Ideology and World War II* (Albuquerque, 2006); Alison Varzally, *Making a Non-White America: Californians Coloring Outside Ethnic Lines, 1925–1955* (Berkeley, 2008); Mark Wild, *Street Meeting: Multiethnic Neighborhoods in Early Twentieth-Century Los Angeles* (Berkeley, 2005).

16. Best-known of the scientific debunkings of racial difference is Stephen Jay Gould, *The Mismeasure of Man* (New York, 1981). The standard work on the social construction of race is Michael Omi and Howard Winant, *Racial Formation in the United States from the 1960s to the 1990s* (New York, 1986, 1994). See also W. E. B. Du Bois, *Black Reconstruction, 1860–1880* (New York, 1935), borrowed by Roediger, *Wages of Whiteness.*

17. See Charles Montgomery, *The Spanish Redemption: Heritage, Power, and Loss on New Mexico's Upper Rio Grande* (Berkeley, 2002).

18. On divisions between Mexicans and Mexican Americans, see David Gutiérrez, *Walls and Mirrors: Mexican Americans, Mexican Immigrants, and the Politics of Ethnic-*

ity (Berkeley, 1995). But see also Foley, "Becoming Hispanic"; Montgomery, *The Spanish Redemption;* Ramón Gutiérrez, "Unraveling America's Hispanic Past: Internal Stratification and Class Boundaries," *Aztlan,* 17, no. 1 (1987): 79–101; and Aída Hurtado and Carlos H. Arce, "Mexicans, Chicanos, Mexican Americans, or Pochos . . . ? Que Somos? The Impact of Language and Nativity on Ethnic Labeling," *Aztlan,* 17, no. 1 (1987): 103–130.

19. See Meeks, *Border Citizens,* 13; Evelyn Nakano Glenn, *Unequal Freedom: How Race and Gender Shaped American Citizenship and Labor* (Cambridge, Mass., 2002), 255–256.

20. Neil Foley, in *The White Scourge,* uses "ethnoracial"; Ellen R. Baker uses "ethnic" in *On Strike and on Film: Mexican American Families and Blacklisted Filmmakers in Cold War America* (Chapel Hill, 2007), esp. 13. On Mexican Americans as a "race," not an ethnicity, see Laura E. Gómez, *Manifest Destinies: The Making of the Mexican American Race* (New York, 2007).

1. A Shared World in Tres Alamos

1. Dunbar's biographical information comes from *History of Arizona Territory Showing Its Resources and Advantages . . .* (San Francisco, 1884), 242; *Grijalba et al. v. Dunbar et al.,* 1889, Cochise County District Court, 1st Judicial District, Case no. 1414, filmfiles 90.6.2 and 90.6.3, ASLAPR, 146–147, 246, quotations on 156, 215, 146. Extant records do not reveal the outcome of the case.

2. Cochise County Marriage Index no. 1, Cochise County Clerk of the Court, Bisbee, Arizona, www.rootsweb.com/~azsvgs/ (accessed 22 July 2002).

3. *Grijalba v. Dunbar,* 227, 207.

4. Ibid., 410.

5. The literature on Mexicans and land is voluminous, but for views close to the one enunciated here about land ownership and status, see esp. David Montejano, *Anglos and Mexicans in the Making of Texas, 1836–1986* (Austin, 1987); and Armando C. Alonzo, *Tejano Legacy: Rancheros and Settlers in South Texas, 1734–1900* (Albuquerque, 1998). Also see Albert Camarillo, *Chicanos in a Changing Society: From Mexican Pueblos to American Barrios in Santa Barbara and Southern California, 1848–1930* (Cambridge, Mass., 1979), Tomás Almaguer, *Racial Fault Lines: The Historical Origins of White Supremacy in California* (Berkeley, 1994); Robert D. Shadow and Maria J. Rodriguez-Shadow, "Rancheros, Land, and Ethnicity on the Northern Borderlands: Works on Social and Agrarian History in the Last Decade," *Latin American Research Review,* 32, no. 1 (1997): 171–198; Maria Montoya, *Translating Property: The Maxwell Land Grant and the Conflict over Land in the American West, 1840–1900* (Berkeley, 2002); Ray H. Mattison, "Early Spanish and Mexican Settlements in Arizona," *New Mexico Historical Review,* 21, no. 4 (October 1946): 273–326; and Martha Menchaca, *Recovering History, Constructing*

Race: The Indian, Black and White Roots of Mexican Americans (Austin, 2001). A rare discussion of Mexican American homesteading appears in Alvar W. Carlson, *The Spanish-American Homeland* (Baltimore, 1990), 53–63.

6. See Shadow and Rodriguez-Shadow, "Rancheros," 177–178.

7. Quoted in Nat McKelvey, "Reckless, Romantic Redington," *Arizona Highways* (May 1958): 36; "Affidavit of N. B. Appel, Territory of Arizona, County of Pima," Appel biofile, AHS.

8. Henry F. Dobyns, Theodore Bundy, James E. Officer, and Richard W. Stoffle, *Los Tres Alamos del Rio San Pedro: The Peculiar Persistence of a Place Name* (Tucson, 1996).

9. James E. Officer, *Hispanic Arizona, 1536–1856* (Tucson, 1987), 50.

10. Dobyns et al., *Los Tres Alamos,* 15.

11. Menchaca, *Recovering History,* 126.

12. See esp. Ross Frank, *From Settler to Citizen: New Mexican Economic Development and the Creation of Vecino Society, 1750–1820* (Berkeley, 2000).

13. Thomas E. Sheridan, *Arizona: A History* (Tucson, 1995), 36–41; Officer, *Hispanic Arizona,* 2–3, 109. The name "Tucson" derived from a Pima Indian word meaning "spring at the foot of a black mountain." See www.arizona.edu/home/tucson-history.php (accessed 13 November 2008).

14. Robert M. Utley, *A Clash of Cultures: Fort Bowie and the Chiricahua Apaches* (Washington, D.C., 1977), 17–18; Officer, *Hispanic Arizona,* 106–110, 148–171, 295; Sheridan, *Arizona,* 47–52.

15. On the Tres Alamos colony, see Jay J. Wagoner, *Early Arizona: Prehistory to Civil War* (Tucson, 1975), 230–231; Menchaca, *Recovering History,* 226; Charles D. Poston, *Building a State in Apache Land,* ed. John Myers (Tempe, Ariz., 1963), 42–43; Joseph F. Park, "The Apaches in Mexican-American Relations, 1848–1861," *Arizona and the West,* 3, no. 2 (1961): 129–146. Land grants are shown in Henry P. Walker and Don Bufkin, *Historical Atlas of Arizona,* 2nd ed. (Norman, Okla., 1986), Map 15.

16. See special issues of *Archaeology Southwest,* 17, no. 3 (Summer 2003) and 18, no. 1 (Winter 2004); Dobyns et al., *Los Tres Alamos;* Sheridan, *Arizona,* 36–38; Edward H. Spicer, *Cycles of Conquest: The Impact of Spain, Mexico, and the United States on the Indians of the Southwest* (Tucson, 1962), 244; Officer, *Hispanic Arizona;* and Wagoner, *Early Arizona,* 229–231.

17. Edward Ellsworth, "Homesteaders in Tres Alamos Rio San Pedro, Pima County, Arizona Territory: The Homestead Act of 1862," unpublished manuscript in author's possession (Benson, Ariz., 1998), 18–21.

18. Dobyns et al., *Los Tres Alamos,* 27.

19. Hunting quotation is from *Grijalba v. Dunbar,* 22; also see 28–29, 44, "dug out" on 66. On crops, see *Arizona Citizen,* 4 July 1874, in Ellsworth, "Homesteaders," 164–165. On natural habitat, see Richard J. Hinton, *Handbook to Arizona, 1877* (Glorieta, N.M., 1970; orig. pub. 1878), 231; McKelvey, "Reckless, Romantic Redington"; J. J. Wagoner,

"Development of the Cattle Industry in Southern Arizona, 1870's and 1880's," *New Mexico Historical Review,* 26, no. 3 (July 1951): 204–224; and Paul Hirt, "The Transformation of a Landscape: Culture and Ecology in Southeastern Arizona," *Environmental Review,* 13, (Fall–Winter 1989): 167–189.

20. Conflicting origins of the Tres Alamos District appear in (Mamie) Mary Belle Bernard Aguirre, "About My First School," typescript, 1890s, AHS; and Elsie Toles, *Rural and Small-Town Schools of Cochise County* (ca. 1920), Elsie Toles Collection, AHS.

21. On squatting and land law, see Paul W. Gates, *History of Public Land Law Development* (Washington, D.C., 1968), esp. 238–240, 387–434; quotations from *Grijalba v. Dunbar,* 40, 274, and from *John Montgomery v. George Wesley,* Probate Case of the County of Pima and Territory of Arizona, in Ellsworth, "Homesteaders," 79–114, "good mercheneble corn" on 79.

22. Quotations from Severiaño Bonillas deposition, *John C. Johnson Estate v. the U.S. and Apaches,* Commissioner of the Court of Claims, Benson, Arizona, 14 March 1913, 6, in Ellsworth, "Homesteaders," 205; *Grijalba v. Dunbar,* 420; also see Probate Case of Antonio Grijalba, Cochise County Probate Court, case no. 437, microfilm, ASLAPR.

23. P.W.G. [Paul Wallace Gates], "Homestead Act," in Howard R. Lamar, ed., *The New Encyclopedia of the American West* (New Haven, 1998), 492–493.

24. Dobyns et al., *Los Tres Alamos,* 41–42; Edward Soza, *Mexican Homesteaders in the San Pedro River Valley and the Homestead Act of 1862: 1870–1908* (Altadena, Calif., 1993, 1994), 28; and idem, *Hispanic Homesteaders in Arizona, 1870–1908* (Altadena, Calif., 1994), 15 (both works by Soza are available at parentseyes.arizona.edu). Nine of the county's thirty-six cash entries before 1890 were by Spanish-surnamed individuals, and ten of seventy-two from 1890–1899 (BLM database).

25. "San Pedro Valley and Vicinity," *Arizona Citizen,* 1 July 1876, 2; Patricia Preciado Martin, *Beloved Land: An Oral History of Mexican Americans in Southern Arizona* (Tucson, 2004), 76–83; Grijalba probate case.

26. Biofiles for Juan, Francisco, and Antonio Grijalba, AHS; Officer, *Hispanic Arizona,* 181, 284–286, 326; *El Fronterizo* (Tucson), 20 January 1894, 3; James M. Murphy, *Laws, Courts, and Lawyers: Through the Years in Arizona* (Tucson, 1970), 4; Menchaca, *Recovering History,* 253. The reference to "owning" whiteness alludes to W. E. B. Du Bois's discussion of the psychological wage of being white, in his pathbreaking *Black Reconstruction in America, 1860–1880* (1935). See also David Roediger, *The Wages of Whiteness: Race and the Making of the American Working Class* (New York, 2007; orig. pub. 1991).

27. Discussion of *casta* and frontier racial systems is based on Magnus Mörner, *Race Mixture in the History of Latin America* (Boston, 1967); José Cuello, "Racialized Hierarchies of Power in Colonial Mexican Society: The *Sistema de Castas* as a form of Social Control in Saltillo," in Jesús F. de la Teja and Ross Frank, eds., *Choice, Persuasion, and Coercion: Social Control on Spain's North American Frontiers* (Albuquerque, 2005), 201–226; Leo J. Garafolo and Rachel Sarah O'Toole, "Introduction: Constructing Differ-

ence in Colonial Latin America," *Journal of Colonialism and Colonial History*, 7, no. 1 (2006), online at muse.jhu.edu (accessed 13 May 2008); Cheryl Martin, *Governance and Society in Colonial Mexico: Chihuahua in the Eighteenth Century* (Stanford, 2001); John Tutino, *Making a New World: Forging Atlantic Capitalism in the Bajío and Spanish North America* (Durham, N.C., forthcoming, 2010); and Cynthia Radding, *Wandering Peoples: Colonialism, Ethnic Spaces, and Ecological Frontiers in Northwestern Mexico, 1700–1850* (Durham, N.C., 1997), esp. 17, 111–115. On race mixing, see esp. Alan Knight, "Racism, Revolution, and *Indigenismo*: Mexico, 1910–1940," in Richard Baker, ed., *The Idea of Race in Latin America, 1870–1940* (Austin, 1990), 71–113; Menchaca, *Recovering History*; idem, "Chicano Indianism: A Historical Account of Racial Repression in the United States," *American Ethnologist* 20, no. 3 (1993): 583–603; Ramón A. Gutiérrez, *When Jesus Came, the Corn Mothers Went Away: Marriage, Sexuality, and Power in New Mexico, 1500–1846* (Palo Alto, 1991); John M. Nieto-Phillips, *The Language of Blood: The Making of Spanish-American Identity in New Mexico, 1880s–1930s* (Albuquerque, 2004); Officer, *Hispanic Arizona*, 41.

28. On race in Sonora, see Miguel Tinker Salas, *In the Shadow of the Eagles: Sonora and the Transformation of the Border during the Porfiriato* (Berkeley, 1997), esp. 26–27. On Arizona, see Officer, *Hispanic Arizona*, esp. 41, 78. On Los Angeles and Albuquerque, see Laura E. Gómez, *Manifest Destinies: The Making of the Mexican American Race* (New York, 2007), 52, 54.

29. Officer, *Hispanic Arizona*, 92, 78.

30. On miscegenation, or race mixing, in the United States, see David A. Hollinger, Thomas E. Skidmore, Barbara J. Fields, and Henry Yu in "*AHR* Forum: Amalgamation and the Historical Distinctiveness of the United States," *American Historical Review*, 108, no. 5 (December 2003): 1362–1414; Gary P. Nash, "The Hidden History of Mestizo America," *Journal of American History*, 82, no. 3 (December 1995): 941–964; Martha Hodes, ed., *Sex, Love, Race: Crossing Boundaries in North American History* (New York, 1998); Peggy Pascoe, "Miscegenation Laws, Court Cases, and Ideologies of 'Race' in Twentieth-Century America," *Journal of American History*, 83, no. 1 (June 1996): 44–69. On *mestizaje*, see Mörner, *Race Mixture*; and Ana María Alonso, "Conforming Disconformity: 'Mestizaje, Hybridity, and the Aesthetics of Mexican Nationalism," *Cultural Anthropology*, 19, no. 4 (November 2004): 459–490. The United States Supreme Court did not overturn anti-miscegenation laws until 1967, in *Loving et ux. v. Virginia*, 388 U.S. 1.

31. On mixed races and racial systems in the United States, see esp. Ramón Gutiérrez, "New Mexico and the Making of North America," in John Tutino, ed., *Mexico and Mexicans in the Making of the United States* (Austin, Tex., forthcoming, 2010).

32. John Ross Browne, quoted in Andrés E. Jiménez, "The Political Formation of a Mexican Working Class in the Arizona Copper Industry, 1870–1917," *SUNY Review* (Binghamton, N.Y.), 4, no. 3 (Winter 1981): 535–569, quotation on 552.

33. Reginald Horsman, *Race and Manifest Destiny: Origins of American Racial Anglo-*

Saxonism (Cambridge, U.K., 1981); Kenneth Greenberg, "The Ideology of Racial Anglo-Saxonism," *Reviews in American History,* 10, no. 3 (1982): 353–357.

34. George W. Stocking, "The Turn-of-the-Century Concept of Race," *Modernism/Modernity,* 1, no. 1 (January 1994): 4–16, quotation on 11; John Higham, *Strangers in the Land: Patterns of American Nativism, 1860–1925* (New York, 1955; rev. ed., 1968), 131–157, quotations on 133 and 134. And see Ivan Hannaford, *Race: The History of an Idea in the West* (Baltimore, 1996), esp. 273–275; Kenan Malik, *The Meaning of Race: Race, History and Culture in Western Society* (New York, 1996), 90–91; Audrey Smedley, *Race in North America* (Boulder, Colo., 1993), 231–254. On "blood" and "race" in New Mexico, see esp. Nieto-Phillips, *Language of Blood.* Also see David J. Weber, "'Scarce More than Apes': Historical Roots of Anglo-American Stereotypes of Mexicans," in *Myth and the History of the Southwest* (Albuquerque, 1988), 53–167.

35. On anti-Mexicanism, see Jiménez, "Political Formation of a Mexican Working Class"; treaty available at www.historicaltextarchive.com (accessed 24 March 2008).

36. Matthew Frye Jacobson, *Whiteness of a Different Color: European Immigrants and the Alchemy of Race* (Cambridge, Mass., 1998), 7.

37. Coles Bashford, comp., *The Compiled Laws of the Territory of Arizona from 1864 to 1871, Inclusive* (Albany, N.Y., 1871), 231.

38. In one such Arizona case in 1921, a judge ruled that Mexicans belonged to the "Caucasian race" unless proven otherwise; see Pascoe, "Miscegenation Laws," 51.

39. On Arizona law, see Menchaca, "Chicano Indianism," 589. James M. Crane, "An Analysis of the Great Register of Cochise County, Arizona Territory, 1884," *Cochise Quarterly,* 18 (1988): 3–9. On citizenship in territories, see Gómez, *Manifest Destinies,* esp. 41.

40. Gutiérrez, *When Jesus Came,* 206.

41. Martha Menchaca offers a different interpretation in *Recovering History,* 328, n. 14.

42. Edward Soza, *Affidavits of Contest vis-à-vis Arizona Hispanic Homesteaders* (Altadena, Calif., 1998), esp. 75–76.

43. Gómez, *Manifest Destinies;* and esp. Ian F. Haney López, *White by Law: The Legal Construction of Race* (New York, 1996); and Pascoe, "Miscegenation Laws."

44. This is clear from the cross-listing of county registries with land records.

45. Evidence on language in *Grijalba v. Dunbar,* 2, 34, 36, 62, 223, 320, and 409.

46. Check stubs and ledgers, 1905–1906, Grijalba probate case.

47. Thomas E. Sheridan, *Los Tucsonenses: The Mexican Community in Tucson, 1854–1941* (Tucson, 1986), esp. 33; "un-American" in Emma Hildreth Adams, *To and Fro, Up and Down* (Cincinnati, 1888), 57; "phlegmatic" in E. [Enoch] Conklin, *Picturesque Arizona: Being the Result of Travels and Observations in Arizona during the Fall and Winter of 1877* (New York, 1878), 295; "more complete" in *History of Arizona Territory,* 256; James Officer, *Arizona's Hispanic Perspective: A Research Report* (Tucson, 1979), 79.

48. Quoted in W. Clement Eaton, "Frontier Life in Southern Arizona, 1851–1861," *Southwestern Historical Quarterly*, 36, no. 3 (January 1933): 173–192, quotation on 182.

49. Sheridan, *Los Tucsonenses,* esp. 37.

50. Dobyns et al., *Tres Alamos,* 57. Cleófila Apodaca had inherited her homestead but would later file her own claim and marry another homesteader. See Soza, *Affidavits of Contest,* 124–125; and BLM database.

51. Lynn R. Bailey, *Henry Clay Hooker and the Sierra Bonita* (Tucson, 1998); also see Ellsworth, *Homesteaders,* 145, 172, 175; *History of Arizona Territory,* 242; Colonel Hodge, *Arizona Citizen,* 28 May 1875, 2; *Grijalba v. Dunbar,* 265; Dobyns et al., *Tres Alamos,* 26, 54; William B. Shillingberg, *Tombstone, A.T.: A History of Early Mining, Milling, and Mayhem* (Spokane, 1999), 89–90, 119, 190.

52. On *norteños'* alliances, see Andrés Reséndez, *Changing National Identities at the Frontier: Texas and New Mexico, 1800–1850* (New York, 2005); and Tinker Salas, *In the Shadow.* On global connections, see esp. Samuel Truett, *Fugitive Landscapes: The Forgotten History of the U.S.-Mexico Borderlands* (New Haven, 2006).

53. On water rights, see R. H. Forbes, "Irrigation and Agricultural Practice in Arizona," *Arizona Agricultural Extension Service Bulletin,* 63 (1911); and Dean E. Mann, *The Politics of Water in Arizona* (Tucson, 1963).

54. Letter to author from Edward J. Ellsworth, Benson, Arizona, August 2001.

55. *Grijalba v. Dunbar,* 78–80.

56. On Teófila León, see Arthur L. Campa, *Hispanic Culture in the Southwest* (Norman, Okla., 1979), 70; Dobyns et al., *Los Tres Alamos,* 26–27, 36; Cochise County Superior Court Marriage Index no. 1, 1881–1963, microfilm file 90.5.69, ASLAPR. In marriage records, there is no way to track ethnic or national origin besides Spanish surnames; obviously the count is not exact. Sheridan, *Los Tucsonenses,* 149.

57. Frank Lockwood, *Pioneer Portraits* (Tucson, 1968), 109–127; Donna J. Baldwin, "A Successful Search for Security: Arizona Pioneer Society Widows," in Arlene Scadron, ed., *On Their Own: Widows and Widowhood in the American Southwest, 1848–1939* (Urbana, Ill., 1988), 228; Howard R. Lamar, *The Far Southwest, 1846–1912: A Territorial History,* rev. ed. (Albuquerque, 2000; orig. pub. 1966), 365; "Notes from Tres Alamos," *Tucson Citizen,* undated clipping, 1885, AHS; List of Cochise County Justices of the Peace, 1881–1901, Sierra Vista Genealogical Society Website, www.rootsweb. com/~azsvgs/JPs1.htm (accessed 12 January 2006).

58. Peggy Pascoe, "Race, Gender, and Intercultural Relations: The Case of Interracial Marriage," *Frontiers,* 12 (1991): 5–18; Jay Wagoner, *Arizona Territory, 1863–1912: A Political History* (Tucson, 1970), 65; Roger D. Hathaway, "Unlawful Love: A History of Arizona's Miscegenation Law," *Journal of Arizona History,* 27 (Winter 1986): 377–390. And see Peggy Pascoe, *What Comes Naturally: Miscegenation Law and the Making of Race in America* (New York, 2009).

59. The "collateral" term is from Rosaura Sánchez, *Telling Identities: The Californio Testimonios* (Minneapolis, 1995), 201.

60. On intermarriage and its dangers, see Deena González, *Refusing the Favor: The Spanish-Mexican Women of Santa Fe, 1820–1880* (New York, 1999), esp. 10, 107–122; but also see Maria Raquel Casas, *Married to a Daughter of the Land: Interethnic Marriages in California, 1820–1880* (Las Vegas, 2007); Miroslava Chávez-García, *Negotiating Conquest: Gender and Power in California, 1770s to 1880s* (Tucson, 2004); Paul R. Spickard, *Mixed Blood: Intermarriage and Ethnic Identity in Twentieth-Century America* (Madison, Wisc., 1989); Pascoe, "Race, Gender, and Intercultural Marriage"; Rebecca McDowell McCraver, *The Impact of Intimacy: Mexican-Anglo Intermarriage in New Mexico, 1821–1846* (El Paso, 1982); Jane Dysart, "Mexican Women in San Antonio, 1830–1860: The Assimilation Process," *WHQ,* 7 (1976): 365–375; Darlis A. Miller, "Cross-Cultural Marriages in the Southwest: The New Mexico Experience, 1846–1900," in Darlis A. Miller and Joan M. Jensen, eds., *New Mexico Women: Intercultural Perspectives* (Albuquerque, 1986); D. A. Brading, *Miners and Merchants in Bourbon Mexico, 1763–1810* (Cambridge, U.K., 1971), 21; Richard Boyer, *Lives of the Bigamists: Marriage, Family, and Community in Colonial Mexico* (Albuquerque, 1995), 47; Diana Balmori, Stuart F. Voss, and Miles Wortman, *Notable Family Networks in Latin America* (Chicago, 1984), 34–35, 101–102; John E. Kicza, "The Great Families of Mexico: Elite Maintenance and Business Practices in Late Colonial Mexico City," *Hispanic American Historical Review,* 62, no. 3 (August 1982): 429–457; and Reséndez, *Changing National Identities,* ch. 4.

61. *Grijalba v. Dunbar,* 14; on *casas chicas,* see Susan L. Johnson, "Sharing Bed and Board: Cohabitation and Cultural Difference in Central Arizona Mining Towns," in Susan Armitage and Elizabeth Jameson, eds., *The Women's West* (Norman, Okla., 1987), 77–78; Phocian Way, quoted in Eaton, "Frontier Life," 184.

62. What follows echoes Manuel P. Servín, "The Role of Mexican-Americans in the Development of Early Arizona," in Servín, ed., *An Awakened Minority: The Mexican-Americans* (Beverly Hills, 1974), 30. On class and color distinctions, see Tinker Salas, *In the Shadow,* 27–29; and esp. Antonia Castañeda, "The Political Economy of Nineteenth-Century Stereotypes of Californianas," in Adelaida R. Del Castillo, ed., *Between Borders: Essays on Mexicana/Chicana History* (Encino, Calif., 1990), 213–236; Almaguer, *Racial Fault Lines,* 58–61; and Amy S. Greenberg, *Manifest Manhood and the Antebellum American Empire* (New York, 2009), ch. 3. Phocian Way, quoted in Eaton, "Frontier Life," 184; Charles D. Poston, *Building a State in Apache Land,* ed. John M. Myers (Tempe, Ariz., 1963), 75.

63. Eaton, "Frontier Life," Way quotation on 184, Pumpelly on 189; see also Jane Samson, *Race and Empire* (Harlow, U.K., 2005), 63.

64. Adams, *To and Fro,* 57.

65. On landholding women in Tucson, see Officer, *Hispanic Arizona,* 19. Unless otherwise noted, my discussion of widowhood and inheritance laws relies on Scadron, ed., *On Their Own;* Carole Shammas et al., *Inheritance in America from Colonial Times to*

the Present (New Brunswick, N.J., 1987); González, *Refusing the Favor;* Yolanda Chávez Leyva, "'A Poor Widow Burdened with Children': Widows and Land in Colonial New Mexico," in Elizabeth Jameson and Susan Armitage, eds., *Writing the Range: Race, Class, and Culture in the Women's West* (Norman, Okla., 1997), 85–96; and Chávez-García, *Negotiating Conquest.*

66. Inheritance and property laws applied to Anglo women too, but this very small group did not have long experience with these marriage and inheritance systems. See Deborah Rosen, "Women and Property across Colonial America: A Comparison of Legal Systems in New Mexico and New York," *William and Mary Quarterly,* 60, no. 2 (2003): 355–381; and Sara Brooks Sundberg, "Legal Systems at Odds: Wills, Marriage Contracts, and Women's Property in Spanish West Florida and Early Louisiana, and Spanish Natchez and Early Mississippi," unpublished paper, 19 March 2005, in author's possession.

67. On children of intermarriage, see Chapter 5.

68. James Muhn, "Women and the Homestead Act: Land Department Administration of a Legal Imbroglio, 1863–1934," *Western Legal History,* 7 (Summer–Fall 1994): 282–307.

69. BLM database; Ellsworth, *Homesteaders,* 76 and Ellsworth letter; Katherine Mejía, oral history transcript, interview by Liz Brenner, 18 April 1997, SPVAHM; and Jesús Maldonado, Probate Case no. 715, Cochise County Probate Court, microfilm, ASLAPR. (Likewise, Francisca Comadurán Díaz de Mejía, clearly a relative of Jesús, had a cash entry and a homestead claim in her own name that appears in Soza, *Hispanic Homesteaders in Arizona.*) Bert Haskett, "Early History of the Cattle Industry in Arizona," *Arizona Historical Review,* 6, no. 4 (October 1935): 3–42, esp. 32; *Grijalba v. Dunbar,* esp. 174–175, 343.

70. Martin, *Beloved Land,* 80.

71. See, e.g., Leyva, "'A Poor Widow'"; and Gonzalez, *Refusing the Favor. Grijalba v. Dunbar,* 175–176, 343.

72. David J. Weber, *The Spanish Frontier in North America* (New Haven, 1992), 336–341, quotation on 336.

73. *The Sonora Exploring and Mining Company, Sonora—and the Value of Its Silver Mines: Report of the Sonora Exploring and Mining Co., Made to the Stockholders* (Cincinnati, 1856), Newberry Library, Chicago, 23; Wagoner, *Early Arizona,* 390–392.

74. *History of Arizona Territory,* 27.

75. Wagoner, *Arizona Territory,* 20–21.

76. Officer, *Hispanic Arizona,* 76, 258–259, 307, 326; Sharon Johnson Mariscal, "The Sosa/Soza Family of Arizona," *Cochise Quarterly* (Summer 1986): 16. But see Edward Soza, "Soza Family History: Antonio Campo Soza, 1845–1915," www.library.arizona.edu/soza/marriages.htm (accessed 11 January 2006); Edwin R. Sweeney, *Merejildo Grijalva: Apache Captive, Army Scout* (El Paso, 1997); and see Brian McGinty, *The Oatman*

Massacre: A Tale of Desert Survival and Captivity (Norman, Okla., 2005). On captive taking, see Karl Jacoby, *Shadows at Dawn: A Borderlands Massacre and the Violence of History* (New York, 2008). Captives and slaves in the borderlands have been a subject of rich debate. See esp. James F. Brooks, *Captives and Cousins: Slavery, Kinship, and Community in the Southwest Borderlands* (Chapel Hill, 2002).

77. On attacks, see Dobyns et al., *Los Tres Alamos*, ch. 1, 27; Legislature of the Territory of Arizona, *Memorial and Affidavits showing Outrages Perpetrated by the Apache Indians, in the Territory of Arizona, for the Years 1869 and 1870* (San Francisco, 1871).

78. *Grijalba v. Dunbar*, 54, 282–283, 413; Arthur J. Benedict et al., "Sunday School Pioneers of Sulphur Spring Valley," 1925, 87, BMHM.

79. Jacoby, *Shadows at Dawn;* Chip Colwell-Chanthaphonh, *Massacre at Camp Grant: Forgetting and Remembering Apache History* (Tucson, 2007).

80. P. Richard Metcalf, "Peace Policy," in Howard Lamar, ed., *The New Encyclopedia of the American West* (New Haven, 1998), 845–847; on Stoneman's report, see Wagoner, *Arizona Territory*, 124–128.

81. [John Montgomery], "From San Pedro Valley," *Arizona Citizen*, 15 April 1871, in Ellsworth, "Homesteaders," 161.

82. William Oury, "Historical Truth: The So-Called 'Camp Grant Massacre' of 1871," Tucson *Arizona Daily Star*, 29 June and 1 July 1879, reprinted in Peter Cozzens, ed., *Eyewitnesses to the Indian Wars, 1865–1890: The Struggle for Apacheria* (Mechanicsville, Penn., 2001), 61.

83. Wagoner, *Arizona Territory*, 131. For purposes of comparison, see "Coddled Murderers," *Tucson Citizen*, 13 June 1885, and *El Fronterizo* (Tucson), 5 May 1882, 2, and 30 June 1882, 2.

84. Dobyns et al., *Tres Alamos*, 40.

85. Jacoby, *Shadows at Dawn;* "From San Pedro Valley," *Arizona Citizen*, 10 August 1872 and 17 May 1873, 2, in Ellsworth, "Homesteaders," 166. Hostilities declined in the early 1870s, thanks to a peace agreement between former Civil War general O. O. Howard and Chiricahua leader Cochise that established the Chiricahua Reservation in the years 1872–1876. The peace agreement unraveled when an unscrupulous whiskey trader provided alcohol to the Chiricahuas, one of whom went on a drunken rampage and murdered two of his sisters. The reservation was disbanded, and active warfare broke out again.

86. A reminder that "Anglo" is a catch-all term. At least six of the Anglos, or about 10 percent, were probably Jews.

87. *Memorial*, 8, 17–18, 21; "A Thousand Murders," *Weekly Citizen* (Tucson), 13 June 1885. For a similar discourse in northern Mexico, see Ana María Alonso, *Thread of Blood: Colonialism, Revolution and Gender on Mexico's Northern Frontier* (Tucson, 1995).

88. Carrillo was a Sonora native and prominent resident of southern Arizona, as well as a landowner in Cochise County. His name is misspelled in *Memorial,* 14–15. This is the copy in the Graff Collection, Newberry Library, Chicago.

89. *History of Arizona Territory,* 242.

2. Race and Conflict in Tombstone

1. In the minefield of Tombstone fact and lore, I have trusted the following sources: William B. Shillingberg, *Tombstone, A.T.: A History of Early Mining, Milling, and Mayhem* (Spokane, 1999); Lynn R. Bailey, *Tombstone, Arizona 'Too Tough To Die': The Rise, Fall, and Resurrection of a Silver Camp, 1878–1990* (Tucson, 2004); Samuel Truett, *Fugitive Landscapes: The Forgotten History of the U.S.-Mexico Borderlands* (New Haven, 2006); Casey Tefertiller, *Wyatt Earp: The Life behind the Legend* (New York, 1997); Steven Lubet, *Murder in Tombstone: The Forgotten Trial of Wyatt Earp* (New Haven, 2004); Paula Mitchell Marks, *And Die in the West: The Story of the O.K. Corral Gunfight* (New York, 1989). On Sherman, see Shillingberg, *Tombstone, A.T.,* 323–324; on the Cosmopolitan Hotel, see Bailey, *Tombstone,* 72–73.

2. William T. Sherman to B. H. Brewster, 12 April 1882, MC 2028; Shillingberg, *Tombstone, A.T.,* 323–325.

3. Tombstone histories neglect Mexicans and the border, but see Allen Barra, "Gunfight at the OK Corral," *New York Times,* 6 November 2006, online at www.iht.com (accessed 1 February 2008); Don Taylor, *The United States of America v. The Cowboys,* 2 vols. (Tombstone, 2006); and Truett, *Fugitive Landscapes,* esp. 64–66.

4. "Embryo city" quotation from Clara Spalding Brown, cited in Tefertiller, *Wyatt Earp,* 37.

5. Marks, *And Die in the West,* 49, 155–160; Odie Faulk, *Tombstone: Myth and Reality* (New York, 1972), 92, 102–127; "sensible, manly fellow" from George Parsons, cited in Bailey, *Tombstone,* 112.

6. Eric L. Clements, *After the Boom in Tombstone and Jerome, Arizona: Decline in Western Resource Towns* (Reno, 2003), 31.

7. James Officer, *Arizona's Hispanic Perspective: A Research Report* (Phoenix, 1981), 83–85; Truett, *Fugitive Landscapes,* 63. Castañeda biofile, AHS; Clements, *After the Boom,* 315, n. 29.

8. Clements, *After the Boom,* 30; Faulk, *Tombstone,* 141; party invitations in MS 1039, MacNeil Collection, AHS.

9. John Gosper to C. P. Dake, 28 November 1881, MC 2028; *Nugget* cited in Shillingberg, *Tombstone, A.T.,* 95; *Stock Report* quoted in Tefertiller, *Wyatt Earp,* 96.

10. James Biddle to (unnamed) Deputy U.S. Marshal, Tucson, 11 June 1881; James A. Zabriskie to B. H. Brewster, 22 January 1885; C. B. Pomroy, Tucson, to Wayne MacVeagh, 23 June 1881, all MC 2028; Clara Spalding Brown, *Tombstone from a Woman's Point of*

View: The Correspondence of Clara Spalding Brown, July 7, 1880, to November 14, 1882, ed. Lynn R. Bailey (Tucson, 1998), 49.

11. Estimates found in various letters within MC 2028; Pomroy to MacVeagh, 23 June 1881; Gosper to (unnamed) Attorney General (MacVeagh), 18 August 1881; *Tombstone Epitaph,* 13 August 1881, transcribed in Crawley Dake to S. F. Phillips, 17 October 1881, all MC 2028.

12. Gosper to Dake, 28 November 1881, emphasis in original; see also Joseph Bowyer to John Gosper, 17 September 1882, both MC 2028.

13. On casual posses, see Lubet, *Murder,* 51. On the blurring of law enforcement and vigilantism, see Brown, *Woman's Point of View,* 42. And see Richard White, "Outlaw Gangs of the Middle Border: American Social Bandits," *WHQ,* 12, no. 4 (October 1981): 387–408.

14. Gosper to Dake, 28 November 1881.

15. Gosper to Secretary of State Blaine, 30 September 1881, MC 2028.

16. Shillingberg, *Tombstone, A.T.,* 248, 265.

17. Richard Maxwell Brown, *No Duty to Retreat: Violence and Values in American History* (New York, 1991).

18. This interpretation is Brown's; and see John Mack Faragher, "The Tale of Wyatt Earp: Seven Films," in Mark C. Carnes, ed., *Past Imperfect: History According to the Movies* (New York, 1995), 154–161. On Southern honor, see esp. Bertram Wyatt-Brown, *Southern Honor: Ethics and Behavior in the Old South* (New York, 1982); and J. William Harris, "Honor, Grace, and War (But Not Slavery?) in Southern Culture," *Reviews in American History,* 30, no. 1 (March 2002): 1–7.

19. Lubet, *Murder,* 24–25; Shillingberg, *Tombstone, A.T.,* 162–164, 188, 199–203; Marks, *And Die in the West,* 25–29, 106. There is some dispute about James's party affiliation, but my reading of the evidence says the Earps were Republican. Email correspondence to author from Bob Boze Bell, Phoenix, Arizona, 15 April 2008.

20. Tefertiller, *Wyatt Earp,* 134.

21. Shillingberg, *Tombstone, A.T.,* 209–212.

22. Pomroy to MacVeagh, 23 June 1881.

23. Gosper to Blaine, 30 September 1881, emphasis in original.

24. John H. Barnhill, "Should the Military Take Charge in Emergencies?" *HNN: History News Service,* www.h-net.org (accessed 28 September 2006); Major Craig T. Trebilcock, "The Myth of Posse Comitatus," October 2000, www.homelandsecurity.org (accessed 9 December 2007). In 2005, President George W. Bush called for revisions to the law that would expand the military's role in "homeland security" duties at the U.S.-Mexico border and on the Gulf Coast after Hurricane Katrina.

25. William T. Sherman to R. T. (Robert Todd) Lincoln, 26 October 1881, MC 2028.

26. Tefertiller, *Wyatt Earp,* 99–100, 196–197. Gosper to Kirkwood, 18 August 1881, MC 2028; 29 November 1881, MC 429; 19 December 1881, MC 429. Clayton David Lau-

rie and Ronald H. Cole, *The Role of Federal Military Forces in Domestic Disorders, 1877–1945* (Washington, D.C., 1997), 75.

27. Head of Scout Operations to Deputy U.S. Marshal and Sheriffs, Pima and Cochise County, marked "Confidential," 16 June 1881, MC 2028; and see Pomroy to MacVeagh, 23 June 1881.

28. On the Opatas, see Truett, *Fugitive Landscapes,* 65; Biddle to Deputy U.S. Marshal, 11 June 1881; 16 June 1881, emphasis in original.

29. J. W. Evans to Crawley Dake, 5 September 1881; Sergeant Kelton to (unnamed) Adjutant General, 14 August 1881; also Adjutant General to Pacific Division, telegram, 14 August 1881, partly illegible (referring to the Cibecue incident, discussed below), MC 2028.

30. Tefertiller, *Wyatt Earp,* 90–98; Bowyer to Gosper, 17 September 1882; Evans to Dake, 4 August 1881; Dake to MacVeagh, 5 August 1881; all MC 2028.

31. Pomroy to MacVeagh, 23 June 1881.

32. Torres to Evans, 5 August 18819; Dake to MacVeagh, 5 August 1881; Evans to Dake, 10 August 1881, MC 2028; Torres to Evans, 24 June 1881, MC 2028; Sherman to Brewster, 12 April 1882.

33. David M. Pletcher, "Mexico Opens the Door to American Capital, 1877–1880," *The Americas,* 16, no. 1 (July 1959): 1–14; "Acts of Lawlessness" quoted in Tefertiller, *Wyatt Earp,* 99; Burton Kirkwood, *The History of Mexico* (New York, 2005), 174–175; Manuel de Zamacona to U.S. Secretary of State, 6 December 1878; John Frémont to Carl Schurz, 6 January 1879; but see also Frémont to Schurz, 18 February 1879, all in MC 429; Gosper to Blaine, 30 September 1881.

34. Pomroy to MacVeagh, 23 June 1881.

35. Gosper to Acting Attorney General, 8 December 1881, MC 2028; Kelton to Adjutant General, 14 August 1881; Legation of Mexico (Manuel de Zamacona) to Blaine, 13 April 1881, MC 429.

36. Gosper to Kirkwood, 29 November 1881; Gosper to Blaine, 30 September 1881. On Earp and Cruz, see Shillingberg, *Tombstone, A.T.,* 315–316. Some blamed the Cowboys' Texas roots for their disregard for Mexican life; see Truett, *Fugitive Landscapes,* 64–65. Rudolfo Acuña claims that the Cowboys kept Mexican labor out of Tombstone. See *Occupied America: A History of Chicanos,* 3rd ed. (New York, 1988), 95.

37. *Arizona Star,* cited in Tefertiller, *Wyatt Earp,* 73.

38. Quotations cited in Tefertiller, *Wyatt Earp,* 97–99. For a similar point, see Truett, *Fugitive Landscapes.*

39. See Ken Gonzales-Day, *Lynching in the West, 1850–1935* (Durham, N.C., 2006); Helen McLure, Ph.D. diss., Southern Methodist University, in progress.

40. See Gosper to Kirkwood, 19 November 1881.

41. Gosper to Kirkwood, emphasis in original.

42. Brown, *Woman's Point of View*, 48–49; *Epitaph* quoted in *History of Arizona Territory, Showing Its Resources and Advantages . . .* (San Francisco, 1884), 156.

43. Pomroy to MacVeagh, 23 June 1881; Phillips to Lincoln, 10 November 1881, MC 2028.

44. On Matías Romero, see Truett, *Fugitive Landscapes*, 3–4, 55–56; Frelinghuysen to Kirkwood, 13 April 1882; Romero to Kirkwood, 6 April 1882, both MC 429.

45. Brown, *No Duty to Retreat*, 81.

46. Peter Cozzens, ed., *Eyewitnesses to the Indian Wars, 1865–1890: The Struggle for Apacheria* (Mechanicsville, Penn., 2001), xxvi–xxvii. Also George Crook, "The Apache Troubles," *Army and Navy Register*, 21 October 1882, in Cozzens, *Eyewitnesses*, 311; and "The Apache Story of the Cibecue," John Bourke Diary, in Cozzens, *Eyewitnesses*, 305.

47. These were the remaining members of the band of Apache leader Victorio, who had fled to Mexico in 1879, and was killed in 1880 by the Mexican army. Naiche is sometimes referred to as Nachez.

48. Dan L. Thrapp, *General Crook and the Sierra Madre Adventure* (Norman, Okla., 1972), 62; Frederick Frelinghuysen, "Mexico: Reciprocal Right to Pursue Savage Indians across the Boundary Line," 29 July 1882, in Cozzens, *Eyewitnesses*, 343–345.

49. Ramón Ruiz, *The People of Sonora and Yankee Capitalists* (Tucson, 1988), 173; Tefertiller, *Wyatt Earp*, 106.

50. See Ana María Alonso, *Thread of Blood: Colonialism, Revolution and Gender on Mexico's Northern Frontier* (Tucson, 1995).

51. George Whitwell Parsons, *A Tenderfoot in Tombstone: The Private Journal of George Whitwell Parsons—The Turbulent Years, 1880–1882*, ed. Lynn R. Bailey (Tucson, 1996), 180–183. I have found no direct evidence that Mexicans were part of the civilian posse, but George Crook relied heavily on Mexican scouts and packers, as did many others.

52. Tefertiller, *Wyatt Earp*, 104–107, Parsons quotation on 106; also see Parsons, *Tenderfoot*, 180–183.

53. Richard J. Perry, *Apache Reservation: Indigenous Peoples and the American State* (Austin, 1993), 104; Elliott West, "Reconstructing Race," *WHQ*, 34, no. 1 (Spring 2003): 7–26.

54. *Arizona Star*, quoted in Tefertiller, *Wyatt Earp*, 73. See also L. Y. Loring, "Report on the [Coyotero] Apaches," Hubert H. Bancroft Collection, Bancroft Library, in Cozzens, *Eyewitnesses*, 195; Anonymous (possibly George Crook), "General Howard's Mission," *Army and Navy Journal*, 9, no. 37 (27 April 1872), in Cozzens, ibid., 113; Charles P. Elliott, "An Indian Reservation under General George Crook," *Military Affairs* (Summer 1948), in Cozzens, ibid., 412; and George Crook, "The Apache Problem," *Journal of the Military Service Institution of the United States*, 7 (September 1886), in Cozzens, ibid., 602, 603. On savagery, "broncos," and "mansos," see Alonso, *Thread of Blood*, ch. 1, esp. 64.

55. Miles's assignment to Wood in Nelson A. Miles, *Personal Recollections and Observations of General Nelson A. Miles* (New York, 1986; rpt. Chicago, 1969), 488; Leonard Wood quotation from "Report of Assistant Surgeon Leonard Wood, U.S. Army, Fort Bowie, A.T., 8 September 1886," in Henry Lawton Scrapbook, Graff Collection, Newberry Library, Chicago.

56. Loring, "Report," 190; on nose cutting, see *The Diaries of John Gregory Bourke*, vol. 1, November 30, 1873–July 28, 1876, ed. Charles M. Robinson III (Denton, Tex., 2003), 92; and H. Henrietta Stockel, *Women of the Apache Nation: Voices of Truth* (Reno, 1993), 20; Miles, *Personal Recollections*, 497, "the husband" on 507.

57. John G. Bourke, "A Conference with Cochise," in Cozzens, *Eyewitnesses*, 153; Geronimo, *Geronimo, His Own Story: The Autobiography of a Great Patriot Warrior*, as told to S. M. Barrett, rev. and ed. Frederick Turner (New York,1996; orig. pub. 1906), 78–83, quotation on 78.

58. Perry, *Apache Reservation*, 67. But see Nancy Shoemaker, "How Indians Got To Be Red," *American Historical Review*, 102, no. 3 (June 1997): 625–644.

59. Frederick Tritle to H. M. Teller, 4 May 1882, MC 429.

60. G. Gordon Adam, "Resolution Adopted at Meeting of Residents of Cochise County, Arizona, Regarding Outbreak of Indians from San Carlos Reservation," in Cozzens, *Eyewitnesses*, 414–424.

61. Miles, *Personal Recollections*, 495; on scouts, see Morris E. Opler, "Chiricahua Apache," in Alfonso Ortiz, ed., *Handbook of North American Indians*, vol. 10 (Washington, 1978), 401–418, esp. 408.

62. Miles, *Personal Recollections*, 521.

63. Perry, *Apache Reservation*, 124–129.

64. Clements, *After the Boom*, 31. An improbable figure of 400–500 is claimed by Faulk, *Tombstone*, 199. In 1890, well after Tombstone's bust, Cochise County had 179 Chinese residents. U.S. Bureau of the Census, *Eleventh Census of the United States, 1890: Population*, part 1, Statistics of Population (Washington, D.C., 1892), 610; Liping Zhu, *A Chinaman's Chance: The Chinese on the Rocky Mountain Frontier* (Niwot, Colo., 1997), 55–56.

65. See Gary Tipton, "Men out of China: Origins of the Chinese Community in Phoenix," *Journal of Arizona History*, 18, no. 3 (1977): 342–344. On smuggling Chinese, see Grace Delgado, "In the Age of Exclusion: Race, Religion, and Chinese Identity in the Making of the Arizona-Sonora Borderlands, 1863–1943" (Ph.D. diss., UCLA, 2000), 192–193, 217–218. On temporary railroad workers and migrants, see Shillingberg, *Tombstone, A.T.*, 130–132; and Truett, *Fugitive Landscapes*, 120–125. On the loophole, see Roger Daniels, *Guarding the Golden Door: American Immigration Policy and Immigrants since 1882* (New York, 2004), 20.

66. The figure of 10 percent is from Tucson in Delgado, "In the Age of Exclusion," 266. On the Page Act, see George A. Peffer, *If They Don't Bring Their Women Here: Chi-*

nese Female Immigration before Exclusion (Urbana, Ill., 1999), xi. Ah Sue in City of Tombstone License Books, Medigovich Collection, MS 1077, AHS. And see Anne Butler, *Daughters of Joy, Sisters of Misery: Prostitutes in the American West, 1865–1890* (Urbana, Ill., 1985).

67. Tombstone even had paid informants who reported on opium dens. See City of Tombstone, City Recorder's Annual Financial Report, 1 October 1887, Medigovich Collection; Florence C. Lister and Richard H. Lister, "Chinese Sojourners in Territorial Prescott," *Journal of the Southwest*, 31 (Spring 1989), special issue; Floyd Cheung, "Performing Exclusion and Resistance: Anti-Chinese League and Chee Kung Tong Parades in Territorial Arizona," *TDR: The Drama Review*, 46, no. 1 (2002): 39–59; Ben T. Traywick, *The Chinese Dragon in Tombstone* (Tombstone, 1989), 13–14. The Chinese could not own property, so they often leased from San Pedro homesteaders. On Chinese professions, see Shillingberg, *Tombstone, A.T.*, 130; Delgado, "In the Age of Exclusion," 152–155; Truett, *Fugitive Landscapes*, 123–124.

68. Shillingberg, *Tombstone, A.T.*, 130–133; Clements, *After the Boom*, 31; Delgado, "In the Age of Exclusion," 102, 138. See also Brown, *Woman's Point of View*, 20.

69. For other campaigns, see Rodman Paul, *Mining Frontiers of the Far West, 1848–1890*, rev. and expanded by Elliott West (Albuquerque, 2001), 243–252; Susan Lee Johnson, *Roaring Camp: The Social World of the California Gold Rush* (New York, 2000), 298–299; Alexander Saxton, *The Indispensable Enemy: Labor and the Anti-Chinese Movement in California* (Berkeley, 1971); Ronald M. James, Richard D. Atkins, and Rachel J. Hartigan, "Competition and Coexistence in the Laundry: A View of the Comstock," *WHQ*, 25 (Summer 1994): 164–184. On Chinese as "illegal aliens," see Erika Lee, *At America's Gates: Chinese Immigration during the Exclusion Era, 1882–1943* (Chapel Hill, 2003); Delgado, "In the Age of Exclusion"; and Lucy E. Salyer, *Laws Harsh as Tigers: Chinese Immigrants and the Shaping of Modern Immigration Law* (Chapel Hill, 1995).

70. See John R. Wunder, "Anti-Chinese Violence in the American West, 1850–1910," in John McLaren et al., eds., *Law for the Elephant, Law for the Beaver: Essays in the Legal History of the American West* (Pasadena, 1992), 212–236.

71. "Exit Chinese: Large and Enthusiastic Anti-Chinese Meeting Held Last Evening," *Tombstone Epitaph*, 17 February 1886; Clements, *After the Boom*, 140–142; George W. Parsons, *The Devil Has Foreclosed: The Private Journal of George Whitwell Parsons— The Concluding Arizona Years, 1882–1887*, ed. Lynn R. Bailey (Tucson, 1997), 202–203. In *Chinaman's Chance*, Liping Zhu makes the point that most people lived in peace with the Chinese.

72. Clements, *After the Boom*, 139–145; *Tombstone Epitaph* and *Daily Tombstone*, passim. On the Chinese and perceptions of disease, see Susan Craddock, *City of Plagues: Disease, Poverty, and Deviance in San Francisco* (Minneapolis, 2004).

73. On Tombstone, see "Exit Chinese."

74. For these gendered claims, see Lister and Lister, "Chinese Sojourners," 12, 60; Joan Wang, "Race, Gender, and Laundry Work: The Roles of Chinese Laundry-men and American Women in the United States, 1850–1950," *Journal of American Ethnic History*, 24 (Fall 2004): 58–99; James et al., "Competition and Coexistence"; Paul A. Frisch, "'Gibraltar of Unionism': Women, Blacks and the Anti-Chinese Movement in Butte, Montana, 1880–1900," *Southwest Economy and Society*, 6, no. 3 (1984): 3–13; and Johnson, *Roaring Camp*, 328–329. But see Paul, *Mining Frontiers*, 251.

75. San Francisco had one laundry called the "Women's and Girl's Protective Laundry." Martha Gardner, "Working on White Womanhood: White Working Women in the San Francisco Anti-Chinese Movement, 1877–1890," *Journal of Social History*, 331, no. 1 (1999): 73–95, esp. 74, 86. On black women's protests, see Delgado, "In the Age of Exclusion," 150. Tombstone quotation in "America for White Men: Another Big Meeting on the Chinese Question," *Tombstone Epitaph*, 28 February 1886.

76. "The Washing Problem Solved," *Tombstone Epitaph*, 24 February 1886; "Anti-Whites," *Tombstone Epitaph*, 25 February 1886; Ad for White Labor Laundry, ibid.; Bailey, *Tombstone*, 200; "America for White Men," *Tombstone Daily Epitaph*, 28 February 1886.

77. "America for White Men."

78. Linda Gordon, *The Great Arizona Orphan Abduction* (Cambridge, Mass., 1999), 30, 50; *Los Dos Republicas*, 27 July 1878; Asunción Sánchez, *El Fronterizo* (Tucson), 10 August 1889, 2. On intermarriage, see, for example, *El Fronterizo*, 29 August 1891, 3; *El Fronterizo*, 20 August 1892, 3. Also see Harry T. Getty, *Interethnic Relationships in the Community of Tucson* (New York, 1976), 213–214; and Roger D. Hardaway, "Unlawful Love: A History of Arizona's Miscegenation Law," *Journal of Arizona History*, 27 (Winter 1986): 377–390. On Mexico, see esp. Evelyn Hu-DeHart, "Racism and Anti-Chinese Persecution in Mexico," *Amerasia*, 9 (1982): 1–28.

79. Adams, in Cozzens, *Eyewitnesses*, 419.

80. Lee, *At America's Gates*, 13, "wetbacks" on 172. On border control against Chinese in Cochise County, Delgado, "In the Age of Exclusion," 190, 216; "Chinks," *BDR*, 8 October 1903, 1; and M. H. Jones Collection, MS 393, AHS.

81. Delgado, "In the Age of Exclusion," 121; Evelyn Hu-DeHart, "Immigrants to a Developing Society: The Chinese in Northern Mexico, 1875–1932," *Journal of Arizona History*, 21 (1980): 275–312.

82. Quoted in Gardner, "Working on White Womanhood," 78; see also West and Paul, *Mining Frontiers*, 251.

83. *Tombstone Epitaph*, 10 April 1882, cited in Delgado, "In the Age of Exclusion," 104; "America for White Men"; "Republican Territorial Convention Platform, 1886," *Tombstone Epitaph*, 1 October 1886.

84. Brown, *Woman's Point of View*, 20; Clements, *After the Boom*, 31, 152.

85. Sherman to Brewster, 12 April 1882.

86. Tritle quoted in Truett, *Fugitive Landscapes*, 65.

3. The White Man's Camp in Bisbee

1. Essential general histories include Lynn R. Bailey, *Bisbee: Queen of the Copper Camps*, 2nd ed. (Tucson, 2002), "Puerta" on 9; Annie M. Cox, "History of Bisbee, 1877–1937" (M.A. thesis, University of Arizona, 1938), "rather slim" on 3; Samuel Truett, *Fugitive Landscapes: The Forgotten History of the U.S.-Mexico Borderlands* (New Haven, 2006); and Carlos A. Schwantes, ed., *Bisbee: Urban Outpost on the Frontier* (Tucson, 1992). Schwantes' volume grew out of the creation of the outstanding Bisbee Mining and Historical Museum. On the town's unique geography, see Richard Francaviglia, *Hard Places: Reading the Landscape of America's Historic Mining Districts* (Iowa City, 1991); and William W. Newkirk, "Historical Geography of Bisbee, Arizona" (M.A. thesis, University of Arizona, 1966). "Built in the heart" is from George Wharton James, *Arizona the Wonderland* (Boston, 1917), 410.

2. Manuscript Census, 1880, "Mule Mountains."

3. Bailey, *Bisbee*, 108.

4. Opie Rundle Burgess, *Bisbee Not So Long Ago* (San Antonio, 1967), 43.

5. Bailey, *Bisbee*, 107–137.

6. Though no comprehensive history of white man's camps exists, useful sources include Charles Howard Shinn, *Mining Camps: A Study in American Frontier Government* (New York, 1970; orig. pub. 1884); Susan Lee Johnson, *Roaring Camp: The Social World of the California Gold Rush* (New York, 2000); Elizabeth Jameson, *All That Glitters: Class, Conflict, and Community in Cripple Creek* (Urbana, Ill., 1998), esp. 140–160; Rodman Paul, *Mining Frontiers of the Far West, 1848–1890*, rev. and expanded by Elliott West (Albuquerque, 2001); and A. Yvette Huginnie, "'Strikitos': Race, Class, and Work in the Arizona Copper Industry, 1870–1920" (Ph.D. diss., Yale University, 1991). On Spanish/Mexican precedents for codes, see Carey McWilliams, *North From Mexico: The Spanish-Speaking People of the United States* (New York, 1968; orig. pub. 1948), 141.

7. Thomas E. Sheridan, *Arizona: A History* (Tucson, 1995), 151; Thomas E. Farish, *History of Arizona*, vol. 2 (Phoenix, 1915), 303, 307, online at southwest.library.arizona.edu/hav2/body.1_div.15.html (accessed 4 April 2007); Manuel P. Servín and Robert L. Spude, "Historical Conditions of Early Mexican Labor in the United States: Arizona—A Neglected Story," typescript, 99, 43–57; Rodolfo Acuña, *Occupied America: A History of Chicanos*, 3rd ed. (New York, 1988), 93–94; A. Yvette Huginnie, "Mexican Labour in a 'White Man's Town': Racialism, Imperialism, and Industrialization in the Making of Arizona, 1840–1905," in Peter Alexander and Rick Halpern, eds., *Racializing Class, Classifying Race: Labour and Difference in Britain, the USA, and Africa* (New York, 2000), 32–56, esp. 40; and Clarence King, *The United States Mining Laws and Regulations*

Thereunder, and State and Territorial Mining Laws, to Which Are Appended Local Mining Rules and Regulations (Washington, D.C., 1885), quotations on 254, 267.

8. Bailey, *Bisbee*, 111–112 ("unanimous" from the *BDR*, 5 December 1903, quoted on 117). For one version of the Chinese-effigy story, see Burgess, *Bisbee Not So Long Ago*, 128; U.S. Bureau of the Census, *Fourteenth Census of the United States, 1920: Population*, vol. 3 (Washington, D.C., 1922), 81. James W. Loewen, *Sundown Towns: A Hidden Dimension of American Racism* (New York, 2006).

9. "Exit Chinese," *Tombstone Epitaph*, 17 February 1886; untitled article, ibid., 24 February 1886.

10. Burgess, *Bisbee Not So Long Ago*, 128; but also see Jane Eppinga, "Ethnic Diversity in Mining Camps," in J. Michael Canty and Michael N. Greeley, eds., *History of Mining in Arizona*, vol. 2 (Tucson, 1991), 57.

11. Juanita Tarin, oral history transcript, interview by Roberta Vaughan, 24 October 1980, BMHM.

12. Victor S. Clark, "Mexican Labor in the United States," *Bureau of Labor Bulletin*, 78 (1908): 466–522, quotation on 512.

13. Much has been written on the dual-wage system. See especially Carl Strikwerda and Camille Guerin-Gonzales, "Labor, Migration, and Politics," and Camille Guerin-Gonzales, "The International Migration of Workers and Segmented Labor: Mexican Immigrant Workers in California Industrial Agriculture, 1900–1940," both in Camille Guerin-Gonzales and Carl Strikwerda, eds., *The Politics of Immigrant Workers: Labor Activism and Migration in the World Economy since 1830* (New York, 1993), 3–45, and 155–174. Also see Mario T. García, *Desert Immigrants: The Mexicans of El Paso, 1880–1920* (New Haven, 1981); Linda Gordon, *The Great Arizona Orphan Abduction* (Cambridge, Mass., 1999); and Joseph Park, "The History of Mexican Labor in Arizona during the Territorial Period" (M.A. thesis, University of Arizona, 1961).

14. Phelps Dodge Corporation, Payroll Records, 1885, MS 0947, AHS.

15. J. C. Ryan testimony, PMC hearings, 241.

16. *BDR*, World's Fair Edition, 1904.

17. On dual-wage differentials in Arizona, see Park, "History of Mexican Labor"; Bisbee specifics in untitled article, *El Fronterizo* (Tucson), 2 February 1891, 2.

18. George F. Leaming, *The Story of Mining in Bisbee* (Marana, Ariz., 1998), 13. Two indispensable but company-endorsed histories of the Phelps Dodge Corporation are Robert Glass Cleland, *A History of Phelps Dodge, 1834–1950* (New York, 1952); and Carlos A. Schwantes, *Vision and Enterprise: Exploring the History of Phelps Dodge Corporation* (Tucson, 2000).

19. And see Gordon, *Great Arizona Orphan Abduction*, 318.

20. For wage decline, I used Phelps Dodge Payroll, 1885–1886, AHS. Quotation from "Labor Conditions in the Southwest," *EMJ*, 76, no. 13 (31 March 1904): 510. See Park, "History of Mexican Labor," 248; Servín and Spude, "Historical Conditions," 48–49.

21. Clark, "History of Mexican Labor," 486.

22. U.S. Immigration Commission, "Immigrants in Industries, Part 25: Japanese and Other Immigrant Races in the Pacific Coast and Rocky Mountain States," *Reports of the Immigration Commission* (Washington, D.C., 1911), 130.

23. I am indebted here to Philip J. Deloria, *Indians in Unexpected Places* (Lawrence, Kans., 2004), Trevor Purvis and Alan Hunt quoted on 10. And see Tomás Almaguer, *Racial Fault Lines: The Historical Origins of White Supremacy in California* (Berkeley, 1994), 17–19.

24. Victor Clark, quoted in Dru McGinnis, "The Influence of Organized Labor on the Making of the Arizona Constitution" (M.A. thesis, University of Arizona, 1930), 18. On Anglo attitudes about Mexican wages, see Gordon, *Great Arizona Orphan Abduction,* 180.

25. Asunción Sánchez, in *El Fronterizo* (Tucson), 10 August 1889, 2.

26. "Caught Like a Thief," *Douglas Examiner,* 11 June 1907, 3.

27. Evan Fraser-Campbell, "The Management of Mexican Labor," *EMJ* 91 (3 June 1911): 1104–1105.

28. See generally Gunther Peck, *Reinventing Free Labor: Padrones and Immigrant Workers in the North American West, 1880–1930* (New York, 2000); and on the Copper Queen Mine, see Dwight E. Woodbridge, "The Copper Queen Mining Company," *EMJ,* 81, no. 24 (16 June 1906): 1134–1135; also see Park, "History of Mexican Labor," 219.

29. John Commons, *Races and Immigrants in America* (New York, 1907), 151, but also see 115.

30. A. Yvette Huginnie, "A New Hero Comes to Town: The Anglo Mining Engineer and 'Mexican Labor' as Contested Terrain in Southeastern Arizona, 1880–1920," *New Mexico Historical Review,* 69, no. 4 (October 1994): 323–344; quotations from Huginnie, 330, and "Labor Conditions in the Southwest," 510.

31. "Confident" from "Bisbee Is the Best Mining Camp in the World," *Cochise Review,* 4 June 1900; "life-sized" from Ralph Rollins, "Labor Situation in Arizona Points to Mexicanization," *Arizona Mining Journal,* 4 (July 1920): 13–14; "Independent spirit" from Arthur Train Jr., "Bisbee: Early History of Bisbee, Home of Copper Queen Branch, Phelps Dodge Corporation" (1941), 40, copy at AHF. See also Matthew Basso et al., eds., *Across the Great Divide: Cultures of Manhood in the American West* (New York, 2001); and Johnson, *Roaring Camp.*

32. Lawrence Glickman, "Inventing the 'American Standard of Living': Gender, Race and Working-Class Identity, 1880–1925," *Labor History,* 34 (Spring–Summer 1993): 221, quotation from 226.

33. Martha May, "The Historical Problem of the Family Wage: The Ford Motor Company and the Five Dollar Day," *Feminist Studies,* 8, no. 2 (Summer 1982): esp. 404 and 419. Also see Martha May and Ron Rothbart, "'Homes Are What Any Strike Is About': Immigrant Labor and the Family Wage," *Journal of Social History,* 23, no. 2 (1989): 267–284; and Alice Kessler-Harris, *A Woman's Wage: Historical Meanings and Social*

Consequences (Lexington, Ky., 1990); Linda Gordon, *Pitied but Not Entitled: Single Mothers and the History of Welfare* (Cambridge, Mass., 1994), 53. On women in mining-town economies, see Gordon, *Great Arizona Orphan Abduction;* Mary Murphy, *Mining Cultures: Men, Women, and Leisure in Butte, 1914–41* (Urbana, Ill., 1997); Dee Garceau, *The Important Things of Life: Women, Work, and Family in Sweetwater County, Wyoming, 1880–1929* (Lincoln, Neb., 1997); Laurie Mercier, *Anaconda: Labor, Community, and Culture in Montana's Smelter City* (Urbana, Ill., 2001); Laurie Mercier and Jaclyn Gier, eds., *Mining Women: Gender in the Development of a Global Industry, 1670 to 2005* (New York, 2006); and Paula Petrik, *No Step Backward: Women and Family on the Rocky Mountain Mining Frontier, Helena, Montana* (Helena, Mont., 1990).

34. James R. Barrett and David Roediger, "Inbetween Peoples: Race, Nationality and the 'New Immigrant' Working Class," *Journal of American Ethnic History,* 16, no. 3 (Spring 1997): 3–44, esp. 8; Glickman, "Inventing the 'American Standard of Living,'" esp. 222; May, "Historical Problem," 407. On women at the Copper Queen, see pay scale for January 1898, AHS.

35. Burgess, *Bisbee Not So Long Ago,* 45.

36. *BDR,* World's Fair Edition, 1904.

37. Park, "History of Mexican Labor," 219; *Thirteenth Census of the United States, 1910: Abstract with Supplement for Arizona* (Washington, D.C., 1911), 584; Gordon, *Great Arizona Orphan Abduction,* 48; Ángel Baldenegro, oral history abstract, interviewer unknown, Tucson, 1973, AHS.

38. Mae Ngai, *Impossible Subjects: Illegal Aliens and the Making of Modern America* (Princeton, 2004), esp. chs. 1 and 2, border-crossing stations on 64; railroad engineer quoted in Vernon Monroe McCombs, *From over the Border: A Study of the Mexicans in the United States* (New York, 1925), 22.

39. But see Anne Kulinovich Medigovich, oral history, interview by Beverly Woods, 29 May 1990, BMHM. On Bisbee's Alianza, see Kaye Lynn Briegel, "Alianza Hispano-Americana, 1894–1965" (Ph.D. diss., University of Southern California, 1974), 66; and "Spanish American Alliance Formed," *BDR,* 20 March 1906; Herlinda Tofoya oral history, interview by Beverly Woods, 12 July 1993, BMHM. On the two-edged sword of barrioization, see Albert Camarillo, *Chicanos in a Changing Society: From Mexican Pueblos to American Barrios in Santa Barbara and Southern California, 1848–1930* (Cambridge, Mass., 1979)

40. Baldenegro, oral history; "J. H. Goodman" from *BDR,* 29 July 1904.

41. U.S. Bureau of the Census, *Eleventh Census of the United States, 1890: Population,* part 1, *Statistics of Population* (Washington, D.C., 1892), 610; U.S. Bureau of the Census, *Twelfth Census of the United States, 1900: Special Reports,* part 2 (Washington, D.C., 1901), Table 95; *Thirteenth Census, 1910,* 584–586; *Fourteenth Census, 1920,* 81; and *Fifteenth Census of the United States, Population,* vol. 3, part 1: *Reports by States* (Washington, D.C., 1932), 157.

42. On Cornish in the West, see J. Rowe, *The Hard-Rock Men: Cornish Immigrants*

and the North American Mining Frontier (Liverpool, U.K., 1974), esp. 172–176, 216–223; Richard E. Lingenfelter, *The Hardrock Miners: A History of the Mining Labor Movement in the American West, 1863–1893* (Berkeley, 1974). On Bisbee, see Cleland, *History of Phelps Dodge,* 110; Corrin family, oral history, interview by Carl Nelson, 26 September 1972, BMHM; and Burgess, *Bisbee Not So Long Ago,* 66–67; Joe Chisholm, *Brewery Gulch: Frontier Days of Old Arizona, Last Outpost of the Great Southwest* (San Antonio, 1949), 113, 117, 20.

43. Barrett and Roediger, "Inbetween Peoples," 23; H. Mason Coggin, "Roots of the Calumet & Arizona," *Cochise Quarterly,* 24, no. 1 (Spring 1995): 3.

44. Noel Ignatiev, *How the Irish Became White* (New York, 1995), esp. 41, 112. On Bisbee's Irish, see Father John L. Howard, oral history transcript, interviewer unknown, ca. 1976–1980, AHS. Millicent W. Kasun, "The Development of Churches in the Bisbee Area," unpublished seminar paper, Cochise College, January 1972, BMHM, 2; Harris Sobin, *St. Patrick's Catholic Church, Bisbee, Arizona: A History* (Tucson, 1998); Mary Eileen Murphy Walsh, Diary, MS 1045, AHS. And see David M. Emmons, *The Butte Irish: Class and Ethnicity in an American Mining Town, 1875–1925* (Urbana, Ill., 1989).

45. The Clifton story is the subject of Gordon, *Great Arizona Orphan Abduction.* Quotation from *BDR,* World's Fair Edition, 1904.

46. PD Mercantile Company Annual Reports, 1915, 1916, BMHM; www.brophyprep. org/academics/history.html (accessed 10 October 2007); Gordon, *Great Arizona Orphan Abduction,* 301–302.

47. Linda Gordon calls this immigrant merchant class "Euro-Latins" (Gordon, *Great Arizona Orphan Abduction*). Sam Levy, interview transcript, Bloom Southwest Jewish Archives, University of Arizona, Tucson; Caretto family files, BMHM; Nick Balich and Mamie Bugen, "Saint Stephen Nemanja Serbian Orthodox Church," *Cochise Quarterly,* 5, nos. 2–3 (Summer–Fall 1975), 21–23. Also useful is Bailey, *Bisbee,* 118–124.

48. Newkirk, "Historical Geography," 49; Schwantes, *Bisbee: Urban Outpost,* "Introduction," 15; Park, "History of Mexican Labor," 219; see also *Thirteenth Census, 1910,* 584; Gordon, *Great Arizona Orphan Abduction,* 48.

49. "No Foreign Labor Wanted," *BDR,* 27 May 1903, 1.

50. Jameson, *All That Glitters,* 140–160.

51. Copper Queen Mine Payrolls, 1898, AHS. Payrolls are available only for scattered years, so it is possible the Caretto and Medigovich sons worked as miners later than this.

52. H. Mason Coggin, "Roots of the Calumet: A Short History of the Calumet and Arizona Mining Company," in J. Michael Canty et al., *History of Mining in Arizona,* vol. 3 (Tucson, 1999), 155–176; Schwantes, *Vision and Enterprise,* 81–88, 135–138; Leaming, *The Story of Mining in Bisbee,* 30; Burgess, *Bisbee Not So Long Ago,* 176–177.

53. John Higham, *Strangers in the Land: Patterns of American Nativism, 1860–1925* (New York, 1968; orig. pub. 1955), esp. 134–137, quotation on 137.

54. Higham, *Strangers in the Land;* Desmond King, *Making Americans: Immigration, Race, and the Origins of the Diverse Democracy* (Cambridge, Mass., 2000); David R. Roediger, *Working toward Whiteness: How America's Immigrants Became White* (New York, 2005).

55. King, *Making Americans,* 50–51.

56. My analysis of Italians relies on Phylis Cancilla Martinelli, "Racial Formation and Italians in Arizona History: Italians as a Partly Racialized Group," unpublished paper, 2001, in author's possession; and idem, "Examining the Relationships of Italians and Mexicans in a 'Mexican Camp' and a 'White Man's Camp': Mexicans and Euro Latins in the Arizona Copper Industry, 1900–1930," in J. E. Worrall, C. B. Albright, and E. G. Di Fabio, eds., *Italian Immigrants Go West: The Impact of Locale on Ethnicity* (New York, 2003). Also see Art Kent, oral history, interview by James Houston, ca. 1975, AHS; Fred Watson, oral history, interview by James Houston, ca. 1970s, AHS; and Maria A. Ayala, oral history, interview by A. Valenzuela, 19 December 1980, BMHM; "John Vercellino Recalls the Bisbee Deportation," no date, audio recording, courtesy of Christine Marín and James McBride, Chicana/o Collection, Arizona State University.

57. "No Foreign Labor Wanted"; Train, "Bisbee," 41; "Old Reliable" from "Cochise County against Prohibition: Voters Are Emphatic for License and Regulation," *BDR,* 27 January 1910; "Must Be Able To Speak English," *BDR,* 28 May 1903.

58. Mamie Bugen, oral history, interview by Beverly Woods, 21 May 1991, BMHM. On the Black Hand, see Petition to City of Bisbee, 19 December 1910, Petitions to City of Bisbee, no. 58, BMHM; Dan Kitchel, oral history, interview by Roberta Vaughan, 6 February 1981, BMHM. In Serbia, nationalists created a Black Hand society later, after 1911.

59. Copper Queen Payroll, 1898; Martinelli, "Racial Formation"; Linda Gordon found a few Italians in "Mexican" wage categories (*Great Arizona Orphan Abduction,* 101–102).

60. "No Foreign Labor Wanted."

61. U.S. Immigration Commission, *Reports,* 130. Thomas A. Guglielmo, *White on Arrival: Italians, Race, Color, and Power in Chicago, 1890–1945* (New York, 2004); Father Howard, oral history; on Louisiana, see Roediger, *Working toward Whiteness,* 62.

62. In 1910, Serbia was still part of the Hapsburg Empire, and Serbs were counted as "Austrians" in the census; *Thirteenth Census, 1910,* 586, and *Fourteenth Census, 1920,* 81. On the Serb community, see esp. Mamie Bugen, oral history, interview by C. Graham, 12 March 1981, BMHM; "Bisbee's Trail Blazers," *BDR,* 3 October 1954; Olga Yuncevich Pincock, oral history transcript, interview by Beverly Woods, 24 May 1997, BMHM; "Viola Yuncevich Shields," Shattuck biofile, BMHM; "First Servian Christmas in Bisbee . . . ," *BDR,* 9 January 1907; and Balich and Bugen, "Saint Stephen Nemanja Serbian Orthodox Church."

63. Copper Queen Payroll, 1898; "A Slavonic Wedding," *Cochise Review,* 15 June 1900; Eppinga, "Ethnic Diversity."

64. Bugen, oral history; Anne Kulinovich Medigovich, oral history, interview by Beverly Woods, 29 May 1990, BMHM.

65. Roediger, *Working toward Whiteness,* 61–64.

66. Few Finns and Italians remained after the Deportation. In 1920, there were 155 Finns in the census, but many were in the rural settlement of McNeal, not Bisbee. See *Fourteenth Census, 1920,* 81; and Manuscript Census, Cochise County, 1920, "McNeal"; "very secretive" from Kitchel, oral history; Einar Saarela, "Memories of Bisbee, Arizona, 1914–1917," 1990, unpublished manuscript, BMHM.

67. Roediger, *Working toward Whiteness,* 66; Peck, *Reinventing Free Labor,* esp. 99–106; Saarela, oral history; "Labor Conditions in the Southwest," cited in Byrkit, *Forging,* 29.

68. See Jameson, *All That Glitters,* 142, 150–152; Huginnie, "Mexican Labour," 40.

69. Quoted in Gordon, *Great Arizona Orphan Abduction,* 104.

70. These low numbers held steady through 1940, according to the census.

71. E. G. Hall, Bisbee, Arizona, to NAACP, New York City, 23 July 1915, Records of the National Association for the Advancement of Colored People, Series 1, Box 69, Library of Congress, Manuscript Division, Washington, D.C. My survey of more than a thousand deputies and deportees did not find definitive evidence of African American involvement.

72. "Negroes Will Perhaps Have Own School," *BDR,* 2 March 1910; Tofoya, oral history. Also see Grace Davis Conroy, oral history, interview by Beverly Woods, Bisbee, Arizona, 13 April 1992, BMHM; "Teachers Wait in Vain for Colored Children," *Bisbee Evening Miner,* 15 September 1910; Art Kent, oral history.

73. Gerald Horne, *Black and Brown: African Americans and the Mexican Revolution, 1910–1920* (New York, 2005), 46–68, quotations on 57, 66.

74. On Douglas and Bisbee as variants of company towns, see Josiah M. Heyman, "In the Shadow of the Smokestacks: Labor and Environmental Conflict in a Company-Dominated Town," in Jane Schneider and Rayna Rapp, eds., *Articulating Hidden Histories: Anthropology, History, and the Influence of Eric R. Wolf* (Berkeley, 1994), 156–174. *BDR,* World's Fair Edition, 1904; Cleland, *History of Phelps Dodge,* 71–74, 165–168; "The Copper Queen Company . . . ," *Arizona Republican,* 7 February 1898, 3; Florence Watkins Chance, "Life in Southern Arizona at the turn of the Century," ca. 1978, unpublished manuscript, BMHM.

75. Bailey, "Bisbee," 168–171; "An Old Timer Returns Here," *BDR,* 16 December 1903, 8. Train, "Bisbee," 45, gives the date of the lynching as 1884; Burgess says 1887 (*Not So Long Ago,* 125). On library holdings, see S. C. Dickinson, "A Sociological Survey of the Bisbee Warren District," Arizona State Bureau of Mines, 1917, UASC, 3.

76. "Somewhat frightful" in Charles S. Sargent, "Copper Star of the Arizona Urban Firmament," in Schwantes, *Bisbee: Urban Outpost,* 35; "Cleanliness" in Bertha M. Mosher, unidentified clipping entitled "The Town," 7 December 1902, courtesy of Mrs. Alice Metz.

77. Gordon, *Great Arizona Orphan Abduction,* 215–219; Don Robinson, "Pioneer Arizona Doctor, 85, Recalls His . . . Early-Day Practice in Territory," unidentified newspaper clipping, BMHM; Schwantes, *Vision and Enterprise,* 139; Burgess, *Bisbee Not So Long Ago,* 84–92; articles on Bisbee and rates of death in *Bulletin: Arizona Board of Health,* 1912–1920, passim; "Foreign population" quotation from Warren District Commercial Club, "Arizona's Treasure House: Bisbee and the Warren Mining District" (Bisbee, 1913), 8, UASC. Significantly, Bisbee was the rare Arizona city that blamed the "foreign" population, not just Mexicans; see, for example, Frank D. Myers, *Cochise County Arizona* (Tombstone, [1910–1911]), 43. On disease and racialization, see Natalia Molina, *Fit To Be Citizens? Public Health and Race in Los Angeles, 1879–1939* (Berkeley, 2006); Amy L. Fairchild, *Science at the Borders: Immigrant Medical Inspection and the Shaping of the Modern Industrial Labor Force* (Baltimore, 2003); and Alexandra Minna Stern, *Eugenic Nation: Faults and Frontiers of Better Breeding in Modern America* (Berkeley, 2005).

78. See John A. Fairlie, *Local Government in Counties, Towns and Villages* (New York, 1906).

79. Isabel Shattuck Fathauer, with Lynn R. Bailey, *Lemuel C. Shattuck: "A Little Mining, A Little Banking, and a Little Beer,"* (Tucson, 1991), 52–53.

80. Ernest E. Brewer, "First Public Utilities," Record Group 91, WPA Manuscripts, Box 7, ASLAPR.

81. Fathauer, *Shattuck,* 52–53, 117; Cox, "History of Bisbee," 145–150. For tax rates and mine valuations, see Table 1 in Tru A. McGinnis, "The Influence of Organized Labor," 210; Schwantes, *Bisbee: Urban Outpost.* And see Amy Bridges, *Morning Glory: Municipal Reform in the Southwest* (Princeton, 1997).

82. Charles Willis, "Report of Cost of Living Investigation in the Warren District" [1919], Phelps Dodge Corporation Archives, Phoenix, Arizona; Map of Bisbee Sewer System, 1908, ASLAPR; *BDR,* 7 October 1902, 22 October 1902; Bisbee-Naco Water Company Register, 1906, ASLAPR; Dickinson, "A Sociological Survey," 80.

83. Newkirk, "Historical Geography," 120; "Mayor Muirhead Denies Charges," *BDR,* 30 March 1902; "Did Mayor Muirhead Consult Mr. Douglas?" *BDR,* 1 April 1902.

84. Robert S. Jeffrey, "The History of Douglas, Arizona" (M.A. thesis, University of Arizona, 1951), 8–10; see also Glenn S. Dumke, "Douglas, Border Town," *Pacific Historical Review,* 17, no. 3 (August 1948): 283–298; Fathauer, *Shattuck,* 117.

85. *BDR,* cited in Park, "History of Mexican Labor," 252–253.

86. The population in 1920 was no doubt lower than its World War I peak, but the number is still telling. Only one block of once-sprawling Lowell still exists; today the rest is gone, replaced by the Lavender Pit.

87. E. A. Putnam et al., Correspondence and Report, Industrial YMCA of the Warren Mining District to C. F. Willis, Consulting Supervisor, 5 July 1919, Phelps Dodge Corporation Archives, Phoenix, Arizona.

88. Ordinance No. 1, published in *BDR,* 23 January 1902; Clara Allen, "Statement of Real Estate and Personal Property . . . , 1902," City of Bisbee records, BMHM; Medigov-

ich Collection, MS 1077, File 288, AHS; and Chisholm, *Brewery Gulch,* 130. The stories of Tombstone's Allen Street and Douglas' Sixth Street follow similar paths.

89. "Bisbee News," *Tombstone Prospector,* 5 March 1894, 7 March 1894.

90. See David J. Pivar, "Purity and Hygiene: Women, Prostitution, and the 'American Plan,' 1900–1930," *Contributions in American History,* no. 193 (Westport, Conn., 2002); and Alan Hunt, *Governing Morals: A Social History of Moral Regulation* (New York, 1999). "City Council: Their Work Is Satisfactory So Far," *BDR,* 24 January 1902; "Saloons Close on the Minute at 12 O'Clock," *BDR,* 1 April 1910; Kitchel, oral history.

91. See, e.g., "Redlight Mixup Is Finally Settled Up," *BDR,* 11 September 1909; "Police Start Crusade," *BDR,* 1 October 1910; Petition to City of Bisbee, 15 December 1905, no. 58, BMHM; Ernest Francis Ruterman, *Ernest Francis Ruterman's Recollections: Bisbee/Douglas, Arizona, 1906–1987* (Syracuse, N.Y., 1994), 39–40. And see Mark Wild, "Red Light Kaleidoscope: Prostitution and Ethnoracial Relations in Los Angeles, 1880–1940," *Journal of Urban History,* 28 (September 2002): 720–742.

92. January and May 1903, City License Book, 1902–1910, microfilm, ASLAPR and BMHM; Manuscript Census, 1910, Cochise County, "Brewery Gulch"; Chisholm, "Brewery Gulch," 29, 124.

93. Butler, *Daughters of Joy;* also see "Bisbee Council Throws City Wide Open," *BDR,* 23 October 1909, 1, 8; on roundups, see "After Lewd Women," *BDR,* 3 January 1903; "Mrs. Thos. Fox Is Found Guilty," *BDR,* 20 June 1905; "Police Start Crusade," *BDR,* 1 October 1910; "Crusade Begins on Open Vice," *BDR,* 2 October 1910; *City of Bisbee v. Mrs. L. Elliott,* 8 October 1910, and *City of Bisbee v. Mrs. L. Elliott,* 5 December 1910, Bisbee Police Court ledgers, BMHM; City of Bisbee License Book, 1902–1910, 66. Ruth Rosen estimates that perhaps only one in six Mexican and African American prostitutes were registered by cities; see Rosen, *The Lost Sisterhood: Prostitution in America, 1900–1918* (Baltimore, 1983), 78. On laws and crackdowns, see also Bailey, *Bisbee,* 180–190.

94. On similar women, see Sarah Deutsch, *No Separate Refuge: Culture, Class and Gender on an Anglo-Hispanic Frontier in the American Southwest, 1880–1940* (New York, 1987); Peggy Pascoe, *Relations of Rescue: The Search for Female Moral Authority in the American West, 1874–1939* (New York, 1990); and Virginia Scharff, *Twenty Thousand Roads: Women, Movement, and the West* (Berkeley, 2002). My definition of maternalism is influenced by Linda Gordon, "Gender, State, and Society: A Debate with Theda Skocpol," *Contention* 2, no. 3 (Spring 1993): 146–147; and, on the ways maternalism differed from paternalism, *Pitied but Not Entitled: Single Mothers and the History of Welfare* (Cambridge, Mass., 1994), esp. 55–56. In the huge paternalism literature, I have found useful Drew Gilpin Faust, *James Henry Hammond and the Old South: A Design for Mastery* (Baton Rouge, 1982), 72–73, 369–370; and Elizabeth Fox-Genovese, *Within the Plantation Household: Black and White Women of the Old South* (Chapel Hill, 1988), esp. 64. On gender and the welfare state, see Linda Gordon, ed., *Women, the State, and*

Welfare (Madison, Wisc., 1990), esp. 9–35. Historian Nikki Mandell also uses the term "corporate maternalism"; see Mandell, *The Corporation as Family: The Gendering of Corporate Welfare, 1890–1930* (Chapel Hill, 2002).

95. Mrs. Alice Metz, "'Thru the Years' with the Bisbee Woman's Club," part 1, typescript, BMHM; also see the Douglas Woman's Club scrapbooks, CCHS.

96. Lori Ginzberg, *Women and the Work of Benevolence: Morality, Politics, and Class in Nineteenth-Century America* (New Haven, 1990). "History of the Bisbee Woman's Club," *Seventy Years in Federation: Bisbee Woman's Club* (March 1972); and BWC Minutes in Metz, "Thru the Years," both at BMHM; "The Woman's Club of Bisbee Concludes Its Year's Work," *BDR,* 27 May 1908. Douglas women embraced reform earlier; see "Pioneers Recall Women's Club Work During Early Development of Douglas," in Douglas Woman's Club Scrapbooks; and "Philanthropic Department," *Douglas Daily Dispatch,* 10 September 1907.

97. *BDR,* Woman's Club Edition, 3 November 1902; Marjorie Wheeler Ross, *History of the Arizona Federation of Woman's Clubs and Its Forerunners* (Phoenix, 1944); "Mrs. French Favors This Juvenile Bill," *BDR,* 10 March 1907.

98. Mrs. C. W. Wilcox, "History of the Bisbee Young Women's Christian Association" and YWCA records, Bisbee Community Y, Bisbee, Arizona; Membership ledgers and list of staff and presidents; Metz, BWC minutes, BMHM; "Educational Work of Bisbee Y.W.C.A.," *BDR,* 1 October 1910.

99. YWCA records; Dickinson, "Sociological Survey," 22. On the national movements, see Nina Mjakij and Margaret Spatt, eds., *Men and Women Adrift: The YMCA and YWCA in the City* (New York, 1997); and Dorothea Browder, "A 'Christian Solution of the Labor Situation': How Workingwomen Reshaped the YWCA's Religious Mission and Politics," *Journal of Women's History,* 19, no. 2 (2007): 85–110.

100. "Quarterly Report of Charity Committee," *BDR,* 2 April 1911; "Worthy Cases for Charity Committee," *BDR,* 12 January 1910; Mary Kidder Rak, *A Social Survey of Arizona,* University of Arizona Bulletin no. 111, University Extension Series no. 10 (Tucson, 1921), 55–56; Esther Cummings, Secretary, Charity Committee of the Board of Trade, to Gov. George W. P. Hunt, 27 August 1914, Governors' Files, Kibbey, Sloan, Hunt, 1905–1916, Record Group 1, Box 1A, ASLAPR.

101. Cummings to Hunt; "Financial Statement and Report of the Warren District Relief Association," 1 September 1915 to 1 September 1917, Phelps Dodge Corporation Archives, Phoenix, Arizona.

102. "Family Was Starving," *Bisbee Evening Miner,* 14 September 1910; "Woman Begged to Support Her Family," *Bisbee Evening Miner,* 15 September 1910; "Quarterly Report of Charity Committee," *BDR,* 2 April 1911; "Financial Statement and Report of the Warren District Relief Association." For context, see Thomas A. Krainz, "Culture and Poverty: Progressive Era Relief in the Rural West," *Pacific Historical Review,* 74, no. 1 (2005): 87–120.

103. See Schwantes, *Vision and Enterprise*, 15; Geoffrey Douglas, *Class: The Wreckage of an American Family* (New York, 1992), 75–79; "Presbyterian Copper," *Fortune* magazine, July 1932, 40–48, 104. On American University in Beirut, see www.aub.edu.lb/about/history.html (accessed 10 October 2007).

4. "A Better Man for Us" in Warren

1. Warren Manning to Mrs. Manning, 19 February 1906, Manning Association Papers, University of Massachusetts Lowell, Center for Lowell History.

2. Cleveland Van Dyke, report to Kendric C. Babcock, president of the University of Arizona, 16 December 1907, Phelps Dodge Corporate Archive, Phoenix, Arizona (hereafter cited as "C&A letters"); and C&A Annual Reports, UASC and MTUCCC.

3. Woodward Architectural Group, "Warren: The City Beautiful," vol. 1, *Historic Building Survey and Historical Overview of the Warren Townsite* (Tempe, Ariz., 1993); population estimates and building numbers culled from "Annual Report: Warren Company," 1915, UASC and BMHM. "Small town" from Mary Eileen Murphy Walsh, Diary, 7 March 1916, MS 1045, AHS.

4. "Copper Country Company Housing," Kim Hoagland, curator, Keweenaw Heritage Center exhibit, Calumet, Michigan, July–August 2003. Arnold R. Alanen, "The Planning of Company Communities in the Lake Superior Mining Region," *Journal of the American Planning Association,* 45 (July 1979): 264. On Calumet & Hecla's town-building and housing efforts, see Larry Lankton, *Cradle to Grave: Life, Work, and Death at the Lake Superior Copper Mines* (New York, 1991), 142–162. The village of Calumet is now a National Historic Park.

5. Board members from C&A letterhead and *C&A Company History* (1922), UASC. I have slightly simplified the early history of Calumet & Arizona, which was created by merging several development companies. See also "Calumet and Arizona Mining Company," Warren, Arizona, September 1916, Report to the American Institute of Mining Engineers, Arizona Meeting, 5–7, MTUCCC; Dwight E. Woodbridge, "Arizona and Sonora, IV," *EMJ* (25 August 1906): 1182; "The Bisbee Consolidation," *EMJ* (26 May 1906): 1003, 1031.

6. "Calumet & Arizona Mining Company: Special Correspondence," *EMJ* (19 October 1907): 739. In this capacity, Powell was also vice president of C&A. See Lewis Powell to Charles Briggs, 7 August 1906; and Briggs to Powell, 13 August 1906, C&A letters. "Annual Report: Warren Company," 1907, 1.

7. A. T. Andreas, *History of the Upper Peninsula of Michigan* (Chicago, 1883), 342; *Men of Progress: Embracing Biographical Sketches of Representative Michigan Men* (Detroit, 1900), 262–263. "Coleraine, 'Model Town,' Thrives on One-Man Rule of Greenway," *Duluth News Tribune,* 9 July 1907, 4; Van Dyke report, 1.

8. This tension is a mainstay in the Progressivism literature, too vast to list. Good overviews include Michael McGerr, *A Fierce Discontent: The Rise and Fall of Progressiv-*

ism in America, 1870–1920 (New York, 2003); Richard McCormick and Arthur Link, *Progressivism* (Arlington Heights, Ill., 1983); Daniel T. Rodgers, "In Search of Progressivism," *Reviews in American History,* 10 (December 1992): 113–132; and Robert H. Wiebe, *The Search for Order, 1877–1920* (New York, 1967). On efficiency versus democracy in relation to housing, see Clinton Rogers Woodruff, "Introduction," in Graham Taylor, *Satellite Cities: A Study of Industrial Suburbs* (New York, 1970; orig. pub. 1915), x.

9. William Dudley Foulke, quoted in Martin J. Schiesl, *The Politics of Efficiency: Municipal Administration and Reform in America, 1800–1920* (Berkeley, 1977), 128.

10. Woodward Group, "Warren," 24–25; Cleveland W. Van Dyke Papers, Arizona Collection, Arizona State University, and obituary in Van Dyke biofile, AHS; Schiesl, *Politics of Efficiency;* on Van Dyke, see sci.tech-archive.net/Archive/sci.archaeology/2005-06/msg00614.html (accessed 12 October 2007).

11. Alanen, "Planning," 258; Powell to Briggs, 7 August 1906; Briggs to Powell, 13 August 1906, C&A letters.

12. Woodward Group, "Warren," 21. On Manning, also see Arnold R. Alanen and Lynn Bjorkman, "Early Twentieth-Century National Planning in the United States: The Vision of Warren H. Manning," in Diane L. Scheu, comp., *Proceedings of the 1999 ASLA Annual Meeting* (Washington, D.C., 1999), 44–46; Arnold R. Alanen and Lynn Bjorkman, "Plats, Parks, Playgrounds, and Plants: Warren H. Manning's Landscape Designs for the Mining Districts of Michigan's Upper Peninsula, 1899–1932," *Journal of the Society for Industrial Archeology,* 24, no. 1 (1998): 41–60; Stephen Conant, "Democracy by Design: Warren H. Manning's Contribution to Planning History" (M.A. thesis, Tufts University, 1984); and Arnold Alanen, "Gwinn: A Model Town 'Without Equal,'" *Michigan History,* 78 (November–December 1994): 33–35.

13. "Aesthetic expression" from Jon A. Peterson, "The City Beautiful Movement: Forgotten Origins and Lost Meaning," *Journal of Urban History,* 2, no. 4 (August 1976): 54. On Harrisburg, see idem, *The Birth of City Planning in the United States, 1840–1917* (Baltimore, 2003), 122, 132–137.

14. Woodward Group, "Warren," 22, 25. Warren also resembled England's garden suburbs (or garden cities). On Manning and garden cities, see Margaret Crawford, *Building the Workingman's Paradise: The Design of American Company Towns* (London, 1995), 70–77. And see Charles F. Willis, "Mining Camp Housing," *Arizona Mining Journal* (November 1918).

15. Crawford, *Building,* 7, 66; Alanen, "Planning of Company Communities," 258.

16. See Richard Maxwell Brown, "The Western Federation of Miners," in *The New Encyclopedia of the American West* (New Haven, 1998), 1196–1197; James D. McBride, "Gaining a Foothold in the Paradise of Capitalism: The Western Federation of Miners and the Unionization of Bisbee," *Journal of Arizona History,* 23 (Autumn 1982): 300–301.

17. "Who Is This Organizer Kennedy?" *BDR,* 12 December 1903; "Written Statement

from Edward Kennedy, Who Came Here to Organize," *BDR*, 17 December 1903; "Bisbee Will Remain as It Was," *BDR*, 15 December 1903; McBride, "Gaining a Foothold," 301–303. "Labor Conditions in the Southwest," *EMJ* (31 March 1904): 510. Byrkit, *Forging*, 29; James C. Foster, "The WFM Experience in Alaska and Arizona, 1902–1908," in James C. Foster, ed., *American Labor in the Southwest: The First One Hundred Years* (Tucson, 1982), 26.

18. The classic work on the IWW is Melvyn Dubofsky, *We Shall Be All: A History of the IWW* (Chicago, 1969). On cross-ethnic organizing in the WFM, see Mellinger, *Race and Labor in Western Copper: The Fight for Equality, 1896–1918* (Tucson, 1995), 17–32.

19. The most complete discussion of WFM organizing and opposition in Bisbee is in the lengthy debate over the 1907 strike in *Proceedings of the Fifteenth Convention of the Western Federation of Miners, 1907* (Denver, 1907), 193–203. See also "The Defeat of Unionism at Bisbee," *EMJ* (24 March 1906): 570–571.

20. "Business Men on Union Situation," *BDR*, 2 March 1906; quotation from "Union Question in Bisbee To Be Settled on March 5," *BDR*, 1 March 1906; vote details in "Open Air Meeting Hears Both Sides," *BDR*, 4 March 1906. On Walter Douglas' opposition to unions, see McBride, "Gaining a Foothold"; "Death Blow to Union," *BDR*, 6 March 1906. Byrkit cites a source saying that there was no union before 1906 and that one organizer had secretly created a WFM local a few weeks before the union vote (Byrkit, *Forging*, 30). The *Daily Review* claimed that there were hundreds of union miners in Bisbee, but the issue was whether there would be a strike. The sources are too unclear to make a final decision on the matter.

21. On Idaho, see J. Anthony Lukas, *Big Trouble* (New York, 1997); and Vernon H. Jensen, *Heritage of Conflict: Labor Relations in the Nonferrous Metals Industry up to 1930* (Ithaca, N.Y., 1950), 197–218. On the Upper Peninsula, see Lankton, *Cradle to Grave*, 208–213.

22. The best source on Cananea is Samuel Truett, *Fugitive Landscapes: A Forgotten History of the U.S.-Mexico Borderlands* (New Haven, 2006), esp. 144–156. Also see Michael J. Gonzales, "United States Copper Companies, the State, and Labour Conflict in Mexico, 1900–1910," *Journal of Latin American Studies*, 26 (October 1994): 651–681. On Cananea and the revolution, see Ramón E. Ruiz, *Labor and the Ambivalent Revolutionaries: Mexico, 1911–1923* (Baltimore, 1993), 3; and the classic Rodney D. Anderson, "Mexican Workers and the Politics of Revolution, 1906–1911," *Hispanic American Historical Review*, 54 (1974): 94–113. See also Jonathan C. Brown, "Foreign and Native-Born Workers in Porfirian Mexico," *American Historical Review*, 98, no. 2 (June 1993): 786–818; and Marvin D. Bernstein, *The Mexican Mining Industry, 1890–1950* (Albany, N.Y., 1965), 65. On the Partido Liberal Mexicano in Cananea, see Chaz Bufe and Mitchell Cowen Verter, eds., *Dreams of Freedom: A Ricardo Flores Magón Reader* (Oakland, Calif., 2005), 47–51.

23. "Mexico: Sonora," *EMJ*, 82 (22 December 1906): 1192; "Sonora," *EMJ*, 84 (11

August 1907): 280; Samuel Truett, email correspondence, 8 August 2005; "Late Capt. Hoatson Was Pioneer of This Region," obituary, no date, Hoatson file, MTUCCC.

24. *Harper's Weekly* quoted in Lankton, *Cradle to Grave*, 144; Jensen, *Heritage of Conflict*, 246–248; Alanen, "Planning of Company Communities," 264, 266; "Impending Labor Changes in Lake Superior Region: Special Correspondence," *EMJ*, 97, no. 16 (18 April 1914): 793–794.

25. "The Defeat of Unionism," 570; Report labeled "Dwellings for Employees" from C. W. Powell, President of Warren Company and third VP of C&A, to Charles Briggs, President of C&A, 7 August 1906; Powell to Briggs, 7 August 1906; Briggs to Powell, 13 August 1906; C. d'Autremont Jr. to Charles Briggs, 15 August 1906, all in C&A Papers.

26. See Lankton, *Cradle to Grave*, 153–159. But see Alison Hoagland, "Homeownership in a Company Town: Workers' Strategies in Michigan's Copper Country," unpublished paper given at the 11th National Conference on Planning History, Coral Gables, Florida, 22 October 2005.

27. Van Dyke report. Labor historians have reinterpreted turnover, malingering, and shoddy work as "worker's control." See David Montgomery, *Worker's Control in America* (New York, 1979). On "wildcat strikes" by Mexican workers in Arizona, with the same underlying purpose, see A. Yvette Huginnie, "'Strikitos': Race, Class, and Work in the Arizona Copper Industry, 1870–1920," (Ph.D. diss., Yale University, 1991).

28. Lankton, *Cradle to Grave*, 157–159; on environmentalism, see Raymond A. Mohl, *The New City: Urban America in the Industrial Age, 1860–1920* (Wheeling, Ill., 1985), 166–179.

29. See Kathryn J. Oberdeck, "From Model Town to Edge City: Piety, Paternalism and the Politics of Urban Planning in the United States," *Journal of Urban History*, 26, no. 4 (May 2000): 508–518; Crawford, *Building*; Stanley Buder, *Pullman: An Experiment in Industrial Order and Community Planning, 1880–1930* (New York, 1967); Jane Addams, "A Modern Lear," reprinted in Taylor, *Satellite Cities*, 68–90; Janice Reiff, "A Modern Lear and His Daughters: Gender in the Model Town of Pullman," in Richard Schneirov et al., eds., *The Pullman Strike and the Crisis of the 1890s: Essays on Labor and Politics* (Urbana, Ill., 1999), 65–86.

30. On Tarbell, see Crawford, *Building*, 57; "organic totality" from Peterson, *The Birth of City Planning*, 139.

31. "Blight" quotation from Henry B. Fuller, "An Industrial Utopia: Building Gary, Indiana, to Order," *Harper's Weekly*, 51 (October 12, 1907): 1482; Van Dyke report, 1; Crawford, *Building*, 42–45, 56; Taylor, *Satellite Cities*, 17–21; "thoroughly" quotation from Willis, "Mining Camp Housing."

32. "Rules for Labor Election Monday," *BDR*, 3 March 1906; McBride, "Gaining a Foothold," 307–308; Byrkit, *Forging*, 31; see also the debates in *Proceedings . . . 1907*, 193–204; "Mother Jones, Remarkable Character," *BDR*, 21 February 1907; "Mother Jones and Socialism," *BDR*, 21 February 1907; "Large Number of Miners Laid Off," *BDR*, 13

February 1907. See also "Eight Hundred Miners are Laid Off by Warren District Mining Companies," *BDR,* 14 February 1907; and "Many Miners Are Leaving the District," *BDR,* 15 February 1907. Edward Crough notebooks, unpaginated, James D. McBride private collection, Tempe, Arizona, copy in author's possession; "Renewing the Attack," *BDR,* 13 February 1907; "Bisbee Miners Get Raise," *BDR,* 17 March 1907.

33. Byrkit, *Forging,* 31. "Bisbee Miners," *ALJ,* 21 August 1913, 46.

34. On these inconsistencies, see Phil Mellinger, "'The Men Have Become Organizers': Labor Conflict and Unionization in the Mexican Mining Communities of Arizona, 1900–1915," *WHQ,* 23, no. 3 (August 1992): 323–347, esp. 335; and "How the IWW Lost Its Western Heartland: Western Labor History Revisited," *WHQ,* 27, no. 3 (Autumn 1996): 303–324, esp. 316.

35. Quotation from "Recognition Is Denied Union," *BDR,* 9 April 1907; on Slavs and organizing, see "Western Federation Is Making Little Headway," *BDR,* 10 March 1907; Crough notebooks.

36. Numbers come from a pro-company source, so they are, if anything, undercounts. "Struggle Is Now On," *BDR,* 10 April 1907; "Mother Gets $50 for Her Services," *BDR,* 28 May 1907; Crough notebooks; "Situation Is Practically Unchanged," *BDR,* 13 April 1907; William B. Gohring, letter to family, no date (ca. 13 April 1907), BMHM.

37. The picketers were not convicted of the vagrancy charges. Crough notebooks; Byrkit, *Forging,* 31–32; McBride, "Gaining a Foothold," 310; Mellinger, *Race and Labor,* 77.

38. Cannon quotation from *Proceedings,* 196; also see Byrkit, *Forging,* 31; McBride, "Gaining a Foothold," 311; Jensen, *Heritage of Conflict,* 355–359; Crough notebooks.

39. On views of the strike, see esp. Mellinger (the only scholar to consider its racial implications), *Race and Labor,* 73–79; Foster, "WFM Experience," 26–27; and Byrkit, *Forging,* 31–33, where the strike is termed a "rehearsal for the 1917 drama." Cannon saw Bisbee as important because it was Arizona's last holdout of anti-unionism. On Cannon and Jones, see *Proceedings . . . 1907,* "more at stake," 195; and Philip S. Foner, ed., *Mother Jones Speaks: Collected Writing and Speeches* (New York, 1983), 370–375. Underground workers' rule is set out in "Rules for Labor Election Monday."

40. Van Dyke report, 3.

41. Ibid., 8.

42. Huger Elliott, "An Ideal City in the West," *Architectural Review,* 15, no. 9 (1908): 137–142. On Mission Revival's "exaltation of obedience and paternalism," see Mike Davis, *City of Quartz: Excavating the Future in Los Angeles* (New York, 1990), 28; zoning laws are in Charles M. Haar and Michael Allen Wolf, *Land-Use Planning: A Casebook on the Use, Misuse, and Re-Use of Urban Land* (Boston, 1989), 164.

43. Van Dyke report, 7–9, quotation on 7. Appearance of Warren from Woodward Group, "Warren," C&A company reports, and personal observation.

44. *BDR* articles quoted in Woodward Group, "Warren," 27, 29; on other plans, see Bjorkman and Alanen, "Plats, Parks, Playgrounds, and Plants"; Alanen, "Planning";

Crawford, *Building*, 34–35, 68. On City Beautiful, see also Charles Willis, "A City of Homes," draft article for *Tucson Citizen*, in A. T. Thomson, Assistant to the President, PD, Douglas, Arizona, 16 September 1919, Phelps Dodge Corporate Archives, Phoenix, Arizona.

45. Morris Knowles, *Industrial Housing* (New York, 1920), quotation on 32, also see 326–330, 334; Manuscript Census, 1920, Cochise County, Warren Precinct.

46. Van Dyke report, 3; *BDR*, World's Fair Edition, 1904.

47. The World's Fair Edition of the *BDR* claimed that two-thirds of the married miners in Bisbee owned their own homes in 1903, but this seems high. "Union Question . . ."; "Open Air Meeting"; "Rules for Labor Election"; Knowles, *Industrial Housing*, 15.

48. Thomas Adams, quoted in Knowles, *Industrial Housing*, 293.

49. Carol Pateman, quoted in Linda Gordon, "The New Feminist Scholarship on the Welfare State," in Gordon, ed., *Women, the State, and Welfare* (Madison, Wisc., 1989), 20.

50. On masculine "independence" and patriarchal household structure, see Stephanie McCurry, *Masters of Small Worlds: Yeoman Households, Gender Relations, and the Political Culture of the Antebellum South Carolina Low Country* (New York, 1995), esp. 35.

51. "The 'Organizers' and the Conditions in Bisbee," *BDR*, 24 January 1906; "Union Question . . ." The newspaper described Cannon as a "local restaurant owner," but he was in fact a national WFM organizer and, later, a CIO organizer, as well as a Socialist political candidate in Arizona and New York. "Wanted at Once: 500 Men," *Douglas Examiner*, 9 June 1907, 3. "Caught Like a Thief," *Douglas Examiner*, 11 June 1907, 3. See also Edward M. Steel, ed., *The Correspondence of Mother Jones* (Pittsburgh, 1985), 87.

52. On mortgage terms, see Van Dyke report and S. C. Dickinson, "A Sociological Survey of the Bisbee Warren District," 31 December 1917, 34, UASC; Arthur Notman, "Welfare Work in the District," *Arizona Mining Journal* (July 1918), 10–13; "Of Interest to the Workers," *Arizona Mining Journal* (April 1920), 24. On complaints elsewhere, see Davis, *City of Quartz*, 28.

53. Elliott, "An Ideal City in the West," 139; Margaret and Gary Dillard, *Warren Ball Park and Its First Game* (Bisbee, 1996).

54. See, for example, *BDR* advertisement, 1 February 1907, cited in Woodward Group, "Warren," 29.

55. Nancy K. Tisdale, "The Prohibition Crusade in Arizona" (M.A. thesis, University of Arizona, 1965), vi; Van Dyke report, 6; but see "Cochise County against Prohibition: Voters Are Emphatic for License and Regulation," *BDR*, 27 January 1910.

56. Foster, "WFM Experience," 27.

57. Conant, "Democracy by Design," 79–80.

58. Marketing information from Charles Willis, "A City of Homes"; Willis, "Mining Camp Housing"; and untitled article, *BDR*, 21 November 1919. On Harrisburg, see Peterson, *Birth of City Planning*, 132–133. On Calumet, see Warren Manning to James Macnaughton, 19 May 1921, MacFarland Papers, Box 70, MTUCCC; Alanen and Bjork-

man, "Plats, Parks, Playgrounds, and Plants"; "Warren Women Have Formed Aid Society," *BDR*, 1 March 1910.

59. "We have learned" comes from Van Dyke report, 8–9, emphasis mine; "free American" from "Union Question . . ." In the copper-mining camp of Jerome, foreign-born residents were more likely to own their own homes; Nancy Lee Prichard, "Paradise Found? Opportunity for Mexican, Irish, Italian, and Chinese Born Individuals in Jerome Copper Mining District, 1880–1910" (Ph.D. diss., Northern Arizona University, 1992), 201–202; see also Elizabeth Jameson, *All That Glitters: Class, Conflict, and Community in Cripple Creek* (Urbana, Ill., 1998), 145–148.

60. *EMJ* quoted in Lankton, *Cradle to Grave*, 144.

61. Mamie Milutinovich Bugen claims this in her oral history, and census data support her. Interview by C. Graham, 12 June 1981, and interview by Beverly Woods, 21 May 1991, both at BMHM.

62. Bugen, oral history, 12 June 1981.

63. On dependency discourses and justifications of slavery and imperialism, see Nancy Fraser and Linda Gordon, "A Genealogy of Dependency: Tracing a Keyword of the Welfare State," *Signs: Journal of Women in Culture and Society* 19 (Winter 1994): 309–336, esp. 315, 317. This is one reason scholars developed the notion of "internal colonialism" to explain the Southwest's racialized class structure and extractive economies. See esp. Mario Barrera, *Race and Class in the Southwest: A Theory of Racial Inequality* (Notre Dame, Ind., 1979); and Gordon, *Great Arizona Orphan Abduction*, 178–185.

64. On Bonillas, see *BDR*, 9 May 1915, Bonillas biofile, AHS; Truett, *Fugitive Landscapes*, 133–134. The Bonillases are not in the 1917 city directory. On the Redondos, see Walsh, Diary, 30 September 1917; Manuscript Census, 1920.

65. Statistics compiled from Manuscript Census, 1910, 1920. Details on wartime crowding come from Walsh, Diary, 20–25 March 1916; "Goat Row" from Bugen oral history, 1991.

66. Willis, "Mining Camp Housing." On Warren's reputation, see, for example, Dan Kitchel, oral history, interview by Roberta Vaughan, 6 February 1981, BMHM. "Aristocrats" from Esker Mayberry, oral history transcription, interview by Colleen Crowlie, 7 November 1950, State Historical Society of Wisconsin, 41. Two scholars state that Warren was built for company executives, but they did not have access to Warren Company documents; see Colleen O'Neill, "A Community Divided: A Social History of the Bisbee Deportation" (M.A. thesis, New Mexico State University, 1989); and Crawford, *Building*, 130.

5. Mormons and Mexicans in the San Pedro River Valley

Unless otherwise noted, all demographic data are compiled from the 1910 and 1920 Manuscript Census schedules, Enumeration District 7, Cochise County, Arizona. Land data rely on the BLM database.

1. *Benson Signal,* 4 September 1915.

2. Henry F. Dobyns, Theodore Bundy, James E. Officer, and Richard W. Stoffle, *Los Tres Alamos del Rio San Pedro: The Peculiar Persistence of a Place Name* (Tucson, 1996); Paul Hirt, "The Transformation of a Landscape: Culture and Ecology in Southeastern Arizona," *Environmental Review,* 13 (Fall–Winter 1989): 167–189; Basil J. Sherlock, "Community Change in the Southwest: The Case of Benson," *Arizona Review of Business and Public Administration* (1965): 1–10.

3. *Grijalba et al. v. Dunbar et al.,* 1889, Cochise County District Court, 1st Judicial District, Case no. 1414, transcripts in Filmfiles 90.6.2 and 90.6.3, ASLAPR, 163; Dobyns et al., *Tres Alamos,* 111–112.

4. See Mark E. Miller, "St. Johns's Saints: Interethnic Conflict in Northeastern Arizona, 1880–1885," *Journal of Mormon History,* 23 (Spring 1997): 66–99. On water, see R. H. Forbes, "Irrigation and Agricultural Practice in Arizona," *Arizona Agricultural Extension Service Bulletin,* 63 (1911): 11; on Mormons as an ethnic group, see Patricia Limerick, "Peace Initiative: Using the Mormons to Rethink Culture and Ethnicity in American History," in Limerick, *Something in the Soil: Field-Testing the New Western History* (New York, 2000), 235–255.

5. Laura Mae Seward, "Annual Report of County Extension Workers," UACES, 1924, Federal Extension Service, Cochise County Office, Willcox, Arizona, and UASC; Louise Fenn Larson, oral history transcript, interview by Nedra Sutherland, 15 January 1993, SPVAHM, 15; Hazel Zimmerman, Southern Arizona Home Extension Agent, quarterly report, September–November 1917, MF T-847, NACP.

6. David R. Berman, *Reformers, Corporations, and the Electorate: An Analysis of Arizona's Age of Reform* (Niwot, Colo., 1992), 16.

7. Richard White, *It's Your Misfortune and None of My Own* (Norman, Okla., 1991), 153; Dobyns et al., *Tres Alamos,* esp. 285–286; on the Benson Canal, see Louise Fenn Larson, *Pomerene, Arizona and the Valley of the San Pedro* (Mesa, Ariz., 1999), 102–118; Forbes, "Irrigation," 57.

8. Dobyns et al., *Tres Alamos,* 125; *Grijalba v. Dunbar,* 163. I have used figures from Forbes, "Irrigation," 50–51, to calculate irrigable acreage. County acreage is from U.S. Bureau of the Census, *Fourteenth Census of the United States,* vol. 7: *Irrigation and Drainage, 1920* (Washington, D.C., 1922), 116.

9. Compiled ledger records of Fairview (the name was changed to Pomerene in 1920) School District no. 64, ASLAPR; Manuscript Census, 1920.

10. F. LaMond Tullis, *Mormons in Mexico: The Dynamics of Faith and Culture* (Logan, Utah, 1987); Pearl Fenn Gashler, entry on Fenn Family in Nelle Spilsbury Hatch and B. Carmon Hardy, eds., *Stalwarts South of the Border* (El Paso, 1985), 188, 191–192. See also Jill Mulvay Derr, "'Strength in Our Union': The Making of Mormon Sisterhood," in Maureen Ursenbach Beecher and Lavinia Fielding Anderson, eds., *Sisters in Spirit: Mormon Women in Historical and Cultural Perspective* (Urbana, Ill., 1987), 153–207, esp. 165; Larson, *Pomerene,* 417–418; James H. McClintock, *History of Arizona:*

Prehistoric, Aboriginal, Pioneer, Modern, vol. 1 (Chicago, 1916), 270; Fenn Larson, oral history, 8.

11. Fenn Larson, *Pomerene,* 417; Fenn Larson, oral history, 15; Fairview School District Census Marshal's reports from 1911–1916, and ledgers for subsequent years, Cochise County School Records, ASLAPR.

12. Cochise County school censuses for 1910, ASLAPR. This practice was pervasive in county Manuscript Census forms.

13. Fairview School District ledger, 1916–1917, ASLAPR.

14. I cross-listed census data with BLM database.

15. Mormons filed perhaps 29 percent of the homesteads in the six townships around Pomerene (T15S-R20E, T16S-R19E, T16S-R20E, T17S-R19E, T17S-R20E, T17S-R21E). I determined religion by cross-referencing homestead records in the BLM database with Pomerene Cemetery Records, and by consulting the Pomerene Latter-Day Saints Branch Directory for 1916 in Fenn Larson, *Pomerene,* 294, 300.

16. Ten of fifty-two households in the 1920 manuscript census were female-headed; Maureen Ursenbach Beecher, Carol Cornwall Madsen, and Lavina Fielding Anderson, "Widowhood among the Mormons: The Personal Accounts," in Arlene Scadron, ed., *On Their Own: Widows and Widowhood in the American Southwest, 1848–1939* (Urbana, Ill., 1988), 123, "replete" on 130; Hatch, *Stalwarts,* 462. Examples of abandoned wives abound in the primary literature; see, for example, Annie Clark Tanner, *A Mormon Mother* (Salt Lake City, 1983). On legal matters, see Marybeth Raynes, "Mormon Marriages in an American Context," in Beecher and Anderson, *Sisters in Spirit,* 229, 233–234; and Beecher, Madsen, and Anderson, "Widowhood among the Mormons," 121–128.

17. Jeanette Done, email correspondence, 6 January 2005. But see news of Naegle's homestead in *Benson Signal,* 17 June 1916.

18. Manuscript Census, 1920. Kind remembrances in Dobyns et al., *Tres Alamos,* 278; Gashler, Fenn entry, *Stalwarts,* 195; and Fenn Larson, *Pomerene,* passim. For anti-Mormon articles, see *El Fronterizo* (Tucson), August 29, 1896, 1; ibid., 7 March 1882, 1.

19. Cochise County Great Register, 1882, microfilm copy from ASLAPR. Doña Jesús Moreno de Soza, "Reminiscences," Soza Family Collection, AHS. On these reminiscences, see Vicki Ruiz, "Nuestra América: Latino History as United States History," *Journal of American History,* 93, no. 3 (December 2006): 655–672.

20. The census taker counted ranchers as farmers in the "Occupation" column, but then specified type of farming in the "Industry, business, or establishment" column. Jesús M. Sánchez and Miguel Gámez had nothing in the "Occupation" column—perhaps an omission—where everyone else had "Stock range" listed.

21. See "Local Items," *Benson Signal,* 19 May 1917; Voter Register, Cochise County, 1914, County Recorder's Office, Bisbee, Arizona. The western riverbank, where most Mexican Americans owned land, supported mainly grazing, with farming on the east side—which is where Pomerene is located. See Dobyns et al., *Tres Alamos,* 117, Map 3.

22. Dobyns et al., *Tres Alamos,* 87; Mrs. Joe Young, Tres Alamos, to Helen Benedict,

Assistant Superintendent of Schools, Tombstone, 13 November 1917, Cochise County Superintendent Series, MS 180, AHS. The last "Tres Alamos News" feature appeared in *Benson Signal*, 3 January 1920.

23. Nineteenth-century homesteading figures compiled from Soza, *Hispanic Homesteaders in Arizona* and *Mexican-American Homesteaders* (parentseyes.arizona.edu); for twentieth century, BLM database. Legal modifications in Pat H. Stein, *Homesteading in Arizona, 1862–1940: A Guide to Studying, Evaluating, and Preserving Historic Homesteads* (Phoenix, 1990), 5–7.

24. Dobyns et al., *Tres Alamos,* 59; *Benson Signal,* 17 June 1916.

25. Data compiled from BLM database and Soza, *Mexican Homesteaders,* esp. "Homestead Proof: Testimony of Witness," Application of Antonio Campo Soza, reproduced in "Exhibits"; Manuscript Census, 1900, 1910, 1920; and "Genealogia," Soza Family Collection, AHS; Sharon Johnson Mariscal, "The Sosa/Soza Family of Arizona," *Cochise Quarterly* (Summer 1986): 16.

26. Mariscal, "The Sosa/Soza Family," 13–16; Thomas E. Sheridan, "Del Rancho al Barrio: The Mexican-American Legacy of Tucson" (Tucson, 1983), 5–6; Moreno de Soza, "Reminiscences."

27. Moreno de Soza, "Reminiscences"; Sheridan, "Del Rancho El Barrio," 5.

28. "Genealogia," Soza Collection, AHS; land ownership data from Soza, *Hispanic Homesteaders of Arizona,* esp. 224–246, and BLM database; Cochise County Superior Court Marriage Index no. 1, 1881–1963, microfilm file 90.5.69, ASLAPR, cross-listed with BLM database.

29. Patricia Preciado Martin, ed., *Beloved Land: An Oral History of Mexican Americans in Southern Arizona* (Tucson, 2004), 54–55.

30. Ibid., 80, 48; Sherlock, "Community Change," 3.

31. Manuscript Census, 1880, Pima County, "On the Road near Tres Alamos"; Dobyns et al., *Tres Alamos,* 174; Cochise County Marriage Index no. 1; Dora Ohnesorgen Oral History Transcript, 27 November 1990, SPVAHM; author conversation with Dunbar descendants, Cascabel, Arizona, 3 November 2006. The wives of John Montgomery and William Ohnesorgen, both María Ruíz, were relatives.

32. Author conversation with Dunbar descendants.

33. Census cross-listed with marriage records; "jungle" image from Edward Ellsworth, Benson, Arizona, letter to author, no date (August 2001).

34. Probate records have only a handful of recorded wills for Mexican Americans. On partible inheritance, see George Alter, "Agricultural Productivity, Partible Inheritance, and the Demographic Response to Rural Poverty: An Examination of the Spanish Southwest," *Explorations in Economic History,* 19 (1982): 184–200; and Theodore E. Downing, "Partible Inheritance and Land Fragmentation in a Oaxaca Village," *Human Organization,* 36, no. 3 (1977): 235–243.

35. Probate Case of Rafaela M. de Rosas, Case no. 474, Cochise County Probate Court. Also see Probate Case of Simón Madríd, Case no. 527. Both in Filmfile no.

90.5.198, ASLAPR. Bernardo S. Gámez, oral history, interview by Nedra Sutherland, 7 May 1994, SPVAHM.

36. Martin, *Beloved Land,* 77.

37. Women accounted for twenty-one of the sixty-two total cash and homestead en-tries by Mexican Americans in townsites on the San Pedro River from T14S-R20E to 18S-21E (BLM database). Figures are based on female first names and Spanish surnames; thus, women with Anglo husbands or ambiguous names may be missing, although I cross-referenced several with census data. On women and homesteading law, see Chap-ter 6 and James Muhn, "Women and the Homestead Act: Land Department Administra-tion of a Legal Imbroglio, 1863–1934," *Western Legal History,* 7 (Summer–Fall 1994): 282–307.

38. BLM database; Soza, *Mexican Homesteaders;* Dobyns et al., *Tres Alamos.* Blas Sánchez's widow was named Dolores; Blas Sánchez, Probate Case no. 309, Cochise County Probate Court, Filmfile 90.5.249, ASLAPR.

39. Mariscal, "The Sosa/Soza family," and Soza Family Brands in Soza Collection, AHS.

40. James Walter Black, "History of Education in Cochise County" (M.A. thesis, Uni-versity of Arizona, 1940); Cochise County School District records, MS 180; Cochise County School District Censuses and ledgers, ASLAPR; Elsie Toles, *Rural and Small-Town Schools of Cochise County* (ca. 1920), Elsie Toles Collection, AHS; Minnie Lintz, "Cochise County School Report, 1915–6," in C. O. Case, "Report of the Superintendent of Public Instruction of the State of Arizona, for the School Years Ending June 30, 1915, and June 30, 1916," ASLAPR.

41. Elsie Toles, "Memoirs of Cochise County Superintendent of Schools Elsie Toles, 1912–1918" (ca. 1920), Toles biofile, BMHM; Shattuck biofiles, BMHM; Joel H. Smith, "A Proposed Plan for the Consolidation of Schools in the San Pedro Valley, Arizona" (M.A. thesis, Arizona State College, 1950); Howard Roberts, "The Evolution of Arizona School Law from Statehood to 1939," unpublished seminar paper, 27 November 1972, AHS; Black, "History of Education."

42. School District Reports, Apodaca School District no. 37, ASLAPR.

43. J. M. Sánchez to Elsie Toles and attached petition, 28 June 1917, and Minnie K. Bisby to Elsie Toles, 29 May 1918, MS 180, AHS.

44. On teachers, see Superintendent Nicholls, Willcox, Arizona, to Miss Bertha Ochoa, 11 September 1901, MS 180, and school district records, ASLAPR; Sadie West-field Martínez biofile, AHS; Bisby to Toles, 18 December 1918, 15 February 1919, 27 May 1918, MS 180, AHS.

45. Bisby to Toles, 18 December 1918, 27 May 1918.

46. Idem, 27 May 1918, 29 May 1918.

47. Idem, 29 May 1918, 15 February 1919, 27 May 1918.

48. See also Eulalia "Sister" Bourne, *Nine Months Is a Year at Baboquivari School* (Tucson, 1968); and Mary Melcher, "'This Is Not Right': Rural Arizona Women

Challenge Segregation and Ethnic Division, 1925–1950," *Frontiers,* 20, no. 2 (1999): 190–214.

49. Undated petition (sent 30 May 1918), MS 180, AHS; Bisby to Toles, 29 May 1918.

50. Bisby to Toles, 29 May 1918.

51. School District compiled records, ASLAPR; Smith, "A Proposed Plan," 45.

52. Sherlock, "Community Change."

53. Thomas E. Sheridan, *Los Tucsonenses: The Mexican-American Community in Tucson, 1854–1941* (Tucson, 1986), esp. chs. 4–5.

54. Joe Chisholm, *Brewery Gulch: Frontier Days of Old Arizona—Last Outpost of the Great Southwest* (San Antonio, 1949), 28; Cochise County Marriage Index, 1880–1890, in Latter-Day Saints microfilm no. 1984688 and available on www.rootsweb.com (accessed 7 December 2007); *Arizona Star,* 5 June 1889, 4; and "Jose Miguel Castañeda," in *Portrait and Biographical Record* (ca. 1901–1902), 903–907, in Castañeda biofile, AHS; for social pages, see, e.g., "Ladies, Attention," *Benson Signal,* 29 September 1917.

55. "Local Items," *Benson Signal,* esp. 9 December 1916, 23 March 1918, 1 June 1918, 7 July 1918, 27 April 1918; "Benson Man Sells Mines at Twin Buttes," *Benson Signal,* 4 March 1916; "Laura Martínez Will Leave Post Office Service," *Benson Signal,* 1 January 1916; Great Register, Cochise County, 1914, Cochise County Recorder's Office, Bisbee, Arizona.

56. *Benson Signal,* 1 March 1919; Martínez biofile. For a similar marriage, see entry for Pedro Aguirre's marriage to Lucy Catlett, 1902, Cochise County Marriage Index no. 1. On father Filiberto Aguirre, a government cattle inspector, see *El Fronterizo* (Tucson), 20 January 1894, 3. On similar marriages in Mexico, see notes to Chapter 1, above.

57. *Benson Signal,* 1916–1920, passim.

58. Voter register, 1914. On woman suffrage, see *El Fronterizo* (Tucson), 22 February 1893, 3; and ibid., 2 March 1895, 2.

59. Great register, 1914. On citizenship, see Victor S. Clark, "Mexican Labor in the United States," *Bureau of Labor Bulletin,* 78 (1908): 466–522, esp. 520–521.

60. Voter register, 1914; Berman, *Reformers,* 114 and 175; *Benson Signal,* 1 March 1919; "Jose Miguel Castañeda," 907; *El Fronterizo* (Tucson), 20 January 1894, 3; Sheridan, *Los Tucsonenses,* 112–122; BLM database and Soza, *Hispanic Homesteaders; Benson Signal,* 18 September 1915, 18 February 1919.

61. Berman, *Reformers,* 54, 92.

62. Ibid., 92.

63. On Alianza, see Tomás Serrano Cabo, *Crónicas: Alianza Hispano-Americano* (Santa Fe, N.M., 1929); Kaye Lynn Briegel, "Alianza Hispano-Americano, 1894–1965" (Ph.D. diss., University of Southern California, 1974); Olivia Arrieta, *Renato Rosaldo Lecture Series, 1989–90,* vol. 7 (Tucson, 1991); Linda Gordon, *The Great Arizona Orphan Abduction* (Cambridge, Mass., 1999), 134–135. Records from Soza family collection, AHS; *La Alianza* Papers, Accession no. 1994-1408, Box 3, Folder 27, Benson Lodge no. 253, Chicano Collection, Arizona State University.

64. Dance notices appeared in the *Benson Signal* almost every month of 1916, and several of 1919. On Fourth of July, see *Benson Signal*, 6 July 1918.

65. Benson School District Teachers' Reports, ASLAPR; also see Christmas program, *Benson Signal*, 20 December 1919; Fenn Larson, *Pomerene*, 67; Bisbee High School, *Cuprite*, various years, BMHM; *Benson Signal*, 21 June 1919; and see *Benson Signal*, 17 March 1917. Soza also won the award for commercial work, two of the six prizes given out that year. "Closing Exercises of the High School," *Benson Signal*, 26 May 1917.

66. "Augustín Martínez Marries Miss Guadalupe Ochoa," *Benson Signal*, 17 July 1915.

67. *Benson Signal*, 27 April 1918, 24 June 1916, 21 September 1918.

68. Inclusion in the railroad brotherhood was mandatory for some jobs; Sheridan, *Los Tucsonenses*, 5, 179. Dobyns et al., *Tres Alamos*, 69–75. On the divisions between Mexicans and Mexican Americans, see David G. Gutiérrez, *Walls and Mirrors: Mexican Americans, Mexican Immigrants, and the Politics of Ethnicity* (Berkeley, 1995).

69. *Benson Signal*, 28 September 1918, 5 August 1916.

70. Charles Montgomery, *The Spanish Redemption: Heritage, Power, and Loss on New Mexico's Upper Rio Grande* (Berkeley, 2002); also see John M. Nieto-Phillips, *The Language of Blood: The Making of Spanish-American Identity in New Mexico, 1880s–1930s* (Albuquerque, 2004).

71. Charles Montgomery, "Becoming 'Spanish-American': Race and Rhetoric in New Mexico Politics, 1880–1928," *Journal of American Ethnic History*, 20, no. 4 (2001), 59–84, quotation on 61; "Jose Miguel Castañeda," 903; on whiteness, see also Gordon, *The Great Arizona Orphan Abduction*, 54–55; and Neil Foley, "Becoming Hispanic: Mexican-American Americans and the Faustian Pact with Whiteness," *Reflexiones: New Directions in Mexican-American American Studies* (1997): 53–70.

72. "José Miguel Castañeda," 903; Helen Genevieve Hurtado Brown, interview by Katherine Benton-Cohen, 11 February 1999, Willcox, Arizona.

73. Sheridan, *Los Tucsonenses*, 84–85.

74. "Benson Planning for Big Fourth of July Celebration," *Benson Signal*, 17 June 1916; "Rally for the Fourth Liberty Loan," ibid., 28 September 1918; "Fire Wednesday Afternoon," ibid., 22 July 1916.

75. Local notes, *Benson Signal*, 23 March 1918; Dobyns et al., *Tres Alamos*, 171; Benson Tong, *Asian American Children: A Historical Handbook and Guide* (Westport, Conn., 2004), 7–8. Tong claims that four daughters never married—a sign, perhaps, of their racial ambiguity.

6. Women and Men in the Sulphur Springs and San Simon Valleys

1. Manuscript Census, 1910, Cochise County, Kansas Settlement Precinct, ED 11B and 12A; Kansas School District no. 20, Census, Cochise County School District Records,

ASLAPR; Katie Flick (daughter of Mary Cowen), undated funeral announcement, typescript in author's possession; George Homrighausen obituary, *Arizona Range News* (Willcox), 6 January 1911.

2. In 1900, Cochise County had 62,992 acres in farms; in 1920, it had 998,242. See Bureau of the U.S. Census, *Fourteenth Census of the United States,* vol. 5, *Agriculture,* part 3 (Washington, D.C., 1922), 232. On fences, see W[illiam] C. Barnes, "The Passing of the Range," *Scientific Farmer,* 2 (December 1906): 109; and R. H. Forbes, "The Future of the Range," *Agricultural Review* (March 1917): 6. On places and schools, Byrd Howell Granger, *Arizona's Names: X Marks the Place* (Tucson, 1983); James Walter Black, "History of Education in Cochise County" (M.A. thesis, University of Arizona, 1940), 49; and Elsie Toles, *Rural and Small-Town Schools in Cochise County* (ca. 1920), Elsie Toles Collection, AHS, 3. Quotation from George Wharton James, *Arizona the Wonderland* (Boston, 1917), 401.

3. On homesteading in this era, see Paul W. Gates, *History of Public Land Law Development* (Washington, D.C., 1968); and E. Louise Peffer, *The Closing of the Public Domain: Disposal and Reservation Policies, 1900–1950* (Stanford, 1951). Unless otherwise noted, all homestead data cited are from the BLM database. I counted all patents between 1905 and 1923, to account for five years to prove up a claim; after 1912, homesteaders could elect to prove up claims in three years, so some patents made in 1922 and 1923 date from claims made after 1918. Figures on Cochise County's failed claims are unavailable, but even a 50 percent success rate would mean at least 5,000 new homestead claims between 1900 and 1918! On failed claims, see Paul W. Gates, "Homestead Act," in Howard R. Lamar, ed., *The New Encyclopedia of the American West* (New Haven, 1998), 492–493.

4. On environmental impact, see Barnes, "The Passing of the Range"; Forbes, "Future of the Range"; Paul Hirt, "The Transformation of a Landscape: Culture and Ecology in Southeastern Arizona," *Environmental Review,* 13 (Fall–Winter 1989): 167–189; John P. Wilson, *Islands in the Desert: A History of the Uplands of Southeastern Arizona* (Albuquerque, 1995); and Conrad J. Bahre and M. L. Shelton, "Historic Vegetation Change, Mesquite Increases, and Climate in Southeastern Arizona," *Journal of Biogeography,* 20, no. 5 (September 1993): 489–504.

5. Using 1920 U.S. Manuscript Census data, I examined five sample homesteader communities (Kansas Settlement, Light, Servoss, McNeal, and San Simon) to get representative percentages of Midwesterners, Southerners, and Texans. I counted all heads-of-household and subtracted Mexican laborers (generally just a handful, and mostly railroad workers in separate neighborhoods) from the totals.

6. Arthur J. Benedict et al., "Sunday School Pioneers of Sulphur Spring Valley" (1925), 23–24, Churches Vertical File, BMHM.

7. "Good Land and Good Water Obtained in the Bowie Valley at Minimum Cost," *Bowie Enterprise,* 16 July 1915; *Bowie Enterprise,* 1 December 1916; S. W. White, "Texans Will Celebrate at McNeal, 22d," *Benson Signal,* 8 April 1916.

8. On "nesters," see Benedict et al., "Sunday School Pioneers," 41. On ranching and environmental degradation, see Note 4 above; Frank D. Myers, *Cochise County Arizona* (Tombstone, [1910–1911]), in Munk Ephemera Collection, Braun Library, ANC; and "Arizona State News," *Bowie Enterprise,* 5 November 1920. Rainfall in Wilson, *Islands in the Desert,* 191.

9. On rainfall variations, see G. E. Thompson and F. G. Gray, "Dry-Farming in the Sulphur Springs Valley," University of Arizona College of Agriculture Agricultural Experiment Station (hereafter cited as UAAES), Bulletin no. 103, 15 April 1925, Tucson, UASC; "burned to death" from E. W. Clothier, UAAES, "23rd Annual Report," Tucson, Arizona, 31 December 1912, 663–664, UASC; Susie Cundiff Patrick, Diary, typescript, ed. Rebecca Orozco, in author's possession.

10. Allan Bogue, "An Agriculture Empire," in Clyde A. Milner, Carol A. O'Connor, and Martha A. Sandweiss, eds., *Oxford History of the American West* (New York, 1994), 300; "Dryland Farming," in Lamar, ed., *New Encyclopedia,* 320–321. See also Mary W. M. Hargreaves, *Dry Farming in the Northern Great Plains, 1900–1925* (Cambridge, Mass., 1957), 85. Surge in claims evident in BLM database; and see Pat H. Stein, *Homesteading in Arizona, 1862–1940: A Guide to Studying, Evaluating, and Preserving Historic Homesteads* (Phoenix, 1990), 7.

11. On national irrigation campaigns, see Donald J. Pisani, "Reclamation and Social Engineering in the Progressive Era," in Pisani, *Water, Land, and Law in the West* (Lawrence, Kans., 1996), 180–194. Also see Laura Lovett, "Land Reclamation as Family Reclamation: The Family Ideal in George Maxwell's Reclamation and Resettlement Campaigns, 1897–1933," *Social Politics,* 7 (2000): 80–100; and idem, *Conceiving the Future: Pronatalism, Reproduction, and the Family in the United States, 1890–1938* (Chapel Hill, 2007).

12. Hydrographic map of Arizona, in C. N. Catlin, "Character of the Groundwater Resources of Arizona," UAAES, Bulletin no. 114, 1 March 1926, Tucson, Arizona; Cochise County School District Records, MS 180, AHS; Willcox, Arizona, Board of Trade, "This Message Is for You—Read It," (Willcox, ca. 1913); C. O. Anderson, "Why Willcox?" (Willcox, ca. 1909), 11, in Munk Ephemera Collection, Braun Library, ANC. On local participation in national promotion, see, e.g., *Proceedings of Sixteenth National Irrigation Congress* (Albuquerque, 1908), 408–409. On mining interests involved in agriculture, see Isabel Shattuck Fathauer, with Lynn R. Bailey, *Lemuel C. Shattuck: "A Little Mining, a Little Banking, and a Little Beer"* (Tucson, 1991), 238–250; Lynn R. Bailey, *We'll All Wear Silk Hats: The Erie and Chiricahua Cattle Companies and the Rise of Corporate Ranching in the Sulphur Spring Valley of Arizona, 1883–1909* (Tucson, 1994), 182; Thompson and Gray, "Dry-Farming in the Sulphur Spring Valley"; Myers, *Cochise County Arizona,* 51.

13. For combined campaigns and candid assessments of dry-farming's limitations, see E. W. Clothier, UAAES, "22nd Annual Report," Tucson, Arizona, 30 December 1911,

530–531, UASC; "Crop Results for Year," *Arizona Farm Improvement News,* 1, no. 1 (April 1915); Clothier, UAAES, "23rd Annual Report," 663–664, UASC; H. D. DuBois, "Sulphur Springs Valley," *Arizona New State Magazine* (September 1913): 4; Forbes, "The Future of the Range," 15; "This Message Is for You—Read It." On the national context, see David Wrobel, *Promised Lands: Promotion, Memory, and the Creation of the American West* (Lawrence, Kans., 2002), esp. 66.

14. Lovett, "Land Reclamation," 86.

15. Douglas Chamber of Commerce and Mines, "Sulphur Springs Valley, Cochise County, Arizona" (Douglas, Ariz., 1910–1911); *San Simon Artesian Belt: Homeseekers' Edition,* 21 March 1914; "Bowie's Land as an Investment," *Bowie Enterprise,* 7 December 1917; W. B. Dickey, "Free Homes for All in the Sulphur Springs Valley, the Homeseekers' Paradise" (Willcox, Ariz., ca. 1908); Karen Merrill, "Whose Home on the Range?" *WHQ,* 27, no. 4 (Winter 1996): esp. 447. On speculation and its critics, see Pisani, "Reclamation and Social Engineering," 185; "Fifty Homestead Filings in Month," *BDR,* 6 September 1907; "Bowie's Land as an Investment," *Bowie Enterprise,* 7 December 1917; "Crop Results for Year," *Arizona Farm Improvement News;* and Myers, *Cochise County Arizona,* 57. On "flippers," see Elsie Toles, "Memoirs of Cochise County Superintendent of Schools Elsie Toles, 1912–1918" (ca. 1920), Toles biofile, BMHM; and Helen Elizabeth Brunner, oral history, interview by E. F. Schaaf, 1971, Cochise, Arizona, AHS.

16. Maxwell quoted in Lovett, "Land Reclamation," 86; "State Land Sale Now On!" *Bowie Enterprise,* 12 November 1915; Anderson, "Why Willcox?"

17. Douglas Chamber of Commerce and Mines, "Sulphur Springs Valley."

18. Lovett, "Land Reclamation," 86.

19. On the Country Life movement, see Katherine Jellison, *Entitled to Power: Farm Women and Technology, 1913–1963* (Chapel Hill, 1993). On its links to western movements, see Jennie Buell, "The Country Life Movement," *Dry-Farming,* 5 (1 November 1911): 275–276; and untitled article, ibid., 5. On Theodore Roosevelt, see Gail Bederman, *Manliness and Civilization: A Cultural History of Gender and Race in the United States, 1880–1917* (Chicago, 1995), 170–216.

20. Dr. Samuel Fortier, "The Greatest Need of Arid America," in *Official Proceedings of the Fifteenth Annual Irrigation Congress,* Sacramento, California, 2–7 September 1907, ed. W. A. Beard (Sacramento, 1907), 119–120; Theodore Roosevelt, "The Man Who Works with His Hands," in *The Works of Theodore Roosevelt,* vol. 16, national ed. (New York, 1926), 133; Hon. W. M. Hays, "Organization of Schools," *Dry-Farming,* 6, no. 1 (January 1912): 157.

21. Fortier, "The Greatest Need."

22. C. C. Williams, "New Mexico: To-day and To-morrow," *Scientific Farmer,* 5, no. 6 (June 1906): 27; and see Wrobel, *Promised Lands,* 165.

23. Nelson A. Miles, *Personal Recollections and Observations of General Nelson A. Miles* (New York, 1969; orig. pub. 1896), 557, 546; R. H. Forbes, "Preface," in J. J. Thorn-

ber, "The Grazing Ranges of Arizona," UAAES, Bulletin no. 65, Tucson, Arizona, 21 September 1910, UASC.

24. Anderson, "Why Willcox?" 7.

25. See Jay J. Wagoner, *Arizona Territory, 1863–1912: A Political History* (Tucson, 1970), 406–417, 431–439; [H. W. Campbell], "Joint Statehood Again," *Scientific Farmer*, 1, no. 4 (April 1906): 24.

26. Quoted in Dee Garceau, "Single Women Homesteaders and the Meanings of Independence: Places on the Map, Places in the Mind," *Frontiers: A Journal of Women Studies*, 15, no. 3 (Spring 1995): 1–26, quotation on 13.

27. See Mrs. Warner, "The Farm Woman's Problems," *Agricultural Review* (February 1918): 19; Mrs. Louise Whitman Palmer, "Where Woman Rules," *Scientific Farmer*, 1, no. 4 (April 1906): 41; "Where Woman Rules: The Telephone and the Farm," *Dry-Farming*, 1, no. 2 (February 1906): 25; Mabel Bates Williams, "The Neighborhood Club," *Scientific Farmer*, 3, no. 4 (April 1907): 245–247; "Rural Home Section: First International Congress of Farm Women," *Dry-Farming*, 5, no. 1 (1911): 6. Analysis of related themes appears in Jellison, *Entitled to Power*; Lovett, *Conceiving the Future*; and Neil Foley, *The White Scourge: Mexicans, Blacks, and Poor Whites in Texas Cotton Culture* (Berkeley, 1997), 141–162. See also Deborah Fink, *Agrarian Women: Wives and Mothers in Rural Nebraska, 1880–1940* (Chapel Hill, 1992).

28. Warner, "The Farm Woman's Problems," 19.

29. Sherry L. Smith, "Single Women Homesteaders: The Perplexing Case of Elinore Pruitt Stewart," *WHQ*, 22, no. 2 (May 1991): 163–183; Garceau, "Single Woman Homesteaders"; BLM database.

30. Garceau, "Single Woman Homesteaders"; Smith, "Single Women Homesteaders." I thank Karen Merrill for pointing out the frontier counterpart image.

31. Lortah K. Stanbery, "Impressions by a New Arrival," *San Simon Artesian Belt*, 21 March 1914, 7; "build up a home" from Douglas Chamber of Commerce and Mines, "Sulphur Springs Valley"; on Stanbery, see School Superintendent Elsie Toles to Harold Steele, Douglas, Arizona, 11 April 1919, MS 180, AHS.

32. Dickey's legal review of homesteading eligibility, "Free Homes for All," strongly emphasized widows' rights; M. Margaret Shaw, "The Homestead Woman," *Arizona: The New State Magazine* (February 1912): 8–9; *Bowie Enterprise*, 21 March 1919, 1 December 1916.

33. On woman suffrage in the West, see Rebecca J. Mead, *How the Vote Was Won: Woman Suffrage in the Western United States, 1868–1914* (New York, 2004); Beverly Beeton, ed., *Women Vote in the West: The Woman Suffrage Movement, 1869–1896* (New York, 1986); Virginia Scharff, *Twenty Thousand Roads: Women, Movement, and the West* (Berkeley, 2003). On Arizona, see Nancy K. Tisdale, "The Prohibition Crusade in Arizona" (M.A. thesis, University of Arizona, 1965), 35; and David R. Berman, *Reformers, Corporations, and the Electorate: An Analysis of Arizona's Age of Reform* (Niwot, Colo.,

1992), 54, 92. On Cochise County, see "Woman's Club," *Arizona Range News*, 12 December 1912; "Woman Suffrage Meeting," ibid., 8 November 1912; untitled articles in *Benson Signal*, 21 December 1918, 5 December 1919; and "Local Items, San Simon," *Bowie Enterprise*, 6 August 1920.

34. Unidentified newspaper clipping, October 1920, Elsie Toles Scrapbook no. 2, AHS. See "Democrats Have Little Use for State Officials," reprint by Republican State Committee of *Glendale News* article, both clippings in Elsie Toles Scrapbook no. 1, AHS; Heidi Osselaer, "'A Woman for a Woman's Job': Arizona Women in Politics, 1900–1950" (Ph.D. diss., Arizona State University, 2001); Elsie Toles to Estelle Boll, Cochise, Arizona, 20 February 1919, MS 180, AHS; Toles, "Memoirs."

35. Elsie Toles scrapbook collection, AHS; "Spent Fourth," *Courtland Arizonan*, 5 July 1917.

36. Stanbery is listed as "Mrs." in *Arizona Farm Improvement News*, 2, no. 1 (1917); Stanbery, "Impressions."

37. Laura Mae Seward, "Narrative Report of Laura Mae Seward, Home Demonstration Agent for Cochise County, Arizona, December 1, 1925, to December 1, 1926," UACES, 1926, 14, UASC; on women's hidden farm labor, see Stephanie McCurry, *Masters of Small Worlds: Yeoman Households, Gender Relations, and the Political Culture of the Antebellum South Carolina Low Country* (New York, 1995), 78, 81–85; Patrick, Diary, 25 August 1914.

38. H. Elaine Lindgren, *Land in Her Own Name: Women as Homesteaders in North Dakota* (Norman, Okla., 1996); Rebecca Orozco, Foreword to Patrick diary. The BLM database contains dozens of family homestead clusters. Legal aspects of women's homesteading in James Muhn, "Women and the Homestead Act: Land Department Administration of a Legal Imbroglio, 1863–1934," *Western Legal History*, 7 (Summer–Fall 1994): 282–307.

39. Patrick diary, 34.

40. On family dynamics, see Katherine Harris, "Homesteading in Northeastern Colorado, 1873–1920: Sex Roles and Women's Experience," in Susan Armitage and Betsy Jameson, eds., *The Women's West* (Norman, Okla., 1987), 165–178; and Orozco, Foreword to Patrick diary. Cochise County contained several family claims spread in a checkerboard over several miles, as well as families with claims in opposite corners of the county.

41. Serial no. 658437, available at www.glorecords.blm.gov (accessed 17 October 2007); letter to author from Carol Wien Brunner, 5 February 1999; Edna Marie Wien, interview by Katherine Benton-Cohen, 10 February 1999, Dos Cabezas, Arizona; Flick, undated funeral announcement. Lindgren, in her sample of North Dakota woman homesteaders, found that as many as 94 percent made the primary decisions about their land. Even discounting the exact figure, which relied on self-reporting, a high percentage clearly maintained control (Lindgren, *Land in Her Own Name*, 118).

42. "Local and Personal," *Arizona Range News,* 29 December 1911; George Homrighausen obituary, *Arizona Range News,* 6 January 1911. Dozens of family stories would follow similar trajectories, including that of diarist Susie Patrick. See also Lindgren, *Land in Her Own Name,* esp. 28, 223.

43. Gates, *History of Public Land Law Development,* 640; Smith, "Single Women Homesteaders."

44. From the first patent in the nineteenth century until 1904 (thus, among all claims filed in nineteenth century, since it took five years to prove up a claim), people with Spanish surnames accounted for 18 (7 of these between 1900 and 1904) out of 135 total homestead patents. From 1905 to 1923, Mexican homestead patents represented 2.39 percent of the total, or 62 out of 2,594 homestead patents. This figure includes Original Homesteads and Enlarged Homesteads, but not Stock-Raising Homesteads or Cash Entries, of which there were far fewer. The increase in the twentieth century must be seen in context. The population was much smaller before 1900, so that the percentage of Mexicans in total numbers of cash entries and homestead claims was significantly more. Secondly, 17 of Mexican Americans' 28 land patents in the nineteenth century were cash entries, which did *not* require residence for five years. Several Tucson families bought plots of land on the San Pedro without living on them. The families who homesteaded in the twentieth century were clearly more permanent residents of the San Pedro River enclaves.

45. "Missouri Democrat" example in *Cochise County Democratic Yearbook, 1913,* Arizona Collection, ASU. On roads, see *Benson Signal,* 2 September 1916; "Will Vote against a Large Bond Issue," *Bowie Enterprise,* 19 November 1915. "Work and Vote against the $1,000,000 Road Bond . . . ," *Bowie Enterprise,* 30 November 1917; but see "Road Bond Issue Meets with Favor," *Courtland Arizonan,* 7 July 1917, 2; "Complete Returns of Road Bond Election," ibid., 8 December 1917, 1. On opposition to "absentee capitalists," see Thomas E. Sheridan, *Arizona: A History* (Tucson, 1995), 173–174, 182; Wagoner, *Arizona Territory;* Berman, *Reformers,* 18–19, 56–57; and George H. Kelly, *Legislative History: Arizona, 1864–1912* (Phoenix, 1926). "Corrupt fund" from *Bowie Enterprise,* 15 September 1916. On environmental damage, see Charles C. Colley, *The Century of Robert H. Forbes* (Tucson, 1977), 33; and "Farmers Rejoice at News That Smelter Smoke Is Doomed," *BDR,* 26 March 1916. "Bisbee!" from "Cochise County Farm Bureau Report, 1924," Agricultural Extension Service Office, Willcox, Arizona; see also Charles J. Willis, "Mines and the Farmer," *Arizona Mining Journal* (October 1918), pages illegible. On splitting the county, see James Arthur Wilson, "Cattle and Politics in Arizona, 1886–1941" (Ph.D. diss., University of Arizona, 1967), 41–44, 68; "Making Legislative Districts," *Bowie Enterprise,* 22 December 1916, 29 December 1916, 20 August 1920, 29 October 1920; "Warren District Takes Little Interest in County Seat Approval," *Courtland Arizonan,* 7 July 1917, 4; "That County Seat Removal," *Bowie Enterprise,* 1 November 1918; "Maybe and Maybe Not," reprinted in *Courtland Arizonan,* 19 January 1918, 2.

46. On Prohibition, see Harry David Ware, "Alcohol, Temperance and Prohibition in Arizona" (Ph.D. diss., Arizona State University, 1995), esp. 161–165, 177, 298–302; "Cochise County against Prohibition," *BDR*, 27 January 1910, 1; Tisdale, "Prohibition Crusade," 63, 104, 118; Carlton H. Parker, "Why Arizona Went Dry," *New Republic*, 1, no. 11 (16 January 1915): 20. County precinct returns are from *BDR*, 4 November 1914, 1.

47. See, for example, *Arizona Range News*, 1 December 1911; Harry Wheeler to Sims Ely, Secretary to the Governor, 23 February 1908, Arizona Ranger Papers, ASLAPR. Thank yous from Sheriff Wheeler, *Bowie Enterprise*, 17 November 1916; and *Benson Signal*, 18 November 1916.

7. The Bisbee Deportation

1. See Joseph F. Park, "The History of Mexican Labor in the Territorial Period" (M.A. thesis, University of Arizona, 1961), 275; Dru McGinnis, "The Influence of Organized Labor on the Making of the Arizona Constitution" (M.A. thesis, University of Arizona, 1930), "greatest" on 87; David R. Berman, *Reformers, Corporations, and the Electorate: An Analysis of Arizona's Age of Reform* (Niwot, Colo., 1992), "worst" on 82.

2. George W. P. Hunt, Diaries, Arizona Collection, Arizona State University.

3. Berman, *Reformers*, 92–93, 121–125; Byrkit, *Forging*, 52.

4. See Philip Mellinger, *Race and Labor in Western Copper: The Fight for Equality, 1896–1918* (Tucson, 1995); William Gohring testimony, PMC hearings, 452.

5. "Cry" quotation cited in McGinnis, "Influence of Organized Labor," 16. And see Eric Meeks, *Border Citizens: The Making of Indians, Mexicans, and Anglos in Arizona* (Austin, 2007).

6. McGinnis, "Influence of Organized Labor," 82–84; Park, "History of Mexican Labor," 276–277; Berman, *Reformers*, 201; "men with families" from "The 80 Per Cent Citizenship Law," *BDR*, 29 October 1914; also see "Do You Want This Law?" *BDR*, 30 October 1914. Mellinger argues that many Arizona labor organizers were not anti-immigrant, but he then cannot explain the popularity of the Alien Labor Law; see Mellinger, *Race and Labor*, 144, but also 85–87.

7. On protests, see Park, "History of Mexican Labor," 269, and Hunt files, especially Gov. George W. P. Hunt, to Mr. J. F. Smith, St. Joseph, Arizona, 9 December 1914, Record Group 1, Governors' Files, Kibbey, Sloan, Hunt, Box 1A, ASLAPR. See also Berman, *Reformers*, 91–92; Fred Watson, oral history, interviewer unknown, ca. 1970s, AHS; "Eighty Per Cent Law Is Not Held Up by the Courts," *BDR*, 3 January 1915, 1; "Eighty Percent Bill Argued before U.S. Judges," *BDR*, 7 January 1915, 1; "Alien Labor Law Has Been Knocked Down in Court," *ALJ*, 4 November 1915, 1; *Truax et al. v. Raich* (239 U.S. 33; 36 S. Ct. 7), 1915.

8. The anti-injunction case, which eventually overturned Arizona's law and nullified all anti-injunction laws, was not decided until after the Deportation. It was upheld by the

state court in 1918, but overturned by the U.S. Supreme Court in 1921. *Truax et al. v. Corrigan et al.* (20 Ariz. 7; 176 Pac. 570); *Truax et al. v. Corrigan et al.* (257 U.S. 312) [1921]; see "Culinary Workers' Campaign against English Kitchen," *ALJ,* 22 June 1916, 1; "Arizona Truax Case under Discussion, A.F.L. Ex. Council," *ALJ,* 30 June 1921, 2; "Truax Case Reversed by U.S. Supreme Court, Picketing Illegal," *ALJ,* 22 December 1921, 1. On the Citizens' Protective League, see PMC hearings, 4, 218–220, 279–280; and Grant Dowell to Lemuel Shattuck, 24 June 1920, Shattuck Collection, MS 1055, AHS. The elder Truax is listed as a deputy in Bisbee Deportation Gunmen List, microfilm, ASLAPR; on the younger Truax, see Byrkit, *Forging,* 188.

9. Colleen O'Neill, "Domesticity Deployed: Gender, Race, and the Construction of Class Struggle in the Bisbee Deportation," *Labor History,* 34, nos. 2–3 (Spring–Summer 1993): 256–273, esp. 258; William Cleary, Los Angeles, California, to Gov. George W. P. Hunt, Phoenix, Arizona, 23 December 1914, Record Group 1, Governor's Files, Box 1A, ASLAPR; Mellinger, *Race and Labor,* 160–162, offers context for the West's anti-immigrant legislation.

10. On the Clifton strike, see Linda Gordon, *The Great Arizona Orphan Abduction* (Cambridge, Mass., 1999), 209–245; and Mellinger, *Race and Labor,* 33–58.

11. Burton Kirkwood, *The History of Mexico* (New York, 2005), 132. See A. Yvette Huginnie, "'Strikitos': Race, Class, and Work in the Arizona Copper Industry, 1870–1920" (Ph.D. diss., Yale University, 1991); Mellinger, *Race and Labor,* 137.

12. Mellinger, *Race and Labor,* 138–149, 159–165; *ALJ,* 1 July 1915, 8 July 1915, 15 July 1915. On Ray, see also James D. McBride, "The Liga Protectora Latina: A Mexican-American Benevolent Society in Arizona," *Journal of the West* (October 1975): 82–90; "Strike Ended," *ALJ,* 15 July 1915, 4.

13. See Mellinger, *Race and Labor,* 141–147; "Company Gunmen in Ray," *ALJ,* 1 July 1915, 1, 4.

14. Robert W. Bruère, *Following the Trail of the IWW* (New York, 1918), 6; President's Mediation Commission, report on Clifton, 514, quoted in Mellinger, *Race and Labor,* 168; Carmichael quoted ibid., 182.

15. Hunt diary, cited in Mellinger, *Race and Labor,* 144; Park, "History of Mexican Labor," 279; *ALJ,* June–August 1915; "Clifton, Morenci Demand a Living Wage," *ALJ,* 22 June 1917, 1; Morenci Branch of Phelps Dodge, Arizona Copper Company, and Shannon Copper Company, "Telegram to Sec. of Labor William B. Wilson," 7 July 1917, Hunt Papers, ASLAPR.

16. "'Citizen Bill' Cleary Landed Verbal Blows," *ALJ,* 15 July 1915, 1.

17. On Warren in the war years, see Mary Eileen Murphy Walsh, Diary, MS 1045, AHS; Carlos A. Schwantes, "Toil and Trouble," 121, and Tom Vaughan, "Everyday Life in a Copper Camp," 60–61, both in Carlos A. Schwantes, ed., *Bisbee: Urban Outpost on the Frontier* (Tucson, 1992).

18. F. A. McKinney, *Bisbee-Warren District Directory, 1914–5* (Bisbee, 1914), 15.

19. Grover H. Perry (secretary-treasurer of Metal Mine Workers' Industrial Union no. 800), Phoenix, Arizona, to William D. Haywood, Chicago, Illinois, 2 February 1917, Exhibits in *State of Arizona v. Harry Waters* and *Michael Simmons v. El Paso and Southwestern Railroad Co., 1919,* Superior Court of Cochise County, AZ 114, Box 1, UASC (hereafter cited as *Simmons v. EPSW*); Colleen O'Neill, "A Community Divided: A Social History of the Bisbee Deportation" (M.A. thesis, New Mexico State University, 1989); Mellinger, *Race and Labor,* 177; membership figures are from Melvyn Dubofsky, *We Shall Be All: A History of the IWW* (Chicago, 1969), 370.

20. "Editorial Comment," *Dunbar's Weekly,* 4 July 1917, 7 July 1917. Editor John Dunbar was the brother of Thomas Dunbar of Tres Alamos.

21. A. S. Embree, Bisbee, Arizona, to Grover H. Perry, Salt Lake City, Utah, 5 June 1917; Embree to Perry, 26 June 1917, in Exhibits, *Simmons v. EPSW.* PD claimed that 50 percent of the men went out, surely an undercount. See Byrkit, *Forging,* 160; "Strikes Tie Up Copper Industry, *ALJ,* 6 July 1917; and Rosa McKay testimony, PMC hearings, 131.

22. From a census conducted by U.S. army official Ben Dorcy at the Columbus Deportation camp, contained in Hunt Papers, ASLAPR (also in PMC hearings). Finn Hall was "cleaned out," according to Art Kent, oral history, interview by James Houston, ca. 1970s, AHS. On women, quotation from Bassett Watkins testimony, PMC hearings, 256. And see Harry Wheeler testimony, PMC hearings, 158; "Sheriff Wheeler's Statement on Strike," *Courtland Arizonan,* 21 July 1917, 2.

23. Mrs. Robert Noble, testimony cited in reports to Gov. George W. P. Hunt, July, 1917, probably from sworn statements to Arizona Attorney General Wiley Jones, Record Group 1, Governor's Office, Hunt Papers, Box 8, ASLAPR (hereafter cited as "statement(s) to AG Jones"), 10–11; similarly, see "Sheriff Forbes Arrests Women in Ajo Strike," *ALJ,* 22 December 1916, 1.

24. As of June 26, 1917, out of 2,201 total surface and underground workers, 314 were Mexicans (compiled from PMC hearings, 287–290). These numbers generally square with the testimony of Copper Queen general manager G. H. Dowell in the PMC hearings. Labor Secretary William B. Wilson had eased immigration restrictions from Mexico in June; see Michael Parrish, *Mexican Workers, Progressives, and Copper: The Failure of Industrial Democracy in Arizona during the Wilson Years* (San Diego, 1979), 18. On influx, see [William J. Beeman], *The I.W.W. Deportation from the Warren District* (Bisbee, ca. 1922), ASLAPR; Mellinger, *Race and Labor,* 188.

25. Figures cited by witnesses ranged from 50 to 85 percent. I. H. Strickland testimony, PMC hearings, 502; Henry Wheeler testimony, PMC hearings, 166, 256.

26. Workforce numbers were compiled from statistics (in PMC hearings) for the two major companies on 26 June 1917, the last day before the strike. Percentage of strikers (which no doubt included people born in Mexico as well as Mexican Americans) compiled from the Dorcy census of deportees is 27 percent; from a database compiled by me,

the figure is 25.4. This Deportation database includes nationality, citizenship, address, occupation, home ownership, marital status, and parental status. The following sources provided data. On deportees, the Dorcy census and plaintiff list for civil case by deportees in *Simmons v. El Paso,* AZ 114, Box 2, Folder 5, UASC. On deputies, Bisbee Deportation List of Gunmen and Witnesses, microfilm, ASLAPR. Data for all participants from Walsh and Fitzgerald (no first names listed), comps., *Bisbee and Warren District Directory, 1917–8* (Bisbee, 1917); and, to track individuals in the 1920 census, the subscription genealogical database www.ancestry.gov (accessed 8 December 2007).

27. Company officials and IWW leaders concurred on this. "Practically" in G. H. Dowell testimony, PMC hearings, 353; and Grover H. Perry to Bill Haywood, 6 July 1917, Exhibits, *Simmons v. EPSW.*

28. Harry Wheeler testimony to U.S. Congress, Senate Committee on Foreign Relations, *Investigation of Mexican Affairs: Hearing before a Subcommittee of the Committee on Foreign Relations,* United States Senate, 66th Congress, First–Second Session, Pursuant to S. Res. 106, "Directing the Committee on Foreign Relations to Investigate the Matter of Outrages on Citizens of the United States in Mexico" (Washington, D.C., 1919), 1884.

29. Some histories of Arizona's Mexican mine workers have underplayed the particular ideological significance of their strike participation in the white men's camps of Bisbee and Globe-Miami. But see Samuel Truett, *Fugitive Landscapes: The Forgotten History of the U.S.-Mexico Borderlands* (New Haven, 2006); Colleen O'Neill, "Community Divided"; idem, "Domesticity Employed," esp. 258; and Rodolfo Acuña, *Occupied America: A History of Chicanos,* 3rd ed. (New York, 1988), 101.

30. Merrill testimony, PMC hearings, 195.

31. A. S. Embree quoted in Mellinger, *Race and Labor,* 178; Jack Norman, Columbus, New Mexico, to Haywood, 25 July 1917, and strike demands, both in Exhibits, *Simmons v. EPSW.*

32. O'Neill, "Community Divided," 82–83; on Doramé, phone conversation with Devra Weber, 24 June 2008; Wheeler testimony, *Investigation of Mexican Affairs,* 1884; Chaz Bufe and Mitchell Cowen Verter, eds., *Dreams of Freedom: A Ricardo Flores Magón Reader* (Oakland, Calif., 2006), 40, 51–52, 61–62, 345; Dubofsky, *We Shall Be All,* 370; "we ran you out" from [Beeman], *The I.W.W. Deportation.* On the Partido Liberal Mexicano north of the border, see Elizabeth Killen, "Hybrid Visions: Working-Class Internationalism in the Mexican Borderlands, Seattle, and Chicago, 1910–1920," *Labor: Studies in Working-Class History of the Americas,* 2, no. 1 (2005): 77–107; and Emilio Zamora, *The World of the Mexican Worker in Texas* (College Station, Tex., 1993).

33. The Presidential Mediation Commission also failed to interview Mexicans in Globe, another white man's camp. Bruère, *Following the Trail,* 3; Frankfurter, quoted in Parrish, *Mexican Workers,* 29–30, miner quoted on 14; on language of freedom, see Lawrence Glickman, "Inventing the 'American Standard of Living': Gender, Race and Working-Class Identity, 1880–1925," *Labor History,* 34 (1993), 222–223.

34. Worker quoted in Parrish, *Mexican Workers,* 11.

35. Thomas E. Sheridan, *Arizona: A History* (Tucson, 1995), 183; James Byrkit, "The IWW in Wartime Arizona," *Journal of Arizona History* (Summer 1977), online at digital. library.arizona.edu/bisbee/docs2/jahbyrk.htm (accessed July 25, 2006); Dubofsky, *We Shall Be All,* 407–408; Vernon Jensen, *Heritage of Conflict: Labor Relations in the Nonferrous Metals Industry up to 1930* (Ithaca, N.Y., 1950), 400.

36. Number of deputies comes from Wheeler's statement, *BDR,* 12 July 1917; *New Republic,* 21 July 1917, quoted in Byrkit, "The IWW in Wartime Arizona.".

37. Quotations are from Press Committee [Embree?] to Perry, 6[?] July 1917; Exhibits, *Simmons v. EPSW;* and PMC hearings, quoted in Byrkit, *Forging,* 151. J. F. McDonald testimony, PMC hearings, 21; and President's Mediation Commission, "Report on the Bisbee Deportation," Washington, D.C., Department of Labor, Office of the Secretary, 6 November 1917, 4. See also Harold Callender, "True Facts about Bisbee," *Dunbar's Weekly,* 15 September 1917, 10–12. Deputy figures come from Wheeler's statement, *BDR,* 12 July 1917.

38. George E. Kellogg testimony, PMC hearings, 13; "Women and Children Keep Off Streets Today," *BDR,* 12 July 1917, 1; "Arizona Sheriff Ships 1,100 IWW's Out in Cattle Cars," *New York Times,* 13 July 1917, 1; Bill O'Neal, *Captain Harry Wheeler, Arizona Lawman* (Austin, 2003), 117. I have relied on dozens of individual sources, but, overall, the standard sources on the Deportation are Byrkit, *Forging* (the only book-length nonfiction treatment); the essential PMC hearings, edited by Melvyn Dubofsky; and Dubofsky's succinct overview in *We Shall Be All.* Fictionalized portrayals appear in Stephen Vincent Benét's first novel, *The Beginning of Wisdom* (New York, 1921); and Robert Houston, *Bisbee '17* (Tucson, 1999; orig. pub. 1979). An outstanding collection of primary and secondary sources has been gathered at www.digital.library.arizona.edu/exhibits/bisbee. I am also indebted to Colleen O'Neill's pioneering attention to race and gender and to her discovery of women's testimonies. And see note 44.

39. A survey found that 2.1 percent of the poorest homes had phones; see S. C. Dickinson, "A Sociological Survey of the Bisbee Warren District," conducted by Arizona State Bureau of Mines, 1917, 82, UASC. Mrs. Richard Denning, statement to AG Jones, 8; Mrs. Bridget Gerity, statement to AG Jones, 6. Mary Frances Lynn, "Women of Bisbee," *Bisbee Gazette,* 20 September 1989, BMHM.

40. Mrs. Myrtle Reep, statement to AG Jones, 19; Susie Rice, statement to AG Jones, 37–38; see also Mrs. John Conner, statement to AG Jones, 10.

41. On Bledsoe, see Parrish, *Mexican Workers,* 36; Anna Payne, statement to AG Jones, 13. See also Colleen O'Neill, "Domesticity Deployed," 268–269; and, especially, idem, "Community Divided," 102–105.

42. "Hurrah" in Mrs. Denning, statement to AG Jones, 8; Payne, statement to AG Jones, 13. "Women Organize," *ALJ,* 15 February 1918, 1; author's conversation with Kenneth Payne, grandson of Anna, April 1998.

43. Horace Daniel Nash, "Town and Sword: Black Soldiers in Columbus, New Mex-

ico, in the Early Twentieth Century" (Ph.D. diss., Mississippi State University, 1996), 100.

44. Important interpretations not previously cited include John H. Lindquist and James Fraser, "A Sociological Interpretation of the Bisbee Deportation," *Pacific Historical Review, 37*, no. 4 (1968): 401–22; Philip Taft, "The Bisbee Deportation," *Labor History,* 13, no. 1 (1972): 3–40; and Christopher Capozzola, *Uncle Sam Wants You: World War I and the Making of the Modern American Citizen* (New York, 2008), esp. 125–131.

45. I have been influenced here by Kristin L. Hoganson, who has linked diverse interpretations of turn-of-the-century imperialism to a crisis of masculinity; see Hoganson, *Fighting for Manhood: How Gender Politics Provoked the Spanish-American and Philippine-American Wars* (New Haven, 1998). Also see Susan Lee Johnson, "'A Memory Sweet to Soldiers': The Significance of Gender in the History of the 'American West,'" in Clyde A. Milner III, ed., *A New Significance: Re-Envisioning the History of the American West* (New York, 1996); and Gail Bederman, *Manliness and Civilization: A Cultural History of Gender and Race in the United States, 1880–1917* (Chicago, 1995).

46. Cullen Cain, managing editor of the *BDR,* to the managing editor of the *San Francisco Bulletin,* undated clipping (September 1917?), John Greenway Papers, MS 311, Box 181 F 2393, AHS. On Roosevelt, see Joseph P. Lash, ed. *From the Diaries of Felix Frankfurter* (New York, 1975), 24. Bruère, *Following the Trail;* Thomas Cole to John Greenway, 16 May 1911, Greenway papers; "Statements of Managers," *Courtland Arizonan,* 30 June 1917, 3.

47. All of the managers' public and private statements demonstrate this commitment. See John Greenway's correspondence during these years in Greenway Collection, AHS; and discussion of Douglas in Byrkit, *Forging,* esp. 32, 87, 99, 139, 178, 187, 299, 301; Bruère, *Following the Trail,* 7; Philip S. Foner, *Labor and World War I, 1914–1918,* vol. 7 of *History of the Labor Movement* (New York, 1947), 269.

48. "These old bags" and "control a quarry" from Felix Frankfurter, quoted in Michael E. Parrish, *Felix Frankfurter and His Times: The Reform Years* (New York, 1982), 93, 95. Other quotations are from Harlan B. Phillips, ed. *Felix Frankfurter Reminisces: Recorded in Talks with Dr. Harlan B. Phillips* (New York, 1960), 118–119, 137.

49. On discrepancies about his service during the Spanish American War, see Wheeler testimony, "Investigation of Mexican Affairs," 1874; and O'Neal, *Harry Wheeler,* 19–20. "Perhaps" quotation, ibid., 108. Capt. Harry Wheeler, General Orders, Naco, Arizona, 1 June 1907, Arizona Ranger Papers, ASLAPR; "man of splended" quoted in Bill O'Neal, "Captain Harry Wheeler, Arizona Lawman," *Journal of Arizona History,* 27, no. 3 (1986): 303.

50. Capt. Harry Wheeler, Naco, Arizona, to Gov. Kibbey, Phoenix, Arizona, 30 October 1908, Arizona Ranger Papers; O'Neal, "Harry Wheeler," 304.

51. George Medigovich, Akron, Ohio, to Clare Ellinwood, 12 April 1979, online at www.library.arizona.edu/exhibits/bisbee/docs/rec_exce.html (accessed 29 November

2007), emphasis in original. *Report of the Arizona Rangers for the Years Ended June 30, 1907, and June 30, 1908* (Tucson, 1908), 7, Munk Ephemera Collection, Braun Library, ANC. On Wheeler's view of the strike, see Wheeler to Sims Ely, Secretary to the Governor, May 1907; "the Copper outfit," ibid., 23 February 1908. Philip Foner, ed., *Mother Jones Speaks: Collected Writings and Speeches* (New York, 1983), 372; see also O'Neal, *Harry Wheeler*, 57–58.

52. Medigovich to Ellinwood, 12 April 1979; Walter Douglas to A. T. Thompson, 29 June 1917, quoted in Parrish, *Mexican Workers*, 21.

53. O'Neal, *Harry Wheeler*; it is possible that he received this sum *after* the Deportation, as a thank-you for services rendered that he did not anticipate. Quotations from PMC hearings, 589, 492.

54. [Beeman], *The I.W.W. Deportation*, 4, 12.

55. "Sheriff Announces He Will Use Force," *Courtland Arizonan*, 30 June 1917, 3, 8; Wheeler testimony, PMC hearings, 155; "Sheriff Wheeler's Statement on Strike," *Courtland Arizonan*, 21 July 1917, 2.

56. Wheeler testimony, PMC hearings, 138; ibid., 137.

57. On Wheeler, see O'Neal, *Harry Wheeler*, 99–100, 108; Linda Hall, "The Mexican Revolution and the Crisis in Naco: 1914–5," *Journal of the West*, 16 (1977): 27–35. On watching the Naco battles, see M. H. Jones, Reminiscence, no date, BMHM. On the battles' impact on Wheeler, see Wheeler testimony, PMC hearings, 161–162. See also Bruère, *Following the Trail*, 13–14.

58. Friedrich Katz, *The Life and Times of Pancho Villa* (Stanford, 1998), 612, 660–664. At one point, Wheeler said he had heard about rifles from a chambermaid, Wheeler testimony, PMC hearings, 148–149; see also 142; "complexion" on 161. On Pancho Villa and his followers, see Wheeler testimony, *Investigation of Mexican Affairs*.

59. Tombstone *Prospector*, cited in O'Neal, *Harry Wheeler*, 115; Byrkit claims that the league was created in the summer of 1917, but its roots were considerably older (*Forging*, 162).

60. Warren District Trades Assembly Committee to President's Mediation Commission, 31 October 1917, 6–7, in Hunt Papers, ASLAPR; Greenway to A. A. Hopkins, Esq., ROTC Company 12, Presidio of San Francisco, 5 July 1917, Greenway Papers, Box 181; the League claimed 1,600 members by early July (Byrkit, *Forging*, 165, national movement on 248). On both organizations, see Dickinson, "Sociological Survey," 30.

61. Wheeler testimony, PMC hearings, 143; see also "Sheriff's Posse Being Organized," *Benson Signal*, 28 April 1917. On its earlier guise, see O'Neal, "Captain Harry Wheeler," 307.

62. Warren District Trades Assembly Committee to President's Mediation Commission; Thomas McGuinness, "The Story of What Happened at Bisbee as Told by Disinterested Eye-Witness," *San Francisco Bulletin*, 11 August 1917; Miles Merrill testimony, PMC hearings, 224.

63. [J.L.P.], police informant, to Sheriff Wheeler, re: "Mexican Matters, 5 June 1916, in Exhibits, *Simmons v. EPSW;* Wheeler quoted in McNeill, "Domesticity Deployed," 263.

64. Hall, "The Mexican Revolution"; O'Neal, *Harry Wheeler,* 99; [Beeman], *The I.W.W. Deportation;* Chester A. Congdon to Greenway, 4 June 1917, Greenway Papers.

65. Bruère, *Following the Trail,* 1.

66. Wheeler testimony, PMC hearings, 165, 140.

67. Ibid., 253.

68. On laundry, see for example, [William Beeman], *The I.W.W. Deportation;* "Sheriff Wheeler's Statement on Strike," *Courtland Arizonan,* 21 July 1917, 2.

69. Strickland testimony, PMC hearings, 502; McGuinness, "The Story"; on rough treatment of Mexicans, see Amado Villalovas statement to AG Jones, 20–21; Wheeler testimony, PMC hearings, 166, 256.

70. The statistics on U.S. citizenship and nativity in Deportation database are lower than estimates based only on Dorcy census, used by other researchers. Because we cannot trace every participant, the exact figures will never be known. My numbers on Mexicans and Slavs are: 225 Mexicans out of total of 894 with identifiable national origin; 227 Slavs/eastern Europeans. I counted the following nationalities as Slavic/eastern European: Austrian (these were largely what would become Yugoslavs), Bohemian, Bosnian, Bulgarian, Croat, Dalmatian, Hungarian, Lithuanian, Montenegrin, Polish, Russian, Serb, and Slav (as listed). On citizenship, the number is 223 out of 894.

71. J. C. Ryan testimony, PMC hearings, 268.

72. Ibid.; "Women of the Warren District at the Bisbee Gymnasium of the Y.M.C.A. Organized the Women's Loyalty League of America," *Bowie Enterprise,* 7 July 1917. For a hostile view of the group as a "ridiculous and indecent organization of women," see John Dunbar, "Editorial Comment: White-Washing Committee," *Dunbar's Weekly,* 1 September 1917, 7; women's throng in Byrkit, *Forging,* 255; statements to AG Jones.

73. Mrs. Gertrude Bailey, statement to AG Jones, 23; on families abandoned, see PMC hearings, 294–308.

74. Frank J. Vaughan to George W. P. Hunt, 25 July 1917, Hunt Papers; Rosa McKay testimony, PMC hearings, 136.

75. Parrish, *Mexican Workers,* 36.

76. Dubofsky, *We Shall Be All,* 389; on vagrancy arrests, see PMC hearings, 71–73, 97, 137, 326, 328, 487, "sandbagging" on 71; [Beeman], *The I.W.W. Deportation;* O'Neill, "A Community Divided," 110. Also see Presidential Mediation Commission, "Report on Bisbee Deportations," 6. The term "kangaroo committee" occurred several times in the PMC hearings; it also occurs in Lemuel Shattuck, Bisbee, Arizona, to Dr. E. B. Perrin, Williams, Arizona, 17 July 1917, Shattuck Collection, MS 1055, AHS.

77. Byrkit, *Forging,* 276–279; Bruère, *Following the Trail;* and Dubofsky, *We Shall Be All,* 389–390.

78. Byrkit, *Forging,* 265–269; Phillips, *Frankfurter Reminisces,* 136–137; Alice Hamilton, *Exploring the Dangerous Trades: The Autobiography of Alice Hamilton, M.D.* (Boston, 1943), 210–211, 219.

79. Parrish, *Mexican Workers,* 44; Fred Watson, oral history.

80. *BDR,* 14 September 1917. Depending on how they were counted (that is, on whether I was liberal about including people with common names), I found thirty-four or forty-five of the original list of deportees in the 1920 census.

81. Vaughan to Hunt; "the men" from Dan Kitchel, oral history, interview by Roberta Vaughan, 6 February 1982, BMHM; "thousands" quotation from Parrish, *Mexican Workers,* 46. On avoiding the blacklist, see Tom Vaughan, "'Muy Gusta Mi Vida,' Says 93-Year-Old Julia Suarez," *BDR* clipping, 19 August 1984, BMHM. On production, see "Report of Directors of Calumet & Arizona Mining Company for the Yr. Ending Dec. 31, 1917," MTUCCC.

82. "Cleaned out" quotation from Art Kent, oral history. The farm town of McNeal became home to many Finnish immigrants. Between 1910 and 1920, the census changed the way it counted people from the region that became Yugoslavia; nonetheless, a total of nearly 800 Slavs had dwindled to 364 Yugoslavs by 1920. The number of Italians fell from 242 in 1910 to 200 in 1920. U.S. Bureau of the Census, *Thirteenth Census of the United States, 1910,* vol. 5, *Population, Abstract with Supplement for Arizona* (Washington, D.C., 1912), 584; U.S. Bureau of the Census, *Thirteenth Census of the United States, 1910,* vol. 3, *Population* (Washington, D.C., 1911), 81; U.S. Bureau of the Census, *Fifteenth Census of the United States, 1930,* vol. 3, part 1, *Population* (Washington, D.C., 1933), 156.

83. As with the deportees, these numbers are an educated guess because of faulty information or the repetition of common names.

84. All examples compiled from city directory and 1920 census using www.ancestry.com. Some people appeared to have moved down in rank from shift boss to miner, but there is no way to tell if these are mistakes in the census, the result of downsizing, or actual demotions.

85. "New Housing Plan Working," *Arizona Mining Journal* (September 1918); Walter Douglas, President, Copper Queen Mining Company, to A. T. Thompson, Assistant to the President, 7 March 1918, Phelps Dodge Corporate Archives, Phoenix, Arizona; also see Truett, *Fugitive Landscapes,* 114–116. There are no single, foreign men listed in Manuscript Census, 1920, Warren Precinct.

86. PMC hearings, 427–428; Walsh and Fitzgerald, *Bisbee and Warren.* On the retention of married workers, see Parrish, *Mexican Workers,* 28; and esp. Charles F. Willis, consulting supervisor to A. T. Thomson, Assistant to the President, PD Corporation, "Summary of Community Service Plan for the Warren District," 9 June 1919, Phelps Dodge Corporate Archives. On C&A, see "Cowperthwaite Talks," *State Safety News* (1 March 1918), State Series no. 28, 2. "Fellas" quotation from Art Kent, oral history.

87. "Address of Senator Sutter of Cochise County," 4 June 1918, State of Arizona, Third Legislature, First Special Session, 13, UASC.

88. "Of Interest to Workers," *Arizona Mining Journal*, October 1920, 34; "Editorial Discussion: Mines Keep Employees Many Years," *Arizona Mining Journal*, 15 July 1922, 12. Married men accounted for 76.5 percent of underground miners, and 76.8 of surface workers; see also Charles Willis, "Per Cent of Employees in Camp 10 Years," *Arizona Mining Journal*, 1 August 1922; "last stand" quotation from "Bisbee, the Most Southern Mile-High City in North America," *ALJ*, 31 May 1929, 27. On labor policies and marital status, see Willis to Thomson, "Summary of Community Service Plan for the Warren District."

89. Parrish, *Mexican Workers*, 33–34, 47; Robert S. Jeffrey, "The History of Douglas, Arizona" (M.A. thesis, University of Arizona, 1951), 113; James H. McClintock, "Laborers Transferred from Mining Districts to Cotton Growing Section," *EMJ*, 5 November 1921, 748. The *Arizona Labor Journal*, after its brief support for Mexican miners' unions, reported on these deportations with approval; see "Alien Mexican Labor," *ALJ*, 12 May 1921, 1; on Willis, "Y.M.C.A. Workers Consider Program," *BDR*, 21 March 1919; Willis to Thomson, "Summary of Community Service Plan for the Warren District"; PMC hearings, 349; Ralph Rollins, "Labor Situation in Arizona Points to Mexicanization," *Arizona Mining Journal*, 4 (July 1920): 13–14. Married women were also laid off; see Walsh diary, 18 December 1918.

90. With rare exception, the Catholic churches in Bisbee had been segregated since 1904. Harris Sobin, *St. Patrick's Catholic Church, Bisbee, Arizona: A History* (Tucson, 1998); "very indignant" from Walsh diary, entry for 30 September 1917. Mandin was the priest who brought the orphans to Clifton; the episode is examined by Linda Gordon in *The Great Arizona Orphan Abduction.*

91. Laura Muñoz, "Desert Dreams: Mexican American Education in Arizona, 1870–1930" (Ph.D. diss., Arizona State University, 2006), 123–124.

92. McKay, statement to AG Jones, 29–30.

93. McKay testimony, PMC hearings, 136, 131; O'Neill, "A Community Divided," 106.

94. "Minimum Wage Law Passes Legislature," *ALJ*, 9 March 1916, 1.

95. Statistics on women given transportation are from PMC hearings, 291–294; Mrs. Bertie Davis, statement to AG Jones, 16–17; Callender, "True Facts."

96. McDonald (first name unknown), Columbus, New Mexico, to Grover Perry, 25 July 1917, Exhibits, *Simmons v. EPSW.*

97. "Jones Gets Excited over Bisbee Situation," *Courtland Arizonan*, 4 August 1917; Alice P. Metz, "'Thru the Years' with the Bisbee Woman's Club," typescript, BMHM, 9; Mrs. Berties Davis, statement to AG Jones, 16–17.

98. Heidi Osselaer, "'A Woman for a Woman's Job': Arizona Women in Politics, 1900–1950" (Ph.D. diss., Arizona State University, 2001), 53–54; "Nellie A. Hayward for Secretary of State," *Arizona Gazette* newspaper clipping, no date, AHS biofiles; "Organized Labor Loses Friend and Supporter," *ALJ*, 24 March 1934, 1.

99. William S. Collins, *The New Deal in Arizona* (Phoenix, 1999), 32; "CWA Project Has Been Closed," *BDR*, 11 March 1934, 5.

100. Wheeler, Merrill, and Bisbee mayor Jacob Erickson quoted in Gerald Horne, *Black and Brown: African Americans and the Mexican Revolution* (New York, 2005), 111; also see 9.

101. Nash, "Town and Sword," 45–48, notes 62–63; E. G. Hall, Bisbee, Arizona, to NAACP, New York City, 23 July 1915, Application for Charter, Bisbee, Arizona, 3 October 1919; Allen C. Jones, Bisbee, to Bagnall, 24 January 1924; all in Records of the National Association for the Advancement of Colored People, Series 1, Box 69, Library of Congress Manuscript Division, Washington, D.C.

102. Presidential Mediation Commission, "Report on the Bisbee Deportations," 6.

103. Discussion of legal battles relies on Byrkit, *Forging*, 285–294.

104. *Bowie Enterprise*, 10 November 1916, 17 November 1916, and July–December 1917, passim; J. H. Hulse, *Texas Lawyer: The Life of William H. Burges* (El Paso, 1982), 206; "No Time for Sympathy and No Worthy Object," *Courtland Arizonan*, 21 July 1917.

105. "The Deportation Verdict," *Bowie Enterprise*, 7 May 1920; "I.W.-ism," *Benson Signal*, 6 March 1920. Hundreds of court affidavits, subpoenas, and complaints found in 2006 have been digitized at azmemory.lib.az.us.

106. "Speaking place" from "Croaff Will Not Speak in Bisbee," *ALJ*, 27 June 1919, 1; "management" from Charles F. Willis, "Industrial Relationship Factors in the Southwest," *Arizona Mining Journal*, 3, no. 1 (1919): 10; declining union membership from untitled article, *ALJ*, 9 June 1921, 3; "Proceedings of 14th Annual Convention of the Arizona State Federation of Labor," *ALJ*, 14 November 1925, 1; "Minutes of the 15th Annual Convention of the Arizona State Federation of Labor," *ALJ*, 18 September 1926, 1.

107. "The Delayed Feature Story of Convention," *ALJ*, 7 November 1918, 1; "Lewis W. Douglas," *ALJ*, 6 October 1926, 2. Spanish-language material reappeared in the late 1920s.

108. "Editorial Comment: Americans Employed," *Dunbar's Weekly*, 21 July 1917, 4.

109. "Editorial Comment," ibid., 7 July 1917, 5.

8. One County, Two Races

1. William S. Collins, *The New Deal in Arizona* (Phoenix, 1999), 22; Madeline Ferrin Paré, *Arizona Pageant: A Short History of the 48th State* (Phoenix, 1965), 307; Robert Glass Cleland, *A History of Phelps Dodge, 1834–1950* (New York, 1952), 162, 198–199; population calculated from 1917 estimates and from Bureau of the U.S. Census, *Fourteenth Census of the United States, 1920*, vol. 1, *Population* (Washington, D.C., 1921), 150, 180, 341; Bureau of the U.S. Census, *Sixteenth Census of the United States, 1940*, vol. 2, part 1, *Characteristics of the Population* (Washington, D.C., 1943), 370–381.

2. Paré, *Arizona Pageant*, 307; Elsie Toles, "Memoirs of Cochise County Superinten-

dent of Schools Elsie Toles, 1912–1918," Elsie Toles biofile, BMHM; survey by Bertha Virmond in "Narrative Report for Cochise County," 15 January 1929 to 1 December 1929, AZ 302, Cochise County Home Extension Reports, UASC.

3. BLM database; Dana T. Milner, "Bowie and the San Simon Valley, Cochise County, Arizona" (Bowie, Ariz., ca. 1920s), unpaginated, Braun Collection, ANC; Toles, "Memoirs." Bureau of the U.S. Census, *Thirteenth Census of the United States, 1910: Abstract with Supplement for Arizona* (Washington, D.C., 1912), 573; Bureau of the U.S. Census, *Fifteenth Census of the United States, 1930: Population,* vol. 3, part 1, *Reports by States,* 159.

4. James Chisholm, *Brewery Gulch* (San Antonio, 1949), 15–19. On the Red Light Saloon, see Bisbee Tax Ledger, 1908, microfilm, BMHM; and "License Will Not Be Lost by Nordenger," *BDR,* 1 October 1910. On Elsie, see Debra Mues, "First County School Superintendent, Bisbee Educated," *BDR,* 6 September 1978, BMHM clipfiles (in fact, Minnie Lintz, Toles's predecessor, was the first female county superintendent); Toles, "Memoirs." Girls consistently outnumbered boys in the high schools of the county.

5. "Elsie Toles for State Superintendent of Public Instruction," *Arizona Mining Journal,* 15 October 1920. Also see Elsie Toles, *Rural and Small-Town Schools in Cochise County* (ca. 1920), 14–16, Elsie Toles Collection, AHS; and "Her Duties Are Much More Difficult . . . ," news clipping in Elsie Toles Scrapbook no. 1, AHS. Exacting standards evident in correspondence with teachers, MS 180, AHS, passim. On sex disparities, see Toles, *Sixth Biennial Report of the State Superintendent of Public Instruction to the Governor of the State of Arizona for the Period July 1, 1920, to June 30, 1922* (Phoenix, 1922), 54–55.

6. Toles, *Sixth Biennial Report,* 10; clipping in Toles Scrapbook no. 2. For editorials pro and con, see Toles Scrapbook no. 2 and beginning of Scrapbook no. 3, AHS. Both of Toles's reforms were defeated soundly. See C. E. Rose, Superintendent of Instruction, Tucson, to Elsie Toles, Phoenix, Arizona, 8 November 1922; and "2,000 Voters in Six Counties 'Singleshot' for Miss Toles and Gov. Campbell, Shown," *Tucson Citizen,* clipping, no date—both in Elsie Toles Scrapbook no. 3.

7. Minnie K. Bisby to Elsie Toles, 15 March 1919, Cochise County Superintendent Series, MS 180, AHS.

8. "Apply City Ideas to Rural Schools, Miss Toles Urges," *Tucson Citizen,* clipping, no date, Toles Scrapbook no. 1. Laura Muñoz, "Desert Dreams: Mexican American Education in Arizona, 1870–1930" (Ph.D. diss., Arizona State University, 2006), "to hear" on 120.

9. "Hundreds of School Marms . . . ," clipping, no date, Toles Scrapbook no. 2; "Will Entertain Guests at Cave Creek Ranch" and "Two Women Politicians Seek Name for Ranch," clippings, no date, Toles Scrapbook no. 2; Debra L. Mues, "Interview with Ms. Myriam Toles," Bisbee, 1979, Toles biofile, BMHM (Myriam was Elsie's sister).

10. Rev. A. D. Raley, "Deportations Justified," *Arizona Mining Journal* (August 1917):

7–8; A. D. Raley et al. to "Dear Brother," 18 August 1920, draft enclosed with letter from Raley to Toles, 19 August 1920; "Mormonism Exposed" and additional clipping, no date, both in Toles Scrapbook no. 2.

11. On Ruth Fuess, see "Non-Partisan Support Given to Miss Toles," clipping, October 1920, Elsie Toles Scrapbook no. 2, AHS; and Zack Wanda Browning, "That Nurse Lady," typescript in Ruth Fuess biofiles, BMHM.

12. On the Home Extension Service, see Amy E. Ross, "'Every Home a Laboratory': Arizona Farm Women, the Extension Service, and Rural Modernization, 1932–1952" (Ph.D. diss., Arizona State University, 1998); Joan Jensen, "Canning Comes to New Mexico: Women and the Agricultural Extension Service, 1914–19," *New Mexico Historical Review,* 57, no. 4 (1982): 361–386; Neil Foley, *The White Scourge: Mexicans, Blacks, and Poor Whites in Texas Cotton Culture* (Berkeley, 1997), 141–162; Sandra Schackel, *Social Housekeepers: Women Shaping Public Policy in New Mexico, 1920–1940* (Albuquerque, 1992), 111–140; Marilyn Irvin Holt, "From Better Babies to 4-H: A Look at Rural America, 1900–1930," *Prologue,* 24 (Fall 1992): 245–255; and Katherine Jellison, *Entitled to Power: Farm Women and Technology, 1913–1963* (Chapel Hill, 1993). On parallels between women's and farm organizing, see Theda Skocpol, "Soldiers, Workers, and Mothers: Gendered Identities in Early U.S. Social Policy, *Contention,* 2, no. 3 (Spring 1993): 172.

13. See "Why Not Cochise?" *Courtland Arizonan,* 19 January 1918; "Miss Sporleder Appointed," *Benson Signal,* 28 September 1918; "Local Items," *Benson Signal,* 20 April 1918; "Hot Lunches for School Children," *Benson Signal,* 31 May 1919.

14. On Pirtleville, see WPA Writers' Projects Manuscripts, Box 7, microfilm, ASLAPR; Henry Wilkinson, "A Personal Interview with Mrs. Mike Gomez," typescript, CCHS; and Eva Buttner Muñoz, oral history, interview by Cindy Hayostek, 3 October 1992, CCHS. Quotation from Minnie Lintz, "Statement Submitted for Cochise County," in C. O. Case, "Report of the Superintendent of Public Instruction of the State of Arizona, for the School Years Ending June 30, 1915, and June 30, 1916," 37, ASLAPR.

15. Louise Sporleder, "Cochise County Home Extension Report," December 1918 to December 1919, 1–2, AZ 302, UACES, UASC; a likely menu appears in Mary Pritner Lockwood et al., "The Hot Lunch for Rural Schools," University of Arizona, College of Agriculture, Circular no. 25, November 1918, UASC; "Fourth Annual Report, Agricultural Extension Service," UACES, 1918, AZ 302, UASC; Mary Pritner Lockwood, "County Home Demonstration Agent Work," UACES, 1919, Cochise County Agricultural Extension office, Willcox, Arizona. Lambert exemplified the women Peggy Pascoe labels "native helpers"; see Pascoe, *Relations of Rescue: The Search for Female Moral Authority in the American West* (New York, 1990).

16. See Josiah M. Heyman, *Life and Labor on the Border: Working People of Northeastern Sonora, Mexico, 1886–1986* (Tucson, 1991), esp. 65; May 1921 membership report for Pirtleville, La Alianza Papers, Chicano Collection, Arizona State University. On the Altar

Society, see Grace Ryan, "Abstracts from Cochise County," UACES, December 1921, AZ 302, UASC.

17. Bertha Virmond, County Home Demonstration Agent, "Annual Narrative Report for Cochise County," 1 December 1933 to 1 December 1934, pages A–C, AZ 302, UASC; "Hot Lunches for School Children."

18. Quotations from Muñoz, "Desert Dreams," 114.

19. Laura Mae Seward, "Narrative Report of Laura Mae Seward, Home Demonstration Agent for Cochise County, Arizona," 1 December 1925 to 1 December 1926, in Cochise County Agricultural Extension office files, UACES, Willcox, Arizona; and see Ryan, "Abstracts from Cochise County," 1921, 1, 3. Also see Paré, *Arizona Pageant,* 307.

20. Ryan, "Abstracts from Cochise County," 1921, 1.

21. Ibid., 8; "antagonism" from Laura Mae Seward, "Annual Report of Home Demonstration Agent," 1 December 1923 to 1 December 1924, 2, UACES, AZ 302, UASC.

22. Ryan, "Annual Report of Home Demonstration Agent," 1 December 1921 to 1 December 1922, 8–9, in AZ 302, UASC; and Virmond, "Narrative Report for Cochise County," 1929, 1–2.

23. Laura Mae Seward, "Narrative Report for Cochise County," 20 July 1927 to 1 December 1927, 29; and Bertha Virmond, County Home Demonstration Agent, "Annual Report of County Extension Workers," 1 December 1929 to 1 December 1930, 18; both in AZ 302, UASC.

24. The children's programs in Dragoon, Pearce, Bowie, and Gleason were all integrated. Laura Mae Seward, "Narrative Report for Cochise County, 20 July 1928 to 1 December 1928," 32–33, AZ 302, UASC; 1920s and 1930s reports, passim; Virmond, "Annual Report," 1934, A–C, emphasis added.

25. On this era and its impact on notions of illegality, see George J. Sánchez, *Becoming Mexican-American: Ethnicity, Culture, and Identity in Chicano Los Angeles, 1900–1945* (New York, 1993), 19–20, 59–62; Mae Ngai, *Impossible Subjects: Illegal Aliens and the Making of Modern America* (Princeton, 2004), esp. 18, 58–71; and Roger Daniels, *Guarding the Golden Door: American Immigration Policy and Immigrants since 1882* (New York, 2004), 57–64.

26. "The Federal Civil Works Administration in the State of Arizona," undated typescript, ASLAPR, 6 (hereafter cited as "CWA report"); Pierce Williams, Field Administrator, to Harry L. Hopkins, Federal Relief Administrator, 31 August 1933, Record Group 69, Records of the Works Progress Administration, FERA Central Files, 1933–1936, State Series, March 1933–1936, Box Arizona—Field Reports, NACP; *Fourteenth Census of the United States, 1920,* vol. 1; *Sixteenth Census of the United States, 1940,* vol. 2; James Walter Black, "History of Education in Cochise County" (M.A. thesis, University of Arizona, 1940), 82; On homeownership, see Florence Warner to Harry Hopkins, 26 June 1933, Record Group 69, FERA Central Files, 1933–1936; State Series March 1933–1936, Box Arizona Official FERA, Folder May–December 1933, NACP.

27. CWA report, 5; Collins, *New Deal in Arizona*, 59; Warner to Hopkins, 26 June 1933; Williams to Hopkins, 31 August 1933.

28. Henry F. Dobyns et al., *Los Tres Alamos del Rio San Pedro: The Peculiar Persistence of a Place Name* (Tucson, 1996), 165–173.

29. U.S. Works Project Administration, *The Federal Civil Works Administration: Interesting Programs in Arizona* (n.p., 1934), 7. Bernardo S. Gámez, oral history, interview by Nedra Sutherland, 7 May 1994, SPVAHM. Two brothers (Miguel D. Gámez and Conrado M. Gámez) did acquire a stock-raising homestead in 1938; see www.glorecords.blm.gov.

30. Helen Genevieve Foster Hurtado, oral history, interview by Katherine Benton-Cohen, 11 February 1999; Herlinda Tofoya, oral history, interview by Beverly Woods, 12 July 1993, BMHM.

31. Discussion of the New Deal in Cochise County focuses on four interrelated kinds of programs: those that provide a comparison of the county's mining and agricultural regions, those that show the ties between federally funded relief efforts and the mining industry, those where information on Mexican American participation is available, and those administered for or by women. Most data is from 1933 to 1936, specifically the progression of relief programs created by the Civil Works Administration (CWA), the Federal Emergency Relief Administration (FERA), and the Works Progress Administration (WPA), as well as programs that cooperated with Homemakers' Extension Agents.

32. "Mass Meeting to be Held Monday Night on Relief Committees," *BDR*, 12 December 1931, 12; "Bisbee," *Arizona Labor Journal*, 18 June 1932, 9. "Systematic Operation of the Local Relief Work Explained to Gathering in Theatre," *BDR*, 15 December 1931, 1–2. And, on deportations, see "Los Mineros," PBS American Experience, videocassette recording, produced and directed by Hector Galán, 1990.

33. Collins, *New Deal in Arizona*, 25–27; see also Pierce Williams to Harry L. Hopkins, 20 July 1933, Record Group 69, FERA 1933–1936, State Series March 1933–1936, Box 10, AZ 400–406, Folder Arizona—Field Reports, NACP. On sales taxes, see U.S. Works Progress Administration, *Federal Civil Works*, 13.

34. Thomas E. Sheridan, *Arizona: A Brief History* (Tucson, 1995), 253; "Presbyterian Copper," *Fortune* magazine, July 1932, 40–48, 104; "every" from Annie M. Cox, "History of Bisbee, 1877–1937" (M.A. thesis, University of Arizona, 1938), 134; "biggest" from *Los Angeles Times*, 20 April 1942, quoted in Glenn S. Dumke, "Douglas, Border Town," *Pacific Historical Review*, 17, no. 3 (August 1948): 285.

35. Byrkit, *Forging*, 168–173; "Lew Douglas Book Attacks Policies of the New Deal," *BDR*, 17 July 1935, 3.

36. Information on female representatives from congress.house.gov (accessed 22 November 2008); Collins, *New Deal in Arizona*, quotation on 139; Forrest R. Rickard, comp., *The Development of Ajo, Arizona* (Ajo, 1996); Elmer Graham, Douglas, Arizona, to Secretary of Labor Frances Perkins, 27 June 1933, Record Group 69, FERA Central

Files, 1933–1936, State Series, March 1933–1936, Box 13, Folder 460 Arizona Complaints, NACP.

37. Williams to Hopkins, 31 August 1933. For a recent overview of race and the New Deal, see Ira Katznelson, *When Affirmative Action Was White: An Untold History of Racial Inequality in Twentieth-Century America* (New York, 2005).

38. U.S. Works Progress Administration, *Federal Civil Works*, 15; on county burden, see F. W. Warner, Secretary, Arizona State Board of Public Welfare, to Aubrey Williams, Assistant Administrator, FERA, Washington, 25 May 1935, Record Group 69, FERA Central Files, 1933–1936, State Series, March 1933–1936, Box 401 Arizona, Folder June 1935, NACP.

39. Collins, *New Deal in Arizona*, 32; "Federal Relief Agencies in State Are Recognized to Carry on Huge Program," *BDR*, 12 July 1935, 5; "Globe Unionists Protest Action of Relief Heads," *Arizona Labor Journal*, 23 May 1935, 1. On PD's influence on programming, see "Chief of WPA Outlines New Plan at Meet," *BDR*, 17 July 1935, 1; "Civil Forces Will Move on Bisbee Today," *BDR*, 24 July 1935, 1.

40. Strike discussion in correspondence dated 14 June–12 August 1935 in March 1933–1936, Box 12, AZ 420–453, Folder 450 AZ Work Relief, NACP. Warner to Williams, 13 March 1935, Box 9, Alaska 401, Arizona 400, Folder October–December 1934; Lee W. Hogan, President and Chairman of Business Agency, et al., Federal Labor Union 18694, Bisbee, to President of the United States, 17 May 1935, Box 13, File AZ Complaints A–F. All in Record Group 69, FERA Central Files, 1933–1936, State Series, 1933–1936, NACP.

41. PD's post-Deportation grievance committee had also excluded Mexican workers, and had given company officials absolute veto power. Collins, *New Deal in Arizona*, 58; minutes of Arizona State Board of Welfare, 14 March 1934, Record Group 69, FERA Central Files, 1933–1936, State Series, March 1933–1936, Box 13, Folder Arizona Minutes, NACP; "Organization Is Formed for Unified Giving on Christmas," *BDR*, 5 December 1931, 3.

42. Graham to Perkins, 27 June 1933. State board secretary Florence Warner, defender of the mining officials, disputed his complaints in Florence Warner, Phoenix, Arizona, to Bruce McClure, FERA Secretary, Washington, D.C., 31 July 1933, Record Group 69, FERA Central Files, 1933–1936, State Series, March 1933–1936, Box 13, 460 Arizona Complaints, G–L, NACP; for another complaint, see L. H. White, IUMMSW Board Member, to Hopkins, 23 June 1935; "tends to promote" from Veterans Employment Committee, VFW Armstrong-Stetson-Campbell Post no. 836, Lowell, Arizona, to President Roosevelt, 28 April 1935, and "resent" from P. J. Lindaman, Secretary, All-American Protective Association, Local no. 1, Douglas, Arizona, to Warner, 27 July 1935, all three in Record Group 69, FERA Central Files, 1933–1936, State Series, March 1933–1936, Box 13, Folder Arizona Complaints, A–N, NACP. On similar complaints in Globe's Gila County, see "Offer Unemployed Low-Pay Work," *Arizona Labor Journal*, 9 May 1935, 3.

43. Business Agency of Bisbee Federal Labor Union no. 18964, Bisbee, Arizona, to President Roosevelt, [17 May 1935], and Nels Anderson, Adviser on Labor Relations, Washington, D.C., to Mr. Lee W. Hogan, President, Federal Labor Union, no. 189644, Bisbee, Arizona, 24 May 1935, both in Record Group 69, FERA Central Files, 1933–1936, State Series, March 1933–1936, Box 13, Folder Arizona Complaints, A–N, NACP. Similarly, see "Globe Unionists Protest Action of Relief Heads," *Arizona Labor Journal,* 23 May 1935, 1.

44. Minutes of Arizona State Board of Welfare, 1934, passim, Record Group 69, FERA Central Files, 1933–1936, State Series, March 1933–1936, Box 13, Folder Arizona Minutes, NACP; "Souers Likes ERA Plan for Idle Workers," *BDR,* 16 March 1934, 2. For other disparities, see "CWA's Payroll Here Saturday Sets New High: Nearly $35,000 Is Paid, with $13,869 Disbursed among Bisbee Workers," *BDR,* 8 January 1934, 1. General figures on disparity are from "Report of Activities, Cochise County Board of Public Welfare," 53–62, ASLAPR. I did not count local street improvements in the roadwork figures; only highway and county roads are included. "Bisbee County" in letter to WPA, 1 November 1935, Record Group 69, WPA Central Files, 1933–1936, State Series, 1933–1936, Box 13, Folder Arizona 453, NACP.

45. Cochise County Board of Public Welfare (Federal Emergency Relief Administration), Bisbee, Arizona, "Report of Activities," 1 May 1934 to 1 August 1935, ASLAPR; "Warren Residents to Receive Free Shade Trees as Soon as Fencing Project Is Complete," *BDR,* 21 July 1935, 6; Ernest E. Brewer, "Bisbee," WPA Arizona Writers Project Manuscripts, 1940–1941, microfilm, ASLAPR; State Board Minutes, 25 April 1934; "$60,000 Asked for San Pedro," *BDR,* 6 January 1934, 1.

46. Corrington Gill, Assistant Administrator, to Senator Carl Hayden, Washington, D.C., FERA, Washington, D.C., 30 January 1935, Record Group 69, FERA Central Files, 1933–1936, State Series, March 1933–1936, Box 13, Folder 460, AZ Complaints A–F, NACP.

47. Collins, *New Deal in Arizona,* 33.

48. A. C. Garcia, Douglas, Arizona, to U.S. Secretary of Labor Frances Perkins, Washington, D.C., 28 March 1935; J. B. Bailey, Executive Secretary, Cochise County ERA, to A. C. Garcia, Douglas, Arizona, 18 March 1935; Lucy M. Brown, to Division of Special Inquiry, Washington(?), 6 May 1935; all in Record Group 69, FERA Central Files, 1933–1936, State Series, March 1933–1936, Box 13, Folder 460, AZ Complaints A–F, NACP; Minutes of Arizona Board of Public Welfare, 10 July 1934, ibid., Folder Arizona Minutes.

49. For complaints about Mexican aid, see S. C. Spencer, Cochise, Arizona, to Whom It May Concern, 24 July 1934, Record Group 69, FERA Central Files, 1933–1936, State Series, March 1933–1936, Arizona Complaints, O–Z, Box 840 (690 AZ), NACP; J. E. Wilkie, Secretary, Arizona Peace Officers' Association, to Sen. Henry Ashurst, Washington, 8 May 1936, ibid.; F. M. Warner, Secretary, to Arthur Goldschmidt, Acting Director

of Professional Projects, FERA, 9 September 1934, Record Group 69, FERA Central Files, 1933–1936, State Series, March 1933–1936, Box Alaska 401, Arizona 400; Folder Arizona Official FERA, August–September 1934, NACP.

50. Cochise County Board of Public Welfare, "Report of Activities," 129.

51. "Alien class" in U.S. Works Progress Administration, *Federal Civil Works*, 2; Minutes of Arizona State Board of Welfare, 19 October 1933, Record Group 69, FERA Central Files, 1933–1936, State Series, March 1933–1936, Box 13, Folder Arizona Minutes, NACP.

52. Complaint in F. M. Warner, Secretary, Arizona State Board of Public Welfare, to Corrington Gill, Assistant Administrator, FERA, 11 February 1935, Record Group 69, FERA Central Files, 1933–1936, State Series, March 1933–1936, Box 9, Alaska 401, Arizona 400, Folder 400 Arizona Officials February–August 1935, NACP; Collins, *New Deal in Arizona*, 72; Graham to Perkins, 27 June 1933.

53. On the relationship between the restriction of European and Asian immigrants and the encouragement of Mexican immigration, see Thomas E. Sheridan, *Los Tucsonenses: The Mexican Community in Tucson, 1854–1941* (Tucson, 1986), 209. Complaints by organized labor about Mexican immigration appear regularly in the *Arizona Labor Journal*, 1928–1930: e.g., "Douglas Central Labor Union Takes Note of Mexican Immigration Evil," 8 March 1930, 1.

54. Camille Guerin-Gonzales, *Mexican Workers and American Dreams: Immigration, Repatriation, and California Farm Labor, 1900–1939* (New Brunswick, N.J., 1994), 114, 93. Galán, "Los Mineros," features a wrenching discussion of the Clifton-Morenci deportations. The federal government did increase deportation of Europeans in this era, but I have found no evidence of this practice in Bisbee. See Ngai, *Impossible Subjects*, 61, 67.

55. "Racial Groups in Arizona," and untitled manuscript on Serbs, both in WPA Writer's Project Manuscripts.

56. Manuscript on Serbs, and "Racial Groups in Arizona," final draft, WPA Writer's Project Manuscripts.

57. *Bisbee Cuprite*, 1934, BMHM; Dobyns et al., *Tres Alamos*, 169, 174; Collins, *New Deal in Arizona*, 116–117.

58. Dobyns et al., *Tres Alamos*, 134–135.

59. Selso Parra and Juanita Parra, oral history, interview by Stella Davenport, 25 March 1982, Tombstone Oral Histories, Tombstone Public Library.

60. Collins, *New Deal in Arizona*, 33–34, 300; [Mrs. Amy H. Gardner] to Mildred J. Wiese, Works Progress Administration, Washington, D.C., 26 January 1939, in Record Group 69, 651.341 Arizona, Box 837, NACP. Cochise County Board of Public Welfare, "Report of Activities," 1. The directorship of the National Youth Administration could be a powerful political post: in Texas, it was held by an ambitious young man—Lyndon Baines Johnson.

61. Collins, *New Deal in Arizona*, 77, 287.

62. On power over whether programs run, see for instance Helen Dail Thomas, Assistant Director of Employment, WPA, Phoenix, Arizona, to Mrs. Mary G. Burke, Douglas, Arizona, 31 March 1939, Record Group 69, Box 662 Arizona, Folder January 1939, NACP. Collins, *New Deal in Arizona,* 300–305; "CWA Project Has Been Closed," *BDR,* 11 March 1934, 5, "Personals"; *BDR,* 13 March 1934, 5; "Mrs. Nellie Hoy, Back from Extensive Trip to Europe, Tells of Her Journey," *BDR,* 20 October 1931, 6; "Shortage of Domestic Help Will Result in NYA Course," *BDR,* 18 January 1940, 1; Mrs. Helen C. (Hubert) d'Autremont, Tucson, Arizona, to Florence Warner, Secretary of Arizona State Board of Public Welfare, 4 April 1936, Record Group 69, Box 661 Arizona, Folder March–May 1936, NACP; but see www.lib.az.us/awhof/women/datremont.cfm. "Snooty" from outline for Preliminary Plans for Household Worker's Training Schools in Arizona, 13 January 1936, Record Group 69, Box 839, 661 Arizona, Folder June–November 1935, NACP. And see Evelyn Nakano Glenn, "From Servitude to Service Work: Historical Continuities in the Racial Division of Paid Reproductive Labor," *Signs: Journal of Women and Culture in Society,* 18, no. 1 (Autumn 1992): 1–43.

63. Pierce Williams, Field Administrator, to Hopkins, 16 August 1933, Record Group 69, FERA Central Files, 1933–1936, State Series, March 1933–1936, Box Arizona 400–406, Folder Arizona Field Reports, NACP; F. W. Warner to Josephine C. Brown, Administrative Assistant, FERA, Washington, 29 September 1934, Record Group 69, FERA Central Files, 1933–1936, State Series, March 1933–1936, Box Alaska 401, Arizona 400, Folder October–December 1934, NACP.

64. On segregation, see for example Bertha Virmond, "Annual Narrative Report for Cochise County," 1 December 1935 to 1 December 1936, 27, UACES, MS 302, UASC; Collins, *New Deal in Arizona,* 299, 313; Jane Rider to Ellen Woodward, 9 September 1936, Record Group 69, Box 663, Folder Arizona August–December 1936, NACP.

65. Bertha Virmond, County Home Demonstration Agent, "Annual Report of County Extension Workers," 30 November 1931 to 1 December 1932, 11, 27, UACES, AZ 302, UASC.

66. Ibid., 46.

Conclusion

1. "In the Matter of Phelps Dodge Corporation, a Corporation and International Union of Mine, Mill and Smelter Workers, Local No. 30," *Decisions and Orders of the National Labor Relations Board,* vol. 19, case no. C-500, decided 16 January 1940, 560.

2. *Phelps Dodge v. National Labor Relations Board,* 313 U.S. 177 (1941). Also see Carlos Schwantes, *Vision and Enterprise: Exploring the History of Phelps Dodge Corporation* (Tucson, 2000), 203.

3. Ellen Baker, *On Strike and on Film: Mexican American Families and Blacklisted Filmmakers in Cold War America* (Chapel Hill, 2007).

4. Supreme Court of the United States, October Term 1940, *No. 387: Phelps Dodge*

Corporation vs. National Labor Relations Board; No. 641: National Labor Relations Board vs. Phelps Dodge Corporation, Transcript of Record, vol. 1, Exhibits 23, 25, 31, 34, 35, 54. See also "Bisbee Miners Tighten Picket Line at P-D," *ALJ,* 20 June 1935, 1; "Phoenix Attorney Called to Bisbee," ibid., 27 June 1935, 1; and *Decisions and Orders of the National Labor Relations Board,* vol. 19, 556.

5. "Globe Unionists Protest Action of Relief Heads," *ALJ,* 23 May 1935, 1; "Miss Warner Too Busy to Discuss Relief Situation," ibid., 28 March 1935, 1; "Ladies Affiliate with Globe Union" and "Prevailing Wage Rate Restored to Globe Women," ibid., 6 June 1935, 1; "Douglas Labor Council Holds Mountain Picnic," ibid., 3 October 1935, 1. Also see E. F. Vickers, "Douglas Groups Cooperate," *ALJ,* Anniversary Edition, 1936, 6; Jane H. Rider to Mrs. Ellen S. Woodard, Assistant Administrator, Works Progress Administration, Attn: Miss Agnes Cronin, 30 November 1935, telegram, Box 661 AZ, Folder December 1935, Record Group 69, WPA Records, NACP.

6. Reid Robinson, President, Mine-Mill, to J. Warren Madden, Chairman, National Labor Relations Board, 22 August 1939 and 19 September 1939, Formal and Informal Unfair Labor Practices and Representation Case Files, 1935–1948, Entry 155, Box 2837, Case C-500, Folder Phelps Dodge Corp., Bisbee, AZ, Record Group 25, Papers of the National Labor Relations Board (NLRB), NACP.

7. A succinct overview of the AFL replacement appears in "Calendar of Important Events," Formal and Informal Labor Practices and Representation Case Files, Entry 155, Box 2839, Folder Phelps Dodge Corp., CQ Mine Bisbee, AZ, Case XXII-0-452, Record Group 25, NLRB, NACP; Ernest G. Trimble to Mr. Lawrence W. Cramer, undated memo, ca. late 1944, Subject: Discrimination in the Southwest, Southwest—Mexicans, Entry 19, Box 339, File Mining, Record Group 228, Papers of the Committee on Fair Employment Practice, also known as the Fair Employment Practices Commission (FEPC), NACP.

8. Complaint of Carlos B. Rivera, Pirtleville, Arizona, 17 August 1942, Legal Division Hearings 1941–1946, Southwest—Mexicans, Folder Entry 19, Box 340, Douglas, AZ (Phelps Dodge Corp.), Record Group 228, NACP.

9. Complaint of Jose Estrada, Douglas, Arizona, 17 August 1942, Legal Division Hearings 1941–1946, Southwest—Mexicans, Folder Entry 19, Box 340, Douglas, AZ (Phelps Dodge Corp.), Record Group 228, NACP. Neither Rivera nor Estrada received direct redress from the FEPC hearings, as discussed below.

10. Complaint of John B. Hart, Douglas, Arizona, 17 August 1942, ibid.

11. Complaint of Jose P. Chavez, Douglas, Arizona, 17 August 1942, ibid. Another example of the use of "Latin American" can be found in the same file, in the complaint of Luis Rubio.

12. On relations between Mexican immigrants and Mexican Americans, see David Gutiérrez, *Walls and Mirrors: Mexican Americans, Mexican Immigrants, and the Politics of Ethnicity* (Berkeley, 1995). On Arizona campaigns centered around being "Cauca-

soid," see Eric Meeks, *Border Citizens: The Making of Indians, Mexicans, and Anglos in Arizona* (Austin, 2007), 174–179, 186–187. For comparison, see Thomas A. Guglielmo, "Fighting for Caucasian Rights: Mexicans, Mexican Americans, and the Transnational Struggle for Civil Rights in World War II Texas," *Journal of American History*, 92, no. 4 (2006): 1212–1237.

13. Daniel R. Donovan and Barron B. Beshoar to Dr. Ernest G. Trimple, undated memo, re: Wage differentials in the copper mines, Legal Division Hearings 1941–1946, Southwest—Mexicans, Entry 19, Box 339, Folder Southwest Hearings, Record Group 228, NACP.

14. See Record Group 228, Papers of the Fair Employment Practices Commission, NACP. For the only complete secondary overview, see *Chicano Workers and the Politics of Fairness: The FEPC in the Southwest, 1941–1945* (Austin, 1991). See also Mario T. García, *Mexican Americans: Leadership, Ideology, and Identity, 1930–1960* (New Haven, 1989), 175–198; and Zaragoza Vargas, *Labor Rights Are Civil Rights: Mexican American Workers in Twentieth-Century America* (Princeton, 2004), esp. 220–223.

15. D. H. Dinwoodie, "The Rise of the Mine-Mill Union in Southwestern Copper," in James C. Foster, ed., *American Labor in the Southwest: The First Hundred Years* (Tucson, 1982), 52.

16. R. J. Bridgewater, Bisbee Miner's Union no. 30 [Mine-Mill], to Dr. Ernest Trimble, FEPC, El Paso, 31 August 1942, Legal Division Hearings 1941–1946, Southwest—Mexicans, Entry 19, Box 339, File Hearing Background Materials, Record Group 228, NACP.

17. Carlos E. Castañeda to Will Maslow, 21 June 1944, "Subject: Area-Wide Mining Industry Investigation, Bisbee, Arizona," Legal Division Hearings 1941–1946, Southwest—Mexicans, Entry 19, Box 339, ES 270, Recapitulation of the Mining Industry for Arizona for the Year 1943, File Southwest Hearings Record Group 228, NACP; Castañeda to Maslow, 1 September 1944, Subject: Southwestern Hearing on Mining Industry, File Mining, Record Group 228, NACP. On Victory campaigns, see Carlos E. Castañeda, Cottonwood, Arizona, to Will Maslow, 5 June 1944, Subject: Progress Report, Area-Wide Mining Industry Investigation, Clarkdale-Jerome, AZ, Legal Division Hearings 1941–1946, Southwest—Mexicans, Entry 19, Box 339, File Southwest Hearings, Record Group 228, NACP; Baker, *On Strike and on Film*, 61–65.

18. Meek, *Border Citizens,* 190–210. Also see extensive holdings on the student Chicano Movement at the Chicano Collection, Arizona State University, created by Dr. Christine Marín, activist, miner's daughter, and archivist. Arizona's first—and thus far only—Mexican American governor was Raul Castro, who grew up in Pirtleville outside Douglas and was the son of a copper miner from Cananea.

19. Jonathan D. Rosenblum, *Copper Crucible: How the Arizona Miners' Strike of 1983 Recast Labor-Management Relations in America* (Ithaca, N.Y., 1995); Barbara Kingsolver, *Holding the Line: Women in the Great Arizona Mine Strike of 1983* (Ithaca, 1996; orig. pub. 1989).

20. See "Environmentalists Hail the Ranchers: Howdy, Pardners!" *New York Times* (national edition), 10 September 2002, D3; Jonathan S. Adams, *The Future of the Wild: Radical Conservation for a Crowded World* (Boston, 2006), 108–140.

21. Jonathan Clark, "No Longer 'Ground Zero,'" *Sierra Vista Herald Review,* 12 November 2006, available at www.svherald.com (accessed 8 December 2007); Marc Cooper, "Last Exit to Tombstone," *Tucson Weekly,* 29 March 2005, www.tucsonweekly.com (accessed 30 March 2005); "CBP Border Patrol Announces Fiscal Year 2008 Achievements for Tucson Sector," 15 October 2008, www.cbp.gov (accessed 24 November 2008); "Cochise County, USA: Cries from the Border," DVD directed by Mercedes Maharis, Genius Entertainment, 2005.

22. Clark, "No Longer 'Ground Zero'"; U.S. Rep. Gabrielle Giffords, Statement on Border Patrol Checkpoint, 21 September 2007, www.giffords.house.gov (accessed 8 December 2007); David L. Tiebel, "Border Deaths Rise 29 Percent in Past Year," *Tucson Citizen,* 29 September 2007, www.tucsoncitizen.com (accessed 9 December 2007); "Indiana Guard Has Big Impact on Border Mission," 17 November 2006, www.ngb.army.mil (accessed 9 December 2007).

23. Megan Mazurek, "Influx of Cash, More Agents Increases Apprehensions," *Tombstone Epitaph,* 12 September 2008, www.theepitaphonline.com (accessed 24 November 2008). Unless federalized by the president, the National Guard is a state militia not subject to the limitations of the Posse Comitatus Act, whose power has eroded over the years. Major Craig T. Trebilcock, "The Myth of Posse Comitatus," October 2000, www.homelandsecurity.org/journal/articles/Trebilcock.htm (accessed 9 December 2007).

Acknowledgments

I grew up in suburban Phoenix, and I can't remember the first time I visited Bisbee. I feel as if I have always been able to picture it in my mind's eye, this Victorian city-in-a-canyon where gourmet restaurants coexist with industrial mining's detritus. I've known the northern part of the county, especially Willcox, where my family went camping and picked apples, at least as long. I lived in Bisbee for six months in 1998–1999, and return whenever I can. I even have a little bit of Cochise County in my blood. My grandfather, Alex Silverman, was born in Douglas in 1913 to Polish Jewish immigrants who had a small shop that sold dry-goods and musical instruments. They stayed in Douglas only a couple of years, moving to Nogales and El Paso, where my mother grew up. My grandfather's life has shaped how I've thought about this book and the people who inhabit it. I never listened carefully enough to his stories about growing up on the border, and I teased him too much when he pestered me to go to Harvard—a place he always admired from afar as a child of the border, of immigrants, and of the Depression. It has not escaped my notice that this is a book about his birthplace and that it is published by Harvard. Maybe, somewhere, it hasn't escaped his notice either.

All of this means that I cannot be said to be "objective," but it does mean that I have tried hard to get the story right. Dozens of people helped me to write this book, and many saved me from foolish errors. The mistakes that remain are mine alone.

Many institutions and organizations have provided financial support for this project's many phases. I have benefited from University Fellowships and travel grants from the University of Wisconsin, the Walter Rundell Award and a Graduate Student Conference Scholarship from the Western History Association, the Irene Ledesma Prize from the Coalition for Western Women's History; the Western Association of Women Historians' Founders Graduate Student Fellowship; a Dissertator Seminar Fellowship from the Mellon Foundation; a Newberry Library Short-Term Fellowship; Michigan Technological University's Copper Country Collection Travel Grant; Louisiana State University's Council-on-Research and Manship Summer Research Grants, Junior Faculty One-Semester Sabbatical Leave, and a Faculty Research Grant; the Autry National Center's Jane and Charlie Butcher Fellowship in Western Women's History; and Georgetown University's Americas Workshop and research funds.

For their helpful responses to versions of this work presented as scholarly papers, I thank participants at conference sessions sponsored by Georgetown University's Americas Workshop, the Autry Western Workshop, the American Historical Association, the Organization of American Historians, the Western History Association, the Rural History Seminar at the Newberry Library, the Nineteenth-Century Studies Conference, the Gender History Workshop at Pennsylvania State University, the "Border Cities / Border Cultures" conference at the University of Wisconsin-Milwaukee, the "Gender in the Borderlands" conference in San Antonio, and the Women's West Conference in Pullman, Washington.

Sections of Chapter 1, 5, and 6 first appeared as "Common Purposes, Worlds Apart: Mexican-American, Mormon and Midwestern Women Homesteaders in Cochise County, Arizona," *Western Historical Quarterly,* 36, no. 4 (Winter 2005): 429–452; copyright by the Western History Association, reprinted by permission. Portions of Chapter 3, 4, and 7 first appeared as "Docile Children and Dangerous Revolutionaries: The Racial Hierarchy of Manliness and the Bisbee Deportation of 1917," *Frontiers: A Journal of*

Women Studies, 24, nos. 2–3 (2003): 30–50; copyright by the Frontiers Editorial Collective, reprinted by permission.

I owe thanks to a vast array of friends, family, acquaintances, historians, genealogists, and talented museum curators and archivists. In Bisbee, Gary Dillard, Annie Dillard, Carrie Gustafson, Boyd Nicholl, Sylvia Smith, and Judith Stafford were indispensable. Rebecca Orozco gave me food, shelter, work, and precious family documents and photos, one of which appears in Chapter 6. In Cascabel, I thank Jacquie Dale (who also lodged me), Steve Ronquillo, Monica Dunbar Smith, Darlene Dunbar Wilkins, and Maria Araiza Troutner, and everyone who attended my talk at the Cascabel community meetinghouse. Harry Ames, Cindy Hayostek, and Mayor Ray Borane taught me about Douglas. Kenja Hassan and Blake Kammann learned with me and ate with me in Cochise County. In Phoenix, Wendi Goen, Don Langlois, Nancy Sawyer, and Melanie Sturgeon have done me many favors at the Arizona State Archives. At Arizona State University, Christine Marín has been an inspiration for the fifteen years I have known her. In Michigan's Upper Peninsula, Erik Nordberg, Kim Hoagland, and Abby Sue Fisher showed me Bisbee's northern roots. Lynn Bjorkman, James Woodward, Samuel Truett, Charles Parrott, James McBride, Heidi Osselaer, Devra Weber, Chris Capozzola, and Karl Jacoby generously shared their research with me. Yvette Huginnie met with me early on, and offered rich insights from her own research. Richard Selbach, at the Bureau of Land Management office in Phoenix, made homestead data available to me, and Yvette J. Saavedra, Sarah Hinman, and Sarah Lipscomb provided research assistance. Philip Schwartzberg drew fine maps on a short deadline. Richard Shelton's book *Going Back to Bisbee* reinforced my feelings that this was a special place. I am also indebted to local historians and genealogists, especially Edward Ellsworth, Edward Soza, and Louise Fenn Larson, as well as to the women whom I interviewed for this project. At the Autry National Center and Braun Library, Carolyn Brucker, Marilyn Kim, Liza Posas, Manola Madrid, Virginia Scharff, Kim Walters, and Stephen Aron made my visit fruitful. Blame Steve for this book, because fifteen years ago, after I handed in my senior thesis at Princeton, he convinced me to become a historian.

At the University of Wisconsin, Arnold Alanen, the late Jeanne Boydston, Camille Guerin-Gonzales, Susan L. Johnson, Steve Kantrowitz, Steve Stern, and Florencia Mallon guided my intellectual development. Bill Cronon and Linda Gordon, especially, modeled distinct—but equally exemplary—ways of being an American historian. Thomas Andrews, Flannery Burke, and Marienka Sokol Vanlandingham learned the ropes alongside me. My career is unimaginable without them. Alexander Shashko did more than he had to, and I am grateful. Thank you for everything. At Louisiana State University, Maribel Dietz, Gaines Foster, David Lindenfeld, Tiwanna Simpson, Mark Thompson, and Meredith Veldman cheered me on. Melea Burney and Heather Sewell Day made sure I felt not-so-desperate, and I miss them all. In Washington, my new Georgetown colleagues have been extraordinarily welcoming. I am grateful to all, and especially (in addition to those listed as readers below) to Tommaso Astanta, Kathleen Buc Gallagher, Amy Leonard, Chandra Manning, Bryan McCann, and Adam Rothman.

I wish to thank those who have read parts of this work; they have pushed me in new directions and saved me from many errors. They include Bob Boze Bell, Carol Benedict, Jenice Benton, Antonia Castañeda, Gaines Foster, Alison Games, Dee Garceau-Hagen, Tom Guglielmo, Michael Kazin, Peter Lee, David Rich Lewis, Laura Lovett, Joe McCartin, Karen Merrill, Laura Muñoz, Colleen O'Neill, Rebecca Orozco, John Tutino, and Devra Weber. Hal Cohen, Karl Jacoby, Samuel Truett, Peggy Pascoe, and my anonymous reviewers bravely read the entire manuscript and improved it much. My editors, Kathleen McDermott and Maria Ascher, did, too, and thank goodness for their advice and kindness. Along with Kathleen Drummy, they have cheerfully tolerated a lot of nervous pestering. I am grateful to all.

My family, of course, deserves my biggest thanks. I'm pretty convinced I have the world's greatest parents. John and Jenice Benton have been role models in so many ways—but particularly important for this project, they bequeathed to me a curiosity about remote places, local culture, and interesting characters. I first came to Cochise County as a child with my parents, and I never forgot it.

As I worked on this book, my brother, J.T., and my sister, Betsy, grew from rambunctious teenagers to thoughtful adult friends who have kept me happy and entertained. J.T. helped me with some mortgage intricacies for Chapter 4, and Betsy tolerated a lot of book talk and made me laugh. Lauralyn Lee, who is like family, deserves my thanks for just that reason. I have also enjoyed the company and support of my second parents, Steve Cohen and Debbie Mendeloff; my sisters-in-law, Jennie and Beth; my brother-in-law, Mike; and my nephew and niece, Miller and Evie. Otis kept me company.

Recently, I explained to my son, Julius, that I was writing a book and needed to work on it for a couple hours. When I got back from the library, he asked confidently, "You finished your book?" Would that it were so simple! Since I began this project more than ten years ago, a lot has happened. I have been single, dating, single, dating, engaged, married, pregnant, nursing, potty training, and now busy sounding out words, answering questions, and folding paper airplanes recycled from my draft manuscripts. The research for this book has traversed this large continent by Ford pickup, Beetle, Eurovan (two, actually), Subaru, and U-Haul. Though nearly all of it takes place in Cochise County, it has been written not just in Arizona, but also in Wisconsin, New York, Michigan, Illinois, Louisiana, Vermont, Nova Scotia, and Washington, D.C.

With me one way or another during all of these adventures has been Hal Cohen. Without him most of what is listed above would have been impossible (and not just the obvious stuff). Hal's insights and editing made this book a million times better. But, really, compared to everything else he's brought to my life, as they say in Louisiana, that's just *lagniappe*. Thanks, P.H. To paraphrase Julius, I am so happy we are all *toGEVer*.

Index

President's Mediation Commission *(continued)*
221, 223, 227–228; Deportation deemed illegal
by, 234; on strikers' fight for "free manhood," 3,
210; Wilson's ties to Phelps Dodge and, 3

Progressive Era, 13, 14, 115, 241; barriers to voting
in, 170; diversity of political affiliation in, 124,
243; Home Extension Service, 243, 244;
homesteading and, 183; "social-purity"
campaigns, 113; white women's ascendancy in,
187

Prohibition, 196

Property ownership, 30, 31, 34–35, 139, 161–162.
See also Homeownership; Land ownership

Prostitution, 51–52, 72, 73, 75; barred from
Warren, 141; in Bisbee, 111–114, *112*; social
reform and, 116

Protestantism, 76, 117

Pullman, Ill., 132, 137

Race (racial system): American debates over
meaning of, 29–30; Apache Wars and, 65;
black-white binary, 13, 27; censuses and, 153;
citizenship and, 30–31; class and gender hierarchies and, 88–89; controversy over meaning
of, 184; Cowboy gang and, 60–61; Darwinian
competition and, 88; dismantling of, 270–271;
fears of "race suicide," 97, 183; ideology of
"white man's camp" and, 87–88; in Mexico, 15,
27–29; nation linked to, 6, 13, 14; racial binary,
13, 27, 265, 274; relief programs and, 255–256;
sources for ideas about, 9; terminological
meanings of, 13–17; in United States, 27, 28,
29–32; women's reform role and, 115. *See also*
"Science," race and

Racial boundaries, 3, 8, 18, 96, 103, 225

Racism, "scientific," 5, 30, 66, 88. *See also*
Eugenics; "Science," race and

Railroads, 12, 23, 149, 172; Benson as hub of,
167–168; Chinese labor and, 73; homesteading
and, 179; Mexican investments in, 59, 63;
Phelps Dodge Co. and, 85. *See also* El Paso &
Southwestern Railroad; Southern Pacific
Railroad

Rancheros, 26, 155

Ranchers and ranching, 53, 155, 171, 174; copper
mining and, 195; economic depression and,
179. *See also* Cattle ranching; Cattle rustling

Ray, town of, 202, 203–204

Red-light districts, 111–112, *112,* 116

Red Scare, 271

Relief boards and societies, 151, 252–256

Republican Party, 54, 55, 56, 78; dominance in

New Mexico, 186; Mexican Americans and,
170; Mormons and, 151, 155; Progressivism
and, 124; women candidates, 189–190

Rider, Jane, 262, 264

Romero, Matías, 63

Rooming houses, 8, 102, 111, 137, 206

Roosevelt, Franklin D., 236, 248, 251, 254, 270

Roosevelt, Theodore, 93, 97, 183–184, 187, 188,
217

Ruíz, Eugenio, 43

Ruíz family, 35, 36

Ryan, Grace, 246, 247

Ryan, J. C., 84, 226

Safford, A. P. K., 36

Saloons, 107, 112, 141, 241

Salt of the Earth (film), 268

Sánchez, Guadalupe, 169

Sánchez, Jesús María, 162, 163–164, 167, 170

Sánchez family, 159, 163, 165

Sanctuary Movement, 273

San Pedro Valley, *20, 34, 53,* 155, 157, *157,* 173, 258;
Apache Wars in, 43–44; Chinese residents, 72;
history of, 21; irrigation enterprises, 150;
"Mexican schools," 162–167, *164*; in Spanish
colonial era, 21

Schieffelin, Ed, 50, 80, 103

Schools, 18, 103–104; Bisbee High School, 241,
261, 263; Franklin School, 231; integration in
Benson, 171–172; kindergartens, 115, 116;
"Mexican schools," 162–167, *164*; segregated, 17

"Science," race and, 29–30, 68, 88, 96–97, 183. *See
also* Eugenics; Racism, "scientific"

Scientific Farmer (journal), 185, 186

Scottish miners, 94, 107, 127

Serbians, 8, 118; Americanization of, 261; Balkan
Wars and, 205; kin and cultural networks,
100–101; on voting rolls, 169; Warren
Americanization scheme and, 143–144;
whiteness and, 94–95, *95,* 101

Settlement patterns, 8, 150

Seward, Laura Mae, 246–247

Shattuck, Lemuel, 95, 107, 109, 217, 250

Sherman, Gen. William T., 44, 48–49, 56–57, 59,
78

Silver City strike, 268

Slaughter, John, 109

Slavery, abolition of, 4

Slavs, 96, 99; Alien Labor Act and, 201;
Americanization of, 260–261; Balkan Wars and,
229; Bisbee Deportation and, 260; Home
Extension Service and, 247; IWW (Wobblies)

and, 202; in Mexican areas of Bisbee, 111; in
midwestern mines, 130; status and wages of,
101; "status of free manhood" and, 3; union
organizing and, 135, 136; in Western Federation
of Miners, 207; whiteness and, 15. *See also*
Serbians
Sloan, Richard E., 199
Slovenia, 100
Smythe, Elwood, 180
Social Darwinism, 96, 131
Socialists, 124, 127, 128, 139, 206
Sonora, Mexican state of, *11, 12*, 29, 38;
anti-Chinese movement in, 76; Apache Wars
in, 22, 64; Cowboys in, 56, 58–60; industrial
mine workers from, 87; Mexican Revolution
in, 203, 221; miners' strike in, 129; *norteño*
identity and, 174; race and class in, 65;
Revolution in, 153
Sonora Exploring and Mining Company, 41
Southern Pacific Railroad, 12, 34, 71, 85, 167, 181;
Great Depression and, 249; New Deal and,
255; racial hierarchy at, 172–173
Soza, Antonio Campo, 42, 155, 157–159, *158,* 170
Soza, Francisco, 172
Soza, Manuel, 159, 170
Soza family, 163
Spain and Spanish Empire, 28, 41–42
"Spanish American," term, 15, 173, 256
Spanish-American Society, 171
Spanish language, 28, 32, 46, 99; children of
intermarriage and, 160; Tucson newspapers in,
76, 87, 169, 175; used by Anglos, 33
Sporleder, Louise, 244–246, 247
Stanbery, Lortah, 188–189, 190, 191
Standard of living, American, 89–90, 96–97, 100,
111, 205, 208; striking Mexican workers and,
211, 238; white women reformers on, 117
Statehood, 13. *See also* Arizona
Stewart, Elinore Pruitt, 188, 191
Strikes, 13, 130; Bisbee (1907), 219; Bisbee (1917),
205–211; during Depression, 267; Empire Zinc
Mine, 268; Mexican workers and, 202–203; in
Michigan, 129; Pullman strike (1894), 132;
Silver City strike, 268
Suárez, Jesús, 24
Suffrage, women's, 13, 169, 186, 196. *See also*
Voting
Sulphur Springs Valley, 177, 181, 182, 189, 195
"Sundown towns," 82–83
Supreme Court, U.S., 201, 202, 233, 234, 267;
Frankfurter as justice, 3
Sutter, Fred, 230, 235, 250

Taft, William H., 199
Tarbell, Ida, 132
Texas Rangers, 57
Tintown (section of Bisbee), 92, 99, 111, 143, 223,
246
Tohono O'odham Indians, 44
Toles, Elsie, 163, 165; elected to statewide office,
189–190; on homesteaders' poverty, 240;
reforming efficiency of, 241–242; relationship
with Helen Benedict, 190, 242–243
Toles, George, 241
Tombstone, town of, 5, 113, 149; African
Americans in, 103; Anglo dominance in, 33;
anti-Chinese campaigns, 6, 16, 71–78, 83;
Cowboy gang, 49, 52–63; in decline, 79, 249;
history of, 50–52, 78; integration of, 262; labor
struggle in, 127; Mexicans in, 76–77; silver
boom, 9, 34, 50, 51, 74; tourism in, 10, 12, 78,
272. *See also* OK Corral shoot-out
Tombstone Epitaph (newspaper), 62, 73, 75,
77–78
Tombstone Nugget (newspaper), 52
Tombstone Prospector (newspaper), 222
Tombstone Rangers, 65–66
Torres, Luis, 59
Town-planning experiments, 8, 16, 132
Treaty of Guadalupe Hidalgo (1848), 7, 20, 23, 30,
68
Tres Alamos settlement, 16, 18–21, 81, 185; Apache
Wars and, 42–46; building of community in,
21–27; decline of, 149–150, 155–156; map, *20*;
racial system, 30, 37; transfer to U.S.
sovereignty, 32–33; Tres Alamos School, 162,
163; water rights conflict, 35–36, 152; women,
39–41
Tritle, Gov. Frederick, 48, 69, 78
Truax, William, Sr. and Jr., 201–202
Truax v. Corrigan, 201–202
Tucson, city of, 23, 26; Apache Wars and, 44–45;
Mexican elites of, 33–34, 36; under Mexican
rule, 27; Sanctuary Movement, 273; Spanish
colonial period, 157; Spanish-language
newspapers, 76, 87, 169, 175

Udall, Morris, 271
Unions, 17, 51, 97, 132; Depression-era gains of,
267–268; gender ideology and, 139–140;
homeownership and, 138–139, 140; merchant
class against, 175; municipal power and, 108;
New Deal and, 254; Progressivism and, 124;
rise in fortunes of, 199–200; "white man's
camp" and, 85–86, 102. *See also* Industrial